MW01273808

The Rise of China and International Security

This edited volume offers diverse and comprehensive views of China's rise and its implications for the East Asian region and beyond.

The economic growth of China, initially started in the late 1970s with domestic and rural reforms, has been increasingly driven by China's industrialization and integration into the regional and global markets. The growth and integration of China, however, has exposed China's closest neighbors and even more remote countries to its various (previously internal) problems, and the lagging political openness of China has often negatively impacted on cooperation with other countries in dealing with these problems (i.e. trans-border pollution, epidemics, illegal migration, organized crime, financial management, etc.). This book integrates geopolitical and domestic political analysis of China with a broad set of transnational security issues, and includes a diversity of regional views. In doing so, it explores further than the dichotomous debate between the American realists and liberals, adding finesse to the often simplified discussions on how to deal with the rising China.

This book will be of interest to students of Asian Politics, Security Studies and International Relations.

Kevin J. Cooney is Associate Professor of Political Science and International Relations at Union University, Jackson, Tennesee.

Yoichiro Sato is Associate Professor at the Asia-Pacific Center for Security Studies, Honolulu, Hawaii.

Asian Security Studies

Series Editors: Sumit Ganguly, *Indiana University, Bloomington* and Andrew Scobell, *US Army War College*

Few regions of the world are fraught with as many security questions as Asia. Within this region it is possible to study great power rivalries, irredentist conflicts, nuclear and ballistic missile proliferation, secessionist movements, ethno-religious conflicts and interstate wars. This book series publishes the best possible scholarship on the security issues affecting the region, and includes detailed empirical studies, theoretically oriented case studies and policy-relevant analyses as well as more general works.

China and International Institutions
Alternate Paths to Global Power
Marc Lanteigne

China's Rising Sea Power
The PLA Navy's Submarine Challenge
Peter Howarth

If China Attacks Taiwan
Military Strategy, Politics and Economics
Steve Tsang (ed.)

Chinese Civil-Military Relations
The Transformation of the People's Liberation Army
Nan Li (ed.)

The Chinese Army Today
Tradition and Transformation for the 21st Century
Dennis J. Blasko

Taiwan's Security
History and Prospects
Bernard D. Cole

Religion and Conflict in South and Southeast Asia
Disrupting Violence
Linell E. Cady and Sheldon W. Simon (eds)

Political Islam and Violence in Indonesia
Zachary Abuza

US-Indian Strategic Cooperation into the 21st Century
More than Words
Sumit Ganguly, Brian Shoup and Andrew Scobell (eds)

India, Pakistan and the Secret Jihad
The Covert War in Kashmir, 1947–2004
Praveen Swami

China's Strategic Culture and Foreign Policy Decision-Making
Confucianism, Leadership and War
Huiyun Feng

Military Strategy in the Third Indochina War
The Last Maoist War
Edward C. O'Dowd

Asia Pacific Security
US, Australia and Japan and the New Security Triangle
William T. Tow, Satu Limaye, Mark Thompson and Yoshinobu Yamamoto

China, the United States and Southeast Asia
Contending Perspectives on Politics, Security and Economics
Evelyn Goh and Sheldon W. Simon

Conflict and Cooperation in Multi-Ethnic States
Institutional Incentives, Myths and Counterbalancing
Brian Dale Shoup

China's War on Terrorism
Counter-Insurgency, Politics and Internal Security
Martin I. Wayne

US Taiwan Policy
Constructing the Triangle
Øystein Tunsjø

Conflict Management, Security and Intervention in East Asia
Third-Party Mediation and Intervention between China and Taiwan
Jacob Bercovitch, Kwei-Bo Huang, and Chung-Chian Teng (eds)

Nuclear Weapons and Conflict in Comparative Perspective
Rajesh M. Basrur

The Rise of China and International Security
America and Asia Respond
Kevin J. Cooney and Yoichiro Sato (eds)

The Rise of China and International Security

America and Asia Respond

**Edited by Kevin J. Cooney
and Yoichiro Sato**

Routledge
Taylor & Francis Group

LONDON AND NEW YORK

First published 2009
by Routledge
2 Park Square, Milton Park, Abingdon, Oxon, OX14 4RN

Simultaneously published in the USA and Canada
by Routledge
270 Madison Avenue, New York, NY 10016

Routledge is an imprint of the Taylor & Francis Group, an informa business

© 2009 Kevin J. Cooney and Yoichiro Sato for selection and editorial matter;
individual chapters, the contributors

Typeset in Times New Roman PS by
Florence Production Ltd, Stoodleigh, Devon
Printed and bound in Great Britain by
Antony Rowe Ltd, Chippenham, Wiltshire

British Library Cataloguing in Publication Data
A catalogue record for this book is available from the British Library

Library of Congress Cataloging in Publication Data
  The rise of China and international security: America and
  Asia respond/edited by Kevin J. Cooney and Yoichiro Sato.
    p. cm.—(Asian security studies)
  1. Security, International. 2. China—Relations—United States.
  3. United States—Relations—China. 4. China—Relations—Asia.
  5. Asia—Relations—China. I. Cooney, Kevin J. II. Sato, Yoichiro, 1966–
  JZ5588.R57 2008
  355′.033051—dc22   2008003171

ISBN10: 0–415–43396–7 (hbk)
ISBN10: 0–203–89363–8 (ebk)

ISBN13: 978–0–415–43396–9 (hbk)
ISBN13: 978–0–203–89363–0 (ebk)

To our children:

Aiyana & Kian Cooney

and

Akihiro & Namie Sato

Contents

List of illustrations   ix
Notes on contributors   x
Abbreviations   xii

1   **Introduction**   1
    Kevin Cooney

2   **The rise of China: Chinese perspectives**   13
    Jian Yang

3   **Chinese–American hegemonic competition in East Asia:
    a new cold war or into the arms of America?**   38
    Kevin Cooney

4   **US strategic relations with a rising China: trajectories
    and impacts on Asia-Pacific security**   59
    Evelyn Goh

5   **Tango without trust and respect? Japan's awkward
    co-prosperity with China in the twenty-first century**   94
    Yoichiro Sato

6   **Taiwan's response to the rise of China**   120
    Denny Roy

7   **Out of America, into the dragon's arms: South Korea,
    a Northeast Asian balancer?**   140
    Seong-Ho Sheen

8   **Southeast Asian responses to China's rise: managing
    the "elephants"?**   159
    Evelyn Goh

 9 **India's response to China's rise**   177
    J. Mohan Malik

10 **Political construction of human rights: with a focus on North
    Korean refugees in China**   213
    Mikyoung Kim

11 **Conclusion: China in the eyes of Asia and America**   232
    Yoichiro Sato

    Bibliography   242
    Index   259

Illustrations

Figures

1.1 A nation practicing realism might choose other options
     for realist reasons   10
3.1 American and Chinese linear GDP growth projections   51
3.2 American and Chinese linear GDP growth projections   52
5.1 Average size of Japanese FDIs   97
5.2 Japan's exports by destination   98
5.3 Japan's imports by source   99
5.4 ODA loans to China   102
5.5 Major sea lanes in East Asia   109

Tables

2.1   Early twenty-first-century state power structure for China,
      France, Britain, Russia, Japan, Germany, and India   24
4.1   Possible scenarios of change in the US–China relationship   83
5.1   Major recipients of ODA loans   101
7.1   2005 Military spending in Northeast Asia   150
7.2   People and wealth in Northeast Asia 2005   150
9.1   Chinese public views on India–China relations   183
10.1 Types of residential support for North Korean refugees   223
10.2 Types of living environments in China   224

Contributors

Kevin Cooney is an Associate Professor of Political Science & International Relations at Union University in Jackson, Tennessee. His recent books include *Japan's Foreign Policy Since 1945* (M.E. Sharpe, 2007) and *Japan's Foreign Policy Maturation: A Quest for Normalcy* (Routledge, 2002).

Evelyn Goh is University Lecturer in International Relations, St Anne's College, Department of Politics and International Relations, at Oxford University. Her recent books include *Reassessing Security Cooperation in the Asia-Pacific: Competition, Congruence, and Transformation* (co-edited, MIT Press, 2007) and *China, the United States, and Southeast Asia: Contending Perspectives on Politics, Security, and Economics* (co-edited, Routledge, 2007).

Jian Yang is a Senior Lecturer in International Relations at the University of Auckland, New Zealand. He is the author of *Congress and US China Policy: 1989–1999* (Nova Science Publishers, 2000).

Yoichiro Sato is a Professor at the Asia-Pacific Center for Security Studies in Honolulu, Hawaii. His recent books include *Growth and Governance in Asia* (edited, Asia-Pacific Center for Security Studies, 2004), and *Japan in a Dynamic Asia* (co-edited, Lexington Books, 2006).

Mikyoung Kim is an Associate Professor at Hiroshima Peace Institute and Hiroshima City University. She was also a Fulbright Visiting Professor at Portland State University. Her research work on North Korean refugees and Northeast Asian regionalization have appeared in several journals.

Mohan Malik is a Professor at the Asia-Pacific Center for Security Studies in Honolulu, Hawaii. He is the author of *Dragon on Terrorism* (Strategic Studies Institute, 2002) and *The Gulf War: Australia's Role and Asian-Pacific Responses* (Strategic and Defense Studies Center, Research School of Pacific Studies, Australian National University, 1992).

Denny Roy is a Senior Fellow at the East–West Center in Honolulu, Hawaii. He is the author of *Taiwan: A Political History* (Cornell University Press, 2003) and *China's Foreign Relations* (Macmillan, 1998).

Seong-Ho Sheen is an Assistant Professor at the Graduate School of International Studies, Seoul National University. His writings on international security, US foreign policy, Northeast Asian politics and the Korean Peninsula have appeared in several journals.

Abbreviations

ABM	Anti-Ballistic Missile Treaty
ACFTA	ASEAN China Free Trade Area
APEC	Asia-Pacific Economic Cooperation
ARF	ASEAN Regional Forum
ASAT	anti-satellite
ASEAN	Association of Southeast Asian Nations
ASEAN +3	Association of Southeast Asian Nations plus China, Japan, and Korea
ASEAN-6	Association of Southeast Asian Nations—Indonesia, Philippines, Singapore, Malaysia, Thailand, and Brunei (original six members)
ASEM	Asia–Europe Summit Meeting
BIMSTEC	Bay of Bengal Initiative for MultiSectoral Technical and Economic Cooperation
CCP	Chinese Communist Party
CFC	Combined Forces Command
CLMV	Cambodia, Laos, Myanmar, Vietnam
CNOOC	China National Offshore Oil Corporation
CNP	comprehensive national power
CTBT	Comprehensive Test Ban Treaty
DPP	Democratic Process Party
DPRK	Democratic People's Republic of Korea
EAC	East Asia Community
EAS	East Asian Summit
EDAC	Economic Development Advisory Conference
EEZ	exclusive economic zone
EPA	economic partnership agreement
FDI	foreign direct investment
FTA	free trade agreement
GDP	gross domestic product
GNP	gross national product
IAEA	International Atomic Energy Agency
IPR	intellectual property rights

JETRO	Japan External Trade Organization
KEDO	Korean Energy Development Organization
KMT	Kuomintang Party
KORUS FTA	Korea–US Free Trade Agreement
LAC	Line of Actual Control
MAD	Mutual Assured Destruction
METI	Ministry of Economy, Trade, and Industry (Japan)
MGC	Mekong-Ganges Cooperation
MOFA	Ministry of Foreign Affairs (Japan)
NAM	Non-Aligned Movement
NATO	North Atlantic Treaty Organization
NGO	non-government organizations
NIC	newly industrialized country
NPT	Nuclear Non-Proliferation Treaty
NSG	Nuclear Suppliers Group
ODA	Overseas (official) Development Assistance
PLA	People's Liberation Army
POC	peacetime operational control
PRC	People's Republic of China
RMA	Revolution in Military Affairs
ROC	Republic of China
ROK	Republic of Korea
SAARC	South Asian Association for Regional Cooperation
SARS	Severe Acute Respiratory Syndrome
SCO	Shanghai Cooperation Organization
SLOC	sea lanes of communication
UNOCAL	Union Oil Corporation of California
UNSC	United Nations Security Council
USFK	US Forces in Korea
WHO	World Health Organization
WOC	wartime operational control
WTO	World Trade Organization
ZOPFAN	Zone of Peace, Freedom, and Neutrality

1   Introduction

Kevin Cooney

China and its spectacular economic rise, and its concurrent military modern-ization, is arguably the most important political event in Asia since the Korean War over 50 years ago. Implications of the "rise of China" are being talked about globally and debated among foreign policy and security policy experts as to what it means for the rest of the world. Of particular importance is the question of what it means for China's neighbors in Asia. Will China be a benign or adversarial power? Will China challenge the current reigning hegemon, the United States, in the near or long-term future or will it never be a challenge to American power? How do the nations of Asia feel about the potential for China to be the next hegemon?

This book seeks to answer these questions while examining how the United States, Japan, North and South Korea, Taiwan, The Association of Southeast Asian Nations (ASEAN) and India are all reacting to China's rise. We have gathered a group of Asian experts in foreign and security policy to examine how each of these nations is responding to the economic and military rise of China. Additionally we have asked Jian Yang to provide a Chinese perspective on the "rise of China" debate. The importance of this is that understanding the perspectives and policies of the major powers of Asia in regard to China, along with the Chinese view of itself, will help us to prevent conflict and tensions in the region. China needs to understand its neighbors' views of its power, and its neighbors need to understand how China views itself. We have further endeavored to make the writing in this book accessible to not just the academic, but the policymaker and the concerned layman.

The book starts with Jian Yang's chapter on China's view of its own rise and why it should be viewed as benign. Yang examines in detail what Chinese scholars call the "China threat theory" and the role of Chinese think tanks in responding to this "theory." He notes that from a Chinese perspective the world is currently neither a unipolar world nor a multipolar world but rather a world in transition from a unipolar one to a multipolar one. This transition is likely to take anywhere from 20 to 50 years from the Chinese perspective. Promoting this new multipolar world is how China intends to claim the high moral ground over the United States in world opinion. This multipolarity is China's short-term goal. Its medium-term goal is to use the peace and stability of a multipolar world to work toward the revising of what it sees as the inherent "unreasonableness" of the current international order, according to Yang. He further argues that China is deliberately being vague as to its future intentions in order to avoid potential conflict with the United States.

The next two chapters look at the American policy and its reaction to China's rise. Writing first in Chapter 3, Kevin Cooney challenges the conventional wisdom that America is in decline both militarily and economically. America rather perceives itself to be still in ascendancy. It sees itself challenged by China, but not in decline vis-à-vis China. This is important because it helps clarify some of the seemingly schizophrenic nature of American policy toward China. Cooney argues that when looking at American policy from the macro point of view one can see an order and coherence that are not as apparent when one looks closely. The United States is trying to engage China economically in such a way as to create a mutually dependant relationship while at the same time refusing to surrender its vast military superiority over China. Miscalculated perceptions of the strength of the United States' advantage present a very real strategic risk for both nations, according to Cooney, and a delicate balancing act is required for the nations of the region caught between these two great powers.

In Chapter 4, Evelyn Goh takes a different approach to the Sino–American relationship. She argues that the United States as the predominant power feels responsible to orchestrate regional order including how much accommodation is to be made for a rising China. Beijing is seen by Washington as unpredictable and reactive, argues Goh. The question that she asks is whether China and the United States can successfully negotiate their relationship toward what the Chinese label "peaceful coexistence." She notes, like Yang and Cooney, that it will be at least many decades for China to catch up with the United States in economic, technological, and military terms. In the meantime, she argues that China will probably be perceived as a systemic disruption under one or more of the five scenarios that she eloquently lays out.

Yoichiro Sato in Chapter 5 examines Japan's reaction to China's rise. He first looks at the long history of Sino–Japanese relations and notes the historical anomaly of Japan's recent domination of China. He then moves on to look at current economic and political relations between these two East Asian powers. His examination includes energy security, trade disputes (including product safety), and territorial disputes between China and Japan. The internal shifting attitudes within Japan toward China are noted with the results being a mixed set of policies toward the rise of China in the coming years. Sato concludes that while Japan is engaging China economically, it (like the United States) is unwilling to cede militarily to China's rise. Potential "shocks" in East Asia have the power to set the agenda for future Sino–Japanese relations.

The sixth chapter contains Denny Roy's examination of Taiwan's reaction to mainland China's rise. He begins by rightfully noting that the intentions of a "rising China" are equally important to its increased capabilities. For Taiwan this is a strategic problem. Roy notes that China has begun to change the tenor of its policy toward Taiwan while maintaining its basic principles.

Taiwan's particular set of circumstances makes it behave like a normal state in balancing China. Taiwan's policy seems to be to conduct both hard and soft balancing versus China's growing power, Roy argues. He highlights Taiwanese President Chen Shui-bian's argument that "democracy is Taiwan's best defense" and that Taiwan's increasing economic investment in China does not necessarily mean political cooperation. He concludes with an analysis of the ongoing cooperation between the two societies and the deep political divisions between the two.

In the seventh chapter, Seong-Ho Sheen looks at South Korea's self-appointed role as a balancer between the United States/Japan and China. He notes the growing uncertainty of relations between Seoul and Washington and the growing anti-Americanism that is causing South Korea to move closer to Beijing. The expanding trade relations between China and South Korea are further cementing this relationship. However, President Roh Moo-Hyun's desire to see South Korea develop a "self-reliant defense capability" is causing him to pursue a role of balancer in the power politics of Northeast Asia. This represents a hedging strategy on the part of South Korea according to Sheen. South Korea wants autonomy from America, but it may never truly be able to achieve it.

In the eighth chapter, Evelyn Goh returns with a tight analysis of how the ASEAN states are reacting to China's rise. She notes the historical importance of China over Southeast Asia including during the Cold War. The ASEAN states, she notes, have been at the forefront of managing the rise of China over the last 15 years. The ASEAN–China relationship has four main problems, according to Goh. First, the relationship has been untested since 1995. Second, divergence of views about China among the members of ASEAN is increasing. Third, the relative unimportance of Southeast Asia continues when compared to Northeast Asia. And fourth, non-traditional security issues are growing in importance in the region. The two main worries for the states of ASEAN are being caught in the middle of a conflict between the United States and China and territorial disputes between China and several ASEAN members in the South China Sea. Overall, all the individual member states of ASEAN seem to be practicing a hybrid form of realism instead of the straightforward institutionalism that one might expect.

In the ninth chapter, J. Mohan Malik looks at India's reaction to China's rise. Malik basically sees India as a rising balancer to China's new-found economic growth and power. He very correctly notes that India is also on the rise and as the world's largest democracy it has its own dreams of being a "big power." He further notes the historical "perceptions and misperceptions" and "expectations and illusions" between these two great civilizations. Primarily he focuses on the historical perception on the part of China that India is not its equal but rather it is an upstart. India is seen by China as at best a regional power but as Malik notes the United States has offered to help make India a twenty-first-century power. India is working with the Western powers to slow the "prowling dragon" of China.

Malik furthers his analysis by looking at the various drivers of the disputes between China and India. Chief among these are the territorial disputes between India and China with India's nuclear status being close behind. Energy security is a further issue for India and China's "complementary yet competitive economies." Malik concludes by noting that China's rise has driven India from a non-aligned foreign policy to a multilateral foreign policy that seeks to balance China.

In the tenth chapter, Mikyoung Kim looks at the awkward relationship between North Korea and its principle sponsor, China. China supplies most of North Korea's electricity and has an interest in keeping the Kim Jong-il regime in place if to be nothing else but a buffer to the United States and South Korea. As North Koreans increasingly flee across the border to China and beyond, Beijing is being forced to round up these refugees and return them as criminals to North Korea. This is seen by the rest of the world as a human rights violation, and China is coming under increasing pressure to improve its human rights record.

The final chapter concludes the book with a summary of what we have learned and what questions remain about China's rise. The many unknowns are noted, however many popular myths regarding China's rise are dispelled as a clear summary is given of all of the differing authors' findings.

Realism in Asia

The last part of this introductory chapter will place the case studies of the Asian nations contained in this book within the context of the established international relations and foreign policy theories. In a study of political science and international relations, it is important to place ideas and observations of state behavior in theoretical contexts. Political theory helps to explain the reasons why nations make the choices that they do, and it helps us to better predict state behavior. This section will also look at the alternative security choices that the nations of Asia face in regard to China's rise. The overarching purpose of this section is to place the reader within common theoretical frameworks for all the case studies in the book. Detailed analysis of the overall direction of foreign policy in Asia is saved for the book's final chapter.

Alternative security

Barry Buzan *et al.*, in their 1998 book, *Security: A New Framework for Analysis*, examine the "wide versus narrow" debate in security analysis.[1] The "wide" debate deals with the tendency of some to view everything as a security matter. An example would be the "War on Drugs" in the United States, in which stopping the flow of drugs into the United States is viewed as a matter of national security. The "narrow" debate focuses almost exclusively on traditional military concerns, such as the balance of forces and the need to protect the territorial sovereignty of the state. In this book we examine the "wide" debate in relation to 'Asia's security policy regarding China. The basic argument is that, by focusing on the "narrow" traditional security issues, we will find it difficult to come to a fuller understanding of American and Asian foreign and security policies relating to China's rise. However, Buzan *et al.* caution against the "intellectual and political dangers of simply tacking the word security onto an ever wider range of issues."[2] There needs to be a balance in any examination of nontraditional security issues. Thus, there is a requirement for some kind of connection or thread to traditional security issues that links to the alternative issue.

According to Hans J. Morgenthau, traditional security encompasses protection of a state's people, territory, and economy from outside attack.[3] For Buzan *et al.*, alternative security issues can be much more wide-ranging (with the caveat about the need for caution against attaching security to too many issues). Issues involving environmental, societal, and political sectors can be incorporated as critical security issues. Furthermore, domestic economic issues that are not subjected to traditional international threats can and should also be included in what Buzan *et al.* call the "securitization process." Buzan *et al.* describe securitization as, "the exact definition and criteria of securitization is constituted by the intersubjective establishment of an existential threat with a saliency sufficient to have substantial political effects."[4] To put it simply, a security threat exists when and if the state recognizes or perceives the threat in a way that has political consequences. For Buzan *et al.*, the danger lies in looking at security in too narrow a perspective. Traditional approaches to security, as well as alternative approaches, must be incorporated in any examination of security. However, security is much more than any specific threat or problem. Such threats or problems may be only political in nature.[5]

It is also important that the issues being securitized are perceived as security issues both by those inside a state and by those outside it. An issue is not securitized until it is accepted as securitized, both internally and externally. The previously mentioned "political consequences" thus need to be apparent both domestically and internationally. Furthermore, there needs to be a "speech act" in which an issue is securitized. The danger must be spoken of in terms of the threat that, if not dealt with, will potentially cause harm to the state. This harm can be ad hoc or institutionalized. However, according to Buzan *et al.*, an issue has not been successfully securitized until those on the outside have perceived the speech act as securitizing the issue. There also needs to be a consideration of the side effects of securitizing an issue that may lead to making the issue a greater threat than previously assumed. In these situations, desecuritization may be the ideal choice.[6] That is to say that the state may want to proclaim that a previously announced threat is no longer a threat. A historical example of this type of desecuritization would be the World War II alliance between the United States and the Soviet Union. The previous nontraditional threat from the ideology of Communism was abandoned because of the need to deal with the immediate and mutual threat of Nazi Germany.

When looking at alternative security issues in Asia, we must recognize that the nation-state does not exist in a vacuum. In terms of security, a nation-state is part of the larger community of states with which it interacts politically, economically, culturally, and adversely. It is common to perceive these sectors of interactions as being independent rather than interdependent. To consider a wider security agenda in Asia, we must consider the interlinking of the security sectors and the ways they affect the overall security of the state. Splitting the sectors into their own subunits is helpful for analysis but troublesome when one needs to examine a state's overall security environment.

Alternative security issues have been made ever more important as the result of the erosion of Western military, economic, and political power by the forces of globalization and in our specific case, the rise of China. Protecting the state is not the same as it once was. Classical security issues of military comparison between bordering states may be a thing of the past in Asia, but competition for resources and over disputed territories are not. Relations between states over a host of issues that can be securitized are now normative in their application. To put it another way, it is normal for states to talk in security terms over almost any issue of concern. As Buzan *et al.* state, "All of the states in the system are enmeshed in a global web of security interdependence."[7] However, insecurity is often associated with proximity, because of the fact that security threats do not travel well.[8] States worry more about their neighbors than they do about distant potential threats. For example, China is a greater worry for Asia than Africa. This circumstance creates what Buzan *et al.* call "security complexes," which are regionally based clusters "whose security perceptions and concerns are so interlinked that their national security problems cannot reasonably be analyzed or resolved apart from one another."[9] These security complexes are "miniature anarchies" that operate as a fully functional subset of the larger system.[10]

When we look at China's rise in light of the arguments of Buzan *et al.*, we can see that China sits in what may be called an Asian security complex. The players in this security complex are Japan; India, the nations of ASEAN, China, including Taiwan; the two Koreas; and the United States, the global hegemonic power with significant interests in the region and a stake in its order and stability. How these players have reacted and are reacting to China's economic and military rise efforts are of vital importance. However, we also need to examine what international relations theories tell us about China's rise in Asia. International relations theories can teach us about what a state hopes to *gain* by the process of securitization and its motives for potentially choosing the process of alternative security.

The theoretical foundations of Asian security

As the late former American Speaker of the House, "Tip" O'Neill, once said, "All politics is local"[11] and Asia is no exception. The phrase widely used during President Bill Clinton's 1992 campaign, "It's the economy, stupid!" rings true in Asia today. Economic welfare and domestic needs drive voters and authoritarian rulers in Asia just like anywhere else. As one Asian government official put it, "the voice for foreign policy *will* come from those who emphasize domestic politics *first.*"[12] The implication here is that the peoples of Asia will elect or support political leadership that will solve domestic economic problems and provide wealth and prosperity, regardless of those leaders' foreign policy agenda. The fear on the part of the official was that an ideologue could seize the policy reins and take a nation such as China in an ill-conceived direction that would risk stability in Asia by pursuing short-term nationalist gains at the expense of absolute gains for the nation. An example of such a security policy disaster could be a "nationalist" foreign policy that leads China to unilaterally, in an unprovoked way, attack Taiwan forcing the United States and the nations of Asia to respond.

Currently there would seem to be no such policy on the rise in China as the Chinese communist government has been very careful to focus its own interests. Since the communist victory in 1949, China has concentrated on a foreign policy based on realism or "self-help." Realism, as described by Joseph M. Grieco:

> encompasses five propositions. First, states are the major actors in world affairs (Morgenthau 1973:10; Waltz 1979:95). Second, the international environment severely penalizes states if they fail to protect their vital interests or if they pursue objectives beyond their means; hence, states are "sensitive to costs" and behave as unitary-rational agents (Waltz 1986:331). Third, international anarchy is the principal force shaping the motives and actions of states (Waltz 1959:224–238; 1979:79–128; Hoffmann 1965:27, 54–87, 129; Aron 1973a:6–10). Fourth, states in anarchy are preoccupied with power and security, are predisposed toward conflict and competition, and often fail to cooperate even in face of common interests (Aron 1966:5; Gilpin 1986:304). Finally, international institutions affect the prospects for cooperation only marginally (Waltz 1979:115–116; Morgenthau 1973:512; Hoffmann 1973b:50).[13]

Since the end of the Cold War, Asian foreign policies have not followed predictions of the traditional power-based realism of Hans J. Morgenthau.[14] Rather, the policies have been largely based on a realistic assessment of the foreign policy limitations of each respective nation. This is especially true for Japan and the nations of ASEAN. Limitations have meant that most of the smaller nations of Asia have been forced to pragmatically pursue an institutionalist–neoliberalist[15] foreign policy.[16] Institutionalists would say that Asia is simply following an institutionally based foreign policy, not realism. However, the institutionalists would seem to be wrong, as Grieco argues:

> In fact, neoliberal institutionalism misconstrues the realist analysis of international anarchy and therefore it misunderstands the realist analysis

of the impact of anarchy on the preferences and the actions of states. Indeed, the new liberal institutionalism fails to address a major constraint on the willingness of states to cooperate which is generated by international anarchy and which is identified by realism. As a result, the new theory's optimism about international cooperation is likely to be proven wrong.[17]

Most of the nations of Asia have depended on the United States and the United Nations for their security needs (China, India, and North Korea being notable exceptions). This institutionalist approach to foreign policy is not based on a belief in institutionalism, but on a realistic assessment of their options, which are few.

The premise underlying this argument is that realism *dominates or influences* all calculations concerning relations between nations. This argument runs counter to the ideas of many political scientists who hold that there are multiple theoretical explanations for the behavior of nation-states. As Sheldon Simon states in his 1995 paper, "International Relations Theory and Southeast Asian Security":

Students of international politics have debated the efficacy of alternative theories of state behavior for decades. Among the most prominent of these debates is the question of whether world politics is a zero-sum conflict in which all state-actors view one another as unmitigated competitors versus the less gloomy vision of a world in which states can best achieve security and prosperity through cooperation rather than conflict. Put simply, advocates of the first school see international politics as a struggle for *relative gains* in which the power and the status of states are determined hierarchically. The second school disagrees, insisting that all members of the system benefit when absolute gains are achieved across the system, virtually regardless of their distribution. Those who follow the first approach are called realists; their more optimistic rivals take the label: *neoliberalists*. These alternative visions currently compete for the attention of many statesmen in the post-Cold War world, who are searching for policies to secure and advance their governments' fortunes.

While realists concede that states may be concerned in the long run with absolute gains, they insist that immediate survival needs take precedence and require independent military and economic capabilities that attenuate cooperation. Neoliberals counter that strong empirical evidence of cooperation in international politics and the creation of institutions to facilitate cooperation show that states do not necessarily concentrate on relative gains exclusively.

Theoretically, under zero-sum conditions, there is no basis for international cooperation regimes because one actor's gain is another's loss. Indeed, in the realist world, a hegemonic state determines the structure or rules of international relations.[18]

Simon argues in his article that both realism and neoliberalism are evident in Southeast Asian security policy. This book does not question this finding; rather, it offers an alternative hypothesis for why nations pursue an alternative or institutionalist foreign policy. An institutionalist foreign policy is a policy based on the use of multilateral forums (rather than traditional alliances), such as the United Nations, ASEAN, and the ASEAN Regional Forum (ARF) for security. It is also important to note why nations in Asia accept absolute gains in cooperation with other states rather than competing over relative gains.

Realists would argue that as the current dominant hegemon, the United States, declines,[19] other nations will vie for the right to be the top dog. Neoliberals argue that states with an investment in the current hegemon's regime will have an interest in preserving or creating frameworks that will continue the rules and regulations imposed by the reigning hegemon.[20] This neoliberal argument is seen as nothing more than an attempt by nation-states to augment their power through institutionalism. Nations are motivated by the need for "self-help," but the realities of the post-Cold War world such as economic interdependence, a lone hyperpower in the form of the United States, and so on are forcing them to pursue *relative gains* through *absolute gains*. States see the competition to be "top dog" as resulting in a net loss in terms of *relative gains* for themselves. Part of the reasoning behind this belief is that, as Grieco writes, "For realists, a state will focus both on its *absolute and relative gains* from cooperation, and a state that is satisfied with a partner's compliance in a joint arrangement might nevertheless exit from it because the partner is achieving relatively greater gains."[21] With survival foremost on their minds, nations practicing realism choose *absolute gains* over a net loss in *relative gains*. States will return to relative gains only when they are more profitable than absolute gains.[22] With the world becoming more interdependent, nation-states are less likely to find themselves pursuing *direct relative gains* when *absolute gains* offer so much more.

To illustrate this concept of relative versus absolute gains, let us look at the case at hand, the rise of China. As the states of Asia are dealing with the rise of China, they realize that they do not want to be caught between the hegemonic power of the United States and the rising power of China. They also do not want to alienate either power in case they need the United States for protection or China for economic opportunity. Realizing their limitations, they will individually try to position themselves for relative gains through absolute-gain methods. Asia needs the stability offered by the regime of the current hegemon, the United States, to continue in order to pursue relative gains, especially vis-à-vis China. This need requires that Asian states pursue a neoliberal approach to their foreign policy and the resulting absolute gains. The calculations of the states in Asia tell them that *absolute gains* will give them a *greater relative gain* than if they pursued only *relative gains*. That is, the *absolute gains* from institutional relationships with the United States *and* China outweigh any conceivable *relative gains* from abandoning institutionalization of either relationship.

A nation may thus choose to pursue a purely realist path or not. It may choose to follow a liberal path because it is the rational thing to do in its localized context. This is a kind of "localized rationality" on the part of many nations within Asia.[23] Part of this logic is based on the belief that people and nations must have incentives to work for goals and interests beyond their immediate selfish needs and agendas. Thus, the behavior of the nations of Asia in relation to China can be explained best in realist terms, no matter what form of policy they seem to be practicing. The circumstances in which they make a "realist" choice may reflect a view of mankind in which a nation can choose to work for the common good because it is in the nation's particular interest. Figure 1.1 illustrates this concept.

This argument adds to the ongoing debate between Joseph Grieco and Robert Powell over the issue of relative versus absolute gains in international relations theory.[24] Neoinstitutionalists argue that states are interested only in their own gains (absolute) and do not care about the gains of other states. Grieco disagrees with this assessment and argues that nations will pursue relative gains over absolute gains *if* they can.[25] Powell tries to marry both these schools of thought by arguing that the choice of relative or absolute gains is situational in nature.[26] A nation will pursue relative gains from a state that it fears as a security threat. If it does not harbor this fear, it will pursue absolute gains. This secondary argument states, particularly in the case of the less powerful nations of Asia such as the ASEAN nations, that in this process, there is a simultaneous element: states will pursue relative gains in any given situation, even when, on the surface, they appear to be pursuing absolute gains. If a state does not have the option or ability to pursue a realist or neorealist strategy, it will attempt a neoliberal strategy, focused on absolute gains in economics and security. In the case of Asia, the economic integration options with China are strong, but their security options are weak, because of their limitations. They thus rationally pursue a pragmatic strategy of diplomacy in order to make relative gains in terms of intangibles, such as goodwill and influence. On the surface, many nations in Asia are currently pursuing absolute gains by using a neoinstitutionalist strategy, but underneath they are seeking relative gains in

Figure 1.1 A diagram illustrating why a nation practicing realism might choose other options for realist reasons

the form of intangibles, since they cannot make relative gains in the traditional forms of economics and security because of their limitations.

China, on the other hand, is forced to do this same calculus but from a different perspective of limitations versus the United States. China needs open sea lanes of communication (SLOC) for energy supplies and export of its products. If China cannot trade internationally, it will decline. To keep the SLOCs open, China must either do so by military force (which it does not currently have the power to do) or work with other nations and the United States through multilateral institutions. China's need to keep the SLOCs open is self-centered, but it carries a benefit for other nations as well, because cooperation in most cases is better than conflict. In realist terms, considering China's current limitations, collaboration with the United States and the nations of Asia is its best option. Furthermore, in realist terms, cooperation adds to China's power by strengthening it as a nation through goodwill and economics, thus giving it status or influence as a power of a kind that it would not have been able to achieve by military means. China has made a relative gain by letting other nations, including the United States, gain in absolute terms.

In sum, the argument is that Asian security policy can be explained primarily through realist doctrines. If one looks at both options and limitations, one can see a realist strategy governing the foreign policies of the region's states vis-à-vis one another, even when, at first glance, there appears to be an institutionalist policy (which on the surface there is). The next chapter begins with Jian Yang's analysis of China's rise and why it should be seen as benign. This is followed by the other authors examining the policies of the United States and the nations of Asia watching China's rise.

Notes

1 Barry Buzan, Ole Wæver, and Jaap de Wilde, *Security: A New Framework for Analysis* (Boulder, CO: Lynne Rienner Publishers, 1998), pp. 2–5 and 239.
2 Ibid., p. 1.
3 Hans J. Morgenthau, *Politics Among Nations* revised by Kenneth W. Thompson (New York: Knopf, 1985).
4 Buzan *et al.*, p. 25.
5 Ibid., pp. 4–5.
6 Ibid., pp. 28–31.
7 Ibid., p.11.
8 Ibid. The rise of global terrorism may change this situation eventually; however, it is important to note that even terrorism (in its current form) does not travel well. It is easier for groups like Al-Qaeda to operate in Iraq than in the United States. Culture, language, and even religion offer formidable barriers to would-be terrorists.
9 Buzan *et al.*, pp. 11–12.
10 Ibid., p. 13.
11 Tip O'Neill and Gary Hymel, *All Politics is Local: And Other Rules of the Game* (Holbrook, MA: Bob Adams, Inc., 1994).
12 Interview with a high-ranking Japanese official who asked that his comments not be attributed or quoted directly with his name attached. Interview by Kevin Cooney, during May–June 1998, Tokyo.

13   Joseph M. Grieco, "Anarchy and the Limits of Cooperation: A Realist Critique of the Newest Liberal Institutionalism," in *Neorealism and Neoliberalism: The Contemporary Debate*, ed. David A. Baldwin (New York: Columbia University Press, 1993), pp. 118–119.

14   Hans J. Morgenthau, *Politics Among Nations*.

15   For the purposes of this chapter, the terms "institutionalism" and "neoliberalism" are used interchangeably and are seen as synonymous.

16   I am indebted to my friend and colleague Tong Ge for introducing me to this concept of a realistic approach to institutionalism. In her master's thesis, Tong Ge argued that, in spite of a longstanding (and continuing) opposition to institutionalist approaches to foreign policy, China is now pursuing institutionalist foreign policy options out of a realistic need for international legitimacy. That is to say, China sees a realist need to use institutions for its foreign policy needs. In the same way, Japan and ASEAN seem to have used an institutionalist approach for realist purposes.

17   Ibid, p. 117.

18   Sheldon W. Simon, "International Relations Theory and Southeast Asian Security," *The Pacific Review*, Vol. 8, No. 1 (1995), p. 6.

19   Kevin Cooney in Chapter 3 argues strongly against this commonly held hypothesis that the United States is currently in decline. He argues that the opposite would seem to be occurring, in that American power is on the rise and that other nations are currently trying to ally themselves with the United States to counterbalance China's rising power or as a hedge against it.

20   Simon, p. 7.

21   Grieco, p. 118.

22   To be clear, a nation facing a *net* loss of, say, 100 points in *absolute* gains versus a *net* loss of 50 points in *relative* gains would be likely to choose the relative gains over the absolute gains in order to keep the "game" close, so that as the situation improves for them, they have less ground to recover. This is a delaying action, if you will. It is important to remember that in this scenario there are no gains, only a choice of greater or smaller losses. Other authors (Robert Powell) have argued as to the types of *gains* that a state practicing realism might choose; this book, however, is arguing as to the choice a state facing two different levels of *losses* might make in order to position itself for the future. In other words, a state will choose to minimize losses and focus on the future.

23   This concept of "localized rationality" partially comes from comments by Paul Bracken and Ralph Cossa at the National Bureau of Asian Research's conference at Arizona State University, Tempe, Arizona, held on April 27, 2000 (the author's personal notes). This localized rationality reflects thinking from the perspective of those locally making the decision. It may not appear to be rational from an outsider's perspective, but it is very rational for those making the decision. Examples of this are Saddam Hussein's decision to invade Kuwait, in spite of the strong interdependent relationship between the two states, and Japan's decision to attack Pearl Harbor, in spite of the fact that it knew that it would most probably lose a war with the United States. Both of these cases led to disaster, but the same does not have to be the case. A "localized rationality" may be the best choice for a nation.

24   Joseph M. Grieco, "Anarchy and the Limits of Cooperation: A Realist Critique of the Newest Liberal Institutionalism," pp. 116–140. Robert Powell, "Absolute and Relative Gains in International Relations Theory," pp. 1303–1320, and "Anarchy in International Relations Theory: The Neorealist-Neoliberal Debate," pp. 313–344.

25   Grieco, "Anarchy."

26   Powell, "Absolute and Relative Gains."

2 The rise of China

Chinese perspectives

Jian Yang

The rise of China has been one of the most important events in post-Cold War international politics. Western analysts and policymakers alike have been debating the implications of and responses to the awakening and rapid rising of the giant in the East. Some are confident that China's rise is a manageable challenge.[1] Others are pessimistic and see China's rise as a threat militarily, economically, and ideologically—what the Chinese call the "China threat theory" (*Zhongguo weixie lun*), a convenient label for all China-threat arguments.

China watchers in the West have made credible contributions to the rise of China debate by making efforts to understand Chinese perceptions of international politics. Although Chinese foreign policymaking process remains opaque, much more information is now available for analysts outside China. One important window to observe Chinese foreign policy is Chinese think tanks and analysts.

This chapter starts with a discussion about the roles of Chinese think tanks and analysts (specialists in think tanks, academics at universities, retired diplomats and commentators in the media) in the making of Chinese foreign policy. It then examines Chinese analysts' perceptions centering on the rise of China, including issues such as the Chinese great power dream, their perceptions of the "China threat theory," Chinese self-perceptions, and their perspectives on the future world.

Think tanks and analysts in Chinese foreign policymaking

Yufan Hao observed in 1998 that "few subjects are more complicated and mysterious than Chinese foreign policy . . . So far there has been little consensus and much frustration in this field of study, to say nothing of the failure to bring it into the mainstream of theoretical inquiry."[2] Despite the impressive progress in the past decade, Chinese foreign policy remains a challenge to China observers.

A good summary of the literature pertaining to the study of Chinese foreign policy before 1992 was Bin Yu's review of six influential books. Yu divides the study into several periods. Until the late 1960s, three schools were most influential: the traditional/historical, the Maoist/communist ideology, and the realist/rational actor. During the late 1960s and the 1970s, the strategic triangle and factional politics schools emerged as dominant approaches. Yu is particularly interested in the current generation who "have grown dissatisfied with the earlier interpretations" and, with the newfound abundance of data, attempt to examine either micro policymaking mechanisms or the pre-policymaking processes.[3]

One influential approach to studying Chinese foreign policy focuses on perceptions held by Chinese foreign policymakers, specialists, and scholars at different levels. According to Yu, the perceptual approach became popular thanks to three developments: (1) China's considerable expansion in research and education in international relations in the post-Mao period, (2) the opening of China to the outside world which has made available to Western scholars a vast array of information on the elaborate foreign policymaking structure, and (3) the cognitive/decision-making approach in the mainstream of international relations and foreign policy studies being integrated into the "atheoretical" field of studying Chinese foreign policy.[4] Representatives of the perceptual approach include Gilbert Rozman's *The Chinese Debate about Soviet Socialism, 1978–1985*, Allen S. Whiting's *China Eyes Japan* and David Shambaugh's *Beautiful Imperialist: China Perceives America, 1972–1990*.[5] "Taken together," Yu judges, "the works break new ground that could open the way to an understanding of the deeper structure of Chinese thinking and its impact on China's foreign behavior."[6]

The discussion of the perceptual approach leads to the issue of key actors in Chinese foreign policymaking process. Gone are the days when a leader, such as Mao Zedong, made the final calls on all major foreign policies. In place of individual leaders, "leading small groups" are emerging which coordinate between different agencies on key policy issues. What is also worth noting for the purposes of this chapter are the roles of think tanks and analysts.

Scholars disagree on the impact of Chinese think tanks and analysts on Chinese foreign policy. In Yu's view, although more actors have become involved in China's foreign policymaking since the 1980s, the central role of the Ministry of Foreign Affairs remains indisputable. Yu suggests that China's foreign policymaking bodies tend to distrust scholarly writing on foreign policy.[7]

However, a majority of China watchers tend to believe that Chinese think tanks and analysts do have an important role to play in China's foreign policymaking process. Thomas J. Christensen's influential 1996 *Foreign Affairs* article "Chinese Realpolitik" is largely based on an analysis of Chinese analysts' views on security. Christensen claims that such kind of analysis is "valuable" because Chinese analysts "influence the thinking of government decision makers and are privy to their thoughts."[8] Bonnie S. Glaser and Phillip C. Saunders made it clearer:

China's more pluralistic and competitive policy environment means that senior leaders and policymakers now receive information and analysis from a range of actors. Some policymakers actively solicit analysis that addresses current policy issues or supports their views. As a result, analysts at Chinese research institutes have more opportunity to influence foreign policy than ever before.[9]

Similarly, in "one of the first" empirical case studies of the growing influence of Chinese foreign policy think tanks, Xuanli Liao argues that the most effective framework for analyzing Chinese foreign policy is what she calls the "pluralistic elitism" approach which combines the ruling elite model and pluralist model. The approach is based on Liao's observation that although China's foreign policymaking remains highly centralized in the hands of "the power elite," "no decision can be made without consensus building among the leadership, or without policy consultation with government departments and foreign policy think tanks."[10]

David Shambaugh agrees: "Undoubtedly the decision-making system has become more consultative over time, with an increased role played by the think tank specialists,"[11] so much so that "today they must be considered important actors in the foreign policymaking process in the PRC."[12] To Shambaugh, the published journals of Chinese foreign policy think tanks "provide very important insights into policy debates that are percolating inside bureaucracies, thus offering important 'early warning indicators' of policies to come."[13]

In his study about the growing influence of Chinese intellectuals and think tanks on Chinese foreign policy, Quansheng Zhao elaborates on three reasons, including the development of civil society, greater demand for policy input and the growing professionalism in the foreign policy apparatus.[14] Professionalization is one of the four "-izations" that David M. Lampton noted in Chinese foreign policymaking. Among other things, professionalization refers to "the proliferation of expert-based bureaucracies in the decision-making process; and the increased reliance by decision-makers on information provided by specialized bureaucracies (and their attention to the quality and diversity of such information)."[15]

The Chinese themselves have been unmasking their think tanks. On November 7, 2006, China's top ten think tanks came together and held a forum in Beijing, the first of its kind. The forum emphasized the importance of think tanks and called on the government to lend more support, especially to independent think tanks. The top ten think tanks are:[16]

Chinese Academy of Social Sciences
Development Research Center of the State Council
Chinese Academy of Sciences
Academy of Military Sciences
China Institute of International Studies

China Institute of Contemporary International Relations
China National Committee for Pacific Economic Cooperation
China Association for Science and Technology
China Institute for International Strategic Studies
Shanghai Institute for International Studies

While it is widely accepted that Chinese think tanks and analysts can influence China's foreign policymaking, it is difficult to assess the actual influence which varies dramatically and depends on a number of factors. Glaser and Saunders have classified four types of influence: expertise influence based on where an analyst works in the bureaucracy, expertise influence based on the analyst's expert knowledge, personal influence based on the analyst's personal connections with policymakers and experiential influence based on the analyst's career history and personal experience.[17]

One other issue in studying the roles of Chinese think tanks and analysts in foreign policymaking is to judge whether these analysts represent the official policies or themselves. After years of evolution, especially after China opened up, it is now widely shared that:

> China's vast socio-economic changes and the loosening ties among leaders, factions, institutions and analysts have greatly eroded old assumptions about when an analyst might "speak for" certain departments, factions or top leaders . . . The great majority of the time, the most that can be assumed is that these analysts speak for themselves or quite possibly their institute. Much less commonly can it be assumed that they represent the official voice of their think tank's parent bureaucratic institution.[18]

Chinese analysts are usually strong defenders of the Chinese government's positions on and policies to counter the "China threat theory." Although their views can be constrained by the political environment they are in, they often do speak their mind. In addition, as Herbert Yee and Zhu Feng point out, "unlike the official response [to the 'China threat theory'] which is largely aimed at explaining China's foreign policy orientations, academics tend to engage in more substantive and theoretical analyses" and "unlike the emotional and sometimes irrational Chinese public, PRC scholars tend to be more restrained and rational."[19]

China's pursuit of great power status

The Chinese history, which stretches over 5,000 years, is not short of powerful and prosperous dynasties. Although the Chinese are not the only people who claimed that they were the center of the world, it was the Chinese who named their nation the center of the world, the Middle Kingdom (*Zhongguo*). China's glorious long history is a sharp contrast to what happened between the 1840s and the 1940s—the "Century of Humiliation" when European powers and Japan carved up China. The "Century of Humiliation" has been the basis for contemporary Chinese nationalism and a key driving force in the Chinese effort to regain China's great power status.

China has been perceived as a great power since the 1940s. However, the perception was not rooted in China's strength but its history as a regional hegemon, vast territory, and large population. The perception was also due to US efforts to deliberately enhance China's international status as a great power to counterbalance other great powers, first Japan and then the Soviet Union.[20] China's great power status was not a strong case whether defined by the traditional "European connotation" of some role in the management of the international system or by today's understanding of "having international interests and a capacity to project (usually military) power to protect or advance those interests."[21] Until the 1980s, "China remained a 'candidate' great power because the communist regime had failed in its efforts to promote domestic development that could provide the basis for comprehensive economic and military clout at world-class levels," observed Avery Goldstein.[22]

Since then, China has been focusing on economic development in its pursuit of comprehensive national power (CNP, *zonghe guoli*). Like Western scholars, Chinese analysts have given different definitions to CNP. The essence is the same however. Some analysts point to the seven elements of CNP, including resources, manpower, economy, science and technology, education, defense, and politics. Others put various elements into four categories: basic power (population, resources, and national unity), economic power (industrial power, agricultural power, scientific and technological power, financial power, and commercial power), national defense power (strategic resources, technology, military strength, nuclear power), and diplomatic power (foreign policy, attitude toward international affairs, foreign aid, etc.).[23]

Michael Pillsbury defines China's CNP as "the combined overall conditions and strengths of a country in numerous areas."[24] Unlike the Cold War years, military might is no longer the main defining factor of strength. Pillsbury further elaborates:

> An evaluation of current and future strength requires the inclusion of a variety of factors, such as territory, natural resources, military force, economic power, social conditions, domestic government, foreign policy, and international influence. CNP is the aggregate of all these factors, as Deng Xiaoping stated: "In measuring a country's national power, one must look at it comprehensively and from all sides."[25]

To enhance comprehensive national power has been China's "national strategy" and economic development has been "the highest goal in making external strategies."[26] The Chinese are aware that a strong economy is the foundation of the military dimension of national security. They often remind themselves that the Soviet Union lost the Cold War to the West mainly because the Soviet economy was not able to sustain the conflict. Equally important, economic development is the key to internal stability. To claim its legitimacy, the Chinese government has to substantially raise the living standard. Thus, it has been widely accepted in China that to develop the economy remains China's "ultimate solution (*genben chulu*) to all internal and external problems."[27] This also applies to the Taiwan issue, not only because economic modernization is the foundation of military modernization, but also because military coercion may not be effective. In fact, military intimidation contributed to the "China threat theory." Economic competition and integration with Taiwan is emerging as a more acceptable and perhaps more effective strategy.

China's economic growth has been breathtaking. Its gross domestic product (GDP) doubled in the 1980s and more than doubled in the 1990s. Beijing used to play down China's economic might in the wake of other countries' concerns over the "China threat." In January 2006, however, the Chinese government announced that China achieved a national economic output of US $2.26 trillion, which sent China soaring past France, Britain, and Italy to become the world's fourth-largest economy only after the United States, Japan, and Germany. Some economists adjust China's figures for the low value of its currency and low domestic prices to suggest that if valued at Western prices, China's output has surpassed Germany's as well.[28] This is in sharp contrast with China's GDP of US $200 billion in 1978. China's rise is one of the most spectacular in history, with its per-capita GDP increasing about 8 percent per year for the 25 years from 1979 to 2004. By comparison, the strongest average per-capita growth for the last rising power—the United States—for any 25-year period since 1830 was less than 4 percent per year.[29] The Chinese economy is expected to be double the size of the German economy by 2010 and to surpass the Japanese economy, the second largest economy in the world, by 2020.[30]

China's economic rise should be put in perspective. Goldman Sachs estimates that China's GDP may overtake that of the US near 2050, but that in per capita terms China will still be far behind the US.[31] Joseph S. Nye notes that if both Chinese and US economies continue to grow at their current rates, the US economy will still be three times larger than China's in 2025 and China's per capita incomes may not reach those of the US until the fourth quarter of the century. Nye also notes that China's economic success rate may not last due to critical economic, social, and political obstacles, including an unsound financial system, inadequate infrastructure, inefficiency of state-owned enterprises, mass internal migration, widening gap between rich and poor, a deficient social safety net, corruption, and weak state institutions.[32]

Nevertheless, China is rising and its influence is increasing. This is especially the case in East Asia. China's rise was an economic concern for the Association of Southeast Asian Nations (ASEAN). China replaced ASEAN as the most desirable destination in Asia for foreign direct investment (FDI), especially after the 1997 financial crisis. FDI in the ASEAN bloc in 2000 was at US $10 billion, a 37 percent decline from US $16 billion in 1999. The figure was US $27 billion in 1997.[33] China became even more competitive in attracting FDI in 2001 when it joined the World Trade Organization (WTO). At the same time, however, China quickly emerged as an economic opportunity for ASEAN. In 1995, China imported goods valued at US \$9.4 billion from ASEAN-5.[34] Japan imported almost five times more at US \$45 billion. However, between 1995 and 2000, Chinese imports from the group grew at a rate six times faster than Japanese imports from the same group.[35] It was against this background that, in November 2000, China and ASEAN announced their decision to start negotiations on a free trade agreement.

Chinese perceptions of the "China threat theory"

China's rise worries some observers and policymakers. Various versions of the "China threat" have emerged, including "China economic threat," "China grain threat," "China environment threat," "China military threat," "China civilization threat," "China energy threat," "China diplomacy threat," and "China model threat." These threats can be categorized into ideological, economic, and military dimensions.[36] A variant of the "China economic threat theory" alerts collapse of the Chinese economy. Gordon G. Chang predicted in 2001 that China "has five years, perhaps ten, before it falls."[37] Five years later, Chang insisted that China was "halfway" to its collapse.[38]

The perception of China as a threat is not new. When the Chinese Communist Party established the People's Republic of China (PRC) in 1949, the US-led West perceived China as an enemy, which was solidified after the Korean War. China became a semi ally of the United States in US rivalry with the Soviet Union in the 1970s. The semi alliance started to collapse in the mid 1980s when Mikhail Gorbachev became the Soviet leader and initiated revolutionary reforms which dramatically improved Soviet relations with the West. With the Cold War coming to an end in the early 1990s, China began to emerge as a threat again.

Chinese analysts noted that although the post-Cold War version of the "China threat theory" first appeared in a 1990 Japanese article,[39] the real source of the theory lies in American and European publications. Sha Qiguang, former director of the Research Division of the PRC State Council Information Office, noted in 2000 that the "China threat theory" reached its peak in 1995. Since then, it has had ups and downs, but never disappeared.[40] According to Chinese analysts, there have been four waves of the "China threat theory."[41] The first wave (1992–1993) started with Ross H. Munro's "Awakening Dragon" published in 1992.[42] The 1995–1996 Taiwan Strait crisis triggered off the second wave, represented by *The Coming Conflict with China*.[43] The third wave followed closely (1998–1999), highlighted by the *Cox Report*,[44] the Wen Ho Lee espionage case[45] and the 1996 US campaign finance controversy,[46] along with the publications of *Year of the Rat*[47] and *Red Dragon Rising*.[48] The most recent "China threat theory" is "the most substantive" (*zui ju shizhixing*).[49] It began with the release of Pentagon's annual report to Congress on China's military power on July 19, 2005,[50] followed by the US–China Economic and Security Review Commission's annual report issued in early November of 2005,[51] the 2006 Quadrennial Defense Review,[52] and a series of "anti-China" articles published by American media such as the *Weekly Standard* and the *New York Times*.[53]

Two other oft-mentioned "China threat" publications are Samuel Huntington's 1993 "The Clash of Civilizations?" and Lester R. Brown's 1995 *Who Will Feed China?: Wake-Up Call for a Small Planet*; both are respected and ridiculed to some extent. While Huntington suggests that the Confucian–Islamic connection "has emerged to challenge Western interests, values and power,"[54] Brown concludes:

> China's emergence as a massive grain importer will be the wake-up call that will signal trouble in the relationship between ourselves . . . and the natural systems and resources on which we depend. It may well force a redefinition of security, a recognition that food scarcity and the associated economic instability are far greater threats to security than military aggression is.[55]

Huntington's concern about the Confucian–Islamic connection does not materialize and Brown's sensational warning has been proved wrong. China completed its transition from aid recipient to international donor in 2005. The World Food Program made its last donation to China in April 2005, marking the end of a 26-year program which started in 1979 and supported more than 30 million hungry people. In the same year, China surpassed Japan to become the world's third-largest food aid donor, following the United States and the European Union.[56]

Just as grain was linked to security, many analysts see China's energy thirst as a much bigger security threat in various ways, from territorial disputes, such as those over the South China Sea and East China Sea, to cooperation with regimes in trouble with the West, including the Iranian, Sudanese, and Venezuelan governments. The deepened relationship between China and Russia is also interpreted as "an axis of oil" and a potential threat to the United States.[57] While the Japanese government has engaged China in a drawn-out competition over an oil pipeline from Russia since 2003, US domestic pressure, especially congressional pressure, forced the China National Offshore Oil Corporation (CNOOC) to withdraw its acquisition offer for Unocal, a US oil company, in 2005.

Initially Beijing simply dismissed the "China threat theory" as "pure fallacy," genuinely believing that China was too weak to threaten Western powers.[58] Although the first article refuting the "China threat theory" appeared in 1992, China did not launch its media campaign against it until 1996.[59] In late 2003, Beijing started to promote the "China's peaceful rise theory."[60] Zheng Bijian, the architect of the "China's peaceful rise theory," emphasizes that one of China's major strategies is to avoid the fate of the rising powers in modern history that used force to grab resources and to seek hegemony.[61] Beijing is so sensitive to "China threat" perceptions that it shied away from the word "rise" and opted for "peaceful development" in late 2004. It is also observed that China even made efforts not to use the word "rejuvenation" as it may remind Chinese neighbors of Chinese imperial system in history.[62]

Chinese analysts have identified some major factors deemed responsible for the rise of the "China threat theory":

Anti-China forces: The "China threat theory" often emerges at times when Sino–American relations are improving, indicating that there are forces in the United States that do not want to see the improvement of the relationship. These anti-China forces hate to see a stable and prosperous China and have been making efforts to divide and contain China.

Institutional interests: The "China military threat theory" reflects the Pentagon's deep-rooted style of making enemies, and its real intention is to secure additional defense funding.

US pursuit of "absolute power": The United States wants to continue to maintain its absolute superiority as "world's political leader," "absolute military hegemony," and "global economic giant." If there is not an enemy, it will be hard for the United States to formulate a major foreign policy to consolidate its power. Since there has been a rapid rise in China's national strength, China has become an "imaginary enemy" to the United States.

Prejudice and a misunderstanding of Chinese culture: The West has little understanding of Chinese non-expansionist culture. Xin Xiangyang argues that unlike the contemporary Western civilization, Chinese civilization is not based on expansion and exploitation. Instead, its growth is based on the growth within itself or the growth of "internal power" (*neigong*). In China's 5000-year history, there was only a short expansionist period of no more than 200 years. In contrast, in the 2500-year Western history since ancient Greece, there was an expansionist history totaling over 1000 years.[63] And in the 200 years (13th and 14th century) when China was indeed expansionist, Chinese analysts tend to point out that China was invaded and ruled by Mongols. Martin Stuart-Fox calls it "Mongol expansionism."[64]

To sabotage security cooperation in East Asia: The United States wants to create tensions and misunderstandings in the region in an effort to undermine regional security cooperation mechanisms in order to weaken Chinese influence and maintain US dominance.

The Taiwan factor: Although Washington may not want to see a military conflict across the Taiwan Strait, the "China military threat theory" will force Taiwan to purchase more arms from the United States. Not only does this satisfy American arms dealers, it also helps to perpetuate the status quo of separate rules across the Strait.

The above perceptions are more or less linked to a fundamental perception; that is, the United States and its allies, such as Japan, regard China as an adversary. Qin Yaqing, Professor of International Studies and Assistant President of China Foreign Affairs College, asserts that although American scholars and policymakers disagree on policy toward China, they "all take China as an adversary . . . They do not disagree about whether China will challenge the United States, but about when China will become strong enough to pose this challenge."[65]

Chinese analysts have advocated different approaches to the "China threat theory." Some argue that China should simply ignore it. These people believe that whatever China does, it will not be able to satisfy the proponents of the "China threat theory." When China was closed and did not develop, it was regarded as a threat. When it is developing well, it becomes a concern for many. China's active diplomacy to take up more international responsibilities is interpreted as China's ill-meant ambition (*yexin*) and China's reserved and low-profile diplomacy is taken as China's strategy of "biding for the time."[66]

Others argue that China cannot and should not simply ignore the "China threat theory." Pang Zhongying, the director of the Institute of Global Studies at Nankai University, argues that the best approach to the "China threat theory" is to face up to it. Under this approach, China could openly question US opposition to the European Union's intention to lift its arms embargo on China. US opposition is based on the argument that to lift the embargo will break the power balance in East Asia and the condition of human rights within China. Pang suggests that China should make it clear that US support for the Taiwan independence movement by approving large scale of arms sales to Taiwan is the real cause of instability in East Asia.[67]

At the same time, Pang agrees that it is important for China to address other countries' concerns and assure the world that it does not pose a threat. "Policy of assurance" appears to be China's official approach to the "China threat theory." According to Jia Qinqguo, professor and associate dean of the School of International Studies at Peking University, a majority of Chinese analysts support China's "policy of reassurance." Only a minority of analysts argue that it is impossible for China to win the trust of the only superpower and that confrontation and conflicts are inevitable. Jia concluded in 2005 that China's "policy of reassurance" was rather successful. He noted that the "China threat theory" "had run out of steam by 2004 in most countries" and that "most countries are willing to give China the benefit of the doubt." Meanwhile, Jia acknowledged that the success of China's policy of reassurance was "still quite limited" and other countries were not completely assured about the rise of China. What was particularly challenging to China were "some structural factors" which had complicated China's efforts to reassure the international community, such as the continued rapid growth of China's military capabilities, China's international influence, and China's political system which is different from Western liberal democracies.[68]

China's military development has been the key component of the "China threat theory." Some Chinese analysts argue that China should avoid "self-inflicted incapacitation" and should persist in the "balanced defense and economic development." On the other hand, Chinese analysts understand the peril of an arms race with the United States. An arms race with the United States "will massively deplete China's national strength."[69]

Chinese self perceptions

The Chinese effort to refute the "China threat theory" is closely related to Chinese national identity. William A. Callahan believes that Chinese responses to the "China threat theory" mainly target domestic audience for identity construction in China.[70] "Chinese identity production involves spreading anti-China discourse within the PRC in order to draw the symbolic boundaries that clearly distinguish Chinese from foreigners," Callahan argues.[71] By refuting "Chinese" threats, China is actually facilitating the production of a series of foreign threats, such as the America threat and the Japan threat. This serves to affirm China's national identity.

There is no clear indication that the "China threat theory" discourse in China is a well-coordinated, purposeful project of identity construction. Yet Callahan's observation has its merit. Historically, China was more a civilization than a nation. It was largely because of foreign invasions in the nineteenth century that "an essentially peaceful and 'Utopian' civilization" lost "many of its admirable features" and gradually developed into "a self-conscious national being in the modern Western sense."[72] Ever since then, victimhood has been part of Chinese identity. China's rise, after years of suffering and humiliation and others' negative reactions to it do help highlight Chinese differences and hence national identity.

An investigation of Chinese national identity by examining Chinese self perceptions is essential to understanding Chinese perspectives on China's rise and their responses to the "China threat theory." Bates Gill notes that "a country's self-perception shapes its approach to the world and the world's approach to it."[73] It should be borne in mind that all nations tend to believe that they are peace-loving. As Ted Osius points out, nation-states "almost uniformly" view their rise in the "benign framework" of posing no threat to other countries.[74]

The Chinese see the rise of China as a result of their pursuit of "rejuvenation of China" (*zhenxing Zhonghua*), beginning with Sun Yatsen, father of modern China, over a century ago. Yan Xuetong, a former senior analyst of the China Institute of Contemporary International Relations and now the director of the Institute of International Affairs at Tsinghua University, notes that the term "rejuvenation" refers to the psychological power embodied in the concept of China's rise to its former great power or even superpower status. This psychological power is reflected in the Chinese belief that China's rise is to regain China's lost international status rather than to obtain something new and that the rise of China is to restore fairness instead of gaining advantages over others. The former explains why the Chinese are continuously dissatisfied with their economic achievements—the economy is simply too weak for China to resume its superpower status. The latter defines Chinese expectation of their nation being a legitimate superpower. China's rise is therefore taken for granted.[75]

With regard to the "China threat theory," Yee and Zhu have noted the following counter arguments put forward by Chinese analysts:[76]

1   The nature of China's socialist system determines that China will never seek hegemony.
2   China's development needs a peaceful international environment.
3   The level of China's economic development is still very backward.
4   China's defense expenditure, which is necessary to ensure national security, is always kept at a low level.
5   China is a peace-loving country with no intention to invade other countries.

The above is by no means an exhaustive list. A few more important self-perceptions are worth mentioning.

China's power status

One of the most provocative studies about China's power status by Chinese analysts is "The Rise of China and Its Power Status" by Yan Xuetong. Yan first points out that for political and technical reasons, differences exist in assessing China's power status. "China threat" proponents tend to overestimate China's power status while many Chinese are inclined to underestimate it in order to dispel "China threat" perceptions or to caution the Chinese government. Yan's own assessment of China's comprehensive national power is that China is much weaker than the United States but stronger than other great powers (Table 2.1).[77]

As Yan is fully aware, some Chinese analysts disagree with his assessment. A retired Chinese ambassador criticized Chinese scholars who advocated that China assume greater international responsibilities. "Some people are carried away by our success and think that China is already a great power," he noted. "But China will be a developing country for a very long time. We should always remember Deng Xiaoping's words."[78] The diplomat was referring to Deng Xiaoping's 16-character principle set after the 1989 Tiananmen Square crackdown, namely *tao guang yang hui* (be skillful in hiding one's capacities and biding one's time), *shan yu shou zhuo* (be good at the tactics of low profile diplomacy), *jue bu dang tou* (never take the lead) and *you suo zuo wei* (take proper initiatives).[79]

Table 2.1 Early twenty-first-century state power structure for China, France, Britain, Russia, Japan, Germany, and India

	China	*France*	*Britain*	*Russia*	*Japan*	*Germany*	*India*
Military power	Strong	Strong	Strong	Strong	Weak	Weak	Strong
Political power	Strong	Strong	Strong	Strong	Weak	Weak	Weak
Economic power	Strong	Weak	Weak	Weak	Strong	Strong	Weak

China's effort to learn the rules of the game

Xia Liping, a senior analyst at the Shanghai Institute for International Studies, emphasizes that since the end of the Cold War, China has been redefining its security concept, from emphasis on military security to comprehensive security and from "zero-sum game" to "mutual security." China has also made more effort to deepen security dialogue and cooperation. Xia acknowledges that there is much room for China to increase its military transparency but argues that it takes time as "Chinese traditional military thinking contained nothing about transparency." As for the development of democracy and rule of law, "ultimately, China will become a democratic country ruled by law with Chinese characteristics," Xia asserts.[80]

China's rise as an opportunity

It is a well-publicized argument that China's rise presents other countries with a "win–win" opportunity. China's rise as an opportunity is not limited to the economic area. Based on the realist balance of power theory, Yan Xuetong argues that China's rise means peace. With the disappearance of the Soviet Union, the United States has become impatient with the slow process of diplomacy and hence resorted to "frequent use of military solutions."[81] The rise of China will help restore a balance of power in the Asia-Pacific region and thus contribute to the stability of the region. This helps to explain why unlike Europe, Africa, the Middle East, and Latin America, East Asia has had no regional wars since the end of the Cold War. "If China had declined like Russia, countries such as North Korea would have been faced with the same fate as Yugoslavia," claims Yan.[82] What Yan is implying is that without a strong China the West would be tempted to use force to resolve North Korea's nuclear issue, just as the 1999 Kosovo War in which US-led NATO bombed Yugoslavia for 78 days and Yugoslavia's former ally Russia was too weak to counterbalance NATO.

One more opportunity related to the rise of China is cultural. Citing long Chinese civilization, Yan argues that the rise of China will make the world more civilized. China's rise will help spread Chinese concept of "benevolence" (*ren*), which is the summation of human virtues like loyalty, reciprocity, wisdom, courage, righteousness, filial piety, and faithfulness, against the political culture created by the West in the past two centuries that emphasized power.[83]

China as an increasingly responsible power

Chinese analysts, like Chinese officials, often point to the fact that China has joined over 100 international organizations and has signed 300 international treaties. Premier Wen Jiabao notes that China stands ready to work together with the international community to facilitate the establishment of a new international political and economic order. China "stands as a staunch force for international peace and stability on such major international and regional issues bearing on peace such as the nuclear issue on the Korean peninsula and Iranian nuclear issue," says Wen.[84]

China's future development

While optimistic about China's future as a responsible great power, Chinese analysts also highlight some uncertainties. China's future development is dependent on various factors, both internal and external. Given that China will continue to focus on its economic development in the years to come and that China has a long, peace-loving culture and history, favorable external relations are essential, including continued economic interdependence, a continued trend of "peace and development," the "positive attitude" of other countries, and the development of "partnerships" between China and other countries.[85]

Challenges to China's rise

While confident that China will continue to rise, Chinese analysts are wary of some major challenges. Externally, China faces economic (market, resources, trade), security (traditional and nontraditional) and political (Westernization) challenges as well as the constraints of the existing international system dominated by the West. Internally, China has to deal with issues like social instability, the widening gap between rich and poor, mass unemployment, rampant corruption, and environmental degradation.[86]

The biggest threat to China is that internal and external threats combine forces. China's late paramount leader Deng Xiaoping used to remind his comrades that the 1989 Chinese students' anti-government demonstrations were the result of the combination of external environment and internal problems. Externally, the West had been trying to "peacefully change China" by exporting Western values to China. Internally, anti-government forces had played upon China's social problems, such as corruption and inflation. Similarly, Falun Gong and separatists in Tibet and Xinjiang have all been accused of plotting with foreign hostile forces for anti-China activities. The Taiwan issue is closely related to China's external security and internal stability. Externally, a military clash across the Taiwan Strait could end up with a China–US military conflict. Internally, a soft stance on the Taiwan issue could trigger off social instability and power struggle in China.

Other than these specific challenges, Chinese analysts have also noted that China faces some dilemmas in its foreign policy. First, it wants to become an important member of the international society and play a more active role in international affairs, which may consolidate its national security. Yet at the same time, to be deeply involved in international conflicts may derail China's economic development. Second, China wants to actively participate in building the international system, which may well benefit its national security. On the other hand, it does not want to be tied up by the system and lose its own autonomy. Third, to counter the "China threat theory," China has interests in international security cooperation. However, given its territorial disputes with a number of countries and the Taiwan issue, China is wary of paying "excessive prices" on sovereignty.[87] While arguing that China should adopt internationalism which advocates international cooperation, a prolific Chinese analyst emphasizes that a precondition for internationalism is to give priority to national sovereignty and national security.[88]

Chinese perspectives on a "fair and rational" international order[89]

An issue related to the rise of China is to what extent Beijing accepts the existing international order. Chinese leaders are not shy in calling for a fairer international order. In his address at the United Nations Summit on September 15, 2005, President Hu Jintao declared that China would "actively participate in international affairs and fulfill its international obligations, and work with other countries in building . . . a new international order that is fair and rational."[90]

As China watchers have noted, Chinese perceptions of the post-Cold War international system experienced some dramatic changes.[91] When the Soviet Union disintegrated and the Cold War came to an end in the early 1990s, many Chinese analysts were of the view that the world, which was in a US-dominated "unipolar moment," was moving toward multipolarity. By the mid 1990s, especially after the war in Kosovo, Chinese analysts realized that the United States as the only superpower was not in a rapid decline and the world would remain unipolar for years to come. This perception was reinforced by the United States war on terror.[92] This unipolar world, or more accurately "one superpower and multiple great powers" (*yi chao duo qiang*), does not serve China's national interests well. Chinese analysts believe that with a preponderance of power and influence the United States opted for unilateralism to strengthen and expand its global domination.

Samantha Blum has noted that although some Chinese analysts argue that the hegemonic order does provide public goods such as economic openness, peace, and security to members of the international community, others emphasize that hegemony and power politics are still rampant, "which is the real root-cause of turmoil in the world today."[93] Rosemary Foot has also observed that Chinese "mainstream strategy analysts" have "overall perceived a consistent and malign US strategy of global domination," and consider US hegemony to be "predatory in nature":

> In Beijing's view, the US is hegemonic, unilateralist, dismissive of international law and the United Nations, and wedded to "zero-sum" concepts of security that ignore non-traditional security concerns and the negative effects of the security dilemma. It is also economically protectionist.[94]

Chinese analysts are nevertheless pragmatic. They understand that China has to and can live with the current international order. After all, "other great powers do not wish to directly confront the US 'hegemonic' position," says Liu Jianfei of the Party School of the Central Committee of the Chinese Communist Party.[95] Some also warn that China should not single-mindedly seek multipolarity. In his quantitative study of international order, Zhou Fangyin criticizes some Chinese analysts for making emotional, instead of rational, assessment about the development of multipolarity. His study shows that there is no definitive evidence that the world is moving toward multipolarity. He emphasizes that the evolution of the international order cannot be forcefully changed or reversed. It can only be carefully guided and utilized at appropriate times. "We must do what we are capable of and make sure that our ambition of becoming a first-class great power will not turn into a burden to the development of our state and nation," warns Zhou.[96]

A majority of Chinese analysts, however, are confident that the international order is evolving as multipolarity is "the trend of the times" and is irreversible.[97] Here we need to clarify the Chinese concept of *duojihua*. In English publications, *duojihua* is normally translated as multipolar-ity or multipolar-ism. While this translation is correct in most contexts, it misses a key element—*hua*. *Duoji* means "multipolarity" while *hua* means "-ization." A difference exists between multipolar-ity or multipolar-ism and multipolar-ization in that the latter could refer to the process of the world moving toward multipolar-ity. Yu Sui, a senior analyst in China Contemporary World Research Centre and Senior Advisor to China Institute for International Strategic Studies, stresses that "the *hua* (-ization) in *duojihua* (multipolarization) demonstrates that the gap between 'multiple great powers' and 'one superpower' is gradually narrowing instead of widening."[98] Qian Wenrong, a senior analyst in Xinhua News Agency's World Affairs Research Center, argues that today's world is neither a multipolar world nor a unipolar world. Instead, it is in the transitional period of moving toward a multipolar world with unipolarity and multipolarity competing against each other. Qian estimates that this transitional period may last 30–50 years,[99] while Ruan Zongze, Vice President of the China Institute of Contemporary International Relations, puts it at 20–30 years.[100]

Chinese analysts tend to claim moral high ground in promoting multipolarity, saying that it "represents China's moral stance and its sense of responsibility to the international society."[101] They do acknowledge that this is also in China's national interest—to facilitate the growth of Chinese strength and to expand China's strategic interests.[102] Wang Yizhou, a senior analyst from the Chinese Academy of Social Sciences, noted in 1998 that "one of the basic goals of multipolarity is to prevent the formation of US-led unipolar world to avoid the consequent negative impact or pressure upon China."[103] This is in fact China's short-term goal, according to Wang. In the medium term, multipolarity would enable all states to seek peace and development. In the long term, a strong China would endeavor to transform the unreasonable (*buheli*) international order.[104] Wang repeated the above argument in his book published in 2003 but added that China should not reject the existing international order outright. Instead, China should try to establish an image that China is behaving as a responsible great power and, in the context of peace and development, is gradually reforming the existing international political and economic order.[105]

Chinese analysts and think tanks made efforts to study the approaches that China should take in helping to construct a new international order. One such think tank is the China Reform Forum headed by Zheng Bijian. A study of the Forum suggests that to help construct a new international order, China should:

1   Enhance its power and expand its interests as the basis for its active participation;
2   Emphasize the importance of values;
3   Emphasize the roles of international regimes;
4   Emphasize the roles of the UN;
5   Start with regional order;
6   Take up great-power responsibilities and establish itself as an active, responsible, constructive and predictable constructor of the international order.[106]

While strongly supporting a multipolar world, Beijing seldom articulates its vision of international order, other than broad principles like "establishing a new international political and economic order," "promoting world peace and common development" and "opposing hegemonism and power politics."[107] There could be multiple reasons for the lack of clarity. It could be that multipolarity is only a distant vision, an ideal and Beijing has not thought about it carefully. It could also be that the concept of multipolarity is clear enough as a common sense and is readily shared by other states.

One other reason could be that China is not prepared to take up more responsibilities. Pang Zhongying notes that the Chinese still tend to only focus on national interests and have little sense of responsibility for the global order. Some are also concerned that if China does assume a more prominent role in both regional and international organizations, it could be misunderstood as China's campaign to expand its sphere of influence, hence the "China threat theory." While acknowledging that as a rising power, China should take on a larger and more responsible role in global affairs, Pang believes that China "is not fully prepared to embrace the notion that it is a custodian of the current international system, with all of the responsibilities that would entail." Pang also points out that China's top priority at present and for the foreseeable future is to deal with domestic problems. "Its capacity in dealing with pressing global issues is relatively limited," concludes Pang.[108]

One more reason why Beijing seldom articulates its vision of international order could be that China deliberately keeps it vague in order to avoid conflicts with the United States. Qian Wenrong suggests that China should not over-emphasize multipolarity as it may offend the United States.[109]

Indeed, a key issue in China's advocacy for a multipolar world is China's relations with the United States, which have become increasingly complex and delicate with China's rise. Evan S. Medeiros and M. Taylor Fravel noted that in the first few years of the twenty-first century there emerged "a critical shift" in Chinese analysts' view of the international system and China's role in it. These analysts advocate that China abandon its long-held victim mentality (*shouhaizhe xintai*). The Chinese should stop using China's "Century of Humiliation" as the main lens in viewing their place in modern international affairs and should instead adopt a "great-power mentality" (*daguo xintai*).[110] Some Chinese analysts believe that China has almost completed the shift. Li Baojun and Xu Zhengyuan assert:

> By establishing various and substantive partnership relations with other great powers, China has resolved the legitimate issue of seeking national power and great power status, completed the conceptual shift on its views about its power and its great-power perspective, started to face and positively evaluate its growing power, formally acknowledged and publicly established its great power status, gradually got rid of the long-held victim psychology.[111]

As mentioned above, Yan Xuetong believes that China is now the second most powerful state after the United States. This does not mean that China is ready to challenge the United States and to transform the current international order. Shi Yinhong, a professor of international relations and the director of the Centre for American Studies at Renmin University of China, argues that China must cooperate with the "first-rate great power and the international regimes supported by it" before "transcending" this accommodation by contributing to the peaceful transformation of international society from one dominated or controlled by Western great powers to one in which the West, and especially the United States, accepts the need to coexist in an equal and reasonable manner with newly rising non-Western states.[112] The official *Beijing Review* also lists "to realize the peaceful and steady development of Sino-US strategic relationship" as one of the challenges to China's peaceful rise.[113]

Conclusion

As "a civilization whose pretensions to superiority are deeply embedded in the national psyche,"[114] China is determined to become a global great power and to regain international standing and respect. Despite many uncertainties, the Chinese believe that they are realizing their great power dream. Seeing China's rise as the nation's "rejuvenation" and perceiving themselves peace-loving, the Chinese reject the "China threat theory" as either anti-China campaigns or Western prejudice. They tend to take it for granted that the international society should accept and accommodate China's rise and believe that future China will be shaped by what others do to China. This is partly due to China's victim mentality. "It also reflects a certain propensity to absolve itself of its own responsibility for its destiny," argues Bates Gill.[115]

It appears that China is increasingly confident in casting itself as a great power. One indication is the twelve-part documentary television series *The Rise of the Great Powers* broadcast on China Central Television in 2006. The documentary discusses the rise of nine great powers since the fifteenth century. It is widely perceived as a serious effort in that the producers were not constrained by ideology and victim mentality. Reportedly, a team of elite Chinese historians contributed to the series and briefed China's *Politburo* about their findings.[116]

A more confident, less ideological and unresentful China could be conducive to the emergence of China as a responsible great power. It would help China to address other countries' concerns about its rise in a more sophisticated, rational manner. Clearly, the acceptance of China's rise by the international society is a core Chinese national interest. Nevertheless, China's rise will remain a challenge to the international society. It is well known that realists see rising powers as trouble makers. Although liberals are not so pessimistic, they are also wary of the challenges to the international society associated with rising powers.

It is noted that China's foreign policy since the end of the Cold War has experienced major changes in a liberal direction. Medeiros and Fravel noted in 2003 that "in the last ten years, Chinese foreign policy has become far more nimble and engaging than at any other time in the history of the People's Republic."[117] Evidence of these changes include the expanded number and depth of China's bilateral relationships, new trade and security accords, deepened participation in key multilateral organizations, widening acceptance of many prevailing international rules and institutions and efforts to help address global security issues.[118]

Noting China's joining of the WTO, its contribution to UN peacekeeping and peace-building operations, and its interest in nuclear nonproliferation since the end of the Cold War, Rosemary Foot concluded in 2006:

> while there were to be many continuities with the Deng [Xiaoping] era, Jiang [Zemin] and his successor Hu Jintao have moved on to emphasize the importance of economic globalization, the multidimensional nature of security, and the need to recognize the responsibility of the great powers, including China, for maintaining global order.[119]

It is fair to say that China is now more versed in and more comfortable with liberal norms. It is more willing to take up responsibilities, domestic and international. It is making more serious efforts to address the concerns of other countries. At the same time, however, realism continues to determine Chinese foreign policy. Yong Deng observed in 1998 that despite the growing *idealpolitik*, the dominant thinking of international relations among Chinese analysts was still realist.[120] Lampton also noted in 2001 that "although there is plenty of evidence of increasing Chinese cooperation and conformity with international norms, there is little evidence that considerations of national interest and realpolitik figure any less prominently in Chinese thinking than they always have."[121]

Similarly, while liberal norms have become increasingly influential, realist understanding of international politics still is the most important factor in shaping Chinese perspectives on China's rise and their responses to the "China threat theory."

Notes

1   Robert S. Ross, "Assessing the China Threat," *The National Interest* (Fall 2005), pp. 81–87.
2   Hao Yufan, "Interpreting Chinese Foreign Policy: The Micro-Macro Linkage Approach" (book review), *American Political Science Review*, Vol. 92, No. 2 (June 1998), p. 510.
3   Bin Yu, "The Study of Chinese Foreign Policy: Problems and Prospect," *World Politics*, Vol. 46, No. 2 (January 1994), p. 244.
4   Yu, p. 246.
5   Gilbert Rozman, *The Chinese Debate about Soviet Socialism, 1978–1985* (Princeton, NJ: Princeton University Press, 1987); Allen S. Whiting, *China Eyes Japan* (Berkeley *et al.*: University of California Press, 1989); David Shambaugh, *Beautiful Imperialist: China Perceives America, 1972–1990* (Princeton, NJ: Princeton University Press, 1991).
6   Yu, p. 247.
7   Ibid, p. 254.
8   Thomas J. Christensen, "Chinese Realpolitik," *Foreign Affairs*, Vol. 75, No. 5 (September-October 1996), p. 37.
9   Bonnie S. Glaser and Philip C. Saunders, "Chinese Civilian Foreign Policy Research Institutes: Evolving Roles and Increasing Influence," *China Quarterly*, Vol. 171 (September 2002), p. 614.
10   Xuanli Liao, *Chinese Foreign Policy Think Tanks and China's Policy toward Japan* (Hong Kong: Chinese University Press, 2006), p. 3.
11   David Shambaugh, "China's International Relations Think Tanks: Evolving Structure and Process," *China Quarterly*, Vol. 171 (September 2002), pp. 575–576.
12   Ibid, p. 581.
13   Ibid.
14   Quansheng Zhao, "Impact of Intellectuals and Think Tanks on Chinese Foreign Policy," in Yufan Hao and Lin Su, editors, *China's Foreign Policymaking: Societal Force and Chinese American Policy* (Aldershot, Hampshire, UK and Burlington, US: Ashgate, 2005), pp. 134–135.
15   David M. Lampton, "China's Foreign and National Security Policymaking Process: Is It Changing, and Does It Matter?" in David M. Lampton, editor, *The Making of Chinese Foreign and Security Policy in the Era of Reform, 1978–2000* (Stanford, CA.: Stanford University Press, 2001), p. 5.
16   Yang Qinglin, "Zhongguo shida zhiku jiti fuchu shuimian" [China's Top Ten Think Tanks Emerge Together], *Ta Kung Pao* (November 8, 2007) at www. takungpao.com/news/06/11/09/MW-647953.htm, accessed March 18, 2007.
17   Glaser and Saunders, pp. 608–613.

18 Murray Scot Tanner, "Changing Windows on a Changing China: The Evolving 'Think Tank' System and the Case of the Public Security Sector," *China Quarterly*, Vol. 171 (September 2002), p. 572.

19 Herbert Yee and Zhu Feng, "Chinese Perspectives of the China Threat: Myth or Reality?" in Herbert Ye and Ian Storey, editors, *The China Threat: Perceptions, Myths and Reality* (London and New York: RoutledgeCurzon, 2002), p. 27. It should be noted that many Chinese articles are not scholarly research but superficial rebuttals to the "China threat theory."

20 Avery Goldstein, "Great Expectations: Interpreting China's Arrival," *International Security*, Vol. 22, No. 3 (Winter 1997), pp. 54–55.

21 Stuart Harris, "The People's Republic of China's Quest for Great Power Status: A Long and Winding Road," in Hung-mao Tien and Yun-han Chu, editors, *China under Jiang Zemin* (Boulder, London: Lynne Rienner Publisher, 2000), p. 165.

22 Goldstein, p. 37.

23 Guo Wanchao, *Zhongguo Jueqi* [*Rise of China*] (Nanchang, Jiangxi: Jiangxi Renmin Chubanshe, 2004), p. 24.

24 Michael Pillsbury, *China Debates the Future Security Environment* (Washington, DC: National Defense University Press, January 2000), www.fas.org/nuke/guide/china/doctrine/pills2/, accessed June 7, 2007.

25 Ibid.

26 Yan Xuetong, *Zhongguo Guojia Liyi Fenxi* [*An Analysis of China's National Interests*], (Tianjin: Tianjin Renmin Chubanshe, 1996), p. 309.

27 Chu Shulong and Wang Zaibang, "Guanyu guoji xingshi he wo duiwai zhanlue ruogan zhongda wenti de sikao" [Some Thoughts on Several Major Issues about International Situation and Our External Strategy], *Xiandai Guoji Guanxi* [*Contemporary International Relations*], No. 8 (1999), p. 6; Yan Xuetong, "Guoji huanjing ji waijiao sikao" [International Environment and Thoughts on Diplomacy], *Xiandai Guoji Guanxi* [*Contemporary International Relations*], No. 8 (1999), p. 10.

28 Keith Bradsher, "Chinese Economy Grows to 4th Largest in the World," *New York Times*, January 25, 2006.

29 Michael J. Mandel, "Does It Matter If China Catches up to the US?" *Business Week*, No. 3911 (December 6, 2004), p. 122.

30 Renato Cruz de Castro, "Exploring the Prospect of China's Peaceful Emergence in East Asia," *Asian Affairs: An American Review*, Vol. 33, No. 2 (Summer 2006), pp. 85–86.

31 Wilson, Dominic and Roopa Purushothaman, "Dreaming With BRICs: The Path to 2050," *Global Economics Paper No: 99*, Goldman Sachs [online article], (October 1, 2003), p. 12 www.usmra.com/china/outlook2004.htm, accessed July 7, 2007.

32 Joseph S. Nye, "Fear of Chinese Guns: The Best Defense is Not to Offer Any Offense," *The San Francisco Chronicle*, April 9, 2006.

33 Isgani de Castro, "Politics: New Pacts May Give China Key Role in Southeast Asia," *Global Information Network*; New York (November 5, 2002).

34 ASEAN-5 refers to the five founding members of the ASEAN: Indonesia, Malaysia, Philippines, Singapore, and Thailand.

35 Datuk Seri Abdullah Ahmad Badawi, "Challenge and Opportunity" (September 17, 2003), p. 10.

36 Tao Jiyi, "Meiguo zhengzhi xuezhe dui 'Zhongguo weixielun' de pibo tanxi" [An analysis of American honest scholars' rebuttal of the "China threat theory"], *Guoji Wenti Yanjiu* [*International Studies*], No. 3 (2005), p. 20; Emma V. Broomfield, "Perceptions of Danger: the China threat theory," *Journal of Contemporary China*, Vol. 12, No. 35 (2003), p. 266.

37   Gordon G. Chang, *The Coming Collapse of China* (New York: Random House, 2001).

38   Gordon G. Chang, "Halfway to China's Collapse," *Far Eastern Economic Review*, Vol. 169, No. 5 (June 2006), pp. 25–28.

39   Wang Yunxiang, " 'Zhongguo weixielun' xi" [An Analysis of the "China Threat Theory"], *Guoji Guancha* [*International Observation*], No. 3 (1996), p. 35.

40   Sha Qiguang, "Dui xifang meiti sanbu 'Zhongguo weixielun' de pingxi" [An analysis of the "China threat theory" spread by Western media], *Guoji Zhengzhi Yanjiu* [*International Political Studies*], No. 3 (2000), pp. 113–114.

41   Yan Bai, " 'Zhongguo weixielun' de sici chaoliu" [The Four Waves of the "China Threat Theory"], *Shishi Baogao* [*Current Affairs Report*], No. 10 (2005), p. 70. For a comprehensive survey and critique of the "China threat theory" works, see Shi Aiguo, *Aoman yu Pianjian: Dongfang zhuyi yu Meiguo de "Zhongguo weixielun" yanjiu* [*Pride and Prejudice: A research on Orientalism and the "China threat theory" in the United States*], (Guangzhou: Zhongshan Daxue Chubanshe, 2004).

42   Ross H. Munro, "Awakening Dragon: The real danger in Asia is coming from China," *Policy Review*, no. 62 (Fall 1992), pp. 10–16.

43   Richard Bernstein and Ross H. Munro, *The Coming Conflict with China* (New York: A.A. Knopf: Distributed by Random House, 1997).

44   On 25 May 1999, the House Select Committee on US National Security and Military/Commercial Concerns with the People's Republic of China issued a declassified version of its report (commonly know as the Cox Report after Representative Chris Cox) on China's acquisition of US technology in a number of sensitive areas, including nuclear weapons, high-performance computers, and missile and space systems. The report's charges and assessment of Chinese acquisition of US nuclear weapons technology have been controversial. www.house.gov/coxreport/, accessed April 22, 2007.

45   In 1999, Wen Ho Lee, a Taiwanese-American physicist, was accused of stealing the "crown jewels" of the US nuclear program and giving them to mainland China. Lee was never charged with spying and the case ended with a plea bargain to a relatively minor charge of mishandling classified data. http://en.wikipedia.org/wiki/Wen_Ho_Lee, accessed April 22, 2007.

46   The controversy was an alleged effort by the PRC to influence American domestic politics prior to and during the Clinton administration. Kevin Cooney, *Japan's Foreign Policy Since 1945*, (New York: M.E. Sharpe, 2007), pp. 103–104.

47   Edward Timperlake and William C. Triplett II, *Year of the Rat: How Bill Clinton Compromised US Security for Chinese Cash* (Washington: Regency, 1998).

48   Edward Timperlake and William C. Triplett II, *Red Dragon Rising: Communist China's Military Threat to America* (Washington: Regency, 1999).

49   Yan Bai, p. 70.

50   The Department of Defense report to Congress on "The Military Power of the People's Republic of China" cites China as a regional power with "global aspirations." Although it welcomes a peaceful and prosperous China, the report considers China at "a strategic crossroads" and notes that China's future military capabilities "could pose a credible threat to other modern militaries operating in the region." www.dod.mil/pubs/china.html, accessed April 22, 2007.

51   The US–China Economic and Security Review Commission is an advisory group to Congress on relations with China. The commission's 2005 report faults China on a number of bilateral issues, including alleged manipulation of its currency, violations of intellectual property rights and subsidies to Chinese industries, as well as technology transfers. www.uscc.gov/researchpapers/annual_reports.htm, accessed April 22, 2007.

52 The Pentagon's 2006 Quadrennial Defense Review notes that China has "the greatest potential to compete militarily with the United States and field disruptive military technologies that over time offset traditional US military advantages." www.defenselink.mil/qdr/report/Report20060203.pdf, accessed April 22, 2007.
53 Yan Bai, p. 70.
54 Samuel P. Huntington, "The Clash of Civilizations?", *Foreign Affairs*, Vol. 72, Iss. 3 (Summer 1993), p. 24.
55 Lester R. Brown's *Who Will Feed China?: Wake-Up Call for a Small Planet* (New York: W.W. Norton & Company, Inc. Worldwatch Institute, Environmental Alert Series. 1995), p. 32.
56 Jonathan Watts, "China shifts from receiving to giving foreign aid as economic boom continues," *The Guardian*, December 15, 2004. www.guardian.co.uk/china/story/0,7369,1373830,00.html#article_continue, accessed July 8, 2007; "China emerges as major food donor," *People's Daily Online*, July 21, 2006 http://English.people.com.cn/200607/21/eng20060721_285296.html, accessed July 9, 2007.
57 Irwin M. Stellzer, "The Axis of Oil," *The Weekly Standard*, February 7, 2005, pp. 25–28.
58 Jia Qingguo, "Learning to Live with the Hegemon: Evolution of China's policy toward the US since the end of the Cold War," *Journal of Contemporary China*, Vol. 14, No. 44 (August 2005), p. 406.
59 Yee and Zhu, pp. 21–42.
60 *Zheng Bijian, Chairman of China Reform Forum, first put forward the "China's peaceful rise theory" in November 2003 at Boao Forum for Asia. Zheng is a close associate and advisor to President Hu Jintao.* Chinese Premier Wen Jiabao first used China's "peaceful rise" in his speech at Harvard on December 10, 2003. Hu Jintao declared that China "should stick to the development strategy of peaceful rise" on February 17, 2004, in his speech at the 110th anniversary of Mao Zedong's birthday. See William A. Callahan, "How to Understand China: The danger and opportunities of being a rising power," *Review of International Studies*, Vol. 31, No. 4 (2005), p. 702; Liu Yi and Wang Xialing, "Dui Zhongguo jueqi de sikao" [Thoughts about the Rise of China], *Dangdai Yatai* [*Contemporary Asia Pacific*], No. 2 (2005), p. 19.
61 Zheng Bijian, "China's 'Peaceful Rise' to Great-Power Status," *Foreign Affairs*, Vol. 84, No. 5 (September/October 2005), pp. 18–24.
62 Zhiqun Zhu, *US–China Relations in the Twenty-First Century: Power Transition and Peace* (London and New York: Routledge, 2006), p. 174.
63 Xin Xiangyang, "Xuer: Da shiye zhong de Zhongguo jueqi" [Prelude 2: The rise of China in a broad context], in Guo Wanchao, p. 3.
64 Martin Stuart-Fox, *A Short History of China and Southeast Asia: Tribute, Trade and Influence* (Crows Nest, New South Wales: Allen & Unwin, 2003), pp. 52–72.
65 Qin Yaqing, "A Response to Yong Deng: Power, Perception, and the Culture Lens," *Asian Affairs, an American Review*, Vol. 28, No. 3 (Fall 2001), pp. 157–158.
66 Pang Zhongying, "Dui 'Zhongguo weixielun' caiqu xin zhitai" [New Attitude toward the "China Threat Theory"], *Liaowang Xinwen Zhoukan* (*Liaowang Weekly*), No. 9 (February 28, 2005), p. 54.
67 Ibid.
68 Jia Qingguo, "Peaceful Development: China's policy of reassurance," *Australian Journal of International Affairs*, Vol. 59, No. 4 (December 2005), pp. 502–504.
69 " 'Experts' warns against 'China threat theory' weakening China's defence," *BBC Monitoring International Reports*, February 15, 2006.
70 Callahan's article attracted the attention of Chinese analysts. An edited version of the article was translated and published in a respected Chinese academic

journal. See Weilian A. Kalahan, "Zhongguo minzu zhuyi de jiexian—
'Zhongguo weixielun': goujia rentong de yizhong shouduan" [William A.
Callahan, "The Limits of Chinese Nationalism: The 'China Threat Theory' as a
Means of Identity Construction"], *Shijie Jingji yu Zhengzhi* [*World Economics
and Politics*], No. 11 (2005), pp. 35–41.
71   Callahan, p. 709.
72   T'ang Leang-Li, *China in Revolt: How a Civilization Became a Nation* (London:
N. Douglas, 1927), p. xv. www.questia.com/library/book/china-in-revolt-how-
a-civilization-became-a-nation-by-tang-leang-li.jsp, accessed June 11, 2007.
73   Bates Gill, "Discussion of 'China: A responsible great power,'" *Journal
of Contemporary China*, Vol. 10, No. 26 (2001), pp. 27–32.
74   Ted Osius, "Discussion of 'The Rise of China in Chinese Eyes,'" *Journal
of Contemporary China*, Vol. 10, No. 26 (2001), p. 42.
75   Yan Xuetong, "The Rise of China in Chinese Eyes," *Journal of Contemporary
China*, Vol. 10, No. 26 (2001), p. 34.
76   Yee and Zhu, pp. 27–29.
77   Yan Xuetong, "The Rise of China and Its Power Status," *Chinese Journal of
International Politics*, Vol. 1, No. 1 (2006), pp. 5–33.
78   As cited in Bonnie S. Glaser, "Ensuring the 'Go Abroad' Policy Serves China's
Domestic Priorities," *China Brief*, Vol. 7, No. 5 (March 8, 2007), p. 4.
79   Jian Yang, "China's Security Strategy and Policies," in Stephen Hoadley and
Jürgen Rüland, editors, *Asian Security Reassessed* (Singapore: Institute of
Southeast Asian Studies), p. 93.
80   Xia Liping, "China: A responsible great power," *Journal of Contemporary China*,
Vol. 10, No. 26 (2001), pp. 17–25.
81   Yan Xuetong, "The Rise of China in Chinese Eyes," pp. 36–37.
82   Ibid. p. 37.
83   Ibid, pp. 37–38.
84   *UPI International Intelligence*, "Chinese PM downplays 'China Threat,'" March
15, 2006.
85   Xia Liping, pp. 17–25.
86   Guo Wanchao, pp. 69–94.
87   Meng Xiangqing, "Lun Zhonguo de guoji juese zhuanhuan yu duiwai aiquan
zhanlue de jiben dingwei" [On the Changes to China's International Role and
the Fundamentals of China's External Security Strategy], *Shijie Jingji yu
Zhengzhi* [*World Economics and Politics*], No. 7 (2002), pp. 12–13.
88   Guo Xuetang, "Guoji zhuyi yu Zhongguo waijiao de jiazhi huigui" [Inter-
nationalism and the Return to Traditional Values in Chinese Foreign Policy],
Guoji Guancha [*International Observation*], No. 1 (2005), p. 38.
89   There is a difference between international order and world order in International
Relations. The former focuses on international system while the latter is
individual-oriented. Chinese analysts normally do not make such difference. They
use international order (*guoji zhixu* or *guoji geju*) more than world order (*shijie
geju*), both referring to international order. This chapter follows Chinese practice
for the purpose of convenience.
90   As cited in Pang Zhongying, "China, My China," *National Interest*, No. 83
(Spring 2006), p. 9.
91   See for example, Rosalie Chen, "China Perceives America: Perspectives of international relations experts," *Journal of Contemporary China*, Vol. 12, No. 35
(2003), pp. 285–297; Samantha Blum, "Chinese Views of US Hegemony,"
Journal of Contemporary China, Vol. 12, No. 35 (2003), pp. 239–264.
92   Xiao Feng, "Shijie 'duojihua' qushi hui nizhuan ma?" [Will the Trend of World
Multipolarity Be Reversed?], *Dangdai Shijie* [*The Contemporary World*],
No. 8 (2002), p. 7.

93 Blum, pp. 241–248.
94 Rosemary Foot, "Chinese Strategies in a US-hegemonic Global Order: Accommodating and Hedging," *International Affairs*, Vol. 82, No. 1 (2006), pp. 82–83.
95 As quoted in Liu Yantang and Liu Xinyu, "Guoji biange: Shijie yu Zhongguo de zhanlue hudong" [International Changes: Strategic Interactions between the world and China], *Liaowang Xinwen Zhoukan* [*Liaowang Weekly*], No. 9 (February 28, 2005), p. 28.
96 Zhou Fangyin, "Dui dangqian guoji gejiu de julei fengxi" [A Categorized Study of Current International Order], *Xiandai Guoji Guanxi* [*Contemporary International Relations*], No. 12 (2000), p. 43.
97 Qian Wenrong, "Duojihua shi dangjin shijie geju fazhan de keguan qushi" [Multipolarization Is the Actual Trend of the Development of Today's World Order], *Heping yu Fazhan* [*Peace and Development*], No. 3 (2004), pp. 16–18; Yu Sui, "Shijie duojihua wenti" [The Issue of Multipolarization of the World], *Guoji Zhengzhi yu Guoji Guanxi* [*International Politics and International Relations*], No. 3 (2004), pp. 15–20.
98 Yu Sui, p. 16.
99 Qian Wenrong, p. 16.
100 Liu Yantang and Liu Xinyu, p. 28.
101 Li Baojun and Xu Zhengyuan, "Lengzhanhou Zhongguo fuzeren daguo shenfen de goujian" [The Construction of China's Identity as a Responsible Great Power since the End of the Cold War], *Jiaoxue yu Yanjiu* [*Teaching and Research*], No. 1 (2006), p. 53.
102 Men Honghua, p. 11.
103 Wang Yizhou, "Sikao 'duojihua'" [Thoughts about "Multipolarity"], *Guoji Jingji Pinglun* [*International Economic Review*], No. 9–10 (1998), p. 26.
104 Ibid, p. 27.
105 Wang Yizhou, *Quanqiu Zhengzhi yu Zhongguo Waijiao* [*Global Politics and China's Foreign Policy*], (Beijing: Shijie Zhishi Chubanshe, 2003), p. 217.
106 Men Honghua, pp. 11–13.
107 Foot, pp. 90–91.
108 Pang Zhongying, "China, My China," pp. 9–10.
109 Qian Wenrong, p. 18.
110 Evan S. Medeiros and M. Taylor Fravel, "China's New Diplomacy," *Foreign Affairs*, Vol. 82, No. 6 (November/December 2003), p. 32.
111 Li Baojun and Xu Zhengyuan, p. 54.
112 Foot, p. 91.
113 "Objectives of China's Rise: Rise for Peace," *Beijing Review*, Vol. 47, No. 24 (June 17, 2004).
114 Stuart-Fox, p. 155.
115 Gill, pp. 27–32.
116 Joseph Kahn, "China, shy giant, shows signs of shedding its false modesty," *New York Times*, December 9, 2006. www.nytimes.com/2006/12/09/world/asia/09china.html?ex=1323320400&en=dad26021a6a1aed8&ei=5088&partner=rssnyt&emc=rss, accessed June 10, 2007.
117 Medeiros and Fravel, p. 23.
118 Ibid.
119 Foot, p. 86.
120 Yong Deng, "The Chinese Conception of National Interests in International Relations," *China Quarterly*, Vol. 154 (June 1998), p. 320.
121 Lampton, pp. 24–25.

3 Chinese–American hegemonic competition in East Asia

A new cold war or into the arms of America?[1]

Kevin J. Cooney

Introduction

The primary task of this chapter will be to examine the hegemonic competition between the United States and China in East Asia. While the United States and the Soviet Union strived to keep their distance (economically and militarily) from each other during the Cold War, the hegemonic competition between the United States and China is remarkable for its all-out economic engagement between the two. At the same time these two nations are preparing their militaries for conflict with each other. When thinking about the Sino–American relationship one could easily get the picture of two men hugging each other in "friendship" with knives poised at each other's back waiting for the other to make a wrong move. Each side needs the other; neither trusts the other.

Examining this intricate engagement between rivals will be no simple task as nothing ever happens in a vacuum, and the bilateral Sino–American relationship is no exception. The relationship is very complex with numerous variables outside the control of either nation. The politics, geography, resources (and the lack thereof), economics, and history of the nations of East Asia all play a role in shaping the policy decisions of Beijing and Washington toward each other. Furthermore, the overall global geopolitical situation provides both opportunities and constraints for both nations.

Before beginning with the analysis an explanation of some of the fundamental assumptions in this chapter is needed. The first and most important is the rejection of the conventional wisdom that the United States is in decline especially vis-á-vis China. This notion is flat out rejected as having no empirical basis in fact when one examines the data in the overall global geopolitical and economic contexts. Furthermore, the data would indicate that overall American military power along with its economic power are not only *not in decline*, but rather that they are still in ascendancy. The global discourse about the "rise of China" (whether one views it positively or negatively) results in a false impression that a hegemonic shift is about to take place. It is not. This hegemonic shift argument fails to account for the overall global political and economic context.[2] This chapter will present the case that a hegemonic shift is not likely in the near future and that it is only likely in the long term

(100 plus years). Evelyn Goh in the next chapter takes the middle range approach by seeing it as a being at least 50-plus years into the future.

This is not to imply that China is not rising; it is in fact rising at a spectacular rate. China is narrowing the gap between itself and the rest of the world. The problem for those that see a hegemonic shift in the process is that neither American military nor economic power are in decline. As will be shown in detail throughout the chapter China's rise will continue but not necessarily at the expense of American economic or military power. Moreover, the rise of China is likely to fuel American ascendancy rather than hasten its decline. This argument for American ascendancy will run parallel to the argument on the rise of China throughout the chapter.

The organization of the chapter will take the following form. First we will examine the "Great China Question" as to the actions and intentions of China toward the United States, East Asia, and globally. This will be followed by an examination of United States policy toward China. The final section will briefly look at how the nations of Asia, both American allies and non-allies alike, are hedging their bets by engaging China economically, while retaining the option of running "into the arms of America"[3] should China prove to be an aggressor nation.

The Great China question

There is a cartoon with Uncle Sam on stage and a hook reaching out to remove him while China waits to the side for its time on stage. The caption reads, "Your 15 minutes are almost up Sammy." China is seen as a nation waiting in the wings to succeed the United States as the dominant global hegemon. If China is a potential threat to American global domination then the fundamental questions of Asian Security (and of global security in general) are:

- What are China's true intentions?
- Is China a growing hegemon that will return the world to a bipolar system?
- Will China be an *aggressor* nation balanced against United States hyper power?
- Will China be seen as a threat by and to Asia as well as America and its principal ally in the region, Japan?
- Or is China simply a developing nation, as it claims, that is peacefully expanding its power base to protect its own interests?

For American foreign and security policymakers, there is currently no greater question that needs to be answered.

The current war on terror is a known factor for American policy. Terrorism is a clear and present danger to America and its allies; however, China is a *possible future* threat to America. Prudence and realism would dictate that the United States prepares for an aggressor China. Idealism on the other hand, suggests that the United States (and the region) should work with China and try to engage China politically and economically in order to encourage the peaceful growth of China politically, militarily, and economically. So what is the United States doing? In many ways it is doing both, under the current administration of George W. Bush. It is prioritizing the more prudent and cautious realist hard line quietly while encouraging the engagement of China economically and to a lesser extent diplomatically. The problem with this policy is that it leads to schizophrenic perceptions of American policy which are justified. The United States is economically heavily investing itself in China as rapidly as possible. This economic investment ties China's future success to the United States and vice versa.

At the same time, America is politically engaging China in disputes over the trade imbalance, the value of the Yuan, and other economic issues in a protectionist way. It is also continuing to challenge China on its human rights record. Concurrently, the American military is preparing for a future where China is the enemy. In its latest report to Congress on the *Military Power of the People's Republic of China 2006*,[4] the Department of Defense questions China's intentions. It notes that China's leaders have "failed to explain" in an "adequate" way the rationale behind their many recent arms purchases that appear to be targeting the United States military.[5] This report to Congress is then used to justify American military expenditures to counter the growing "China Threat" to American security.

When one looks at all of these policies individually the schizophrenia of American policy is obvious. It would seem to be that the American Treasury, Commerce, Defense, and State Departments are all reading from different scripts or are at least not on the same page. The critics of the George W. Bush Administration (of which there are legions) see this as one further example of his incompetence. However, when one looks at the Administration's policy from the macro point of view, one can see a level of coherence that is not evident at first when looking at the individual policies. The Bush Administration is protecting American interests at all levels. It is engaging China in such a way that China will have a hard time separating itself from American interests. If China's interests are America's interests and vice versa, the chances of conflict are greatly reduced. However, it is not in America's interests to be politically or economically bullied or to be challenged militarily.

The Bush Administration is in many ways continuing the policies of the administrations of his father and Bill Clinton which was to keep China guessing as to American intentions. American policy, it would seem, is to "walk softly, but carry a big stick" as Teddy Roosevelt once said. In many ways the current Bush Administration is letting the market decide China's future intentions—the market being the global capitalist economic system that China has invested itself so heavily in. President Bush's policy is thus to engage China politically and economically while continuing to protect American interests in both economic and military hegemony. In sum, current American policy is hoping that China will have too much at stake to become an aggressor nation.

Only time will tell whether this is the best policy or not, however the policy does have some very real risks. The next section will look at these risks for both the United States and China.

Strategically speaking

Strategic theory dictates that a nation never wants to put itself in a position of making itself a tempting target for an aggressor state. There are two ways to make a state a tempting target. The first and more obvious one is to unilaterally disarm to the point of weakness. An aggressor state would see the weak state as a tempting target or a target of opportunity for expansion, domination, or pre-emptive neutralization. The second way a state can make itself a target of aggression is to grow its military capabilities to a level that make it a potential threat to the more powerful state, thus potentially causing the more powerful state to pre-emptively attack it out of its own security concerns. Examples of this currently are China and North Korea, with Japan and the United States being the more powerful states. The East Asian military status quo is currently acceptable to the United States and its principle ally in the region, Japan. However, the military build-up in China could alter the balance of power and will likely cause Japan and the United States to pursue a more aggressive policy toward China with the possible (though unlikely) result being conventional or (in worst case) nuclear conflict.

China is in many ways counting on American greed for cheap products to avoid a new cold war while it builds the People's Liberation Army (PLA) into a modern military force that can compete with the US military at least regionally if not eventually globally. China is hoping to build up its military capacity to the point of advantage or parity with the United States while continuing to trade with the United States at a large surplus partially helped by its artificially weak currency. China hopes to put the United States in a position where the latter cannot afford militarily or economically to defend Taiwan, Japan, or any other imperial aspirations the former has in East Asia.

The United States on the other hand is hoping to keep China engaged economically to the point that the latter is economically too dependent on the Western markets to risk economic sanctions and the resulting collapse of its economy by invading Taiwan or taking a military action in any other state in Asia. In many ways the United States is counting on China's greed for more profits and growth to keep it from becoming more aggressive. However, China appears to be crossing the line to being a true threat to both America and the region, as the political leadership of both major political parties in Washington see China as a growing threat. China seems to be announcing to the world through its actions (not words) that it is planning to engage the United States militarily in the future. Probably not in the near future, but someday in the future China plans to be America's military enemy and is preparing its military for that day. As former CIA Director R. James Woolsey put it, "China is pursuing a national strategy of domination of the energy markets and strategic dominance of the western Pacific."[6] Cragg Hines in an editorial for the *Houston Chronicle* described the problem based on a conversation he had with a former American policymaker:

> It's the "notion of tectonic plates shifting" the geopolitics of the region and the world, said Randy Schriver, who until recently was deputy assistant secretary of State for East Asia and Pacific affairs. We are in danger of a steady but discernible drift into a strategic rivalry.[7]

China's military modernization is not a recent phenomenon. The Chinese military and political establishments were truly shocked during the First Gulf War when the United States so quickly and easily defeated Saddam Hussein's battle-tested Iraqi Army including the Republican Guard. Only after the war did China come to recognize that the most recent Revolution in Military Affairs (RMA) had occurred and that China needed its own military modernization and internal RMA. This recognition can be seen throughout Chinese military journals in the few years following the 1991 Persian Gulf War. Previously China had counted on its own sheer numerical superiority in manpower to challenge and intimidate the United States from any hostile action including defending Taiwan. The First Gulf War taught China that numerical superiority alone would not tip the balance against the United States military. Only technological equality/superiority and numerical advantage combined would make China a true challenger to the American hegemony.[8]

Challenging America

Since the wake-up-call of the Gulf War in the early 1990s, China has embarked on a rapid military modernization and overall numerical downsizing program with the United States armed forces in mind as the potential enemy. China recognizes that while they do have a need for overall numerical superiority over the United States military, they do not need the massive numerical superiority that Mao envisioned and used effectively during the Korean War. The emphasis is now on quality over sheer quantity. The numerical downsizing of China's army is seen as a practical necessity in order to free up resources to build a more professional and well-trained army while remaining numerically superior. This restructuring of China's military is an ongoing process, as the *Xinhua News* reported on July 13, 2005, under a headline, "Chinese Military to be Restructured." The article stated that:

> According to a statement issued by the Headquarters of the General Staff of the PRC People's Liberation Army (PLA), the PLA is expected to shift its traditional structure by adding new battle units and cutting outdated ones in an effort to create new combat effectiveness. The PLA program is attempting to change the structure of the PLA by cutting its divisions and

increasing brigades, reported the *Liberation Army Daily*, the traditional mouthpiece of the Chinese armed forces.[9]

In order to modernize quickly China has pursued both internal military development and external purchases. China has purchased the latest weaponry and technology from Russia, Israel,[10] and also the European Union[11] as much as it has been able to under post Tiananmen Square sanctions. It has also begun to build up its own technological military industrial complex in order to be less dependent on foreign sources of arms. An example of the recent Chinese development is the J-10 all-weather fighter plane. The J-10 is very similar to the now canceled Israeli *Lavi* program and is widely acknowledged to be based on technology purchased from Israel, given the similarities between the two aircraft.

A further example of China's military build-up is its pursuit of cruise missile technology in order to offset the power of the United States Navy and its growing anti-ballistic missile systems. China is particularly interested in obtaining/developing supersonic cruise missile technology in order to force the American carrier battle groups to stay further out to sea in order to protect the asset.[12] It has also purchased four *Sovremenny* destroyers from Russia. These ships were specifically designed to attack aircraft carriers and carry Russian *Moskit* anti-carrier missiles (SS-N-22 Sunburn) that can be armed with conventional or nuclear warheads.[13]

China is also engaging the United States in cyber warfare or computer-based spying. Through the internet, China has an ongoing program of hacking American military, government, and private commercial computers in order to acquire technology and military secrets along with private commercial technology. This new cyber-based threat could be enhanced in time of crisis to bring down the American economy which has become so technologically dependant.[14] The United States government has code named this effort by the Chinese "Titan Rain."[15]

China is also intent on demonstrating its technological advancements through its space program. On October 15, 2003, China became just the third nation to independently send a man into space and return him successfully to earth when Lieutenant Colonel Yang Liwei became China's first astronaut (or *Taikonaut* in Chinese). Almost two years later on October 12, 2005, China repeated the feat by sending two men into space for almost a week. The Chinese have had a space program since the 1970s. However, much of its recent success is due to its close working relationship with the Russian space program. Collaboration with the Russians permitted China to leapfrog over many technological hurdles that otherwise might have delayed China's independent space program.[16] China has a stated goal of putting a man on the moon by the year 2020, something only America has done previously (and currently is trying to repeat by 2018).

Of much greater concern to the United States was China's test of an anti-satellite missile on January 11, 2007. The test missile shot down an aging

Chinese weather satellite over 500 miles above the earth's surface. This makes China only the third nation after the United States and the former Soviet Union to successfully test an anti-satellite weapon. The United States owns 53 percent of all satellites currently orbiting the earth. This test was seen by commentators and governments around the globe as a direct challenge to the United States and its heavy dependence on high technology, communications, and imaging-based defensive systems. China seems to be signaling to the world that it does not intend to use space in a peaceful way only. An example of the worldwide condemnation of China's action can be seen in the comments by Japanese Foreign Minister Taro Aso, responding to the test, in a news conference, "We told China that we doubt if we could call this a peaceful use (of space)."[17] This militarization of space by China could signal a new cold war: this time between the United States and China.

The United States is well aware of China's military build-up. *Voice of America* reports that Admiral William Fallon, commander of the combined United States forces command in the Pacific, on a visit to China suggested that the PRC's ongoing military build-up might be too extensive for a country not facing any outside threats. He stated:

> I'm not about to sit here and determine what percentage of GDP or how many Yuan or whatever ought to be devoted, but my sense is that I don't see a particular threat to China, so military capabilities expansion, [it] seems to me, ought to be commensurate with the growth and development of a country.[18]

The point Admiral Fallon was making was that the United States is not a threat to China and that China was wasting money on military development that could be better used to help develop China. Implicit in the admiral's comment was that if America were planning to attack China (for whatever reason), it would have done so already when China was in a much weaker position than it is today. China's "city buster" nuclear deterrent is more than adequate reason for America to keep conflicts with China under control including any efforts by Taiwan to declare independence.[19] However, even if a conflict could be limited to the conventional (if both sides feared using nuclear weapons or using them first), a conventional conflict with China is not in America's or China's interests as it could wreak economic havoc on both nations.

However, China in spite of statements to the contrary does seem to be keeping a "first use" policy on the table as an option. On July 14, 2005, the *Financial Times* reported from Beijing that Zhu Chenghu, a major general in the People's Liberation Army who is also a professor at China's National Defense University said that China is prepared to use nuclear weapons against the United States if it is attacked by Washington during a confrontation over Taiwan.[20] Zhu Chenghu is quoted as saying: "If the Americans draw their missiles and position-guided ammunition on to the target zone on China's territory, I think we will have to respond with nuclear weapons." He added that China's definition of its territory includes warships and aircraft.[21]

A *Wall Street Journal* reporter is quoted as saying:

> [R]ecent warnings about Beijing's military buildup took on a very real significance, when Chinese Maj. Gen. Zhu Chenghu of the People's Liberation Army warned last week that US military "interference" in a conflict over Taiwan could lead to a Chinese nuclear attack on the US, and he reinforced every worst fear of a "China threat." ". . . it was clear to those of us who witnessed last Thursday's warning that *it was no accidental outburst.*"[22]

China seems confident and willing to play a game of nuclear brinkmanship with the United States. This is of concern not only to the United States, but also its main ally in the region, Japan. China's new-found confidence to challenge the United States is not limited to military acquisitions; China is also looking for economic domination by globally securing access to raw materials. China is basically taking a play out of America's Cold War playbook by adopting the policy of encirclement. During the early days of the Cold War, the United States had a policy of encircling its rival, the Soviet Union, by making allies on all of its sides. Besides the North Atlantic Treaty Organization in the West, there were the US–Japan Security treaty in the east, the Southeast Asian Treaty Organization in the Pacific, and the Middle East Treaty Organization (later renamed Central Treaty Organization) in the Middle East.

What the United States did through military alliances, China has been doing through economic alliances. China has been aggressively pursuing economic/ resource alliances in Africa, Latin America, Central Asia, and even Europe. China has been taking advantage of the American distraction with the war on terror and the occupation of Iraq to secure resources, trading rights, and investments with regimes that are hostile to America or have spotty human rights records in places such as Sudan, Zimbabwe, and Venezuela. China is using its new-found wealth to buy friends and allies around the world. China, unlike the United States, is willing to ignore corruption and human rights abuses in exchange for raw materials and economic opportunity. China hopes that by securing resources from politically corrupt regimes they can buy loyalty in its battle for hegemony with America, and China is very confident in its ability to do this.[23]

Much of China's new-found confidence comes from not only its surging economy, which in purchasing power parity terms has already passed Japan and reached the second largest in the world, but also in a general perception that the current hegemon—the United States—is in decline. However, unlike in major EU countries where such a perception of American decline is common, American ascendancy is widely recognized within Asia capitals. Japan in particular seems to recognize this in its choice to continue its alliance with the United States. Nevertheless, China, it seems, is preparing for a long drawn-out challenge to American power that could be over 100 years in the making. Of course this is in the absence of currently unknown intervening variables that might cause a rapid decline in American power.

Japan's role in America's China strategy: utilities and limits

This brings us to our next important area of inquest, China's challenge to Japan, America's most important ally in the region. This is very important because of the enhanced security role that Japan plays in overall American policy. The inclusion of Japan in our study of America's reaction to China's rise is very important in that Japan, it would appear through successive Prime Ministers and governments, has and is willing to bet its future in Asia and thus globally on continued American global hegemony. China's growing expansionism and hegemonism were begun by Jiang Zemin and succeeded by Hu Jintao. More than anything else except the threat of North Korea, the threat of China is propelling Japan forward with its efforts to alter its constitution. The United States welcomes the revision of Japan's constitution as American policy desires a more fully capable Japan to support American policy in Asia. China has been called a sleeping dragon, but in reality Japan is the real sleeping dragon, which China may be taunting recklessly. In fact, Deng Xiaoping is said to have warned his successors about Japan by telling them to "let sleeping dogs lie," but they have been loath or unable to follow his advice. Japan's constitution has truly limited Japan in its military development and its ability to project power. However, if the threat of China ever causes Japan to abandon its constitutional limitations, China might regret its recent bullying of Japan.

An example of China overplaying its hand occurred on September 9, 2005, just two days before national elections in Japan. China, in what appeared to be an effort to intimidate Japanese voters the way it intimidates voters in Taiwan, sent warships to patrol an area surrounding disputed islands and natural gas fields in the East China Sea. If it was meant to intimidate Japanese voters then it had the opposite effect when the right-wing and more nationalistic Junichiro Koizumi and the LDP won re-election in an overwhelming landslide victory over a more pacifist orientated opposition.

This was not an isolated incident. In recent years and months, China has gotten bolder about fomenting anti-Japanese nationalism within China. This includes riots and street demonstrations outside of Japanese consulates and business assets within China. Many of these protests are triggered by Japanese actions like visits to Yasukuni Shrine (where several class "A" war criminals have been enshrined) by Japanese leaders and the publication of revisionist textbooks approved by the Japanese Ministry of Education that whitewash Japanese atrocities during World War II. In the past, these event have sparked official protests by China (and Korea), but what is different now is that the Chinese government and Communist Party seem to have given sanction to the street protests.[24] However, the Chinese street protests have had the unintended result of awakening the average Japanese citizen to the challenge and potential threat that China is to Japan.

It would appear that China was hoping to marginalize and intimidate Japan so that it is a less effective ally of the United States. This marginalization seems to be having the opposite effect. The problem for China in the long run is that in awakening large-scale anti-Japanese sentiment among its general population it may find it politically impossible in the future to repair relations with Japan when it needs to. This can lead to generational hatreds like the world witnessed in the former Yugoslavia. However, the current state of relations is not solely China's fault in that Japan could have done more in the last 60 years to heal the Sino/Japanese relationship by demonstrating greater sensitivity to Chinese suffering under its rule and offering a more sincere apology for its actions that China could accept. The United States could also have encouraged this process along. Nevertheless, the current state of relations between the two great powers in Asia does not bode well for the future.

Historically since World War II, Japan has been very circumvent about naming threats to Japan. The 1997 *Guidelines* signed between the United States and Japan simply referred to "situations in the areas surrounding Japan" as the threat. However, Japan is beginning to openly voice its concerns about China's growing military power. In its annual 2004 Defense White Paper it noted China's increasingly bold maritime ambitions. The defense paper, which echoes concerns expressed about China's military build-up in the United States Defense Department, said Japan's public was "exceedingly concerned" about the intrusion of Chinese vessels, including a nuclear submarine, into Japanese waters. "Regarding the pick-up in China's maritime activity, the trends need to be watched," it said. "It has been pointed out that the Chinese navy is aiming to become a so-called 'blue-water navy,'" it added, referring to development of a deep-water fleet.[25] This trend continued in 2005 with a new defense white paper that argued that Japan needed to start to respond to Chinese military spending.[26] This could mark the beginnings of an arms race in East Asia and pull Japan further away from Article Nine and toward constitutional revision and normalcy.

It is important to note that China really has nothing to fear from Japan militarily. Japan no longer has the imperial capability (or desire) that it once had due to an aging and declining population and a changed world. Each nation has the capacity to harass the other, but neither can really invade or conquer each other. This current status quo should be good enough to allay any Chinese fears about a resurgent imperial Japan, but China does not seem to be satisfied with the status quo. On the other hand, China's internal anti-Japan message has been very successful at raising a generation of anti-Japanese Chinese with the unintended consequence of growing nationalism within Japan as well. Faced with growing and potent hostility from China, the Japanese have become more patriotic and open to a militarily stronger and more assertive Japan and thus a much more valuable ally of American policy in the region. This more assertive Japan is something that the United States sees as a very desirable counter to growing Chinese military influence and assertiveness in the region.

China's Achilles' heel

China's new-found assertiveness is not without risks to itself. China's new economy is energy dependant. Oil is China's great weakness or rather the lack of adequate oil reserves to fuel its industrial appetite. China is not like the United States which has greater oil reserves than Saudi Arabia (the problem for the United States is that the cost of extracting the oil is cost prohibitive even at $70 a barrel, but not technically or fiscally impossible if needed). China needs new energy sources to feed its growing new industries and continuing access to its current imports. Brownouts are frequent and common in some major cities of China. Many Chinese factories need to keep generators on standby just to keep the factories running. Evidence of China's energy problem can be seen in this *Associated Press* report from July 19, 2005:

BEIJING POWER CRUNCH PROMPTS SHUT DOWN (2005–07–19)

(It was) reported that workers at thousands of Beijing companies are about to get an unscheduled vacation thanks to the scorching summer heat. Beginning this week, 4,689 businesses will take mandatory weeklong breaks on rotation to cut down on energy use in the PRC capital and avoid pushing up already rapidly climbing power prices, the official *Xinhua News Agency* said Tuesday.[27]

It is important to note that China is still a developing economy and that its energy needs are growing with it. China is rushing to develop hydroelectric power at the cost of massive environmental upheaval and population displacement. The Three Gorges Dam on the Yangtze River is but one example of this.

China has also lobbied furiously with Russia for a pipeline from the Siberian oilfields to Manchuria. Japan, on the other hand, lobbied just as furiously for the pipeline to be built to the Siberian coast as not to be dependent on China for the free flow of oil. Both nations got part of what they wanted in that the pipeline will split and go to both Manchuria and the Siberian coast as Russia wants China to be a major market for its oil but does not want to be dependent on China's control of the spigot to market its oil to international customers. The problem will now be to build this new pipeline in a politically and economically volatile Russia.

While Japan and China share the common need for a secure energy supply, Japan as America's ally is approaching the issue from a much different perspective. Japan sees the United States as an ally that it can depend on so it works with the United States to secure its energy needs. China, on the other hand, sees the United States as a potential rival and does not like its dependence on the United States Navy's Seventh Fleet for securing safe passage for its energy supplies from the Middle East to its coastal ports in southeastern China.

China's energy needs have risen as spectacularly as its economy. China has gone from a net exporter of oil in 1992 to the world's second largest importer of oil behind the United States. China is very aware of its oil problem and is doing everything it can to secure energy resources on the open market. Its recent attempt to buy the American Oil giant UNOCAL (Union Oil Corporation of California) and its August 2005 purchase of *PetroKazakhstan* are evidence of this effort to secure the oil reserves through these companies. If China were ever to attack Taiwan, it would likely lose its access to Middle Eastern oil through combined maritime interdictions from the United States Navy's Seventh Fleet, Japan's Maritime Self Defense Force, Royal Australian Navy, and possibly the Indian Navy. This could force China into a desperate attempt to militarily seize the Russian oil fields (particularly those that are owned, in whole or in part, by Chinese oil companies) bringing Russia into a conflict between the United States and China on the side of the United States. This would result in a two-front war for China of which its probabilities of a positive outcome would be almost zero. It could only use its nuclear weapons to ensure that there is no winner, only losers. China's dependence on energy in the form of Middle East oil is the Achilles heel of its military ambitions in East Asia.

With this weakness in mind, China has been working to obtain new sources of oil and natural gas in order to diversify its suppliers. Chief among these efforts have been China's diplomatic efforts in Africa, especially in Sudan and Nigeria. It is also making efforts in America's own backyard among Latin American nations, such as Venezuela and Ecuador, in clear conflict with the Monroe Doctrine.

Energy is not China's only Achilles heel. The environment in China is also an important threat to Chinese power. China's virtually unregulated industrial expansion has produced an environmental disaster of biblical proportions. Reports of untreated toxic waste flowing freely into rivers, workers and children growing up with near toxic levels of air pollution, and a near total breakdown in preventative public health services as evidenced by the growth of "snail fever"[28] and the SARS outbreak of 2004 have led to almost daily reports of riots in rural China by peasants demanding that the government protect them. The government in China has been doing very little to curb or control pollution, and in the absence of government control, the peasants are taking the law into their own hands and shutting the offenders down.[29] The cost of cleanup will be prohibitive when China is finally forced to deal with the problem.

China's third Achilles heel: its new-found wealth or in reality the lack thereof. China is accumulating wealth at an unprecedented rate due to its trade surpluses with the United States and Europe. However, China is hoarding this wealth rather than investing it in itself. While it is spending (almost recklessly) on the PLA, it is neglecting its own infrastructure, people, the environment, and its future stability. China's current domestic policy is like a person who takes a cash advance from his credit card, puts it in the bank, and declares himself rich. The problem is that the interest and payments will eventually destroy him. China, in the same way, by investing in its military and by neglecting its people and domestic needs will eventually pay a price that it cannot afford to pay.

A fourth and final Achilles heel of China: China's position in the world system. China represents an opportunity for the world economy, but it is not currently an essential element. China produces goods cheaply, but the goods that it produces are for the most part not essential commodities for the West. This is why in a conflict over Taiwan the United States and its allies could embargo oil going into China and not be threatened by the loss of Chinese goods being exported. There is nothing that China currently produces that cannot be produced elsewhere if needed. There would be a temporary loss of supply, but the long-term result would be the relocation of the industries. The world basically does not depend on China, China depends on the world. It is for this reason that the world and the United States are willing to continue their engagement of China while being aware of the military threat it poses the region. They see China as the eventual loser of any conflict because the world can turn its back on China, but China cannot turn its back on the world. The next section will briefly look at American ascendancy.

American ascendancy

While many scholars may lament (or rejoice depending on one's perspective) in the seeming decline of American power, there is no conclusive empirical evidence of American hegemonic decline. The only evidence of imminent American decline is anecdotal. Rather the empirical evidence would indicate that American power is still in overall ascendancy. The American economy is currently the largest in the world (with the exception of the combined nations of the European Union). It is currently growing at 4.9 percent for the year 2007. This means that the American economy will grow by nearly $700 billion by 2007. China on the other hand is growing at the rate of 9–12 percent annually. Using the larger figure of 12 percent the Chinese economy will grow by $310 billion in 2007. Using an average growth rate of 4 percent for the United States and 10 percent for China, China will pass the United States in the year 2036. This can be seen in Figure 3.1.

The major problem with this type of economic projection is that it is linear. The real world is not linear; there are economic ups and downs and constantly changing variables. Historically there has never been a correct 50 year linear projection of GDP for any nation. Linear assumptions assume that such things as population, size of workforce, productivity, investments in infrastructure, and military spending all remain constant over time. In the real world they do not. This is especially true in rapidly developing nations such as China which are constantly in a state of change. More developed economies such as the United States and the Member States of the European Union tend to have more stable growth rates with less radical changes in GDP over time. To illustrate this, if the United States economy were to grow at a steady 3.5 percent (the average GDP growth rate of the United States over the last 30 years) over the next 100 years and China was to continue to grow at 12 percent for the next 5 years (2008–2012), and then continue to grow at 10 percent over the following 5 years (2013–2017), and then slow to a solid 6 percent over the next 10 years

US and China GDP

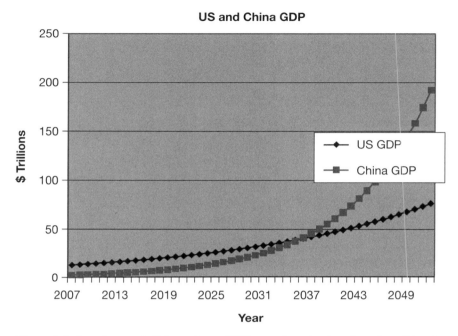

Figure 3.1 American and Chinese linear GDP growth projections based on 4% and 10% annual growth rates respectively over 45 years starting in 2008

(2018–2027), and finally settle to a steady and stable growth rate of 4 percent of a developed, mature economy over the next 80 years, there would still be a $97 trillion gap in GDP between the two nations in the United States' favor. This can be seen in Figure 3.2.

China's growth in the last 20 years has been nothing short of spectacular; however the problem for China in its quest to pass up the United States is America's overall lead in terms of GDP and overall economic wealth. The United States economy grows as much each year as some economies are in size. Gerard Baker described it well in *The Times* of London:

> Given that the United States is a $12 trillion (£6,700 billion) economy, the new data mean that in the first quarter the US added to the global output an amount that, if sustained at that pace for a year, would be about $600 billion—roughly the equivalent of adding one whole new Brazil or Australia to global economic activity every year, just from the incremental extra sweat and heave and click of 300 million Americans.
>
> Think of it another way. In an era in which China embodies the hopes and fears of much of the developed world, the US with a growth rate of half that of China's, is adding roughly twice as much in absolute terms to

the global output as the Middle Kingdom, with its GDP (depending on how you measure it) of between $2 trillion and $4 trillion and its growth of about 10 percent.[30]

David Brooks of the *New York Times* furthers this argument of America not being in decline by examining the economic competitiveness rankings and he finds that in regard to American decline:

> . . . that's just not true. In the first place, despite the ups and downs of the business cycle, the United States still possesses the most potent economy on earth. Recently the World Economic Forum and the International Institute for Management Development produced global competitiveness indexes, and once again they both ranked the United States first in the world.
>
>   In the World Economic Forum survey, the US comes in just ahead of Switzerland, Denmark, Sweden and Germany (China is 34th). The US gets poor marks for macroeconomic stability (the long-term federal debt), for its tax structure and for the low savings rate. But it leads the world in a range of categories: higher education and training, labor market flexibility, the ability to attract global talent, the availability of venture capital, the quality of corporate management and the capacity to innovate.[31]

This is not to say that there could not be currently unknown intervening variables that would change this equation and America's fortunes; this is merely to

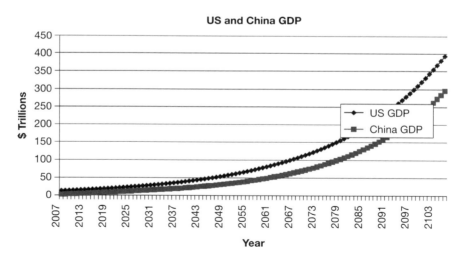

Figure 3.2 American and Chinese linear GDP growth projections based on 3.5% annual GDP growth rate for the United States and 12% (2008–2012), 10% (2013–2017), 6% (2018–2027), and 4% (2028–2106) growth rates for China

emphasize the sheer size of the gap between American and Chinese wealth and economic power. To put this in a different perspective, if you were offered 5 percent of a million dollars or 15 percent of one hundred thousand dollars which would you choose? The smart person would choose the 5 percent as it is equal to $50,000. The 15 percent is only equal to $15,000. Over time the 15 percent will pass the 5 percent but it will take a long time not a short time. While the gap between the United States and China is not as large as the illustration, it is large enough to make the point that Gerard Baker makes above, China still has a very long way to go even if the annual percentage of GDP growth is double the size of the United States'. As the Chinese economy matures its growth will level out to a more stable and steady rate. China may catch up but it will not likely be soon. This economic argument does not even touch the incredible asymmetrical difference between American military power and Chinese military power (the next section will talk about this in more detail).

Furthermore, unlike the major powers of the European Union, it would seem that this economic and military ascendancy is widely recognized within Asia capitals. Japan in particular seems to recognize this in its choice to continue its alliance with the United States. Japan is betting everything on American ascendancy. They are seeking no new allies. Every Japanese leader has followed this path since World War II. This is a staggering vote of confidence in the United States. India is also moving forward with closer security relations with the United States. George W. Bush's February 2006 visit to India clearly was aimed at China on the part of New Delhi and Washington. It would seem that Washington, like China, has renewed the old Cold War policy of encirclement. American policy seems to be to keep China worried about *ALL* its borders so that it is not tempted to *EXPAND* its borders.

The other nations of the region are also concerned about the lack of transparency in Chinese defense strategy and are hedging their bets by avoiding conflicts with both Washington (war on terror and Iraq) and China (economic and military). They know that in case of a threat or conflict that the United States will willingly accept allies and that they can always run to the United States in face of (potential) Chinese aggression as it is in American interest to contain China rather than to let it run unhindered. The next section will look at why United States policy toward China is so confident in its ability to contain possible Chinese aggression in East, Southeast, and South Asia.

Preparing to fight the last war?

In spite of China's recent spending spree, China is poised to fall further behind as the next Revolution in Military Affairs (RMA) takes place over the next three to five years. American military power is about to leap forward once again. In the study of military history there is the old adage the generals always prepare to fight and win the last war, only to learn too late that they are fighting with outdated equipment and tactics. The American military has made a conscious effort to avoid this potential pitfall. However, the same may not be said of China.

China, it would appear is preparing to fight the United States in a 1991 Persian Gulf War scenario or at the very best a 2003 Iraq War scenario. The problem for China is that they may be preparing to fight a conflict with equipment and tactics that are one to two generations out of date. As the United States is deploying its missile defense and developing the first generation of airborne directed energy weapons.[32] Directed energy weapons have the potential to revolutionize the battlefield in ways that have not been seen since the invention of the bow and arrow. This is "*Star Wars*" or "*Star Trek*" for real without the Hollywood special effects. China's missile-based nuclear deterrent could be rendered obsolete in the face of possible United States directed energy weapons.

It is important to understand that the United States is investing heavily in technology not just for economic advantage but in an effort to obtain capabilities. Framed from a position of capability this technology is just a way to obtain capabilities. The directed energy weapons mentioned in the preceding paragraph give capability to intercept supersonic/hyper sonic weapons that could be launched at American military assets, particularly American aircraft carriers. If America acquires the capability to deploy these new technologies China's weapons strategy is irrelevant. China is trying to level the playing field through investment in current weapons systems while the United States is determined to maintain superiority through technological advances. As mentioned earlier Japan has bet its future on the United States continuing to dominate a unipolar world. If the United States acquires these capabilities then the high stakes gamble placed by Japan will have paid off.

The potential for problems here are twofold if China's nuclear deterrent is rendered obsolete by the weapons still in development. The first problem is the more obvious problem which is the scenario where China initiates a conflict with the United States thinking that it will be able to contain or control the United States military response. When Chinese military capacity proves to be inadequate, China will be faced with a huge humiliation and loss of face that may cause it to prolong the conflict unnecessarily to its own detriment. The second problem is for the United States in that the United States will be in a position were it could become overconfident and less willing to work for a peaceful resolution to a potential conflict. This could put the United States in a position of making policy choices that actually precipitate conflict.

Another way to look at potential and ongoing Sino–American hegemonic competition is from a decision-making perspective. Based on most of the decision-making research, we know that people and leaders are risk averse and are motivated by potential regret. They ask themselves "what is the worst that could happen," and if the answer is unpalatable they do not choose to take the risky action. The modernization and acquisition of greater military assets has the potential to make China less aggressive since they will have more to lose in a conflict with the United States. For example, in a conflict with the American Navy, the more ships they have, the greater the potential losses if they engage the Pacific Fleet.

To put it another way, the value of China's new military assets is context dependent. In a regional conflict with smaller countries such as Malaysia, the Philippines, or Vietnam, the modernized Chinese navy measurably improves China's bargaining position. The modern Chinese "blue water navy" would have no trouble intimidating the smaller naval, coastal defense forces of the region. On the other hand, in a hegemonic showdown with the United States, China's modern blue water navy would have very little impact except to potentially cost the United States more ammunition given current American technological superiority. Therefore, the modernization of the PLA Navy means that China risks losing its newly acquired power vis-à-vis regional actors with very little to no potential for gain in a conflict with the global hegemonic power, the United States. Therefore, from an American perspective, China will likely become a little more willing to avoid naval confrontation or to put it simply, it will be less aggressive. Thus in this coming era of greater American supremacy it behooves the American government to continue to engage China in a Liberal-institutionalist way in order to avoid conflict. One problem however is that the American supremacy could be quickly nullified if China (and others) were to obtain the technology and the wherewithal to deploy whatever weapons are state of the art. American economic supremacy would remain, but its military lead could be gone.

Conclusion: American policy toward China's rise is taking the long view

When examining long-term American policy toward China's rise, the assumption must be made that conflict between America and China would be disastrous for China, America, the region, and the world in general and that American policymakers know of this potential for disaster and will work to avoid it. The problem is that the boundaries defining "peaceful coexistence" may be different for Beijing and Washington. Whether the two sides can negotiate the boundaries remains to be seen. Over the last several American presidential administrations and dating back to Nixon's Secretary of State, Henry Kissinger, the American policy regarding China has taken the long view, engaging China through trade and economics while containing China security-wise. This policy has worked well for both countries. China is growing economically and is thus becoming more dependent on the global economic system—which would theoretically make it more cooperative and less adversarial. However, China's new-found wealth is being channeled heavily into the modernization of the PLA.

What *should* be America's policy toward China given the overall unknowns about China's intentions? If China's quest for supremacy is a multigenerational quest, then there is a real chance that diplomatic and economic engagement will make the question moot. A new generation of Chinese and Americans may not desire to see each other as strategic rivals. However, if the Chinese leadership grows impatient, then we may see an aggressor China assert itself into a conflict with the United States, which it currently stands to lose.

Given the choice between containment and engagement, American policy seems to be to simultaneously pursue both with equal effort. The current asymmetrical nature of any potential conflict with China gives the United States greater ability to pursue liberal institutionalist options without sacrificing its advantage from a realist perspective. However, direct conflict with the United States aside China's ability to destabilize the region through its ongoing weapons modernization program gives the United States great concern as to its ability to manage a non-direct conflict with China and pushes it toward a more realist policy toward China. It is for this last reason that the United States has been so willing to talk publicly about the "China threat" and China's status as a rising challenger to American hegemony.

This "China threat" is very important for United States policy in that it gives a focus (or an enemy if you will) for the United States military to focus on. As previously mentioned, without an enemy the United States military would lose support and funding in Washington's budget battles. China provides a real world threat that seemingly "must" be contained. It also fuels American ascendancy by spurring American hegemony to greater heights. In the ancient world, the Roman Empire grew in power as long as there were external threats to it. Once it realized that it had no challenger it began to crumble from within. Only when it was in an irreversible decline could others swoop in and divide up the pieces of a once great empire. America, like ancient Rome (and other empires throughout history) needs an outside threat to keep it from crumbling from within. China is currently providing this threat, intentionally or not. Accordingly, as the data indicates and contrary to conventional wisdom, American power is still growing and will likely continue to do so. America has still not reached the zenith of its power.

America is dealing with China's rise by engaging China economically while attempting to contain China security-wise. Little has changed in this policy over the last two decades of Republican and Democratic Administrations. Barring a "clear and present danger" security threat or crisis from China, America is likely to continue to take the long view toward Chinese growth by continuing to bank on the idea that China desires to grow economically more than it desires hegemonic domination. This long view is based on a liberal institutionalist belief that working with China is better than opposing China. However, this belief is still in line with the realist belief in the need to contain potential adversaries. The United States can always fall back on its economic and military superiority if China proves to be too aggressive or pose a direct threat to American security.

As long as China does not try to neutralize the American strategic advantage and an overconfident America does not unintentionally initiate a crisis, conflict is likely to be avoided as each nation develops a mutually dependant economic relationship. However, if China does pursue efforts to neutralize the American strategic advantage, the American reaction will likely be containment of the

"China threat" by both military and economic means, thus increasing the likelihood of conflict. The American cultural tradition to deal with threats, real or imagined, is a long one, and the pre-emptive nature of the Bush Doctrine is not new to American policy.

Notes

1 Earlier versions of this chapter under different titles were originally presented at the International Studies Association 2006 Annual Convention in San Diego, California, USA March 22–25, 2006 and the ASPC 2007 Annual Convention at the East-West Center in Honolulu, Hawaii, USA June 15–17, 2007.
2 For more on this please see: Yochiro Sato and Satu Limaye, *Japan in a Dynamic Asia: Coping with the New Security Challenges*, (Lanhan Maryland: Lexington Books, 2006), Chapters 1 and 3.
3 With apologies to U2 and their song "Bullet the Blue Sky" which is where this line comes from.
4 Department of Defense, *Annual Report to Congress: Military Power of the People's Republic of China 2006*. Accessed at: www.defenselink.mil/pubs/pdfs/China%20Report%202006.pdf
5 Ibid.
6 Steve Lohr; Andrew Ross Sorkin, and Jad Mouawad, "Unocal Bid Denounced At Hearing," *New York Times*, Section C, Page 1, Column 5 www.nytimes.com and *The China Daily*, July 14, 2005. www.chinadaily.com.cn/english/doc/2005-07/14/content_460173.htm.
7 Cragg Hines, "Why Hu needs the ranch instead of the South Lawn," *Houston Chronicle*, September 7, 2005. www.chron.com/cs/CDA/ssistory.mpl/editorial/outlook/3342368.
8 James C. Mulvenon, Murray Scot Tanner, Michael S. Chase, David Frelinger, David C. Gompert, Martin C. Libicki, and Kevin L. Pollpeter, *Chinese Responses to US Military Transformation and Implications for the Department of Defense*, (The RAND Corp., 2006).
9 Compiled and paraphrased by this author from NAPSnet daily report July 13, 2005. www.chinadaily.com.cn/english/doc/2005-07/13/content_459875.htm.
10 Israel has currently stopped publicly selling weapons to China under US diplomatic pressure, but is thought to be still selling some weapons and technology to China quietly.
11 The European Union currently does not sell advanced weapons to China because of its human rights record. It was contemplating dropping the arms sales ban in the spring of 2005 when China passed the anti-succession law against Taiwan. The passage of this law made it politically unpalatable to resume arms sales.
12 Supersonic cruise missile technology escaped the Soviets' technological abilities and to this day no nation has been able to overcome the technological hurdles. If the hurdles are overcome and China obtains the technology and the weapons, there will be a dramatic shift in the balance of power in East Asia unless the United States develops effective countermeasures to defend its aircraft carriers.
13 Summary from Naval-Technology.com. www.naval-technology.com/projects/sovremenny/.
14 Examples of this can be found from multiple sources: www.time.com/time/magazine/article/0,9171,1098961-1,00.html. www.theregister.co.uk/2006/10/09/chinese_crackers_attack_us/.
15 Computer World, www.computerworld.com/securitytopics/security/story/0,1080 1,105585,00.html.

16   Jing-dong Yuan, "Shenzhou and China's Space Odyssey," *The Jamestown Foundation*, Volume 5, Issue 24 (November 22, 2005) Accessed at: www. jamestown.org/images/pdf/cb_005_024.pdf.

17   "US, allies protest China's anti-satellite test," www.CNN.com, January 19, 2007.

18   Voice of America, July 9, 2005 as reported by *NAPSnet Daily Report*, July 9, 2005.

19   China's "city buster" deterrent is not based on Mutual Assured Destruction (MAD) like the US and the Soviet Union during the Cold War. China deterrent is based on being able to inflict the loss of 20 or more major cities on America as too high a price for aggression against China. The US nuclear arsenal would be able to destroy China several times over, but at the price of the US losing its largest cities.

20   Financial Times, July 14, 2005. http://news.ft.com/cms/s/28cfe55a-f4a7-11d9-9dd1-00000e2511c8.html.

21   Ibid.

22   As quoted by *ViewPoints* July 14, 2005 US Forces Japan www.usfj.mil. From: http://ebird.afis.mil/ Emphasis added.

23   Joseph Kahn, "China Courts Africa, Angling for Strategic Gains," *New York Times*, November 3, 2006. www.nytimes.com.

24   It is interesting to note that when Prime Minister Koizumi made his promised post election visit to Yasukuni Shrine in October 2005, China reverted back to making only official protests rather than permitting street demonstrations. The leadership in China had perhaps recognized that their policy was having undesired consequences.

25   2004 Defense of Japan White Paper. www.jda.go.jp/e/pab/wp2004/.

26   2005 Defense White Paper summary. www.fpcj.jp/e/mres/japanbrief/jb_560. html.

27   As quoted by *NAPSnet Daily Report*, July 19, 2005.

28   Jim Yardley, "A Deadly Fever, Once Defeated, Lurks in a Chinese Lake," *New York Times*, February 22, 2005, A1.

29   Edward Cody, "China's Rising Tide of Protest Sweeping Up Party Officials as Village Chiefs Share Anger Over Pollution," *Washington Post Foreign Service*, September 12, 2005, A01.

30   Gerard Baker, "America's Economic Hegemony is safe," *The Times*, April 25, 2006. http://business.*Timesonline.co.uk*.

31   *David Brooks, New York Times*, November 27, 2009. www.nytimes.com/2007/11/27/opinion/27brooks.html.

32   Doug Beason, *The E-Bomb* (Cambridge, MA: Da Capo Press, 2005).

4 US strategic relations with a rising China

Trajectories and impacts on Asia-Pacific security[1]

Evelyn Goh

Introduction

In spite of the world's attention having been focused on Central Asia and the Middle East in the aftermath of the September 11, 2001 simultaneous terror attacks on the United States, a significant number of potential key points of international conflict remain congregated in the Asia-Pacific region. These include the nuclear stand-off with North Korea; uncertainties associated with China's rising economic, political, and military power; the potential flashpoint of Taiwan; and incidences of Islamic extremism and terrorist activity in Southeast Asia. Overarching these issues is the question of a gradual systemic change, as the rise of China impinges upon the influence of the United States, the incumbent dominant power in the region. The security of the Asia-Pacific region thus rests in large part upon the United States and China, both in the sense of their involvement in specific areas of potential conflict, especially the Korean Peninsula and Taiwan, and also in terms of ongoing structural changes in the balance of power.

The existing discourse appears to work from the position that it is incumbent upon the United States as the predominant power, to orchestrate regional order, and to decide how much room it should make for a rising China. Beijing is seen as somewhat unpredictable, yet mainly reactive, and is by Washington expected to adjust itself to fit into the US-dominated status quo if peace is to be preserved in the region.[1] In contrast, this chapter begins with the premise that effective management of the changing structural conditions in the Asia-Pacific must be based upon a reassessment of the relative interests, positions, and roles of the United States and China in the region. Rather than the alternative scenarios of conflictual power transition or the stark choice between containment and accommodation, it argues that a sustainable regional stability may be determined by whether, in the process of building a new basis for US power in the post-Cold War era, a stake can also be crafted for China as an emerging regional great power. In other words, the question is whether these two countries can successfully negotiate their relationship toward what the Chinese label "peaceful coexistence," in a new regional order.

There have been conflicting interpretations of the implications of China's growing power. Realists warn that the resurgence of China, while still in its early stages, portends a structural transformation in the Asia-Pacific system in that the relative power matrix in the region is being altered in way that deepens the security dilemma.[2] Liberal institutionalists and constructivists argue against the assertion that power competition inevitably leads to war, suggesting that the processes of interdependence, institutional norms and socialization can play a critical role in shaping how Chinese power is exercised.[3] This controversy is not likely to be resolved in the near future because of divergent interpretations of Beijing's intentions. However, on balance, while it may take China many decades to catch up with the US in terms of economic, technological, and military capabilities, in the interim, China's rise might be perceived as a systemic disruption under one or more of the following circumstances:

1   If growing Chinese capabilities are accompanied by evidence of ambitions for domination—that is, a powerful China that poses a demonstrable intentional *threat* beyond the inevitable displacement of some American (or Japanese or Russian) influence in the region as its economy grows.[4]

2   If it becomes clear that Beijing possesses the will to challenge the status quo in order to aggrandize itself. In other words, if China shows evidence of being a *revisionist* power. This is a particularly controversial measure of Chinese intentions as Alastair Iain Johnston has argued, if one acknowledges that the existence of a widely accepted international status quo for major international rules is debatable, and given the analytical difficulties in matching Chinese rhetoric with action in terms of power distribution preferences.[5]

3   The existence of persistent *flashpoints*, which pose the problem of potential conflict by miscalculation or proxy and which require constant monitoring. In the region, the Taiwan issue and the competing claims over islands in the South China Sea are hotspots which directly involve China and which continue to worry policymakers and observers.[6]

4   If China is willing to risk and is planning for *asymmetrical conflict* with the United States. This is the intervening variable which will overcome the arguments that China will be deterred by the huge current gap in capabilities between the United States and itself. As will be discussed later, Beijing could exploit selected numerical and situational advantages in specific areas such as Taiwan, and it is also developing technological warfare capabilities to target the current American edge in war fighting.[7]

5   China's ability to *destabilize* the general strategic climate of the region even without intending to do so, because of the unsettling effects of its growing power on its neighbors. This may take the form of fears of the rising economic competition posed by China across the whole range of industrial

and service sectors, as well as the fuelling of regional weapons acquisitions as part of hedging strategies.[8]

Understandably, the debate over Chinese power continues to turn mainly on the central issue of Beijing's intentions, and secondarily on the displacement effect of China's growing ambient power. This debate has featured prominently liberal optimists stressing the socializing impact of interdependence and political and economic liberalization on the one hand, and pessimistic realists intent on the prospect of China's growing capabilities intensifying the security dilemma and creating a power transition on the other.[9] One means of advancing the current debate is to examine key possibilities for relative power transformation in the Asia-Pacific region. Deriving "concept-driven" generalizations can help us to assess the various likely states, parameters, and scenarios of change as China rises. Working from the assumption that China's economic growth and national integrity will continue for the foreseeable future,[10] the following analysis examines three alternative "models," which help to assess some of the possible processes and outcomes in negotiating Sino–American coexistence in the Asia-Pacific. The three models may be described in shorthand as: status quo, negotiated change, and power transition. For each model, the following discussion examines the impact of relative power distribution, each side's perceived regional image and role, and their priority national interests and objectives in the region. It suggests different aspects of power and influence that may be negotiable for each side. The likelihood of each model prevailing and alternative evolution scenarios is then assessed.

Many scholars and analysts have focused their anxieties on the potential power transition if and when China grows to the extent that it can challenge US hegemony. I suggest, however, that the power transition model belongs within the mid- to long-term range of possibilities (Kevin Cooney argues in his chapter that it is long term), and that in the intervening time period, a variety of different scenarios and developmental paths may be postulated under certain circumstances. In the immediate term, we are witnessing Chinese domestic preoccupation and adjustment to the status quo of US regional hegemony and to regional modes of international interaction. Within the medium term, there is the possibility of a negotiated change in regional order toward what I term a "hierarchical duet" of power. The chapter concludes that we are likely to see tacit coexistence and even some negotiated power share in the short to medium term. In the long term, however, if the two powers are not able to sustain a negotiated regional order either in the form of a hierarchical duet or by moving toward a security community, the region will be left facing the destabilizing scenario of power transition.

Model I: status quo

In the first model, both China and the US maintain the status quo in the Asia-Pacific security system. This primarily involves China conceding and not challenging the fact of existing United States strategic dominance over the region. Instead, Beijing concentrates on internal consolidation and on developing its economy. It also adjusts to global and regional United States dominance in a number of ways: it intensifies trade and other relations with the US; pursues membership in key US-led international institutions such as the WTO; does not challenge United States alliances in East Asia; and publicly proclaims no challenge to the US-led status quo except for Taiwan, which is deemed a domestic issue. At the same time, China adopts prevailing modes of international interaction at the regional level, including a similar volume and style of diplomacy, membership in regional institutions, and a tight focus on economic cooperation.

In this model, there is an underlying structural change in terms of the narrowing gap in relative power between the two largest players in the region, but as yet no power competition. Instead, the key change will occur in Chinese national characteristics, in terms of China's growing economic strength and national consolidation. But United States strategic dominance over the Asia-Pacific will persist, and will not be contested by China.

Many important aspects of this model are reflected in the current state of affairs in the region. A significant degree of Chinese adjustment and accommodation exists relative to United States predominance. In terms of policy, Chinese leaders have evinced their desire to make room for and to avoid open contestation of (if not entirely conform to) United States dominance in recent years. There has been, for instance, a marked moderation in rhetoric against "American hegemony" and United States alliances and bases in East Asia.[11] Chinese actions also do not suggest that it is seeking a strategy of counter-dominance against the US. On the Korean peninsula, Beijing has refrained from exploiting its close relationship with Pyongyang to intensify the antagonism against the United States and South Korea, but has rather shifted toward being a mediating partner of the United States in the Six Party Talks.[12] And while some see renewed Sino-Russian relations as a spot of soft balancing behavior by Beijing, the limits on their strategic cooperation partnership are considerable, including their divergent primary aims, which are arms acquisition on China's part and economic gain on Russia's part, rather than anti-American in focus.[13] Also of note was Beijing's support for the Bush Administration's campaign against terrorism and war in Afghanistan after September 11, 2001, in spite of its growing discomfort with the American presence in Central and South Asia which works to Chinese strategic disadvantage.[14] Moreover, the Chinese government's relatively quiet opposition to the war against Iraq in 2003 indicated that China is willing to allow room for the United States to flex its muscles, even when critical principles such as sovereignty are at stake.[15] On the one hand, Beijing has gained breathing room within the Sino–American relationship as a result of Washington's new preoccupation with anti-terrorism and the Middle East, and has also managed to hitch its controversial domestic anti-insurgency cause to the terrorism bandwagon.[16] On the other hand, China's accommodation of American strategic priorities at this time derives also from the renewed realization of its own relatively inferior technology and war-fighting capability after the demonstrations of American prowess in the recent battlefields.[17]

As a result of the perceived large power differential, and because of their urgent economic imperative, Chinese policy elites are now doubly anxious to maximize what they perceive as the breathing space afforded by the United States war on terror to concentrate on economic development and growth. This accords well with the strategic thinking which has prevailed since the economic reforms of the 1980s. Premier Deng Xiaoping's guiding principles for foreign policy were to seek peace and development (*heping yu fazhan*) while keeping a low international profile and building up China's abilities (*taoguang yanghui*).[18] In meetings and interviews, the Chinese policy community tends to emphasize the large gap between the United States and China in terms of wealth, technology, and military capability. They acknowledge US superiority and China's inability to be a real competitor for the next few decades at least. This pragmatism is accompanied by Beijing's strong strategic focus on domestic economic development and national stability. Chinese leaders publicly acknowledge that the country faces a plethora of developmental problems that "are enough to keep us busy"—Beijing will not have time to spare to "seek hegemony" when it is going to take the "arduous endeavors of generations for China to catch up with developed countries."[19] Thus China cannot afford either to try to forge a counterbalancing coalition against the United States, or to dabble in foreign policy adventurism. By this logic, China is a "satisfied" power.[20]

As one Chinese academic put it, the central problem in Sino–American relations may be conceptual: Washington harbors a "China threat" mentality and perceives bilateral relations to be those between a superpower and a rising challenger.[21] The Chinese, on the other hand, characterize the relationship as one between "the largest developing country" and "the largest developed country."[22] There is a strong recognition that the American unipolar moment will last for some time and that while China does benefit from deeper integration into the world economic system maintained by the United States, it has no alternative developmental path. Thus Beijing's current aim is to "de-securitize" China's rise in order to allay regional concerns. The Chinese foreign policy community has made a concerted effort to represent China's re-emergence as essentially an economic and developmental one, rather than a strategic development. It is not revisionist vis-à-vis the international system but in fact in line with the aims and values well-understood by others because this development is modeled along the well-traveled global capitalist path. Thus, instead of shunning or promoting alternatives to the established institutions, China recognizes that "the world will not let China have a free ride, and because it wants to take the ride, China has no choice but to pay the price for the ticket" for entry into institutions such as the WTO.[23]

As a result, Beijing publicly identifies cooperation rather than conflict as the main characteristic of current and future Sino–American relations. It is hoped that China's economic development will act as the foundation for US–China cooperation on technological advancements, and to ensure bilateral and regional stability to allow concentration on domestic development. In other words, as the emphasis of Beijing's foreign policy is retained upon issues of trade and international economic system membership, key foreign affairs interlocutors in Beijing foresee a broadening and deepening of the overlap in Sino–American interests in maintaining regional stability.[24]

In policy terms, this orientation is evident both at the conceptual and diplomatic levels. Under the presidency of Jiang Zemin, China adopted a more consciously constructive tone in the key foreign policy aims of "increasing trust, reducing problems, developing cooperation, and refraining from confrontation" (Jiang's sixteen-character principles of *zhengjia xinren, jianshao mafan, fazhan hezuo, bugao duikang*). At the international level, Chinese diplomacy con-sciously concentrated on demonstrating China's long-term goodwill, at times more so than on the pursuit of common interests.[25] However, Beijing has also taken some important and consistent steps toward conforming to the status quo in terms of participating in international institutions and adopting norms of conduct. This is most notable at the regional level, especially in Chinese par-ticipation in the ASEAN Regional Forum, an Asia-Pacific gathering devoted to the discussion of security issues and under whose aegis China issued its first defense white paper in 2002.[26] Beijing has also negotiated or settled a number of its outstanding territorial disputes with five neighboring countries.[27] On the economic front, China has undertaken to set up a free trade area with Southeast Asia by 2010, and is actively promoting ASEAN+3, which brings together Southeast Asian countries along with China, Japan and the Republic of Korea (ROK).[28] It would seem that President Jiang's attempt to develop a more activist approach toward "accomplishing some deeds in the diplomatic arena" (*yousuo zuowei*) has borne fruit. Within East Asia, China has managed its "deeds" in a manner consistent with the prevailing diplomatic style of the region, called the "ASEAN way," which emphasizes informality, consensus, non-intervention in internal affairs, and moving at a pace that is comfortable for all members.[29] Further, in a gesture toward its acceptance of the subregion's norms of peaceful settlement of conflicts and nuclear non-proliferation, Beijing signed on to ASEAN's Treaty of Amity and Cooperation at the end of 2003.[30] In the international arena, Samuel Kim has also detected "no evidence of any revisionist or norm-defying behaviour" from China within international institutions (except regarding the Taiwan issue), but rather argues that China has tended to act as a "system maintainer."[31]

According to this "status quo" model of US–China relations, therefore, the impact of systemic power distribution is muted for the time being. China is a rising power, but not one sufficiently strong enough to threaten the United States' preponderance for the next 20 years at least. By this measure, we are not yet living in a time of transition from unipolarity. Thus, in considering the impact of Sino–American relations on regional security, the interesting ques-tions shift from the structural to the ideational and behavioral realm. It would seem that it is in each country's perceived regional image and role for itself and for the other, that some interim answers may be found. Here, there is evidence that China has been cautiously trying to re-represent its resurgence in developmentalist terms and to pursue regional cooperation—and to some extent, leadership—using diplomatic and institutional means acceptable to other states. In this sense, China's determined portrayal of itself as the rising, but considerate and responsible power helps to sustain the status quo in the form of the preferred processes of international relations. It is competing with the United States, but not over power or primacy as yet. Rather, the subtle contest is for diplomatic and economic influence, mainly in East Asia, primarily in order to stabilize its periphery and to forge economic ties, so as to advance its national drive for economic development.

Prospects

Beijing's attempts to limit its goals and to reassure the United States and others in the region about the consequences of its growing power may (or may not) succeed for the next decade. However, there are three key determinants of its success. First, there will need to be greater transparency in Chinese defense strategy and policies in order to persuade others of its intentions. More sophisticated articulation of China's security concepts and strategy would also help to clarify its objectives in the region. For instance, while it still remains opaque compared to US strategic documents, the latest Chinese Defense White Papers issued in 2004 and 2006 provide more information than before on the PLA's doctrine, policies, and international cooperation; give some details on developments in the Chinese defense industry; and shed better light on China's concerns about Taiwan.[32]

Second, the degree of American acceptance of the China's foreign policy approach may be limited by domestic pressures, especially the Taiwan lobby, which can be expected to continue pressing for closer defense ties with the island as Chinese military power grows. Also, as China develops economically, disputes over trade deficits, dumping, tariffs, and copyright protection will increase. The twin conflicts over the undervaluation of the Chinese currency—a dozen bills have been introduced in the newly elected Congress in 2007, including proposals to declare China's cheap currency an illegal export subsidy—and the attempt by a Chinese company to buy over the United States oil and gas company UNOCAL in 2005 demonstrate that important constituencies in the United States readily view China's growing economic power as threatening to their economic competitiveness and national security.[33] Furthermore, the institutionalization of human rights concerns into China policy-making structures within the United States will ensure the continued salience of this set of issues.[34] The two elements were reflected in the 2006 National Security Strategy, which stated that the future character of the Sino–American relationship will be conditional upon improvement in Beijing's record of military transparency, mercantilist trade policies, support for rogue regimes, and ensuring "basic freedoms and universal rights" at home. The strategy document promised to "encourage China to make the right strategic choices for its own people, while we (the United States) hedge(s) against other possibilities".[35]

Finally, to what extent is the developmentalist strategy a means of buying time for Beijing to build up its national base, from which to project its power once it is strong enough? Some American analysts see China's building of comprehensive national power as a short-term strategy, to be replaced by a second phase (to be implemented in 20 to 50 years' time) during which Beijing will enhance its major power status by applying its new power base more aggressively with less regard for a stable regional environment.[36] While this is a reasonable assumption, based on the expectation that a more powerful state is better able to pursue and advance its own interests, some regional observers have pointed out that this window allows us time to try to "socialize" the Chinese policy elite into a longer-term acceptance of international norms and order.[37] Also, there remain the possibilities of cognitive change in the strategic outlook of this generation of Chinese leaders as they engage in greater interaction with the international community.[38]

Moreover, the degree to which China may be restrained by rules and institutions, or Chinese ambitions moderated by relative gains, may be crucially affected by the United States' conceptions of its own position and role in the region. Currently, the Bush Administration's apparent pursuit of perpetual predominance as articulated in its National Security Strategy exacerbates the security dilemma for China. The George W. Bush Administration not only pledges to build up armed forces "strong enough to dissuade potential adversaries from pursuing a military build-up in hopes of surpassing, or equaling, the power of the United States," but has also introduced the principle of pre-emptive strikes against potential adversaries that threaten American national security.[39] Such rhetoric, together with the "China threat" discourse, suggests that the Asia-Pacific is a zero-sum chessboard on which there is no room for China to develop without threatening the US position.[40] Worryingly, from this reading of the US point of view, there are potentially no aspects of strategic power that may be considered negotiable. For instance, Assistant Secretary of State for East Asian and Pacific Affairs James Kelly told a House Committee hearing in June 2004 that China "is challenging the status quo aggressively" in some areas, citing as the only example Beijing "expanding its influence in Southeast Asia by enhancing its diplomatic representation, increasing foreign assistance, and signing new bilateral and regional agreements".[41] Southeast Asians are not likely to agree with Kelly's portrayal of recent Chinese initiatives toward the region, and it would needlessly exacerbate the security dilemma if the United States begins systematically to categorize growing Chinese economic and political influence in its surrounding region as aggressive challenges to the status quo.

On the other hand, since August 2004, the second Bush Administration has revealed elements of its global posture review, which indicate a shift toward a more global (as opposed to region-specific) focus in what is to be a more flexible military strategy.[42] Given the current emphasis against terrorism and weapons of mass destruction, it is expected that Washington's focus will shift toward the Middle East, Central Asia, and South Asia. Coupled with the draw-down of troops from Korea, the Bush Administration may be seen as easing its attention in East Asia and tacitly conceding the region to Chinese influence. While the Bush Administration insists that the impacts of the review will not affect the US commitment to allies or its military capabilities in each theatre,[43] the perception that Washington is more preoccupied with its overall global strategy and conflicts in other regions could be dangerous. It might lead to greater complacency and assertiveness on the part of the Chinese in East Asia. In sum, it is advisable for the United States neither to construct a zero-sum power contest against China, nor to appear to be paying less attention to the region.

A crucial first step to adjusting to a rising or developing China is to acknow-ledge the inevitable concomitant growth in its regional influence. While this entails the parallel realization that the status quo of American and Japanese *dominance* in the region in strategic and economic terms may be altered as a result,[44] a more constructive reaction would be to seek ways to deepen United States engagement in the region in order better to secure its interests.

It is important to understand that growing Chinese influence in the region need not necessarily occur at the expense of American influence. First, power and influence in the Asia-Pacific does not present a zero-sum game. As the Southeast Asian states are fond of reiterating, for example, not only may the size of the economic pie itself be enlarged without their most important traditional trading partners losing out to China; but many states in the region still prefer continued US strategic dominance and urge the closer involvement of both the United States and China in regional security issues and dialogue to enhance stability.[45] Second, the apparent decline in United States influence in the region in recent years may be more the result of the unpopularity of the Bush Administration's conduct of the war against terrorism and in Iraq than it is related to growing Chinese power.[46]

Thus, it would seem that a key feature of the short-term "status quo" model is the hope that time might also be bought for the United States to "acclimatize" itself to a changing regional strategic environment that is moving toward containing two major powers, albeit of somewhat different leagues. In other words, the "status quo" scenario discussed here does not assume a continuation of the current relative power distribution, since the gap between Chinese and American power in the region will close to some extent. However, the status quo is retained insofar as the United States maintains its dominance per se and rising China occupies a second-tier position in the regional hierarchy.

Model II: negotiated change

If China and the United States are able, over the next decade or so, to maintain their relationship along the lines of the status quo model outlined above, it would have been in large part the result of a gradual adjustment on both sides to the changing power dynamics in the region engendered by China's rise and the United States' continued predominance. Over time, this process can be expected to take on a life of its own, if the two sides continue to perceive the importance of coexistence. Over the medium term, it is possible that we may see the relationship move toward a second model of negotiated change, by which the two powers coordinate to manage a structural transformation. Model II differs from Model I in that it involves a more conscious and coherent process of *negotiating* power sharing, rather than the more ad hoc adjustments described in the first model. It also differs in that the aim would be to negotiate a structural *transition* from US hegemony to a concert (or duet) of power between the United States and China in the Asia-Pacific region.

This model is informed by the observation and argument—advanced by institutionalists and constructivists against stark realist logic—that peaceful power transitions are possible.[47] However, here we are concerned not with how to manage China's displacing and taking over American hegemony in the international system, but rather with exploring the potential of finding some form of power sharing between them as the vast power gap between the United States and China is gradually reduced.[48]

Within the historical record, the main example of power sharing among major states is the nineteenth-century European concert system. The great power concert consisting of Great Britain, Russia, Austria, Prussia, and France was most effective in the period between the Napoleonic and the Crimean wars, from 1815 to 1854. It was distinguished by "an unusually high and self-conscious level of cooperation" among these powers, whereby each exercised self-restraint and sought multilateral means of dealing with problems. Concert conduct is distinct from balance of power behavior in the fundamental acceptance that sustained cooperation between great powers is possible and that war is undesirable as a policy tool.[49] In the European case, after the upheaval of the Napoleonic wars, the great powers concerned developed certain common values—the avoidance of major war and a shared stake in economic prosperity—which constituted a change in their conception of self-interest. Thus, as "statesmen thought more in terms of the international system and what was necessary to keep it functioning," the process was accompanied by a "change in [their] values and beliefs about how politics can and should be conducted."[50] This led in turn to the negotiation of a system whereby the great powers would maintain postwar international order using the key norms of crisis management through conference diplomacy, sanctioning territorial change only by consensus, protecting essential members of the system, and granting each other due respect.[51] A concert system essentially involves conscious coordination between great powers in managing international relations, mediating conflicts, and legitimizing acceptable revisions to the status quo.

Does the European concert of power provide a model of negotiated change for US–China relations in the Asia-Pacific today? Other authors have applied the concert concept to the region wholesale to varying degrees of satisfaction.[52]

Given our focus on the Sino–American bilateral relationship, however, this analysis concentrates on drawing from some of the *key* notions of concert systems in developing its own model of negotiated change. We might begin by noting a divergence: concerts are usually deemed to exist in multipolar systems, whereas we are considering a case of two powers that may still exhibit a significant power disparity. While the European concert system was in fact a two-tiered one, consisting of only two great powers (Great Britain and Russia), it is difficult to draw generalizations from the European case for an Asia-Pacific bipolar system.[53] However, it is possible to consider how the general principles of a concert system might be applied to achieve a "duet" of power between the United States and China in this region. Bearing in mind that a concert is a system that requires "explicit and self-conscious management" on the part of the great powers,[54] developing a potential "duet" between Washington and Beijing would involve negotiation on at least the following four aspects of their power and influence:

1   Potential spheres of influence,
2   Desired status quo power distribution,
3   How power is to be exercised, and
4   Modes of conflict management.

The first two categories deal with preferences in terms of structure and the last two with agreement on processes.

Spheres of influence

A major characteristic of a great power concert is the explicit acceptance of each power's respective sphere of influence within the system, within which other powers are not expected to encroach. Thus one crucial means by which the United States and China can negotiate peaceful change in the Asia-Pacific region may be through agreeing upon mutual spheres of influence. In this regard, Robert Ross' suggestion that the extant geographical and geopolitical conditions in East Asia make China the incumbent continental power and the United States the dominant maritime power, is useful. He argues that this division of influence can persist because the United States and China each has a defensive advantage in its own theater sufficient to match each other's military developments. Also, the de facto bipolarity is stable because of weak potential regional powers: Russia is limited in its ability to deploy east, while Japan is too small.[55] Ross' implicit presentation of a Chinese continental versus American maritime sphere of influence is attractive in light of Washington's maritime arc of alliances (the "San Francisco system") stretching from Japan and the ROK to the Philippines to Australia and given China's current lack of maritime power projection capability.

However, for the current de facto division of influence to be better consolidated into a tacit or explicit understanding about spheres of influence over the medium term, some important developments must be taken into account. For instance, to what extent will China exercise what Ross terms "hegemony" over the Korean Peninsula and continental Southeast Asia? It is not clear that Beijing desires a strong reunified Korea at its doorstep because it could pose a challenge to potential Chinese regional dominance; neither can it be taken for granted that countries like Vietnam, with its history of fighting Chinese occupation and of fierce independence, would succumb to the Chinese orbit. At the same time, the processes of globalization and China's integration into the global economy and international community mean that the traditional Monroe doctrine style of exclusionary spheres of influence may not in fact be possible in today's context.[56]

Furthermore, Ross' sanguine view of the existing balance of power between the United States and China in East Asia is contestable. First, in spite of its recent moderate stance on its territorial claims in the South China Sea, the Chinese government did issue a Territorial Waters Law in February 1992, laying claim to the whole of the South China Sea, and it is engaged in upgrading its blue water naval capabilities, potentially blurring the lines between maritime and continental influence.[57] Second, the balance may be disturbed through the implementation of the proposed American Missile Defense system. The project has made slow progress under the George W. Bush Administration, with initial ground-based interceptors deployed on US territory, and Japan having agreed to invest in and jointly develop with the US an East Asian missile defense system to meet the North Korean threat. If it comes into effect, the United States will critically pierce Beijing's offensive deterrence capacity.[58] Finally, Ross' argument underrates the preferences and policies of countries in East Asia, which have adopted relatively successful hedging strategies aimed at cultivating close relations with both the United States and China and not falling into one exclusive sphere of influence.[59]

For these reasons, it would seem that negotiating spheres of influence as such might not be a viable central element of the negotiated change model. Rather than relying on a geographical division of powers, we may have to look instead toward negotiating other means of regulating the relationship between these two major powers with their increasingly overlapping spheres of influence. At the structural level, an alternative to spheres of influence would be to negotiate a mutual understanding about the preferred status quo distribution of power within the Asia-Pacific region.

Power distribution

There are two sets of debates to consider when thinking about the medium- to long-term power distribution in the Asia-Pacific. First is the set of speculation about when China will "catch up" with the United States in terms of economic productivity and military capability.[60] Estimates greatly vary but it is safe to say that over the medium term (20–30 years), assuming that China continues to develop and the United States does not decline, we will still be experiencing the process of China narrowing, but not closing, the gap. Second is the controversy about what type of power distribution gives rise to the most stable kind of international system. Neorealists favor bipolarity because of the reading of the Cold War as a period of "long peace," but classical realists and contemporary Chinese politicians and analysts prefer multipolarity, while some American scholars have argued that the current United States unipolarity will endure for both structural and normative reasons.[61] Again, regardless of the eventual outcome, over the medium term, we are likely to continue to see the *run-up* to a period of potential transition away from unipolarity.

Therefore, over the short to medium term, it is important for the United States and China to negotiate a shared understanding of and interest in the existing status quo, which we may expect to be hierarchical in the sense that the United States would remain the dominant world superpower, while China increasingly becomes the regional great power within East Asia. I would argue that within the medium term, prospects for a negotiated peace would be best secured by the acceptance of this status quo two-tiered power distribution by both sides. This argument is premised upon the assumption that chances for negotiated change are higher if it is clear that the hegemonic position per se is not under contention.[62] Having a hierarchy of powers within a concert is not unusual—as noted above, the nineteenth-century European concert consisted of only two great powers, while the others were a defeated great power (France) and two middle powers (Austria and Prussia). China and the United States could form a hierarchical duet. For this to come to pass though, a fundamental alteration of mutual perceptions is necessary. Washington must come to recognize China's significant regional impact and accord it a legitimate leading role in regional affairs, while Beijing must accede to not only the superiority but also the relative benignity of American power. Both these processes require major changes in mutual perceptions.

Here, the key concert principle of according each great power respect and the cardinal rule that none should be humiliated are particularly important, since a key facilitating factor for such a two-tier duet system would be the norms of equality and mutual respect that Beijing emphasizes but often does not feel that it gains from the United States. As David Kang argues, East Asia has traditionally been more comfortable with hierarchy in its international affairs than is the West.[63] This means that China expects—and will receive from the region, if not the United States —the regard due the largest country in the region. Without going so far as to argue, as Kang does, that countries in the region would necessarily bandwagon with China, it is important to note that they are very likely to accommodate China's rising regional great power status whatever happens. Yet Washington need not worry excessively about losing East Asia to China as an exclusive sphere of influence, as these countries also worry about Chinese hegemony and so are equally likely to continue facilitating an active US presence and engagement in the region.[64]

Over the medium term, establishing mutual Sino–American understanding of their relative hierarchy would be merely a holding operation in the run-up to China becoming strong enough to challenge United States hegemony, if not for the development of the following two elements of concert behavior, which represent crucial socializing processes involving the negotiation of measures of self-restraint and forms of great power systemic management.

Exercise of power

The most critical element of how power is to be exercised is clearly the use of force. Any viable negotiated change scenario would therefore require a commitment on the part of the two major powers to seek and exhaust diplomatic solutions to problems and to reserve the use of force as a very last resort. Worries about Chinese "revisionism" are centered on the concern that Beijing stubbornly maintains its right to use force to settle the Taiwan issue in particular. However, apart from Taiwan, which it considers a domestic issue, Beijing has proclaimed adherence to the principle of peaceful resolution of conflicts through diplomacy in a variety of norms, including the Five Principles of Coexistence, which have guided Chinese foreign policy since the mid 1950s, and ASEAN's Treaty of Amity and Cooperation. It has also begun to negotiate settlements on some of its territorial disputes with India and with Vietnam in recent years, and has committed to dealing with the South China Sea dispute through multilateral diplomacy.[65] Indeed, Premier Deng Xiaoping suggested in 1988 that the Five Principles, initially developed for the Bandung Meeting of non-aligned states, could form the basis of norms for international relations.[66] On the other hand, China and much of the rest of the world is currently worried that the United States may regard the use of force abroad as a sovereign right, particularly after Washington eschewed United Nations sanctions for the war in Iraq in 2003.

The two sides will also have to pay attention to other ways, short of war, in which their strategic policies could deepen the security dilemma. In China, the improvement of its power projection capabilities by means of arms acquisition and modernization and augmentation of its offensive capabilities using the selective development of specific technology fuel American suspicions.[67] The United States, for its part, has been strengthening its key alliances in the region, particularly those with Japan and Australia, and is looking to expand military cooperation with other friendly states such as Singapore. The Bush Administration has identified East Asia as an area of "enduring" national interest to the United States that no other state can be allowed to dominate. China has been indirectly but clearly identified as a potential threat to United States interests in the region, and the Pentagon has emphasized "East Asian littoral" (or maritime East Asia) as a region in which the United States would want to develop additional access and infrastructure agreements to overcome the long distances and its relatively low basing density.[68] These trends, if not accompanied by regular bilateral high-level assurances and military exchanges, will contribute to a spiraling security dilemma. At the same time, other critical arms control issues have to be discussed on a high-level basis as Chinese capabilities improve, as disagreement about nuclear proliferation continues, and as the United States has withdrawn from the Anti-Ballistic Missile (ABM) treaty and is developing a Missile Defense system. The most important achievement of détente diplomacy during the Cold War was arguably the elaborate and extended series of arms control negotiations between Moscow and Washington. The key lesson here is that the United States and China should not need to wait for a Cuban missile crisis to provide belated impetus for such negotiations.

Beyond the "hard" strategic calculations, one problem is that, unlike the United States and the Soviet Union during the Cold War, the United States and China do not currently exercise power in the Asia-Pacific region using a similar mix of instruments. The United States is the more established hegemon with formal alliances and an undeniable political and economic clout that is largely taken for granted, while China is the rising power with growing economic leverage and a marked sensitivity to cultivating diplomatic influence. There is a need for some mutual understanding of the extent to which these types of power are fungible across sectors. For instance, does Chinese domination of a growing slice of the Asian economic pie necessarily translate into a reduction in American strategic hold over its allies? The degree to which economic and strategic aspects of power are negotiable or zero-sum is not well understood. The US–China Economic and Security Review Commission's annual reports to Congress since 2002 have recommended the active use of trade penalties to ensure China's full compliance with WTO regulations.[69] However, as some analysts have pointed out, China's growing regional and international economic role means that such simple "us" and "them" divides do not apply in reality. Because China has become so "deeply embedded with key global supply chains and increasingly has become the final assembly point for products that incorporate the value-added components made by many of America's friends throughout the region," any economic retaliation against China will also hurt Washington's allies and friends. Moreover, the United States will find it difficult to sanction economically one of the biggest engines recycling global trade dollars back into the home economy—China is the second largest United States treasury notes holder after Japan.[70] Thus, in addition to negotiating rules of economic conduct, the United States has also to work out how best to compete peacefully with China in terms of economic and political influence in the region.

Modes of conflict management

Conflict management under the concert system exhibited three main characteristics: territorial change by consensus, multilateral conference diplomacy, and restraint of minor allies by each great power. Applying the first principle to the current US–China relationship, an ideal would be the negotiation of an explicit understanding that potential changes in the political status quo surrounding Taiwan would be acceptable only if both major powers agree. There is a case to be made that in essence, such a tacit principle already exists, since given the agreement on "one China" and the American commitment to counter any unprovoked use of force by China, the only solution agreeable to both sides—a unilateral declaration of independence from Taipei notwithstanding— is some form of peaceful "one country, two systems" reunification. This is a controversial assertion, but one that holds potential for a clearer negotiated understanding than the deliberate ambiguity that currently exists, from a great-power-centered point of view.

Other possible areas of revisionism, such as China's claims in the South China Sea or potential US aims for forcible regime change in other countries, would be more difficult to manage. The rapid development of a number of multilateral security fora in the region since the end of the Cold War may provide some avenue for the United States and China, along with other regional powers such as Japan, Korea, and India, to engage in concert-type diplomacy in times of crisis. However, some of these institutions, such as the ASEAN Regional Forum, currently suffer from malaise because of the divergent views of the two major powers on their purpose and scope.[71] Perhaps the better example is the Six Party Talks regarding the Korean peninsula, which evolved from the American insistence on a multilateral process to involve the United States, China, Japan, Russia, and the two Koreas. This appears in some ways to resemble a concert, with the United States exercising its influence over the ROK and China restraining the DPRK, but both brokering negotiations, while the other two regional powers are brought into the process to accord it legitimacy. Whether such nascent concert diplomacy can mediate revisionism and promote self-restraint remains to be seen. Furthermore, over the medium term, whether such efforts can be further institutionalized to form region-wide norms of conflict management and mediation would depend on whether the United States and China are willing to incorporate such institutions as part of their new negotiated order. One way would be the fulfillment of the aspiration to expand the talks into a Northeast Asian security dialogue.[72]

Prospects

Overall, the conditions for some form of negotiated change in the US–China relationship toward a concert-type "hierarchical duet" are daunting but not unimaginable. First, the presence on both sides of strong leadership and the capacity for tight executive decisions will aid the process of building up a significant level of confidence and trust. Ironically, the Nixon/Kissinger–Mao/ Zhou combination of the early 1970s might provide the ideal model for such a process of re-conceptualizing the relationship. While the Chinese leaders relied on their domestic authority, the American leaders relied on secrecy to negotiate a reduction of mutual threat perceptions, and to cultivate cooperation or coordination on major international issues.[73]

Second, the existence of a significant common interest—a shared external threat is often the best unifying factor—may be crucial to kick-starting the process.[74] In the post-Cold War era, common Sino–American interests include economic development, peaceful reunification on the Korean peninsula, and counter-terrorism. It is not clear whether these are sufficiently salient common causes though. As a goal that is shared by almost every state in the world, it is doubtful whether economic development can act as a gel specific to US–China relations. Furthermore, there is growing domestic sentiment within the United States that Chinese economic growth might engender unhealthy dependence of certain critical US economic sectors on China, and that cheaper Chinese production costs and the undervalued Chinese currency are costing American jobs.[75] In spite of the Bush Administration's rhetoric, whether the "war on terror" might become the next big crusade remains to be seen, especially as China's support of the campaign apparently carried the important consideration of winning American backing for its own domestic struggle with separatists in Xinjiang province. Without the initiation of meaningful arms control talks between Washington and Beijing, counter-proliferation is unlikely to provide the focus for cooperation, as Washington's disagreements with Beijing on the latter's provisions of nuclear technology to countries such as Pakistan remain an issue of contention.[76] As suggested above, the Korean peninsula may provide a promising arena for Sino–American coordination and perhaps the prime avenue for an exercise of concert over the medium term. However, unless it can provide the basis for a more coordinated effort led by the United States and China to institutionalize regional security cooperation, it will remain a limited issue area that cannot provide an overarching ideological bond.

Furthermore, the constraints provided by domestic politics on both sides must be weighed. Any negotiated power sharing arrangement would require a reversal of Chinese attitudes toward American "hegemony" and "imperialism,"[77] and the reconciliation of growing Chinese nationalism with self-restrained exercise of power. The difficulties of this process for Chinese leaders who have to contend with strong nationalist opinion that the time has come to make up for China's century of humiliation cannot be underestimated.[78] On the other hand, however, the specific expressed objectives of Chinese nationalist discourse should not be ignored. The top priority is national reunification. One of the most crucial determinants of a sustainable negotiated regional order may therefore be the US ability to cede Taiwan to the Chinese sphere of influence. If this is achieved, a fundamental obstacle to negotiated change may be removed, and the vital determinant of China as a "revisionist" power negated.

On the other hand, it is important to recognize that the negotiation of a power share will work to China's advantage in the medium term when it is still unable to challenge United States supremacy. This is reflected in Beijing's current posture toward the United States in the Asia-Pacific. Chinese leaders have reportedly told Washington that China (a) will not challenge United States military presence in the Asia-Pacific (which is useful to China because it contains Japanese re-militarization); (b) will not put pressure on neighboring countries to drop their relations with the United States (with the exception of

Taiwan's military relations); and (c) will actively participate in regional security fora and economic development.[79] These undertakings, if translated into consistent practice, could form the basic understanding for a negotiated hierarchical regional power structure.

Faced with international debates about how to deal with a rising China in the 1990s, Beijing also issued its own, relatively moderate national security statement in the form of President Jiang Zemin's "new security concept" (*xin anquanguan*) in 1997. This formulation consciously moved away from the old Cold War security outlook that emphasized great power competition, collective defense, unilateralism, and absolute security. Instead, the new security concept is based on the central notions of mutual trust (*huxin*), mutual benefit (*huli*), equality (*pingdeng*), and cooperation (*xiezuo*). In rhetoric at least, the concept represents new developments in Chinese security thinking in three ways. First, as well as the Five Principles of Peaceful Coexistence (sovereignty and territorial integrity, non-aggression, non-interference in internal affairs, equality and mutual benefit, and peaceful coexistence), it stresses the importance of norms governing international relations, particularly the role played by the United Nations. Second, the new concept is concerned with comprehensive security—in the form of economic, political, technological, environment, and cultural security—as well as military security. It also encompasses non-traditional security issues such as terrorism and transnational crime. Finally, the new security concept is underscored by an emphasis on the growing interdependence of security issues. The understanding, particularly post-September 11, that a nation's security is intrinsically bound up with the security of neighbors in an era of multifaceted and global threats, has led to a new emphasis on common security interests and the need for cooperative security approaches.[80] Furthermore, the Chinese foreign policy community is intensifying its presentation of a peculiarly Chinese style of exercising power. This emphasizes a gradual, incremental, "peaceful rise" (*heping jueqi*) to power. Indeed, in recent years, the term adopted is "peaceful development" (*heping fazhan*), as Beijing pursues the method of deep engagement through economic cooperation for "mutual benefit" with its neighbors, supplemented by the appeal of similar culture and cultural styles in terms of "Asian values" and the "ASEAN way."[81] Under the new leadership of President Hu Jintao and Prime Minister Wen Jiabao, Beijing has also manifested a successful diplomatic "charm offensive" in East Asia in the last two years.[82]

On the other side, the radical change required in American attitudes about China, the United States role in the Asia-Pacific, and its exercise of power as the unipolar power will arguably be much more difficult to achieve. At the bilateral level, there is first the general suspicion and assessments of China as posing a military threat to the United States, which stem from realist convictions, cultural perceptions, and ideological opposition to the largest remaining communist state in the world. While many studies list the outstanding issues of contention between the two countries, it is not clear what China must or can do in order to change American perceptions. Second is the related ideological problem Americans have of dealing with an authoritarian communist government after the Cold War. Finally, it is difficult to gauge under what conditions domestic political pressure with the United States might ease on the Taiwan issue, and how subsequent administrations would calibrate the "ambiguous" commitment to Taiwan's defense.

Fundamentally, the most critical consideration is whether any power sharing arrangement will necessarily be regarded as compromising US influence in the region, a factor that may stymie progress if the Bush Administration's declared objective of preventing any other power from challenging US global hegemony is taken seriously. In order to begin to negotiate a *Modus Vivendi* with China, Washington will have to make room for China at the international and regional tables on issues of importance to China, take seriously and participate in regional fora for cooperation on security issues, and be prepared to even think about conceding to some form of a "one China" solution on the Taiwan issue, for instance, by clearly calling upon Taipei not to seek *de jure* independence. China already sits on the vast majority of the most important negotiating tables in international diplomatic and economic issues, except perhaps for the G8. On the other hand, at the regional level, China has been taking more of an interest in cooperative institutions (such as the ARF, ASEAN+3, East Asian Summit, and Shanghai Cooperation Organization) than the United States, which still uses its alliance structure as the basic foundation of Asia-Pacific strategy.[83] While the region believes that China may be socialized into being a responsible great power by its participation in regional institutions, the parallel aim to socialize the United States into non-military cooperative security modes of behavior has not received equal attention. At the same time, while there is now greater recognition of China's new focus on boosting its profile and participation in international diplomatic arenas and institutions, there is not sufficient consideration in Washington about how to react to and interact with China in these settings instead of in a head-to-head contest.[84]

Still, a start may be made in the current climate to redress the negative images of China as a threatening rising power in the United States now that Washington has found other enemies in the form of global terrorism and rogue states proliferating in weapons of mass destruction. One key possibility is that the argument in favor of an "offshore balancing" strategy in the Asia-Pacific may gain greater currency as the United States remains intensely engaged in the Middle East.[85] This strategy is fatalistic about China's ascendance, but rationalizes the withdrawal of the US security commitment in the region by recourse to the expectation that Japan will rise to balance China. Without accepting the whole extent of this argument, we might suggest that power sharing is an intermediate solution to the potential problem of overextension should Washington persist in the strategy of preponderance. The advantages of negotiated power sharing include lower costs, the constraining of a potential challenger by means of norms and rules, as well as the benefits of cooperation and joint management of regional affairs, which may include quid pro quo Chinese support for American policies in other regions of the world.

The main point here is that in the medium term, the peaceful integration of China into the regional power fabric will require negotiation, rather than simple adjustment. China must be allowed and expected to change a few things too, such as to increase its share of regional trade and influence, and to check the pace of certain institution-building for its own comfort. Of course, there are fundamental rules which all parties should be expected to uphold, for instance, the use of force in settling disputes. Yet, from a negotiating point of view, such bottom lines are harder to maintain if one or both parties are inconsistent or bear a controversial record on such issues. More fundamentally, Washington will want to think about the impacts of China's growing leadership role in East Asia. Beijing's unassailable Asian identity, its sustained engagement with the region as a whole, its emphasis on regional economic development, and its astute diplomacy have all boosted its legitimacy as regional leader, even as its material capabilities lag far behind those of the United States. In contrast, while American economic and strategic preponderance continues in the region, its emphasis on bilateral relationships rather than region-wide engagement, its core reliance on alliances rather than more comprehensive socio-economic aspects, and Washington's apparent high-handedness may seriously undermine United States' leadership in the region.

Trajectories

There are three possible trajectories from this medium term model of negotiated change. First, some form of a hierarchical duet could be sustainable into the longer term, if no major crises occur to undermine the period of mutual negotiation, if China does not overtake the US in terms of economic power too quickly, and if America's relative power advantage is maintained. Second, it is possible that we could see progress toward a Sino–American concert-type arrangement, as Chinese capabilities increasingly catch up with those of the United States. Over the longer term, as the two powers negotiate rules and coordinate their management of regional affairs, it is likely that greater similarity of interests and identity would emerge between them. This, of course, is the constructivist notion of fundamental change in preferences arising from norm- and institution-building.

The most optimistic long-term negotiated change scenario would have the United States and China cultivating multilateral collective security approaches with the other powers in the region, moving toward a regional security community.[86] This process will be arduous, and the goal may be unattainable because of the degree of dominance of the two major powers and the underdeveloped precedence for collective security in this region. On the other hand, some progress has been made at the initiative of ASEAN to propagate its style of diplomacy throughout the region, and regional security dialogue has begun. China has also demonstrated its willingness to adopt ASEAN-style multilateral approaches, and more importantly, appears to be reformulating its security thinking to take greater account of the notion of cooperative security.

Such developments remain mainly rhetorical, regional security dialogues still do not impinge upon some of the most crucial security issues such as Taiwan and the Korean peninsula, and the United States appears to share very little interest in cooperative or collective security approaches. But embarking on the process itself is important, because of the belief that the journey cultivates values and ways of behaving that can moderate behavior and shape preferences, even if the states concerned never reach the end of a European Union-like community.[87] The most important basic change will be the cultivation of the expectation and belief that structural shifts in power do not need to be accompanied by war but can instead be negotiated.[88]

The last possible trajectory is one during which the negotiated change process breaks down. This might occur if a major crisis happens, such as a war over Taiwan; or if over the medium term other powers in the region begin to rise (or, in Japan's case, to rearm significantly), thus disrupting and possibly destabilizing the regional power structure. If this process breaks down, then we are likely to move to the situation of power transition discussed in Model III below.

Model III: power transition

Scenarios of power transition pit the United States as the incumbent hegemon against China as the rising challenger. Such situations with changes in relative power at the structural level are associated with competition over positions within the international hierarchy and concepts of international order. The incumbent power will tend to emphasize system preservation (along with its dominant hierarchical position within it), while the rising challenger will tend to be revisionist, focusing on exerting territorial claims and changing international rules and norms. The ultimate aim of the challenger would be to usurp the dominant position of the incumbent.[89]

Translated into the US–China context, the power transition model portends at least three possible outcomes:

1   China successfully challenges US hegemony in the region, and there is a power transition to Chinese dominance;
2   There is a failed power transition following a crisis and conflict, which sees the reassertion of US hegemony and/or Chinese implosion; or
3   A transition to a new bipolar balance of power occurs in which China and the United States stake out separate spheres of influence and exercise mutual deterrence and containment, with occasional contained conflicts.

The third possible outcome may appear similar to Model II discussed in the previous section, but the substantive outcome and process here would be different—it may involve more conflicts or near-conflicts and lessons learned, such as during the early Cold War years, as opposed to the sustained negotiation in Model II.

Realist and neorealist theorists are pessimistic about prospects for peaceful power transitions. Notably, Robert Gilpin's hegemonic instability theory asserts that the incongruity between a rising power's capabilities and its continued subordinate position in an international system dominated by an erstwhile hegemon triggers a security dilemma that can only be resolved by major war.[90] His is a stark neorealist view that regards states as driven by zero-sum power concerns that make negotiation on hierarchy, rules and values impossible. On a meta-historic glance, it would seem that neorealists are correct: a large majority of power transitions are accompanied by war, with the modifications to the international order made by the victors of military confrontation. However, their theories, almost entirely derived from non-Asian cases of power transition, seem to lack predictive ability that can be applied to the US–China relations for four main reasons.

First, war is usually the necessary determining factor of the transition to the reign of a new hegemon.[91] However, closer historical examinations reveal that the relationship between the incidence of war and power transitions is not clear-cut. Some wars between rising and declining powers—such as the Thirty Years War—do not result in power transition; in other cases—such as the end of the Cold War—peaceful power transitions are achieved when the contending power acknowledges defeat and gives in to a new international order; and in yet other cases—such as the American takeover of British hegemony in the first half of the twentieth century—the major war occurs after the challenger has already over-taken the incumbent power. Thus, it would seem that there are specific conditions under which the incongruity between capabilities and status felt by the rising and declining powers may or may not necessarily lead them to war.[92]

Second, the specific disparity in power between the incumbent power and the challenger is important. The quantitative aspects of power transition—the perceived type and potential scope of the competing power, as well as the relative rates of ascendance and decline—are critical scales on which the balance of threat is calculated by fading or incumbent powers. However, the relationship between power imbalance and war remains a highly contested issue.[93] Intuitively, one would assume that the smaller the disparity of power, the greater the likelihood of conflict as the challenger becomes more confident.[94] However, it is possible that the incumbent power might decide to launch a preventive war against the competition before the challenger becomes too strong; while there is historical evidence that rising dissatisfied powers have tended to challenge hegemons before they have attained the latter's level of power.[95] Thus, for the US–China case, power transition theories cannot help us to identify which power is likely to start a war, or when.

Third, according to power transition theory, the dominant power is usually simultaneously in decline in parallel to the competing power's rise. In the situation of the United States and China currently, this is far from the case: the United States enjoys a preponderance of power which is virtually unparalleled in history, and China may need up to 50 years or more to draw head-to-head with it. In this case, a classic overtake scenario is very unlikely, barring a major domestic crisis, an economic collapse in the United States, or technological change.

Fourth, the dynamics of power transition are by no means simple. The process of power transition often involves more than just the rising and fading powers; there are often multiple rising contenders and simultaneous power challenges, and their involvement in the wars that characterize periods of transition is not clear-cut.[96] Successful new hegemons have tended to rise from the ranks of supporting rather than challenging states.[97] The very high costs of competition between the direct challenger and the old hegemon prohibit success, while the cooperative/competitive relationship between the old hegemon and its supporting partner paves the way for a successful power transition.[98] In this regard, it may be crucial to pay attention to other significant third parties in the Asia-Pacific transition, especially Japan, which is a United States ally, and which, if given a choice, the United States might prefer to cede greater regional power to, or construct a concert of sorts with, to strengthen the face-off with China.[99] Alternatively, India may be another rising regional power that could benefit from a potentially destructive Sino–American conflict.

Thus, great power transition is a complicated process and power transition or neorealist theories alone are inadequate predictors of outcomes. Fundamentally, whether we will see a challenge for dominance by China in the Asia-Pacific depends on two variables: potential power parity between the United States and China, which would provide Beijing with the capability to launch a bid for dominance, and dissatisfaction with the status quo, which will indicate Chinese intention and willingness to challenge the United States. It would appear that outright confrontation between the United States and China is unlikely in the short to medium term simply because of the existing power differential. More importantly, Chinese policymakers are consciously aware of and very wary about their shortcomings vis-à-vis the United States, and especially in light of the demonstrations of American military and technological prowess in the 1990s campaigns, and the recent war against Iraq.[100] Although some suggest that the region is already bipolar because China is the established dominant continental power in East Asia, the reality remains one in which the sheer power disparity, when weighed up in material rather than simple geographical terms, indicates a highly asymmetrical bipolarity, if it might be called that.[101] Indeed, China's eventual capacity to develop as a more even counterweight to the United States can be called into further doubt on the grounds that China's rise may be impeded down the line by the potential power balancing behavior of its immediate neighbors—Russia, Japan, possibly Korea, and Southeast Asian states.[102]

Scenarios of hegemonic challenge remain a long-term prospect in the Asia-Pacific. While power transition and neorealist theories predict a Sino–American power contest, we are more likely to see limited tensions and managed frictions over specific issues, such as the Taiwan question, than outright war. There remains, nevertheless, the possibility of China pursuing asymmetrical conflict with the US, an eventuality that, by definition, would precede the condition of power parity that underlies power transition theories. Thomas Christensen has drawn attention to scenarios of such asymmetrical warfare, but suggests a combination of specific circumstances under which these might occur. A weaker China might well challenge the United States if the leadership sees itself as incurring greater regime costs from not attacking than from attacking (Taiwan is an issue that could lead to this reasoning); if actual or potential American casualties seem sufficiently high to force an early United States withdrawal from any conflict; if the US is tied down militarily in other parts of the world; and if Chinese leaders believe that regional US allies can be encouraged to adopt policies different from America's own.[103] Other indications of China preparing for asymmetrical confrontation include the attention paid to building up missile strike capability against Japan as leverage against the United States and the Chinese strategic focus on developing "assassin's mace" techniques and weapons that can exploit the American technological advantage by targeting critical hi-tech information, intelligence, command, and other logistics systems in a conflict situation.[104] In this context, the apparent anti-satellite weapons test carried out by Beijing in January 2007, when a Chinese medium-range ballistic missile was launched to destroy an old Chinese weather satellite, was especially alarming to Washington. While the anti-satellite (ASAT) test did not come as a complete surprise to American intelligence, the delay and reticence of China's civilian leadership's response to international protests raised concerns about Chinese crisis anticipation and management capabilities, bureaucratic coordination, and civilian control over the military.[105]

Conclusion

We began with the suggestion that in order to obtain security and stability in the Asia-Pacific, the United States and China must negotiate their relationship. This would entail the clarification of each side's regional/global strategy, and a two-way process aimed at finding areas of common interest and possible cooperation and coordination and at hammering out conflict management procedures. As a first cut, this chapter has examined three possible models of how this process might take place: (1) the preservation of the strategic status quo whereby China concentrates on domestic development and accepts US hegemony; (2) negotiated change by which perhaps a bipolar power sharing arrangement and eventually possibly a multilateral cooperative security system is worked out; and (3) a classic power transition entailing competition between the United States as the incumbent hegemon and China as the rising challenger.

There are four main findings in this chapter. First, while much of the conventional argument, especially in the United States, has been centered upon the expectation that China will challenge United States hegemony, leading to a power transition scenario, what we are seeing now is in fact more akin to the status quo model. The evidence indicates that China is playing according to the international rules and will concentrate on domestic consolidation for the short to medium term if it is allowed to do so. Second, the power transition set of outcomes belongs rather to the medium- to long-term range of possibilities. Third, before we reach that point of power transition though, there exists a range of possible trajectories that the US–China relationship could traverse. These alternative scenarios are summarized in Table 4.1.

Scenario A is clearly the most optimistic scenario, which assumes that the two countries manage to negotiate regional order based upon understandings on power sharing, the exercise of power and conflict management, and then to involve other states in the region in building a security community. Even if China and the United States manage to move some way toward power sharing, there is the possibility that this process of negotiation or concert might be

Table 4.1 Possible scenarios of change in the US–China relationship over the long term

Scenario A	1 → 2A → 2B	Successful negotiation of power sharing arrangements, moving eventually to constructing a regional security community
Scenario B	1 → 2A	Continual negotiation of power sharing in the form of hierarchical duet, persisting into concert behavior, possibly including other regional powers
Scenario C	1 → 2A → 3	Move toward power sharing arrangements, but these break down due to dissatisfaction on either or both sides, power transition outcome uncertain
Scenario D	1 → 3	No power sharing as Chinese power accumulation proceeds—either China challenges United States hegemony and/or United States engages in pre-emptive action or active containment against China. Outcome uncertain although Cold War balancing and containment-type scenario more likely if China can find allies to forge countervailing coalition; systemic war more likely if key flashpoint of un-negotiable importance is triggered—e.g. Taiwan crisis in which China manages to fight the United States to stalemate
Scenario E	1	Persistence of clear United States hegemony and potential Chinese rise IF Chinese development stymied by economic problems or by conflict over Taiwan in which United States and Taiwan win

1 = Model I (status quo); 2A = Model II (negotiated change/hierarchical duet); 2B = Model II (negotiated change/security community); 3 = Model III (power transition).

perpetuated and regional stability maintained (Scenario B). If such efforts were to fail, or if they are not undertaken at all, the region will move into a power transition phase, but with uncertain outcomes, depending upon the reactions of key countries in the region and upon the particular areas of conflict that ensue (Scenarios C and D). Alternatively, there is the possibility that the status quo of clear US hegemony might persist if China's growth is undermined by domestic problems or by the outbreak of hostilities in the Taiwan Straits (Scenario E).

Future research projects might investigate in more detail the conditions under which each of these scenarios might occur. For now, the discussion in this chapter shows the current state of affairs within the contemporary "status quo" situation, identifies key areas of dialogue and bargaining needed for negotiated power sharing to occur, and highlights the difficulties of drawing preliminary conclusions about the outcomes of a future power transition. My preliminary evaluation is that Scenario B is most likely to obtain over the medium term, as we may expect rising Chinese power to be circumscribed by slowing economic growth rates and increasing domestic developmental problems that will preoccupy Beijing. At the same time, the massive United States edge in economic and technological terms is likely to continue. Scenarios C and D are clearly the most worrying, and we will need to pay attention to two key trends within Chinese domestic politics that might push Beijing toward adopting more uncompromising or aggressive stances toward the United States. First is domestic unrest arising from uneven development, which will undermine the regime's legitimacy and stability; and the second is the rising salience of nationalism as China grows, which the regime may feel compelled to pander to given the demise of communist ideology as a mobilizing force in domestic politics.

Finally, it is clear that the onus lies equally with both China and the United States to find ways to accommodate the changing power balance between them. This applies not only in traditional military balance of power terms, but also entails the consideration of the more complex competition of influence in the arenas of economics and diplomacy, which may have unprecedented strategic significance in the increasingly interdependent and globalized Asia-Pacific today. Fortunately, the latter are not necessarily zero-sum arenas and could provide critical opportunities for mutual socialization and for the two-way negotiation of new norms of conduct and rules for power sharing.

Notes

* This is an updated version of the article, "The US–China Relationship and Asia-Pacific Security: Negotiating Change," *Asian Security* 1(3), 2005, pp. 216–244, and is reprinted here with the permission of Taylor & Francis (www.informaworld.com).

  1 See, for instance, Richard K. Betts, "Wealth, Power, and Instability: East Asia and the United States after the Cold War," *International Security* 18(3), (Winter 1993/4), pp. 34–77; David Shambaugh, "Sino–American Strategic Relations:

From Partners to Competitors," *Survival* 42(1), (Spring 2000), pp. 98–104; Richard Weitz, "Meeting the China Challenge: Some Insights from Scenario-Based Planning," *Journal of Strategic Studies* 24(3), September 2001, pp. 19–48.

2   Neorealist views are represented by Kenneth Waltz, *Theory of International Relations* (Reading, MA: Addison-Wesley, 1979); John Mearsheimer, *The Tragedy of Great Power Politics* (New York: Norton, 2001), pp. 396–402.

3   For a sample of the debate, see Michael E. Brown *et al.*, eds, *The Rise of China* (Cambridge, MA: MIT Press, 2000); Richard Bernstein & Ross Munro, "The Coming Conflict with America," *Foreign Affairs* 76(2), (March/April 1997), pp. 18–32; Robert S. Ross, "Beijing as a Conservative Power," *ibid.*, pp. 33–44; Alastair Iain Johnston, "Socialization in International Institutions: The ASEAN Way and International Relations Theory," in G. John Ikenberry & Michael Mastaduno, eds, *International Relations Theory and the Asia-Pacific* (New York: Columbia University Press, 2003).

4   See Denny Roy, "Rising China and US Interests: Inevitable vs. Contingent Hazards," *Orbis*, (Winter 2003), pp. 125–137. The classic work distinguishing between threat and power per se is Stephen Walt, *The Origins of Alliances* (Ithaca: Cornell University Press, 1987).

5   Alastair Iain Johnston, "Is China a Status Quo Power?" *International Security* 27(4), (Spring 2003), pp. 5–56.

6   Robert S. Ross, "Navigating the Taiwan Strait: Deterrence, Escalation Dominance, and US–China Relations, *International Security* 27(2), Fall 2002, pp. 48–85; Leszek Buszynski, "ASEAN, the Declaration on Conduct, and the South China Sea," *Contemporary Southeast Asia* 25(3), (December 2003), pp. 434–463.

7   For this argument, see Thomas Christensen, "Posing Problems without Catching Up: China's Rise and Challenges for US Security Policy," *International Security* 25(4), (Spring 2000), pp. 5–40.

8   Pessimists and neorealists predict that an arms race or Chinese economic domination is inevitable—for instance, Aaron Friedberg, "Ripe for Rivalry: Prospects for Peace in a Multipolar Asia," *International Security* 18(3), Winter 1993, pp. 5–33; Gerald Segal, "The Coming Confrontation between China and Japan," *World Policy Journal* 10(2), (Summer 1993), pp. 27–32; Denny Roy, "Hegemon on the Horizon? China's Threat to East Asian Security," *International Security* 19(1), Summer 1994, pp. 149–168. In comparison, the argument here is more moderate, referring only to the de-stabilising effect of growing ambient Chinese power, which, over time, may or may not in fact exacerbate the regional security dilemma, depending on how its neighbors choose to react.

9   See Aaron Friedberg, "The Future of US–China Relations: Is Conflict Inevitable?" *International Security* 30(2), (Fall 2005), pp. 7–45.

10 This assumption can be debated—among those who suggest that it is just as likely that China might experience significant international political fragmentation or prolonged economic upheaval, are Gerald Segal, *China Changes Shape*, Adelphi Papers 287 (London: IISS, 1994) and Gordon G. Chang, *The Coming Collapse of China* (London: Random House, 2001).

11 David Shambaugh, "China Engages Asia," *International Security* 29 (3), (Winter 2004/5), pp. 70–72, 91.

12 Assistant Secretary of State for East Asian and Pacific Affairs Christopher Hill acknowledged that "The new and highly constructive role of China as the convener of the Six-Party Talks is especially important, and our coordination with them in this area is outstanding"—Hill, testimony to House Foreign Affairs Committee, (February 28, 2007). See also David Shambaugh, "China and the Korean Peninsula: Playing for the Long Term," *The Washington Quarterly*, Spring 2003, pp. 43–56; Ming Liu, "China and the North Korean Crisis: Facing Test and Transition," *Pacific Affairs* 76(3), (Fall 2003), pp. 347–374.

13 Denny Roy, "China's Reaction to American Predominance," *Survival* 45(3), Autumn 2003, pp. 64; Johnston, "Is China a Status Quo Power?" pp. 39. For an interesting analysis of China's promotion of various levels of "partnerships" with major powers, including the US, see Joseph Y. Cheng & Zhang Wankun, "Patterns and Dynamics of China's International Strategic Behavior," *Journal of Contemporary China* 11(31), (2002), pp. 235–260.

14 Brendan Taylor, "US–China Relations after 11 September: A Long Engagement or Marriage of Convenience?" *Australian Journal of International Affairs* 59(2), June 2005, pp. 179–199; Kevin Sheives, "China Turns West: Beijing's Contemporary Strategy Toward Central Asia," *Pacific Affairs* 79(2), (2006), pp. 205–224. Together with Moscow, Beijing has used the Shanghai Cooperation Oragnisation as a vehicle for political posturing, notably in its encouragement of Uzbekistan's closure of US bases in 2006.

15 Jing-Dong Yuan, "Making Sense of China's Iraq Policy," (October 3, 2002), PacNet Newsletter #40; Bonnie Glaser, "China and the US Disagree, but with Smiles," *Comparative Connections* January–March 2003; David M. Lampton & Richard Daniel Ewing, *The US–China Relationship Facing International Security Crises* (Washington DC: Nixon Center, 2003), Chapter 2.

16 But some have been quick to point out that the key underlying sources of Sino–American tensions, especially the Taiwan issue, have not disappeared—see Aaron Friedberg, "11 September and the Future of Sino–American Relations," *Survival* 44(1), (Spring 2002), pp. 33–50.

17 Li Nan, "Chinese Views of the US War in Iraq: Warfighting Lessons," IDSS Commentary, June 2003. A Council on Foreign Affairs report reaffirms that China lags at least 20 years behind the US in terms of military technology and capability—see Adam Segal, Joseph Prueher & Harold Brown, *Chinese Military Power* (New York: CFR, Independent Task Force Report, May 2003).

18 See Li Nan, "The Evolving Chinese Conception of Security and Security Approaches," in See Seng Tan & Amitav Acharya, ed., *Asia-Pacific Security: National Interests and Regional Order* (Armonk, NY: M.E. Sharpe, 2004).

19 Prime Minister Wen Jiabao, speech at dinner hosted by nine American organizations, December 9, 2003, Washington DC; "Wen: China will never seek hegemony," *Xinhua* News Agency, (June 28, 2004).

20 For an example, see the exchange in Lanxin Xiang, "Washington's Misguided China Policy" and David Shambaugh, "China or America: Which is the Revisionist Power?" *Survival* 43(3), (Autumn 2001), pp. 7–30. One concrete demonstration of satisfaction with the status quo has been China's settlement of some of its border disputes—notably with Russia and Vietnam—in recent years.

21 Scholar from Tsinghua University at a closed-door seminar on Asia-Pacific security, Beijing, July 19, 2002.

22 Wen, December 9, 2003 speech.

23 Author interview with Chinese policy analyst, Beijing, July 22, 2002.

24 See, for instance, Bonnie Glaser, "A Familiar Pattern: Cooperation with a Dash of Friction," *Comparative Connections*, (January–March 2004). Although note that within the general community of international relations specialists, many continue to see the US as aiming basically to contain China's rise—see Rosalie Chen, "China Perceives American: Perceptions of International Relations Experts," *Journal of Contemporary China* 12(35), 2003, pp. 285–297.

25 Bin Li, "Absolute Gains, Relative Gains, and US Security Policy on China," *Defense and Security Analysis* 19(4), (December 2003), pp. 309–317; Zhang Juyan & Glen T. Cameron, "China's Agenda Building and Image Polishing in the US: Assessing an International Public Relations Campaign," *Public Relations Review* 29(1), March 2003, pp. 13–28.

26   Foot, Rosemary (1998) "China in the ASEAN Regional Forum: Organizational Processes and Domestic Modes of Thought," *Asian Survey* 38(5), pp. 425–440; Evelyn Goh & Amitav Acharya, "The ASEAN Regional Forum: Comparing Chinese and American Positions," in Melissa Curley, ed., *Advancing East Asian Regionalism* (London: Routledge, 2007). The defense white paper, entitled *China's National Defense in 2002*, is available at: http://service.china.org.cn/link/wcm/Show_Text?info_id=50743&p_qry=defense%20and%20white%20and%20paper. The Chinese government has since issued a white paper on Xinjiang in May 2003, one on nuclear non-proliferation in December 2003, and a new defense white paper for 2004, available at http://service.china.org.cn/link/wcm/Show_Text?info_id=116032&p_qry=global%20and%20posture%20and%20review.

27   See Taylor Fravel, "Regime Insecurity and International Cooperation: Explaining China's Compromises in Territorial Disputes," *International Security* 30(2), (Fall 2005), pp. 46–83.

28   John Wong & Sarah Chan, "China–ASEAN Free Trade Agreement," *Asian Survey* 43(3), (May/June 2003), pp. 507–526; Markus Hund, "ASEAN Plus Three: Toward a New Age of Pan-Asian Regionalism? A Skeptic's Appraisal," *Pacific Review* 16(3), (August 2003), pp. 383–417.

29   For a discussion of the "ASEAN way," see Hiro Katsumata, "Reconstruction of Diplomatic Norms in Southeast Asia: The Case for Strict Adherence to the 'ASEAN Way'," *Contemporary Southeast Asia* 25(1), (April 2003), pp. 104–121.

30   "China snuggles up to Southeast Asia," (October 7, 2003), *Asia Times*. ASEAN has invited all its dialogue partners—including the US and the ROK—to sign the treaty. China was the first to accede to the treaty, along with India, and they were followed in 2004 by Japan and in 2005 by Australia.

31   Samuel S. Kim, "China in World Politics," in Barry Buzan & Rosemary Foot, eds, *Does China Matter? Essays in Memory of Gerald Segal* (London: Routledge, 2004), pp. 51. See also Johnston, "Is China a Status Quo Power?"

32   Note that, over the short term, more information about Chinese defense thinking may adversely affect US–China relations. For example, recent worries in Washington about China are related to the new awareness of the PLA's progress military modernization and particularly in building up its capacity against Taiwan—see, e.g. "Chinese Buildup seen as threat to region," *Washington Post*, July 20, 2005; and Department of Defense, *The Military Power of the People's Republic of China 2005: Annual Report to Congress* (Washington, DC: DoD, 2005).

33   For arguments that these sentiments were misplaced and reflected an ignorance of the degree of economic interdependence that now exists between the US and Chinese economies, see Thomas Friedman, "Joined at the Hip," *New York Times*, (July 20, 2005); Paul Krugman, "China Unpegs Itself," *New York Times*, (July 22, 2005).

34   See Rosemary Foot, "Bush, China and Human Rights," *Survival* 45(2), (Summer 2003), pp. 167–186.

35   www.whitehouse.gov/nsc/nss/2006/.

36   Michael Swaine, "China," in Zalmay Khalilzad, ed., *Strategic Appraisal 1996* (Santa Monica: RAND, 1996).

37   See, for instance, Yuen Foong Khong, "Making Bricks without Straw in the Asia Pacific?" *Pacific Review* 10(2), (1997), pp. 289–300. On socialization, see Alastair Iain Johnston, "Treating International Institutions as Social Environments," *International Studies Quarterly* 45, (2001), pp. 487–515; Jeffrey T. Checkel, "International Institutions and Socialization in the New Europe," ARENA Working Paper 01/11, (May 2001).

38   For a brief discussion of key psychological theories which help to explain cognitive change, see Deborah Welch Larson, *Origins of Containment: A Psychological Explanation* (Princeton: Princeton University Press, 1985), chapter 1.

39   *The National Security Strategy of the United States of America*, (September 2002), available at: www.whitehouse.gov/nsc/nss.html.

40   This worry has been expressed repeatedly by Chinese analysts—see, for instance, "Global Times—Big Power relations enter period of cooperation," *People's Daily*, (August 2, 2002), pp. 4–5. English translation available at www.china. org.cn.

41   James A. Kelly, "An Overview of US-East Asia Policy," Testimony before the House International Relations Committee, Washington D.C., (June 2, 2004), available at www.state.gov/p/eap/rls/rm/2004/3306pf.htm.

42   "Bush Tells Veterans of Plan to Redeploy G.I.'s Worldwide," *New York Times*, (August 17, 2004).

43   "Department of Defense Background Briefing on Global Posture Review," (August 16, 2004), available at www.defense.gov/transcripts/2004/tr20040816-1153.html. See also www.defense.gov/home/features/global_posture/gp2004 0924pm1.html.

44   Although, in Southeast Asia for instance, note that the pre-eminent position of the US as ASEAN's major trading partner is unlikely to be assailed in the near future—the US export market (importing US$92 billion worth in 2005) for ASEAN is nearly twice as large as that of China (US$52 billion in 2005); and the US is by far the top single-country foreign direct investor in ASEAN (US$18 billion in 2001–2005), compared to China (US$1.5 billion in 2001–2005). Source: ASEAN Secretariat Statistics.

45   See Friedrich Wu *et al.*, "Foreign Direct Investments to China and ASEAN: Has ASEAN Been Losing Out?" *Economic Survey of Singapore*, (Third Quarter 2003), available at www.mti.gov.sg/public/PDF/CMT/NWS_2002Q3_FDI1. pdf?sid+92&cid=1418; Michael Richardson, "China seen by ASEAN as market," *International Herald Tribune*, (April 26, 2002); Lee Kim Chew, "ASEAN back in spotlight as big players come a-wooing," *The Straits Times* (Singapore), April 26, 2002; Evelyn Goh, "The Role of Great Powers in Southeast Asian Regional Security Strategies: Omni-enmeshment, Balancing and Hierarchical Order," IDSS working paper no.84, (July 2005).

46   Shambaugh, "China Engages Asia," pp. 90–91; Evelyn Goh, ed., *Betwixt and Between: Southeast Asian Strategic Relations with the US and China*, IDSS Monograph No. 7 (Singapore: Institute of Defence and Strategic Studies, 2005).

47   See particularly Charles A. Kupchan, Emmanuel Adler, Jean-Marc Coicaud & Yuen Foong Khong, *Power in Transition: The Peaceful Change of International Order* (Tokyo: United Nations University Press, 2001).

48   That is, we are concerned here with a pre-transition scenario—the possibility of some negotiated understanding prior to the point at which the gap is narrowed enough for the rising power to contemplate a challenge for the hegemonic position.

49   Robert Jervis, "From Balance to Concert: A Study of International Security Cooperation," *World Politics* 38, (1985), pp. 59–61.

50   Robert Jervis, "A Political Science Perspective on the Balance of Power and the Concert," *American Historical Review* 97(3), (June 1992), p.723. See also Robert Jervis, "Realism, Game Theory, and Cooperation," *World Politics* 40, (1988), pp. 317–349.

51   See Richard B. Elrod, "The Concert of Europe: A Fresh Look at an International System," *World Politics* 28, (January 1976), pp. 159–174.

52 See, for instance, Douglas T. Stuart, "Toward Concert in Asia," *Asian Survey* 37(3), March 1997, pp. 229–244; Amitav Acharya, "A Concert of Asia?" *Survival* 41(3), (Autumn 1999), pp. 84–101.
53 Paul W. Schroeder, "Did the Vienna Settlement Rest on a Balance of Power?" *American Historical Review* 97(3), (June 1992), pp. 683–706.
54 Jervis, "A Political Science Perspective," p. 724.
55 Robert Ross, "The Geography of the Peace: East Asia in the Twenty-first Century," *International Security* 23(4), (Spring 1999), pp. 81–118.
56 See Amitav Acharya, "China's Monroe Doctrine? Implications for US Policy," draft mimeo, June 2004. A detailed discussion of the traditional characteristics of a great power's influence over territories in its sphere is found in Geddes W. Rutherford, "Spheres of Influence: An Aspect of Semi-Suzerainty," *American Journal of International Law* 20(2), (April 1926), pp. 300–325.
57 See Shee Poon Kim, "The South China Sea in China's Strategic Thinking," *Contemporary Southeast Asia* 19(4), (March 1998), pp. 369–387.
58 See Thomas Christensen, "Theatre Missile Defense and Taiwan's Security," *Orbis* 44(1), Winter 2000, pp. 18–32; Kori Urayama, "China Debates Missile Defense," *Survival* 46(2), Summer 2004, pp. 123–142; Philip Coyle, "The Limits and Liabilities of Missile Defence," *Current History*, (November 2006), pp. 391–394.
59 See Evelyn Goh, *Meeting the China Challenge: The US in Southeast Asian Security Strategies*, Policy Studies Monograph No. 16 (Washington, DC: East-West Center Washington, 2005); Shannon Tow, "Southeast Asia in the Sino-US Strategic Balance," *Contemporary Southeast Asia* 26(3), (2004), pp. 434–459.
60 See, for instance, "Chinese Military Power: Council on Foreign Relations Independent Task Force Report," (June 2003), available at www.cfr.org/pdf/China_TF.pdf.
61 Waltz, *Theory of International Relations*, Chapter 8; Karl W. Deutsch & J. David Singer, "Multipolar Power Systems and International Stability," *World Politics* 16(3), (April 1964), pp. 390–406; William Wohlforth, "The Stability of a Unipolar World," *International Security* 24(1), (Summer 1999), pp. 5–41. On China's preference for a multipolar world order after the Cold War, see Michael Pillsbury, *China Debates the Future Security Environment* (Washington DC: National Defense University Press, 2000), Chapter 1; "Nation backs multipolar world," *China Daily*, (December 13, 2000); "Chinese, Russian Presidents host joint press conference," *Xinhua*, (May 28, 2003).
62 Contest over hegemonic power is at the heart of most studies of power transition, e.g. Robert A. Gilpin, *War and Change in World Politics* (Cambridge: Cambridge University Press, 1981). The stakes are much higher if hegemonic power is being contested. In Gilpin's preferred economic parlance, the marginal benefits to be gained from a move to the primate position are significantly larger than any other upward move within the hierarchy for the challenger and the marginal losses significantly larger for the incumbent.
63 David C. Kang, "Getting Asia Wrong: The Need for New Analytical Frameworks," *International Security* 27(4), (Spring 2003), pp. 57–85. Kang suggests that East Asian states might be willing to "accept subordinate positions in a Sino-centric [regional] hierarchy" and further implies that this is evidence of bandwagoning behavior, but he does not attempt to substantiate the claim systematically in the contemporary context.
64 See Yuen Foong Khong, "Coping with Strategic Uncertainty: The Role of Institutions and Soft Balancing in Southeast Asia's Post-Cold War Strategy," in J.J. Suh, Peter J. Katzenstein, Allen Carlson, eds, *Rethinking Security in East Asia: Identity, Power, and Efficiency* (Stanford, CA: Stanford University Press, 2004); Goh, *Meeting the China Challenge*; Goh, *Betwixt and Between*.

65   Pramit Mitra, "A Thaw in India–China Relations," *South Asia Monitor* 62, September 1, 2003; Ang Cheng Guan, "Vietnam–China Relations since the End of the Cold War," *Asian Survey* 38(12), (December 1998), pp. 1122–1141; Buszynski, "ASEAN, the Declaration on Conduct, and the South China Sea."

66   Deng Xiaoping conversation with Rajiv Ghandi, 21 December 1988, in *Selected Works of Deng Xiaoping 1982–1992* (Beijing, Foreign Language Press, 1994), pp. 274–276.

67   Adam Ward, "China and America: Trouble Ahead?" *Survival* 45(3), (Autumn 2003), pp. 43–45; DoD, *The Military Power of the People's Republic of China 2005.*

68   Department of Defense, *Quadrennial Defense Review*, 2001, available at www.defenselink.mil/pubs/qdr2001.pdf; "US may half forces in Germany," *Washington Post*, (March 25, 2004).

69   These reports are available at www.uscc.gov/annual_report/recommendations.php.

70   David M. Lampton, "China's Growing Power and Influence in Asia: Implications for US Policy," testimony before the US–China Economic and Security Review Commission, (February 13, 2004), available at www.nixoncenter.org/Program%20Briefs/PB%202004/LamptonUSCCTestimony2-13-04.pdf.

71   Washington wishes to institutionalise preventive diplomacy while Beijing prefers to maintain confidence building measures only—see Goh & Acharya, "The ASEAN Regional Forum."

72   The idea began at the unofficial Track II level, when, in 1993, academics from the US, China, Russia, Japan, and South Korea gathered at the first meeting of the Northeast Asia Cooperation Dialogue (NEACD). In 1996, the governments of these states agreed to create a parallel set of official talks, the Northeast Asia Security Dialogue (NEASD), but the talks were never held, partly because of the deterioration of Sino–American relations after the 1996 Taiwan Straits crisis. For a recent argument for the push toward such a dialogue from the American point of view, see Jason T. Shaplen & James Laney, "The new Asia: China's ascent weakens US influence," *International Herald Tribune*, (July 13, 2004).

73   See Patrick Tyler, *A Great Wall: Six Presidents and China An Investigative History* (New York: Century Foundation, 1999), pp. 105–180; Evelyn Goh, *Constructing the US Rapprochement with China, 1961–1974: From Red Menace to Tacit Ally* (New York: Cambridge University Press, 2005).

74   Although, note from the Sino–American experience in the 1970s–80s that a common threat alone is not necessarily sufficient to sustain a partnership in the absence of the cultivation of broader common interests and the resolution of fundamental conflicts. See Harry Harding, *A Fragile Relationship: The United States and China since 1972* (Washington DC: Brookings Institution, 1992); Robert Ross, *Negotiating Cooperation: The United States and China, 1969–1989* (Stanford: Stanford University Press, 1995).

75   The many recommendations of the US–China Economic and Security Review Commission (op. cit.) include the compilation of reports on areas of the US defense industrial base that may depend or come to depend on Chinese imports or Chinese-owned firms.

76   See Jing-dong Yuan, "Assessing Chinese Nonproliferation Policy: Progress, Problems and Issues for the United States," prepared statement for the US–China Security Review Commission, (October 12, 2001), available at http://cns.miis.edu/pubs/other/jdtest.htm.

77   Note, though, that Chinese views of US hegemony are by no means uniform—there is disagreement at the official and academic level on whether the US has

indeed achieved hegemony, whether it has a grand strategy, and about the weaknesses and vulnerabilities in the American economy and in its relations with allies. See Samantha Blum, "Chinese Views of US Hegemony," *Journal of Contemporary China* 12(35), (May 2003), pp. 239–264.

78 For an analysis of trends in Chinese nationalism, see Alastair Iain Johnston, "The Correlates of Nationalism in Beijing Public Opinion," IDSS working paper no.50, September 2003.

79 Author interviews, Beijing, July 2002. Some Chinese policy experts make the distinction between US "hegemonic power" and "hegemonic behavior," with the former being more acceptable—Tang Shiping & Zhang Yunling, "China's Regional Strategy", in David Shambaugh, ed., *Power Shift: China and Asia's New Dynamics* (University of California Press, 2006); Evan Medeiros & M. Taylor Fravel, "China's New Diplomacy," *Foreign Affairs* 82(6), (Nov/Dec 2003), p. 22–33.

80 See "China's Position Paper on the New Security Concept," (July 31, 2002), available at www.fmprc.gov.cn/eng/wjb/zzig/gis/gizzyhy/2612/2614/t15319. htm; Li Qinggong & Wei Wei, "Chinese Army Paper on New Security Concept," *Jiefangjun Bao* December 24, 1997, translation available at FBIS-CHI-98-015, January 15, 1998. For critical views, see David Finkelstein and Michael McDevitt, "Competition and Consensus: China's 'New Concept of Security' and the United States Security Strategy for the East Asia-Pacific Region," Pacnet Newsletter # 1, January 8, 1999, available at www.csis.org/pacfor/pac0199.html; Carlyle A. Thayer, "China's 'New Security Concept' and ASEAN," *Comparative Connnections* (CSIS Pacific Forum), Vol. 2, No. 3, (Third Quarter 2000), pp. 65–71, available at www.csis.org/pacfor/cc/003Qchina_asean.html.

81 For a theoretically informed elaboration of this point, see Alice Ba, "Who's Socializing Whom? Complex Engagement and Sino–ASEAN Relations," *Pacific Review* 19(2), (June 2006), 157–179.

82 Evelyn Goh, "A Chinese Lesson for the US: How to Charm Southeast Asia," *The Straits Times*, October 31, 2003; Amitav Acharya, "China's Charm Offensive in Southeast Asia," *International Herald Tribune*, (November 8–9, 2003).

83 See Jing-dong Yuan, "Regional Institutions and Cooperative Security: Chinese Approaches and Policies," *Korean Journal of Defense Analysis* XIII(1), Autumn 2001, pp. 263–294; Rosemary Foot, "China in the ASEAN Regional Forum: Organizational Processes and Domestic Modes of Thought," *Asian Survey* 38(5), pp. 425–440; Tang Shiping, "The Future of the Shanghai Cooperation Organization," IDSS Commentary, (October 2002); Evelyn Goh, "The ASEAN Regional Forum in United States East Asian Strategy," *Pacific Review*, 17(1), (2004), pp. 47–69.

84 See Medeiros & Fravel, "China's New Diplomacy."

85 See Christopher Layne, "From Preponderance to Offshore Balancing: America's Future Grand Strategy," *International Security* 22(1), (Summer 1997), pp. 86–124.

86 See Amitav Acharya, *Constructing a Security Community in Southeast Asia: ASEAN and the Problem of Regional Order* (London: Routledge, 2001), esp. Chapter 6. This is what Muthiah Alagappa terms "order through transformation"—see Alagappa, ed., *Asian Security Order: Instrumental and Normative Features* (Stanford, CA: Stanford University Press, 2003), pp. 60–64.

87 For an excellent analysis of the ways in which membership of the ARF has shaped the behavior of Chinese officials, see Johnston, "Socialization in International Institutions."

88 Emmanuel Adler, "The Change of Change: Peaceful Transitions of Power in the Multilateral Age," in Kupchan *et al.*, *Peaceful Power Transitions*.

92   *Evelyn Goh*

89   Notable works on power transition are A.F.K. Organski, *World Politics* (New York: Knopf, 1958); A.F.K. Organski & Jacek Kugler, *The War Ledger* (Chicago: University of Chicago Press, 1980); Paul Kennedy, *The Rise and Fall of the Great Powers* (New York: Random House, 1987).
90   Gilpin, *War and Change in World Politics.*
91   *Ibid.*; Organski & Kugler, *The War Ledger*; Charles F. Doran & Wes Parsons, "War and the Cycle of Relative Power," *American Political Science Review* 74(4), (December 1980), pp. 947–965.
92   On the possibilities of peaceful power transition, see Kupchan et al, *Power in Transition.*
93   See, for instance, Indra de Soysa, John O'Neal & Yong-Hee Park, "Testing Power Transition Theory Using Alternative Measures of National Capabilities," *Journal of Conflict Resolution* 41(4), (August 1997), pp. 509–528.
94   Woosang Kim & James Morrow, "When Do Power Shifts Lead to War?" *American Journal of Political Science* 36(4), November 1992, pp. 896–922; Douglas Lemke & Suzanne Werner, "Power Parity, Commitment to Change and War," *International Studies Quarterly* 40(2), (June 1996), pp. 235–260.
95   Jack S. Levy, "Declining Power and the Preventive Motivation for War," *World Politics* 40(1), (October 1987), pp. 82–107; Organski & Kugler, *The War Ledger*, pp. 13–63.
96   For instance, the two World Wars did not begin as a result of direct challenges by the rising power, Germany, against the declining power, Britain. Rather, the two wars began as conflicts involving other neighboring states which subsequently spread to pit the rising and declining powers against each other. See John Vasquez, *The War Puzzle* (New York: Cambridge University Press, 1993).
97   It was not Spain, the direct challenger to Portugal, which emerged as the new hegemon at the end of the seventeenth century, but Holland. By fighting Spain, the Dutch took up where the Portuguese left off, subsequently acquiring independence and inheriting Portuguese world trade. In the eighteenth century, it was not the French challengers who achieved hegemony, but rather Britain, which had fought alongside Holland in the Napoleonic wars. Again in the twentieth century, Germany failed in both bids for hegemony against Britain, while the United States emerged as the new hegemon after fighting as Britain's ally in both World Wars.
98   See Immanuel Wallerstein, *The Politics of the World Economy* (Cambridge: Cambridge University Press, 1984) and George Modelski, "The Long Cycle of Global Politics and the Nation State," *Comparative Studies in Society and History* 20 (1978), pp. 214–235.
99   Ironically, this may partially return us to the early post-Cold War concern with Japan as a potential challenger to US hegemony—see, for instance, Reinhard Drifte, *Japan's Foreign Policy for the Twenty-first Century: From Economic Superpower to What Power?* (New York: St Martin's, 1991); Chalmers A. Johnson, "Japan in Search of a 'Normal' Role," *Daedalus* 121, (Fall 1992), pp. 1–33.
100   On the PLA's cautious assessments, see David Shambaugh, *Modernizing China's Military: Progress, Problems and Prospects* (Berkeley: University of California Press, 2003); Li Nan, "Chinese Views of the US War in Iraq: Warfighting Lessons," IDSS Commentary, (June 2003).
101   Ross, "The Geography of the Peace."
102   This argument is critical in William Wohlforth's thesis that US unipolarity is sustainable. See Wohlforth, "The Stability of a Unipolar World." This suggests that it is important to consider China's relative capabilities vis-à-vis its neighbors

too, not just the US Over the short and medium term, China's power relative to Taiwan and Japan may be the most critical, but note that the capabilities of these two countries are crucially affected by their defense relations with the US.

103 Christensen, "Posing Problems without Catching Up." But compare his analysis with others who argue that China's limited capabilities and concentration on economic development would deter Beijing from such considerations— Ross, "Navigating the Taiwan Strait"; Robert Ross, "Engagement in US China Policy," in Alastair Iain Johnston & Robert S. Ross, eds, *Engaging China: The Management of an Emerging Power* (London: Routledge, 1999).

104 See Michael Pillsbury, "China's Military Strategy Toward the US: A View from Open Sources," (November 2, 2001), at www.uscc.gov/researchreports/ 2000_2003/pdfs/strat.pdf and Pillsbury, *China Debates the Future Security Environment*, Chapter 6.

105 For a survey of official American reactions, see Bonnie Glaser, "US–China Relations," *Comparative Connections*, (April 2007), available at: www.ciaonet. org/olj/cpc/cpc_apr07/cpc_apr07c.pdf.

5   Tango without trust and respect?

Japan's awkward co-prosperity with China in the twenty-first century

*Yoichiro Sato**

Introduction

China has occupied a special place in Japan's external relations throughout its recorded history. It has been a source of culture, a partner in commerce, and the foremost political and military rival in the region. In the modern history of Northeast Asia, Sino–Japanese relations have mostly been characterized by Japan's dominance over China. This historical anomaly is entering its closing stage after some 120 years since Japan's military defeat of the Qing Dynasty China during the Sino–Japanese War of 1883–1884.

The present realities of China's rapid economic growth and military modernization are partially restoring the historical pattern of mutual prosperity and military rivalry. While Japanese admiration for certain aspects of Chinese culture has persisted, Japan has consolidated its democratic political culture and more closely aligned itself with the Western developed world in condemning the current authoritarian practices of governance in China. At the same time, Japan's revision of modern Northeast Asian history and particularly its own role during the late-nineteenth and twentieth centuries are closely linked with the rapidly altering power balance between the two countries and Japan's perception of the bilateral relations. These changes have worked to transform Japan's postwar diplomacy of apology toward China. The repeated apologies of the past three decades were made under Japan's confidence in its own overwhelming economic superiority and relative absence of security threats from China. Japan's evolving post-Cold War diplomacy toward China is inevitably more fearful of China and more realist. It is based on Japan's desire to restore and maintain an equal partnership with a clear recognition of some diverging economic and security interests.

Despite the diplomatic cooling between the two countries, China's geographical proximity to Japan has naturally made it a major partner of commerce. For the warring samurai leaders of fifteenth- and sixteenth-century Japan, monopolizing trade with China was a means to build war chests to beat their rivals. Japan's industrialization and joining the ranks of colonial powers in the nineteenth century resulted in expansion of Japanese economic activities in China. Japan's defeat in World War II, withdrawal of Japanese settlers from

China and Manchuria, and the communist takeover of mainland China in 1949 severed Japan's historically strong economic ties with China. However, China's economic reform since the late 1970s and the resulting growth gradually brought back the historical geo-economic pattern of close Sino–Japanese integration.

While Japan enjoys its share of economic benefits from China's rapid growth, the growing economic ties have also caused some frictions. The rapid shift of production in manufacturing industries from Japan to China has raised the fear of industrial hallowing in Japan and numerous sector-specific trade disputes. Japan's confidence in its own technological superiority and its strength in designs and brand recognition have also been shaken by China's blatant disregard for intellectual properties.

Furthermore, China's growing political influence in the region and military strength has awakened Japanese leaders to an emerging security threat. The Japanese perception of the "China threat" has been in the background of the upgrading of the US–Japan military alliance and Japan's increasing military role in the collective pursuit of security. Diplomatically, Japan competes against China in order to preserve its favorable relations with other Asian countries.

The Japanese perception of the "China threat" is not only based on tangible economic and military growth, but also on more intangible historical and cultural factors. Despite numerous criticisms against Japan's "whitewashing" of history, especially in regard to the military's violence against Chinese civilians, postwar liberal Japanese education has by and large defined Japan as the offender and China as the victim of the war. This deep-rooted self image of the Japanese, which supported Japan's conciliatory diplomacy toward China since the normalization of bilateral relations in 1972, has so far survived despite the conservative revisionists' attempts to alter it. However, the same self image today also serves as a source of fear, since the Japanese now face the victim of its past misbehavior from a position of relative weakness. China's continuous use of the "history card" amplifies the Japanese perception of the vengeful Chinese, thereby making the Japanese feel more vulnerable.

While state leaders in both China and Japan have attempted, and to a large extent managed, to avoid conflictive aspects of the bilateral relations from hindering mutually beneficial economic cooperation, deepening of the bilateral relations in the societal domains has introduced new uncertainties into the management of this relationship. The growing awareness of the Japanese of their democratic polity has made the Japanese more critical of China's undemocratic governance. However, Japanese skepticism about healthy development of Chinese nationalism and more specifically fear that such nationalism may take anti-Japanese tones have aided Japan's awkward support for the authoritarian regime in China.

Japan's perceptions of the Chinese government and people have also been influenced by transnational issues of Chinese origins, including pollution, food and product safety, disease control, and organized crime. The inability and unwillingness of the Chinese government to cooperate with Japan in addressing these issues have eroded some of the goodwill the Japanese held toward China.

Economic relations

Japan's economic relations with China have rapidly expanded since the early 1990s. Despite the cooling of political relations during the five years of the Koizumi administration, the sizzling economic relations continued as indicated by the volume of trade and overall investments. The closer economic relations have inevitably caused sector-specific trade disputes, and the lack of experience has often unnecessarily exacerbated the problems. At the same time, the increasing presence of Japanese transplants in China has called for a free trade agreement and enhanced provisions for investor protections and intellectual property rights (IPR) protection. While China's joining the WTO brought about an expectation of its improved disciplines (rule abiding behaviors), China has fully exploited the weaknesses in global rules since then. As a result, Japan's approach to China strongly reflects its desire to discipline China's economic behaviors through bilateral and multilateral venues.

Japanese investments in China

Japanese investments in China have played a key role in the latter's rapid growth. Despite the uncertainties about China's political future after the Tiananmen Square incident in 1989, investments from Japan continued to flow. The continuity, however, did not prove that political factors were irrelevant. Compared to Japan's investments in North America or the United States, the size of the average Japanese investment in China has remained small. Lack of democratic politics and, more importantly, a reliable legal system—rule of law—have kept the Japanese investors in China cautious about committing to large investments. In this sense, as far as Japanese investments are concerned, China has not reached its geo-economic potential, despite a boom in 2003 (see Figure 5.1).

The growing presence of Japanese direct investments in China and their continuing problems with the host government policies have resulted in a call for an updated official investment agreement with China. Upon an agreement at the trilateral summit meeting on the side of the ASEAN meeting in October 2003, Japan, China, and Korea launched an official joint study group to examine the prospects of a trilateral investment agreement. The group announced its recommendations in November 2004.[1] While Japan wanted rigorous investor rights protections, equivalent to those in the Japan–Korea investment agreement, China was more interested in a free trade agreement with Japan

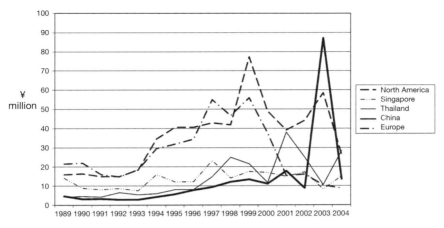

Figure 5.1 Average size of Japanese FDIs
Source: Ministry of Finance

and Korea. While Japan's Federation of Economic Organizations (Keidanren) lobbied for an early signing of a "high-level" investment agreement,[2] cooling of the political relations and suspension of the summit meetings with China and Korea during the Koizumi government stalled the government-level preparatory discussions, which started in 2005.

China–Japan trade

Japan's trade with China has also expanded rapidly during the last 15 years. Uncharacteristic of Japan's Asian trade partners, China has consistently achieved a trade surplus with Japan. China's proportional shares in Japan's overall trade have also increased. By 2005, China had replaced the United States as Japan's number one trade partner in terms of export and import volume combined. For Japan's exports, China remains the third largest market as of 2006 (see Figures 5.2 and 5.3).

As trade between the two economies has increased, sector-specific trade disputes have become more common. While the Chinese government may have been more shielded from domestic pressure against Japanese imports than the governments of Japan's other major trade partners such as the United States, this did not warrant cordial resolutions of trade disputes. Quite the contrary, China's strong reactions to Japan's protectionism against primary and light manufacturing products from China resulted in highly publicized and disproportionate retaliations by China.

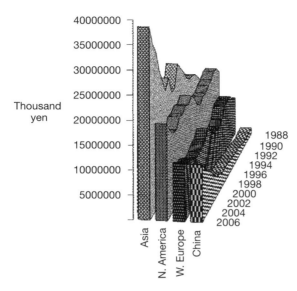

Figure 5.2 Japan's exports by destination
Source: Japanese Customs

In April 2001, Japan invoked provisional safeguards against imports of shiitake mushroom, green onion, and mat rush (*igusa* used for traditional *tatami* flooring) from China. China retaliated by slapping a 100 percent retaliatory tariff on importation of luxury automobiles from Japan, but a series of bilateral negotiations resulted in removal of both the Japanese safeguards and the Chinese tariff by the end of the year.[3] However, the heightened attention on imported farm products from China amounted to political pressure in Japan for more rigorous inspections starting in January 2002.[4] China saw the Japanese move as a cover for protectionism specifically aimed at Chinese exports, and retaliated by banning rice imports from Japan in 2003, noting possible pest contamination. The ban was eventually lifted in June 2007 as a goodwill gesture in return for Prime Minister Shinzo Abe's pledge to revise his predecessor's policy and repair relations with China. However, the resumed sales of Japanese rice faced serious trademark disputes with the Chinese firms which pre-emptively registered famous Japanese rice brand names, like *koshihikari* and *hitomebore*, in Chinese characters.[5]

Japan's handling of a safeguard petition from the domestic hand towel industry in February 2001, on the other hand, averted a potentially serious dispute with China. Japan delayed its investigation and final ruling until April 2004, when the petition was declined.[6]

Japan seeks survival of its high-end rice productions in the export market in China at the time of trade liberalization pressure under the WTO. However, none of the bilateral trade disputes carried the intensity of the major US–Japan trade disputes in the past, largely due to a better international division of labor (less overlap in competing industries) between Japan and China.

Given the growing size of Japan–China trade, the Japanese industrial sector is largely in favor of pursuing an economic partnership agreement (EPA) that includes free trade with China. Backed by lobbying of the Federation of Economic Organizations (*Keidanren*), the Ministry of Economy, Trade, and Industry (METI) is seeking a possible Free Trade Agreement (FTA) with China, but its negotiation tactic is to conclude an investment agreement first by using FTA considerations as incentives for China. China expressed its interest in a trilateral FTA with Japan and Korea as early as November 2002, but Japan was cautious.[7] Progress in the initial process toward a trilateral investment agreement in 2003–2004 encouraged the start of studies on a trilateral FTA. In October 2004, METI's semi-public think tank, the Japan External Trade Organization (JETRO), launched a joint study group with a Chinese counterpart to examine a possible Japan–China FTA.[8] However, deadlock over the investment talks since late 2005 has also retarded the FTA process. *Keidanren* in its position paper in 2006 called for the start of an official joint study group made of business persons, bureaucrats, and academics to study a trilateral FTA with China and Korea—but only on condition that the official negotiations on an investment agreement kick off within 2006.[9]

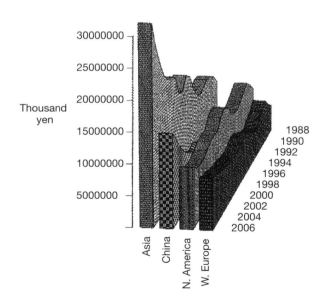

Figure 5.3 Japan's imports by source

Source: Japanese Customs

As Japanese products received wide acceptance into the Chinese market, the issue of intellectual property rights (IPR) protection came to the forefront of the bilateral economic issues. Initially, damage to Japanese companies was concentrated in knowledge intensive products that were easily reproduced, such as movies, music recordings, and computer game software. As manufacturing operations of sophisticated manufactured products moved into China and the local consumers developed a taste for Japanese brand products, trademark violations by domestic Chinese firms became issues for such products as motorcycles and consumer electronics. While Japan enhanced customs inspections to prevent importation of pirated products, protection of Japanese IPRs in the Chinese market has been slow. Bilateral discussions to address this matter have yielded little. The frustration against China's lax IPR protection is shared by the United States, which in August 2007 requested the opening of a panel at the World Trade Organization. Japan and the EU have joined the panel as observers.[10] China has not joined the multilateral discussion toward a treaty against counterfeit and pirated products—which includes Japan, United States, the EU, Switzerland, New Zealand, Mexico, Korea, and Canada.[11] Japan has not adopted a comprehensive EPA strategy toward China to package trade, investment, and IPR together, which might induce China to accept more stringent IPR protection. The Japanese government has only taken defensive initiatives to educate the Japanese investors about the poor state of IPR protection in China and measures to protect themselves against piracy.

ODA

China has held the position of the number-one recipient of Japanese Overseas Development Assistance (ODA) loans for many years (See Table 5.1 and Figure 5.4). Savings from the concessionary interest rate of the Japanese loans assisted China's infrastructure development, and the loans served as a catalyst for FDIs by Japanese and other foreign companies.[12] Japan, since the late 1990s, has revised its emphasis on China, partly for China's rising economic status into the newly industrializing countries (NICs) category. The cooling of political relations since the failed visit of President Jiang Zeming in 1998 has also resulted in an increased call from the ruling party politicians to phase out the ODA loans to China.[13] The Japanese government in April 2005 announced, and China reluctantly agreed, that new approval of ODA loans to China would cease by the time of the Beijing Oympics in 2008.[14]

Political relations

China has occupied a prominent place in Japan's post-World War II Asia diplomacy. Starting from peace settlement with the Nationalist government in Taiwan in 1951, through the shift of the diplomatic recognition to Beijing in 1978 and a de facto anti-Soviet alliance during the 1980s, Sino–Japanese relations have been a critical component of the international system in East Asia.

Table 5.1 Major recipients of ODA loans

Ranking	2000 Country	Amount	2001 Country	Amount	2002 Country	Amount	2003 Country	Amount	2004 Country	Amount	2005 Country	Amount
1	China	2144	China	1614	China	1212	India	1250	India	1345	India	1555
2	Philippines	1288	Philippines	1144	India	1112	Indonesia	1046	Indonesia	1148	Indonesia	930
3	Indonesia	992	Indonesia	908	Indonesia	889	China	967	Turkey	987	Vietnam	908
4	Thailand	957	Vietnam	743	Malaysia	820	Vietnam	793	China	859	Thailand	355
5	Vietnam	709	India	657	Vietnam	793	Thailand	449	Vietnam	820	Sri Lanka	316
6	Brazil	463	Sri Lanka	461	Thailand	452	Turkey	268	Romania	287	Azerbaijan	293
7	Peru	449	Kazakhstan	214	Sri Lanka	336	Brazil	216	Sri Lanka	279	Pakistan	276
8	Sri Lanka	303	Costa Rica	167	Philippines	272	Egypt	215	Ukraine	191	Morocco	272
9	Romania	256	Bulgaria	129	Uzbekistan	250	Kenya	106	Uzbekistan	164	Paraguay	214
10	India	189	Morocco	128	Bangladesh	92	Macedonia	97	Armenia	159	Costa Rica	150

Exchanged Note Basis (in 100 million yen)
No note was exchanged with China in 2005.
Source: Ministry of Foreign Affairs

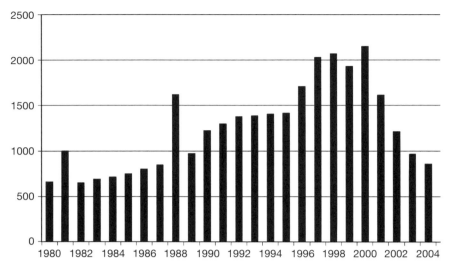

Figure 5.4 ODA loans to China (exchanged note basis; in 100 million yen)

For Japan, the role of the United States as a key determinant of Sino–Japanese relations has derived from US dominance over Japanese foreign policy, but Japan's search for a maneuvering space for more independent foreign policy has increasingly centered on its China policy.[15] Conversely, Japan's utility for the United States in the changing contexts of US–China relations has also affected Sino–Japanese relations.

Chinese memories of Japan's invasion of China have been manifestations of not only the general public opinion in China, but also the changing international power dynamics in the region and the changing Chinese policy toward Japan.[16] Likewise, historical interpretations of the World War II in Japan have also been influenced by particular foreign policy goals of the political groups, and the balance among diverse views has shifted with changing international contexts. While this view supposes a realist view of predominance of inter-state relations over domestic factors, maturing of the Japanese democracy has also raised the importance of values (including those of democracy) in Japan's relations with authoritarian China.

Prime Minister Koizumi's visits to the Yasukuni Shrine during his tenure resulted in a five-year vacuum in diplomatic relations at the summit level. China's harsh reaction to the Japanese leader's visits to this shrine was not new, but Koizumi's strong determination to pursue the visits demonstrated an externally assertive Japan and a new domestic political environment which supported Japan's new direction. Postwar Japanese diplomacy toward East Asian countries, and in particular South Korea and China, derived from a basic stance of apology for the wartime aggression in the region. The extent to which

Asian countries granted forgiveness has varied, based on a number of factors, including but not limited to historical context, local culture, domestic ethnic composition, and political system. After sixty years since the end of World War II, China has remained the least forgiving country for Japan,[17] despite the rapidly advancing economic integration between the two countries.

The "history card" China and Korea have used in their dealings with Japan was effective as long as Japanese liberals closely echoed the two countries' complaints, but Japan in the twenty-first century was no longer willing to limit its international role based on the legacies of its wartime history. A new generation of postwar politicians has steadily entered national politics in the 2000 and 2003 lower-house elections, but particularly en masse as a result of the ruling Liberal Democratic Party's massive electoral success under Koizumi in the 2005 lower-house election. Supported by the conservative-leaning electorate, Koizumi pursued a break from the postwar pattern of apology diplomacy.[18]

Media focuses on Prime Minister Koizumi's Yasukuni Shrine visits produced a common perception that Koizumi, who had little diplomatic experience, picked this issue as a unifying nationalist cause primarily for domestic political reasons and that the relations with China were estranged mainly by this symbolic issue. However, the real significance of the Yasukuni saga was that both Japan and China used this issue for tangible international political goals. Through his visits to Yasukuni, Koizumi declared Japan's metamorphosis into an active global diplomatic and security actor unconstrained by its wartime history and expressed Japan's desire for international acceptance of its new role.[19] China has used history issues, including the Yasukuni issue, to deny Japan what it wanted and keep Japan in its constrained postwar position.[20]

This section will review key regional issues in which Japan's and China's tangible interests diverge (including Japan's pursuit of a permanent membership in the UN Security Council, upgrading of the US–Japan alliance, competition for Asian leadership, Taiwan's future, and North Korea's nuclear ambitions), and how Japan views China's role in these issues. Then, it will also describe Japan's perceptions of Chinese nationalism, prospects of democratization, and its implications on bilateral relations.

UN Security Council reform

As one of the five permanent members of the United Nations Security Council (UNSC), China has exerted diplomatic influence disproportionate to its economic or military strength in the past. On the other hand, Japan started its entry into the UN as a "former enemy" state and has only managed to hold a seat as a non-permanent member of the UNSC on a rotational basis among major Asian countries. Japan's active drive for a permanent UNSC seat in the twenty-first century met strong opposition from both China and South Korea. South Korea's opposition to giving Japan a permanent UNSC seat had much to do with the particular formulation of Japan's proposal for the UNSC reform, which would have closed the door for Korea's entry. On the other hand, China's opposition was more directly targeted at Japan's entry per se. Japan holds a realistic view about China's anticipated opposition to a Japanese seat.[21] Japan's best hope is to gather enough support not only among the four permanent members (other than China) and other developed countries, but also among as many developing countries as possible, in order to make China's exercise of its veto power more difficult. Unfortunately, Japan has even failed to line up American support for its proposed formula to expand the UNSC, allowing China to sit on the sideline without making its opposition explicit.

US–Japan alliance upgrade

The incremental upgrading of the US–Japan alliance since the mid-1990s has kept pace with the rise of China. While Japan's motivations behind this change are multifold including domestic, regional, and global considerations, China has prominently occupied a place in Japan's considerations. Japan's attempts to cement the alliance through increased security cooperation with the United States in regional contingencies have manifested in the 1997 revised guidelines for security cooperation and related enabling legislation since 1998,[22] amendments to the Self Defense Forces Law, and the revised Acquisitions and Cross-Servicing Agreements of 2004—which collectively expanded Japanese Self Defense Forces' roles in supporting the US forces in regional contingencies and defense of the Japanese territories.[23] Japan has also stepped up its missile defense cooperation with the United States in the wake of the North Korean test-firing of the Taepodong missile over the Japanese archipelago in 1998 and the multiple missile tests in the Sea of Japan in the summer of 2006.[24] While North Korean provocations accelerated Tokyo's participation in missile defense, the United States and Japan have attempted to diplomatically assure the Chinese that missile defense is not aimed at neutralizing Chinese nuclear missiles.[25] On the other hand, China has been modernizing its nuclear missile force since before Japan officially decided to participate in joint missile defense research with the United States.

Strengthening of the US–Japan alliance, however, does not automatically mean Japan's (nor America's) intension to militarily contain China. Japan's foremost expectation is to enhance its diplomatic power and security role in Asia with a solid backing of the US alliance. Japan is, however, quickly learning that the Chinese perception of the US–Japan alliance as a deterrent against a revival of Japan's unilateral militarism is fading.[26] The emerging Chinese perceptions of US–Japan co-hegemony and an anti-China containment network that also enlists Australia and India are well understood by the Japanese. Japan's increasing high-level security discussions with Australia and India have not produced immediate and tangible defense cooperation against China, but are clearly aimed at sending diplomatic messages to China.

Asian leadership

Japan sees China's increasing political influence in Asia as a major challenge to its own predominance in the region. Japan's defeat in World War II caused a temporary retreat of Japanese influence from the region, as Japan was stripped of its Asian colonies and incorporated into the US alliance system. However, the Cold War and threats of communist insurgencies throughout Asia shifted the US position on Japan's role in Asia. The United States recognized Asia's importance as Japan's source of natural resources and destination of its product exports. While the United States militarily and diplomatically aided pro-capitalist regimes throughout Asia, Japan focused its efforts on rebuilding lost economic relations with Asia. With growing economic relations, Japan worked to improve its diplomatic relations with Southeast Asian countries and South Korea during the 1960s.

Japan's strategy to maintain its political leadership in Asia while simultaneously courting a close alliance partnership with the United States worked well in Asia during the Cold War. The strategy assured Asia that Japan's economic and political influences in the region would not develop into a military dominance, for the alliance with America would serve as a check against Japan's strategic independence.

China's role in Japan's regional design has been an ambiguous one. China's historical role as the regional hegemon and its long-standing rivalry with Japan on one hand place China into a category distinct from the rest of Asia where Japan more explicitly claimed leadership. China's slow start in economic development due to its failed models from the 1950s through the 1970s gave Japan a de facto economic leadership in Asia. Japan attempted to translate this leadership into a political one. However, Japan did not seek a hegemonic political role in the region and preferred to create a more inclusive multilateral setting that connected Asia with the Western world. Cohesion of the ASEAN grouping also made it hard for one external country (such as Japan or China) to be dominant in a regional setting. In earlier formations of multilateral groupings, Japan's leadership in Asia was partly aimed at borrowing the collective strength of Asia in dealing with external powers. Formation of Asia-Pacific Economic Cooperation (APEC) in 1989, for example, was viewed as Japan's strategy to deter the United States and European countries from pursuing exclusive economic blocs with the lure of combined and opened Asian markets including China's.[27] In recent formulations, Japan's multilateral strategy is geared more toward diluting China's influence within the bloc by inviting broader participation of external powers, as seen in its support for invitations to Australia, New Zealand, and India to join the East Asian Summit in 2005.

While Japan's economic success pushed its predominant economic status in Asia through the 1990s, China's challenge to Japan's predominance since has been swift. In the post-Cold War era, China quickly shed its negative image as the external patron of communist insurgencies in Asia and approached the Asian countries with the lure of its growing domestic market. In 2002, China proposed a free trade agreement with ASEAN countries at the expanded ASEAN Summit meeting and surpassed Japan which was warming its own regional free trade design. Japan has since activated its FTA negotiations with individual ASEAN countries as well as collectively with the whole of ASEAN.[28]

Diplomacy over Taiwan

Taiwan continues to be a thorny issue between Japan and China. In addition to the naval-strategic significance of Taiwan (to be discussed in the section on military security), the island's democratic political system attracts much sympathy among Japanese conservatives.[29] In particular, the former president Lee Teng-hui's praise of Japanese legacies in Taiwan sound comfortable to the Japanese ears. Lee's visits to Japan have become a source of rift between Tokyo and Beijing since his long-attempted and finally successful visit in 2001, and the Japanese government has used this issue to warn Beijing about overusing its "history" card against Japan.

China's policy toward Taiwan is clearly a key ingredient in the Japanese perception of China. Japan has repeatedly emphasized its opposition to involuntary incorporation of Taiwan by China, and any Chinese provocation against Taiwan has met strong Japanese protests. However, Japan's sympathy toward Taiwan based on democratic values has stopped short of actively supporting Taiwan's de facto independence drive under President Chen Shui-bian.

North Korea and the Six-Party Talks

Japan sees China as North Korea's patron state, whose cooperation is essential in diplomatic negotiations with North Korea. China's handling of this issue, to the Japanese, is a test of China as a responsible regional and global security partner. While recognizing China's distinct security interests in North Korea, Japan is cautiously assessing Chinese commitments to nuclear non-proliferation and regional peace and stability.

Japan's limited backdoor relations with North Korea via Socialist Party politicians during the Cold War and the immediately following period did not involve close consultations with China. However, the first crisis over North Korea's nuclear development during the mid-1990s, emergence of multilateral diplomacy in the Korean Energy Development Organization (KEDO), second crisis since 2002, and the resulting emergence of the Six-Party Talks brought about closer discussions between China and Japan on the Democratic People's Republic of Korea (DPRK) issues. Japan's expectations of China's brokership are inevitably mixed. Japan desperately needs Chinese cooperation, having witnessed the failures of the bilateral approach to North Korea by the United States and exhausted its own negative inducements against North Korea. At the same time, current consensus on the first step implementation of the agreed denuclearization by December 31, 2007, would be fragile in the event of North Korean non-compliance or procrastination. Having passed the denuclearization, Japan's other security concerns about North Korea, including its ballistic missile development, would likely introduce more divergence with China, and Japan's expectations about utility of the Chinese brokership may gradually diminish.

Views about Chinese nationalism and democratization

China's authoritarian one-party rule has been the source of both Japan's concern and comfort. It has been a concern, especially since the military crackdown of the student demonstration in Tiananmen Square in 1989. At the same time, Japan has relied on the authoritarian Chinese government to crack down on anti-Japanese demonstrations. While past demonstrations may have often been orchestrated by the Chinese government, the growing dissatisfaction of the Chinese people against the government due to various social, economic, and political problems have turned many anti-Japanese demonstrations into highly volatile ones, which could easily turn against the Chinese authorities. Witnessing the volatility of the anti-Japanese demonstration in Shanghai on April 16, 2005, during which the Japanese consulate building was damaged, the Japanese view toward China's democratization is mixed.

Prime Minister Shinzo Abe inherited a damaged relation with China from the Koizumi administration and pledged to repair this relation. However, Abe's commitment to this cause conflicted with his other emphasis on democratic values to solidify relations with the United States, Australia, and India—all China's potential adversaries. With Abe's sudden resignation in fall 2007, the new Prime Minister Yasuo Fukuda's emphasis on Asia diplomacy is expected to bring Japan's China policy back—closer to its traditional non-ideological stance.

Japan's skepticism about the prospects of democracy in China is based on a pragmatic recognition that friendship with the political leaders of the authoritarian Chinese government has served to stabilize postwar bilateral relations. This ambivalence also affects Japan's relations with Taiwan. Taiwan's democratization in the late 1980s—at the end of the Cold War—was partly the Nationalist Party's effort to augment the weakening ties with the United States with common political values. The same logic appeared to have supported Japan's slight tilt toward Taiwan during the Koizumi and Abe administrations. However, it is more accurate to say that the common values were emphasized to justify the policy shifts which were based on changes in the underlying geostrategic balance. In other words, the limited pro-Taiwan shift of Japanese foreign policy was a product of subtle changes in the regional strategic balance, which for the time being do not warrant an overall review of Japan's China policy.

Conflicts in security interests

China and Japan have historically been military rivals. This geopolitical rivalry in premodern days was largely confined to control of the Korean

Peninsula. In modern days of naval warfare development, Taiwan's maritime strategic importance was clearly recognized as Japan won this island as war indemnity from the Qing China in 1895. Just as the Japanese archipelago held a critical geostrategic importance for the United States during the Cold War, Taiwan's status continues to be of Japan's maritime strategic interests. The alliance of two maritime powers (the United States and Japan) in the Western Pacific and the changing Chinese perception of this alliance further complicate the strategic picture in this region. In the present context, China's industrialization and the associated rise in oil consumption and import have expanded the scope of geopolitical rivalry between the two countries. While some overlap of security interests between the two countries is evident (like a secure and stable supply of oil), the two countries pursue conflicting unilateral and bilateral strategies rather than a more inclusive multilateral strategy. The growing politico-military rivalry between Japan and China is focused on the maritime domain and closely linked with the controlling of energy resources.[30]

Chinese military build-up and naval activities

East Asia's geography has played a major role in the strategic thinking of the major powers. China's setting as a major land power on the Eurasian Continent and Japan as an archipelagic country that lies between China and the vast Pacific Ocean have to a large extent influenced their external relations and military strategies. During the early Cold War, when China and the Soviet Union were viewed as members of a single Communist bloc, Japan allied with the United States to participate in containment, mainly through naval force, first that of the United States alone, but gradually that of Japan as well. The anti-Soviet political alliance between China and the United States during the 1980s (second Cold War) did not fundamentally alter the geopolitical reality of the region. The United States encouraged Japan to be the key naval partner in the Western Pacific, and Chinese forces remained focused on ground territorial defense. In the post-Cold War era, China increasingly sees this US–Japan naval alliance as threatening to its key maritime interests, most importantly freedom of passage for its tankers and sea control in contingencies involving the Taiwan Strait.[31] With its rapid economic growth, China has increased its military budget and spent a large sum on modernization of its naval force. Japan sees the Chinese naval build-up as a major challenge to the status quo of combined dominance by the United States and Japan.

Taiwan's significance in maritime security

While Taiwan's democratic polity is one factor that attracts Japan's emotional attachment to this island, sea lane security has continued to be the dominant factor since the Sino–Japanese War of 1894–1895. Japan's southwestern sea lane runs off Taiwan's east coast, and eastward expansion of China's sea control beyond the island would be a worrisome situation for Japan (Figure 5.5).

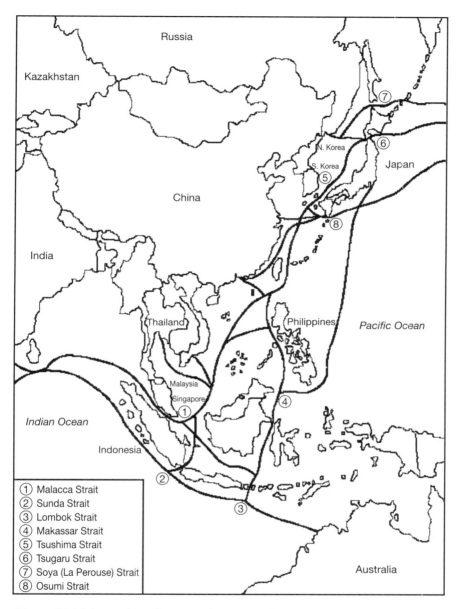

Figure 5.5 Major sea lanes in East Asia (Source: Ji Guoxing, "SLOC Security in the Asia-Pacific," Occasional Paper, Honolulu: Asia-Pacific Center for Security Studies, 2000)

Although Japan renounced its own claim to Taiwan in the San Francisco Peace Treaty in 1951, Japan's "understanding of" and "respect to" the principle of "one China" does not mean Japan's support for Beijing's takeover of Taiwan whether through peaceful means or not.[32] This point was vividly demonstrated by Japan's protest together with the United States against UN Secretary-General Ban Ki-moon's statement in September 2007 that the UN has recognized Taiwan as a part of China.[33]

East China Sea EEZ and continental shelf

Absence of agreed maritime boundaries between Japan and China is a further complicating factor for regional security and has been linked to many other issues. Most importantly, potential gas fields in the East China Sea have been a source of disputes between the two countries. The dispute over the maritime boundary originates in conflicting clauses in the Law of the Sea. China claims a continental shelf into the bulk of the East China Sea reaching the Okinawan Trough. Japan extends its exclusive economic zone (EEZ) claim from its baseline through the Ryukyu (Okinawan) chain of islands to the middle line with China's baseline. The dispute over the ownership of the Senkaku Islands (Daiyoutai in Chinese) further complicates the maritime boundary dispute.

China has built gas rigs at four locations in the East China Sea near (but outside) Japan's claimed EEZ boundary. Due to the perceived likelihood that the gas fields stretch across the boundary, Japan has requested China to share geological survey data. China has instead sent five missile frigates to show force around the disputed gas field.

When Prime Minister Shinzo Abe's visit to China in 2006 broke the icy bilateral relation during Koizumi's tenure, Abe and the Chinese Premier Hu Jintao agreed to start working group discussions toward joint development of gas resources. Japan proposed cost sharing for joint development of the four fields under China's control and other potential fields that lie across Japan's claimed EEZ boundary. China on the other hand only proposed joint development on the Japanese side of Japan's claimed boundary—which is still within the Chinese EEZ according to China's claimed boundary. No concrete agreement has been achieved on joint development or data sharing to date.[34] However, signaling to work on improving the bilateral ties by Prime Minister Yasuo Fukuda has resulted in moving this issue up from an administrative to a political level. A foreign ministers' meeting on December 1, 2007, produced an expression of desire to solve this issue with the planned visit to China by Prime Minister Fukuda in late December 2007.[35]

Okinotori-shima

The lesser known of Japan's territorial claim contested by China is the Okinotori Islands in the Pacific—Japan's southernmost islands lying between Taiwan and Guam. China rejects both Japan's claims that these are islands and that Japan possesses a 200-nautical mile EEZ around the islands. Unlike the case of the Senkakus, China does not lay its own claim over the Okinotoris. However, the strategic significance of the islands' location on the path between Taiwan and Guam—the home of the US Navy's Pacific submarine fleet—is that the international legal status of the surrounding sea based on the Japanese claim favors Japan and its ally—the United States—in naval competition vis-à-vis China. China's most immediate objective in its naval modernization is to achieve an effective denial power against the US Navy in crisis scenarios in the Taiwan Straits. In particular, China's acquisitions of modern submarines and the accompanying research activities to map the sea bottom in and out of the Japanese EEZs are viewed by the Japanese and Americans to be threatening. A submerged Chinese nuclear-powered submarine's incursion into Japan's territorial water through the Sakishima (west of Okinawa) island chain in November 2004 and the later revelation that this same submarine had circled Guam prior to violating the Japanese water clearly alerted the Japanese and American leaders.[36] Voiding Japan's EEZ around the Okinotoris would remove all international legal restrictions against China's research activities in this important area of submarine operations and rob Japan of its legal basis to deny hostile Chinese passage in a crisis. Japan guards these islands not only against natural erosion, but also against possible demolition by hostile agents.

Energy security

China's rapid industrialization has resulted in an exponential increase in its energy consumption. Traditionally, China has depended on a domestic supply of coal for energy. While this reliance continues to some extent, China's import of oil has steadily increased.[37] Securing the supply of oil requires a comprehensive strategy for both China and Japan, and their separate unilateral and bilateral strategies have been a source of conflict.

Due to concentration of economically accessible oil in the Middle East, China and Japan have engaged in diplomatic competitions over access to oil in this region. Japan had reduced the role of public firms in oil import as part of its administrative reform, but China continues to use its national oil company for overseas contracts. China's thirst for oil has driven up international prices not only because of its large purchases, but also because of its inefficient purchasing policies. Japan reversed privatization of its overseas oil explorations and has re-enhanced the role of public corporations and government banks in assisting private oil companies win concessions in the oil-producing countries.[38]

China's maritime import route for crude oil overlaps Japan's. China's critical reliance on a secured passage through the Malacca Strait so far has yielded mixed responses from Japan. On one hand, Japan is on guard against increases in China's influence in Southeast Asia in general, and key SLOC states (such as Indonesia, Malaysia, and Singapore) in particular. The combined naval advantage of the United States and Japan is to be maintained to deter China's naval expansion into this region. Japan's security assistance to Indonesia in the form of three patrol boats in 2006 can be seen in the context of this rivalry. At the same time, China's increasing usage of the strait has frustrated Japan, which underwrote the bulk of the cost of maintaining safety of this international strait.[39] Japan has launched multilateral initiatives to share information against piracy and the cost of maintaining the strait's safety and invited China into these frameworks.

In order to diversify energy supply routes and secure transport through the Indian Ocean, China has approached several countries facing the Indian Ocean including Pakistan, Burma, and Bangladesh.[40] China's naval presence in the Indian Ocean alerts not only India and the United States, but also Japan. Japan's dispatches of the maritime security forces into the Indian Ocean region under the "Anti-Terrorism Special Measures Law" (2001–2007) and the "Iraq Humanitarian Reconstruction Special Measures Law" (2004–2006) provided valuable training opportunities for Japan's more active naval presence in the region.

While China's growing energy consumption directly competes against Japan, Japan sees that it is in its interest to assist China in using energy more efficiently for two reasons. In addition to easing pressure on international energy supply through reducing China's demands, Japan also benefits from reduced pollution from China's energy use. Japan has shifted its ODA from mega infrastructure projects to environmental projects, and the Abe–Hu meeting during the APEC summit in 2007 reaffirmed Japan's cooperation with China in this area.[41]

China as a transnational security threat

While Japan has increasingly considered the Chinese state as a political and military rival, Japan's broader security is being threatened by a multitude of transnational security issues originating inside Chinese territories. Crossing of borders by these transnational entities may be aided by the ignorance and incompetence of the Chinese government authorities, but often without deliberate intensions to harm Japan or the Japanese people. Dealing with this type of threat requires the active cooperation of the Chinese government, and Japanese perceptions of China worsen when such cooperation is not readily availed.

Trans-border air pollution/global warming

China's industrialization has brought about major trans-border pollution issues to its regional neighbors including Japan. Sulfur byproducts from Chinese burning of coal have caused acid rain over Japan, which threatens Japan's forests and wetlands. While Japan went through a similar path of industrial pollution during the 1960s and 1970s, the two oil shocks of the 1970s and the following de-industrialization and relocation of the polluting industries overseas resulted in some improvements in Japan's air quality. The renewed threat of air pollution from China is viewed with much disdain. China surpassed the United States in carbon dioxide emissions in 2007 to become the world's largest emitter,[42] China's objection to the strict national emission quota for carbon dioxide under the Kyoto Protocol mechanism also caused the Japanese populace to view China as an uncooperative country.

Pandemic diseases

With the increased volume of air traffic, communicable diseases have come to the attention of security practitioners. Most notably in recent years, the outbreak of Severe Acute Respiratory Syndrome (SARS) in China and its global spread in 2002–2003 shocked the world when it was revealed that poor handling of the disease in China caused the otherwise preventable global outbreak. For the Japanese, revelation of the suspected linkage between SARS and the eating of ferret species by rural Chinese was an additional factor that enhanced the Japanese stereotype of the Chinese people as uncivilized.

Advances in scientific research have increasingly confirmed the long speculated theory about the origin of flu inside China. Recurrences of massive avian deaths were linked to the new strain of avian flu virus, and the mechanism of its passing from wild birds to captive chickens and ducks in China and beyond has been established with increasing certainty. As the new strain caused some human deaths and the possibility of viral mutations to enable human-to-human transmissions was debated, poor handling of the disease by the Chinese authorities again was perceived as a security threat by the Japanese and others outside China.

Food safety

Japan's increasing economic integration and close proximity to China have pushed the volume of food imports from that country. Japan's strict food safety regulators have frequently discovered pesticide residues on fruits and vegetables imported from China that were over the permissible levels, or sometimes even banned chemicals on these imports. Japan's protests and import restrictions were often met with denials, counter-attacks that Japan was engaging in protectionism, and retaliations against Japanese exports to China.

When China's lax supervision of its export products met Japanese nationalism, a powerful stereotype of Chinese products emerged. Ridiculing of Chinese practices is tacitly accompanied by the notion that the Japanese would not go that far to abandon business ethics for the sake of profits. While this ethnic stereotyping can be challenged by poor Japanese handling of food safety in such cases as the widespread recycling of old milk, some revelations of Chinese practices such as stuffing Shanghai crabs with lead pellets to inflate their weights were simply beyond the Japanese imagination and had disproportionately negative and lasting impacts on the Japanese consumer mentality.[43]

In 2007, disputes over Chinese food safety spread to the United States. Numerous deaths of household pets in the United States were attributed to Chinese-made ingredients in pet food, resulting in a major recall campaign.[44] The news was widely reported in Japan as well because it matched the Japanese stereotype of low Chinese business standards. Discovery in the United States of carcinogenic banned antibiotics in imported farm-raised eel products from China in the summer of 2007 immediately resulted in an import suspension in both the United States and Japan.[45]

China in 2007 launched a major public relations campaign to counter the image of tainted Chinese food and accused its trade partners, including Japan of using safety issues as a cover for their protectionist trade policies. During the campaign, a television reporter was sentenced to one year in jail and a 1,000-yuan (US$132) fine for staging a news story about the mixing of meat and corrugated cardboard material by a Chinese meat bun maker.[46] At the same time, China finally took the issue of food safety more seriously, inspecting and suspending many of the export firms.

Illegal migration

China is by far the largest supplier of illegal migrants into Japan. Despite sensationalistic television coverage of human smuggling in cargo containers, the bulk of illegal migrants in Japan are those who overstay their visas and workers without proper authorizations.[47] Their entry and continued presence are the result of Japan's economic needs (labor shortage), China's relative lack of opportunities, existence of brokers (both legitimate and illegitimate), and lax enforcement of law against illegal employers in Japan. Nevertheless, occasional crimes involving these illegal migrants have triggered xenophobic reactions in Japan. In particular, intrusion of organized crime syndicates in human trafficking and smuggling, organized theft, racketeering, and other criminal activities have alerted the Japanese authorities and the public alike.

Conclusions

China–Japan relations today face two conflicting forces of geo-economics and geopolitics, wrapped in a unique historical circumstance and its subjective interpretations. Economically, Japan as a whole enjoys growing benefits through cheaper imports from and expanded export opportunities to China, as well as enhanced competitiveness of Japanese products in third country markets through relocation of production into China. The integration of regional economies is raising China's significance in the overall health of the Japanese economy. In terms of geopolitics, Japan as a maritime power closely aligned with the United States (another maritime power) faces China as the rising land power with maritime ambitions. The coexistence of economic cooperation and military–diplomatic rivalry is further complicated by the politics over interpretations of World War II history especially in regard to Japan's role in it.

Japan sees emerging conflicts with China in its growing economic relations, especially in the areas of intellectual property rights protection and protection of foreign investments. While China's entry into the World Trade Organization has brought China under the discipline of multilateral trade rules, these rules do not sufficiently protect Japan's interests in intellectual property and investment rights. However, given the growing business opportunities in China, Japan sees that these conflicts are manageable through enhancing multilateral rules, bringing China into such legal regimes, working together with the United States and the European Union to apply pressure on China, and assisting domestic firms in taking defensive action.

Competition over global and regional political leadership between China and Japan has intensified as China has emerged with its growing economic might and nationalism. Facing the Chinese veto power at the global UN arena and possible Chinese dominance in the regional (Asian) arena, Japan defensively seeks a new definition of regionalism, as seen in the East Asian Summit, which includes China but aims at diluting its influence within. Japan's attempt to break from the postwar pattern of never-ending apologies to China with the backing of the enhanced alliance with the United States has faced Chinese attempts to use the history card in order to prevent Japan's metamorphosis into a fully fledged diplomatic and military power.

The rivalry between China and Japan, however, has not completely ruled out cooperation over issues of overlapping (if not identical) concerns. North Korea's nuclear weapons development has provided an opportunity for the two countries to work together on a security matter within a multilateral framework. Japan is willing to hitch a ride on China's regional clout when it serves Japan's interests.

In order to maintain this pragmatic policy toward China, Japan has largely refrained from lodging any harsh criticism about China's internal governance issues. As a result of a combination of China's close proximity and its status as a de facto Cold War ally, Japan has actively engaged China's authoritarian government since the switching of diplomatic recognition in 1978. This non-ideological approach to downplay the importance of democratic governance and human rights protection survived China's bloody crackdown of the student protestors at Tiananmen Square in 1989 and the ideological rightward drift of Japan during the Koizumi and Abe administrations.

Japan's perception of China has also been driven by the regional geopolitical shift, which resulted from China's rapid economic growth. China's growing military budget, compared with Japan's fiscal reform and zero budget growth for the military, enabled rapid military modernization including expansion of the naval force. The post-Cold War dominance of the Western Pacific by the combined naval strength of the United States and Japan has been increasingly challenged by metamorphosis of the Chinese navy from a brown water (coastal) navy into a blue water navy. The intensifying maritime rivalry stretches from the area of sea control (including sea lane control), resources transportation (notably oil from the Middle East), to resource exploration and exploitation.[48]

The means of this competition also stretch over the military, diplomatic, and international legal tools.

While government-to-government relations between Japan and China fluctuated, China's growth has turned Japan into a frontline showcase for a whole range of transnational problems originating in China. Pandemic diseases in the previously isolated rural Chinese communities have become serious concerns for the Japanese, with faster and more voluminous air traffic. Growth in imports from China has brought the issue of product safety to the forefront, especially that of food items. Transnational criminal organizations have always been an issue in East Asia, but their increasing exploitation of global communication and transportation in the post-Cold War era has raised their relative prominence within the issues of security concerns.

Japan's mixed views about China are likely to persist in the coming years, provided that there will not be a major disruption in the prevailing economic, political, and military trends. One such negative shock event would be China's return to heavily mercantile economic policies as a result of either an economic crisis similar to the Asian economic crisis of 1997–1998 or a more incremental series of political–economic crises involving international trade disputes and domestic worker disputes. Another negative shock event might be a military conflict in the Taiwan Straits or a new political crisis following a major crackdown on political demonstrations. Short of such shock events, the mix within Japan's conflicting perceptions of China is likely to remain stable, despite ups and downs caused by events of lesser magnitudes and shorter residual effects.

Notes

*   The views expressed in this chapter are those of the author and do not reflect the official policy or position of the Asia-Pacific Center for Security Studies, Department of Defense, or the US Government.

1   *The Report of the Joint Study Group on the Possible Trilateral Investment Arrangements among China, Japan, and Korea.* Downloaded on November 28, 2007 at: www.meti.go.jp/policy/trade_policy/jck/data/041129ifdi-e.pdf.
2   Nihon Keizai Dantai Rengoukai, Chugoku Iinkai Kikaku Bukai [Federation of Economic Organizations, China Commission Planning Section], "Nicchu Tsusho Keizai Kankei no Saranaru Kakudai ni Mukete—Nicchu Tsusho Taiwa Mission Position Paper [Toward Further Expansion of Japan–China Trade Relations—Japan–China Trade Dialogue Mission Position Paper]," February 23, 2005. www.keidanren.or.jp/japanese/policy/2005/016.html.
3   China Japan Net Bridge (Japanese version), January 10, 2002. http://people.ne.jp/zhuanti/Zhuanti_43.html.
4   *Nourin Kinyu*, May 2002, p. 3. www.nochuri.co.jp/report/pdf/n0205re1.pdf.
5   Jiji Tsushin, July 7, 2007. Reproduced by Nouzai.com. www.nouzai.com/news/webdir/277.html.
6   China Japan Net Bridge (Japanese version), April 4, 2004, http://j.peopledaily.com.cn/2004/04/04/jp20040404_38230.html.
7   *Yomiuri Shimbun* (online), November 5, 2002. www.yomiuri.co.jp/02/2002 1104i513.htm.

8   *Yomiuri Shimbun* (online), October 18, 2004. www.yomiuri.co.jp/business/news/20041018ib01.htm.
9   Nihon Keizai Dantai Rengoukai, Chugoku Iinkai Kikaku Bukai [Federation of Economic Organizations, China Commission Planning Section], "Dai 3 kai Nicchu Tsusho Taiwa Mission Position Paper" [The third Japan–China Trade Dialogue Mission Position Paper], March 16, 2006. www.keidanren.or.jp/Japanese/policy/2006/015.html.
10   *Asahi Shimbun* (online), September 26, 2007. www.asahi.com/international/update/0926/TKY200709260140html.
11   *Asahi Shimbun* (online), October 23, 2007. www.asahi.com/business/update/1023/TKY200710230105.html.
12   Tsukasa Takamine, "The Role of Yen Loans in China's Economic Growth and Openness," *Pacific Affairs*, 79(1), Spring 2006, p. 30.
13   Reinhard Drifte, "The Ending of Japan's ODA Loan Programme to China—All's Well that Ends Well?" *Asia-Pacific Review*, 13(1), 2006, pp. 99–101.
14   *Yomiuri Shimbun* (online), November 8, 2007. www.yomiuri.co.jp/politics/news/20071108i214.htm.
15   Takashi Inoguchi, "Japan Goes Regional," in Inoguchi, editor, *Japan's Asia Policy: Revival and Response*, New York: Palgrave, 2002, pp. 15–18, 29–31.
16   Lee Jung Nam, through his survey of Chinese intellectuals mainly in social sciences, revealed that the Chinese not only recognize a rise of nationalism in China, but also its positive utility in international negotiations. Lee, "The Revival of Chinese Nationalism: Perspectives of Chinese Intellectuals," *Asian Perspective*, 30(4), 2006, pp. 159–162.
17   Shogo Suzuki provides a detailed discourse analysis of China's self identity as a "victimized state," its view of Japan as an "other," and how the two relate. Suzuki, "The Importance of 'Othering' in China's National Identity: Sino-Japanese Relations as a Stage of Identity Conflicts," *Pacific Review*, 20(1), March 2007, pp. 23–47.
18   The enhanced role of the prime minister's office in conduct of foreign policy during Koizumi's tenure clearly played a role. Koizumi's long-term policy secretary and the chief advisor to the prime minister, Isao Iijima, notes in his memoir that the office in consultation with the Ministry of Education and Science actively revised the "history" aspects of the MOFA drafted speech to be given by the prime minister at summit meetings. Iijima, *Jitsuroku Koizumi Gaikou* [Documentary of Koizumi Diplomacy], Tokyo: Nihon Keizai Shibunsha, 2007, pp. 38, 41–42, 238–240.
19   Iijima notes that Koizumi repeatedly explained that his prayers at Yasukuni were for Japan not to repeat the mistake of starting a war and troubling its neighbors, thereby differentiating Japan's emerging multilateral security roles from the militarist past. Iijima, *Jitsuroku Koizumi Gaikou*, pp. 35–36.
20   Robert G. Sutter, *China's Rise in Asia*, Lanham, MD: Rowman and Littlefield, 2005, pp. 135–136; Gilbert Rozman, "China's Changing Images of Japan, 1989–2001: The Struggle to Balance Partnership and Rivalry," *International Relations of the Asia-Pacific*, 2(1), 2002, pp. 95–129; Suisheng Zhao, "A State-Led Nationalism: the Patriotic Education Campaign in Post-Tiananmen China," *Communist and Post-Communist Studies*, 31(3), 1998, pp. 287–302; Allen S. Whiting, *China Eyes Japan*, Berkeley: University of California Press, 1989.
21   Yang Bojiang argues that China at the time of Japan's initial declaration in 2004 of its effort to seek a permanent UNSC seat was "not negative." He quotes a Chinese Foreign Ministry spokesman as saying "We [the Chinese] understand the will of [the] Japanese to play a greater role in international affairs." Yang Bojiang, "Redefining Sino–Japanese Relations after Koizumi," *Washington Quarterly*, 29(4), Autumn 2006, pp. 134–135. It should be remembered,

however, that "understanding" in the diplomatic world indicates far less attachment to the position than "supporting."

22   Yoichiro Sato, "Will the US–Japan Alliance Continue?" *New Zealand International Review*, XXIV(4), July/August 1999, pp. 10–12.

23   Yoichiro Sato, "Role of Norms in Japan's Overseas Troop Dispatch Decisions," in Sato and Keiko Hirata, editors, *Norms, Interests, and Power in Japanese Foreign Policy*, New York: Palgrave, forthcoming; Sato, "Nihon no Kaigai Hahei Kettei no Bunseki [Analysis of Japan's Overseas Troop Dispatch Decisions]," in Kimie Hara, ed., *Zaigai Nihonjin Kenkyusha ga Mita Nihon Gaikou* [Japanese Diplomacy As Seen by Overseas Japanese Scholars] (tentative title), Tokyo: University of Tokyo Press, forthcoming.

24   Yoichiro Sato, "Japan's Reactions to the DPRK Missile Tests of July 2006," in Yongjin Zhang, editor, *Whither the Six Party Talks? Issues, Stakes and Perspectives*, Auckland: New Zealand Asia Institute, pp. 35–44; Sato, "US North Korea Policy: the 'Japan Factor,' " in Linus Hagström and Marie Söderberg, eds, *North Korea Policy: Japan and the Great Powers*, European Institute of Japanese Studies, East Asian Economics and Business Series Number 9, London: Routledge, pp. 73–94.

25   Ted Osius, *The US–Japan Security Alliance: Why It Matters and How to Strengthen It*, Washington Papers Number 181, West Port, CT: Praeger and Washington, D.C.: Center for Strategic and International Studies, 2002, pp. 89–90.

26   Yang, "Redefining Sino–Japanese Relations after Koizumi," pp. 133–134; Wu Xinbo, "The End of the Silver Lining: A Chinese View of the US–Japan Alliance," *Washington Quarterly*, 29(1), Winter 2005–2006, pp. 119–130.

27   Edward J. Lincoln, *East Asian Economic Regionalism*, Washington, D.C.: Brookings Institution, Press, 2004, pp. 148–149.

28   Yoichiro Sato, "Japan and the Emerging Free Trade Agreements in the Asia-Pacific: An Active Leadership?" in Sato and Satu Limaye, editors, *Japan in a Dynamic Asia: Coping with the New Security Challenges*, Lanham, MD: Lexington Books, 2006, pp. 56–61.

29   Gregory W. Noble, "New Breakthroughs and Enduring Limitations in Japan's Special Relationship with Taiwan," in Sato and Limaye, eds, *Japan in A Dynamic Asia*, pp. 106–108.

30   This is not to undermine the importance of ground supplies of energy, such as Sino–Japanese competition over Russian oil and gas pipelines, but these pipeline issues at present are handled within the domain of diplomacy and lack military dimensions. See for a more inclusive discussion: Xuanli Liao, "The Petroleum Factor in Sino–Japanese Relations: Beyond Energy Cooperation," *International Relations of the Asia-Pacific*, 7 (2007), pp. 23–46.

31   Kent Calder, "Coping with Energy Insecurity: China's Response in Global Perspective," *East Asia*, 23(3), Fall 2006, p. 54.

32   The People's Republic of China was not a party to the San Francisco Peace Treaty, but the Republic of China (the government in Taiwan) was. For a detailed discussion of Taiwan's postwar status, see Kimie Hara, *San Francisco Heiwa Jouyaku no Mouten* [The Blind Spots of the San Francisco Peace Treaty], Hiroshima: Keisui-sha, 2005, chapter 2 (pp. 81–112).

33   *Asahi Shimbun* (online), September 8, 2007. www.asahi.com/international/update/0908/TKY200709080239.html. The Japanese protest emphasized that Japan "understand and respect" the Chinese position but does not agree with it. The shift of UN representation from the *Kuomintang* (nationalist) government in Taiwan to the communist government in Beijing only meant a withdrawal of UN endorsement for the nationalist claim to the mainland. While there is only one China, whether that includes Taiwan is a question deliberately left unanswered.

34 *Yomiuri Shimbun* (online), September 19, 2007. www.yomiuri.co.jp/politics/news/20070919it05.htm.

35 *Asahi Shimbun* (online), December 2, 2007. www/asahi.com/politics/update/1202/TKY200712010287.html.

36 Denny Roy, "Stirring Samurai, Disapproving Dragon: Japan's Growing Security Activity and Sino–Japan Relations," in Sato and Limaye, eds, *Japan in A Dynamic Asia*, pp. 73–74.

37 Calder, "Coping with Energy Insecurity," pp. 49–51; Pak K. Lee, "China's Quest for Oil Security: Oil (Wars) in the Pipeline?" *Pacific Review*, 18(2), June 2005, pp. 267–269.

38 *Asahi Shimbun* (online), May 18, 2006. www.asahi.com/politics/updates/0518/004html.

39 Kenji Nagamatsu, "Malacca, Singapore Kaikyo Mondai—Kokusaiteki Kyoryoku no Wakugumi Kouchiku ni Mukete [Malacca-Singapore Straits Problems—Toward Building a Framework of International Cooperation]," Speech at the 35th Kaiyo Forum, July 11, 2006. www.sof.or.jp/ocean/forum/35/pdf/35.02.pdf; Yoichiro Sato, "Southeast Asian Receptiveness to Japanese Maritime Security Cooperation," Asia-Pacific Papers, Honolulu: Asia-Pacific Center for Security Studies, 2007.

40 Henry J. Kenny, "China and the Competition for Oil and Gas in Asia," *Asia-Pacific Review*, 11(2), 2004, pp. 42–43.

41 *Yomiuri Shimbun* (online), September 9, 2007. www.yomiuri.co.jp/politics/news/20070909i204.htm.

42 *Asahi Shimbun* (online), November 8, 2007. www.asahi.com/international/update/1107/TKY200711070345.html.

43 Lead and cadmium contamination of crabs and other sea food from Chinese waters, however, is a more serious problem, and resembles the history of serious pollution in Japan during the 1960s and 1970s.

44 David Barboza, "Second Chemical Eyed in Chinese Pet Food Scandal," *International Herald Tribune* (online), May 8, 2007. www.iht.com/articles/2007/05/09/business/petfood.php#end_main.

45 Xinhua News, November 28, 2007. http://news.xinhuanet.com/english/2007-11/28/content_7160088.htm.

46 "China Sentences Reporter Who Faked Cardboard Buns Story to 1 Year in Jail," *International Herald Tribune*, August 12, 2007. www.iht.com/articles/ap/2007/08/13/asia/AS-GEN-China-Cardboard-Buns.php#end_main. The swift ruling in authoritarian China is viewed in Japan with skepticism that the reporter—who might have been a real whistle blower—instead was made a scapegoat.

47 Katsuko Terasawa, "Labor Law, Civil Law, Immigration Law and the Reality of Migrants and Their Children," in Mike Douglas and Glenda S. Roberts, eds, *Japan and Global Migration: Foreign Workers and the Advent of a Multicultural Society*, Honolulu: University of Hawaii Press, 2003, pp. 224–227.

48 Liao, "The Petroleum Factor in Sino–Japanese Relations."

6 Taiwan's response to the rise of China

Denny Roy

The "Rise of China" refers to increased capabilities. Equally important are China's intentions, or the ways Chinese leaders choose to employ their growing capabilities. Taiwan and other Asia-Pacific states are reacting not merely to the rise of China, but to the policies of the People's Republic of China (PRC) accompanying that rise. Beijing well understands that the increase in PRC capabilities still leaves open a number of possibilities in China's relationships with the region ranging from amicable cooperation to cold war. This explains why Chinese officials have assiduously worked to persuade other Asian states that there is no need for them to form a defensive coalition against a rising China. Thus, Taiwan's reaction to the rise of China is highly contextualized, and the degree to which policy decisions in Beijing shape Taiwan's behavior should be recognized. China's capacity to build hundreds of short-range ballistic missiles creates a certain security environment for Taiwan, but this capacity combined with the policies of aiming the missiles at Taiwan and asserting the right to use force against the island creates a far more threatening environment. The same "rising" Chinese military, political, and economic capabilities combined with a relaxed and conciliatory PRC cross-Strait policy would constitute quite a different security environment, eliciting correspondingly different reactions from Taiwan. It is important to understand that the question of Asia-Pacific reactions to the rise of China involves not simply decisions by regional governments in relation to a growing but implicitly passive PRC. Rather, along a dimension separate from and in addition to its growing capabilities, Beijing actively shapes the environment in which regional governments make their decisions, and therefore bears part of the responsibility for the character of those decisions.

China as a strategic problem for Taiwan

The iterative interaction of policymaking between Beijing and neighboring governments is particularly clear in the case of Taiwan. No other country in Asia currently faces such bellicosity from Beijing, which is generally seeking to reduce tensions with all of its other neighbors and to promote a peaceful, non-threatening image in the wider Asia-Pacific region. China's position is that Taiwan is destined to be a province of the People's Republic of China, and that the status quo of a de facto independent Taiwan must eventually yield to China's claim of ownership. The Chinese argue that since the Taiwan question is an internal matter, Beijing's relationship with Taipei is outside the principles of China's relations with sovereign foreign governments. The PRC's diplomacy with its other neighbors usually features efforts to reduce tensions, shelve difficult disputes, and engage in multilateral dialogue. In contrast, the PRC's approach to Taiwan includes a standing threat to use force if necessary to keep the Taipei government from formally separating the island from China. Based on the capabilities the People's Liberation Army (PLA) has or is acquiring, an attack on Taiwan might take the form of a missile bombardment or blockade intended to force Taipei to renounce a declaration of independence. Alternatively, the PLA could attempt to invade, seize control of the organs of government, and replace the regime in Taipei. On several occasions this decade China has conducted war games on and around Dongshan Island, which lies off the coast of Fujian province directly across the Strait from Taiwan. Lest anyone miss the point, PRC media reported that the purpose of the Dongshan exercises "is to declare to the 'Independence' elements, should they remain impenitent and dare to disintegrate the country someday, the PLA is capable and confident in settling the Taiwan Issue by military forces."[1] Chinese research vessels, which Taiwan suspects are engaged in collecting signals intelligence and other military-relevant information, have frequently sailed near or into Taiwan's territorial waters, promoting the Republic of China (ROC) to dispatch naval or coast guard vessels to escort or chase away the Chinese ships.

As with other governments, autonomy and sovereignty are among Taipei's highest values. Beijing's interests are a direct threat to the survival of the Republic of China (ROC) as a state. Accommodating China's wishes would require the extinction of the ROC, the government of which found an offshore haven on Taiwan in 1949 as the mainland fell to Chinese Communist Party forces. The PRC threat to Taiwan goes beyond state security. It is also a national security threat for those residents of Taiwan who see themselves as part of a distinct "Taiwanese" nation. The Chinese government views Taiwan's people as part of the Chinese nation and would erase this distinction. China is also a threat to Taipei's regime security. At minimum, absorption by China would force a downgrade in the status of Taiwan's rulers from national leaders to provincial leaders. Some, particularly those branded as "separatists" or worse, would be at risk of losing their positions entirely if China had its say. Finally, China threatens human security on Taiwan in a lesser and indirect way by restricting Taiwan's opportunities to participate in international activities and in a major and direct way by maintaining the potential for military attacks against Taiwan. Even peaceful unification of Taiwan with the much less economically and politically advanced PRC could endanger the well-being of Taiwan's people through mismanagement and the revocation of civil liberties.

The PRC has welcomed cross-Strait trade as a means of eroding Taiwan's resistance to unification. The PRC gives business people from Taiwan preferential treatment and tolerates a trade surplus in Taiwan's favor. Beijing hopes the Taiwanese brought to China by business opportunities will lose their distrust and negative misconceptions of China and become a constituency in Taiwan for seeking peace with Beijing. Taiwan's government has long worried that economic dependence on its large neighbor would give Beijing additional weapons to wield in an attempt to force unification on PRC terms (by denying Taiwan crucial supplies, nationalizing Taiwan-owned assets on the mainland, or even holding Taiwan citizens in China as hostages). For decades Taipei has fought a losing battle with its own people in its attempts to limit cross-Strait trade, gradually and grudgingly removing the restrictions while encouraging Taiwanese to diversify their business to countries other than China.

Beijing strives to isolate Taiwan internationally, rejecting notions of making the cross-Strait dispute a subject of multilateral security discussions, fighting to minimize the number of states that diplomatically recognize Taiwan, and demanding that the international community makes no gestures that imply Taiwan is a state. This has costs to Taiwan beyond affronts to Taiwanese pride and additional inconvenience when they travel abroad. When a serious earthquake struck Taiwan in 1999, groups from several countries quickly organized assistance, only to confront a demand from the PRC chapter of the Red Cross that all those outside Taiwan offering help must obtain advance permission from Beijing. After Taiwan became one of the hubs of the SARS outbreak of 2002–2003, China opposed direct collaboration between the World Health Organization and Taiwan's health authorities. Taiwan understandably sees China's cross-Strait policy as hostile, notwithstanding the positive inducements that are also a part of Beijing's approach.

Beijing typically requires that any country seeking normal diplomatic relations with China should first affirm the "one-China principle" and sever official ties with Taiwan. China's rising economic and political power gives it insuperable advantages over Taiwan in this zero-sum contest. Beijing offers financial assistance, technical advice, attractive trade agreements, and even arms sales as incentives for foreign governments to recognize Beijing rather than Taipei. By 2007 the number of countries officially recognizing Taiwan was down to 25, comprised mostly of small, poor states in Latin America, Africa and the Pacific isles. China pressures countries with which it has diplomatic relations not to host visits by high-ranking ROC officials (generally cabinet-level and above). Beijing, for example, recalled its ambassador when the United States allowed the visit of ROC President Lee Teng-hui in 1995. In subsequent visits to the United States by Lee's successor Chen Shui-bian, the US government has restricted his itinerary. When ROC Vice-President Annette Lu made a surprise visit to Indonesia in 2002, Beijing warned that diplomatic relations between the two countries were in jeopardy and Jakarta insisted Lu's visit was not officially planned or sponsored. Chinese opposition to such visits does not necessarily end when high-ranking Taiwan political figures leave office and become private citizens. Beijing also formally protested the three visits of ex-President Lee to Japan. In 1997 Beijing went so far as to veto a United Nations proposal to send peacekeepers to monitor a cease-fire in Guatemala because that country maintained diplomatic relations with the Republic of China. The PRC also generally opposes membership for Taiwan in international organizations. China has relented in some cases. It has agreed to Taiwan's participation in the Olympic Games and the World Trade Organization only under awkward names that suggest Taiwan is not a sovereign country: respectively, "Chinese Taipei" and "Separate Customs Territory of Taiwan, Penghu, Kinmen and Matsu." Beijing, nevertheless, continues to oppose Taiwan's membership in the World Health Organization despite the international community's obvious interest in extending the global health-management regime to cover a populous area that is close to southern China. Cases such as this highlight the risk to China of counter-productivity in its policy of isolating Taiwan—that is, international support for Taiwan stemming from sympathy over Beijing's repressive efforts might exceed the damage to Chinese interests caused by Taiwan joining an international organization.

Arms sales is another area where Beijing seeks to limit Taiwan's international opportunities, but here there is a strategic rationale to go along with the political symbolism. The Netherlands sold two modern submarines to Taiwan in 1982. In retaliation, Beijing downgraded its diplomatic relations with Amsterdam. The Dutch thereafter ceased selling arms to Taiwan. Under heavy Chinese pressure, France agreed to stop new arms deals with Taiwan after 1994.

Tactical adjustments in China's Taiwan policy

While the basic principles have been consistent, the tenor of the PRC's policy toward Taiwan has shifted in recent years, largely due to feedback from both Taiwan and the United States. Beijing's attempts to employ open military coercion to influence politics in Taiwan have been at best unsuccessful, if not counter-productive. The PLA missile exercises and other military maneuvers conducted in 1995–1996, a reaction to Lee's efforts to expand Taiwan's "international space" and particularly his invitation to visit the United States and speak at his alma mater Cornell University in June 1995, apparently led to Lee's re-election by an even wider margin in the ROC presidential election of March 1996. The missile firings also elicited a strong gesture of military support for Taiwan from the United States, which sent two aircraft carrier battle groups to the waters near Taiwan during this third Taiwan Strait Crisis, and gave impetus to a strengthening of US–Japan defense ties. A similar but less militarized attempt at coercive diplomacy occurred in conjunction with Taiwan's 2000 presidential election, when PRC Premier Zhu Rongji gave a stern public warning implying great peril if Taiwan's people elected Chen Shui-bian. Chen, Beijing's least-preferred of the major candidates, won anyway. These actions also played poorly internationally. Threats against Taiwan intensified criticism of China within the United States and became an obstacle to improved bilateral relations. They also contrasted sharply with China's attempts to reassure its other Asian neighbors that a stronger China would be peaceful and conciliatory. The inescapable lesson of these events was that Beijing needed a less adversarial means of combating what the Chinese viewed as Taiwan's drift toward formal independence. A change in the PRC's approach to Taiwan was visible after the Chinese Communist Party's Sixteenth National Congress in 2002. Beijing placed greater reliance on the hope that sustained, long-term economic and social interaction would lead to unification, obviating the need for political or military pressure.[2]

At the end of the 1990s, the Chinese leadership had concluded that their goals for economic development in the twenty-first century depended on maintaining a constructive working relationship with the United States. The incoming George W. Bush Administration seemed prepared to downgrade that relationship. The Chinese therefore made a persistent effort to assure Washington that China would not actively oppose American alliances and military bases in the Asia-Pacific region. After the temporary and unplanned setback of the aircraft collision and detention of the American flight crew on Hainan Island in April 2001,[3] Sino–US relations attained a strength that far surpassed the expectations set by the Bush team's campaign rhetoric. This was reflected in US policy toward Taiwan. President Bush began his first term with what appeared to be a shift toward stronger support for Taiwan, manifest in his pledge to do "whatever it takes" to defend the island in the event of PLA attack and his administration's offer of a strong arms sale package that included advanced submarines. In late 2003, however, Bush stood next to Chinese Premier Wen Jiabao and rebuked Chen, saying, "the comments and actions made by the leader of Taiwan indicate that he may be willing to make decisions unilaterally to change the status quo, which we oppose."[4] Beijing had secured the assistance of Taiwan's most important ally, the United States, in preventing Taiwan independence. This was vastly preferable from China's point of view: it was more likely to be effective, it was a step toward reversing what the Chinese viewed as the serious problem of US support for the "Taiwan authorities," it broadened the common ground in the US–China relationship, and it spared China the costs of playing the role of bully.

Balancing and bandwagoning

Smaller states facing the rise of a potential hegemon in their region have an array of policy options.[5] Given Taiwan's particular circumstances and current political and economic conditions in the Asia-Pacific region, two clear strategic choices that form a useful conceptual basis for analyzing Taiwan's China policy are balancing and bandwagoning.

Balancing refers to a state making efforts to strengthen itself against a potential adversary either by shifting internal resources toward this purpose (internal balancing) or by cooperating with another, less-threatening state that also fears the same potential adversary (external balancing). Balancing can vary in intensity. High intensity balancing involves a large commitment of resources toward military capabilities and relatively deep security cooperation with a partner state or states. Typically the highest level of security cooperation is formalized in a treaty. In such a case the perceived threat is dire and imminent. The relationship with the threatening state has deteriorated to the point where the balancing state is beyond concern that it might pay additional costs by alarming or offending its potential adversary. By contrast, in the case of low intensity balancing, the danger is not perceived to be imminent; fewer resources need be involved; cooperation might be minor, indirect, and without a formal defense agreement; and the balancers might simultaneously attempt to maintain favorable relations with the targeted state, including offering assurances to control or offset the political damage caused by the balancing behavior. At this stage the argument "If you treat China as an enemy, China will become an enemy," and its implied corollary might apply.[6]

"Bandwagoning" is a somewhat problematic concept. The term has at least two distinct meanings in the international relations literature. The first definition refers to the strictly security-oriented phenomenon of aligning with a threatening country to avoid being attacked by it.[7] This usage is similar to what some international relations theorists call "binding." If Taiwan joins with the PRC, for the sacrifice of a degree of its autonomy and the unfulfillment of the aspirations of Taiwanese nationalism, it stands to gain the removal of what is now its greatest security threat. This is the essence of bandwagoning as a security policy.

The second meaning of the term places it in an economic context: this is Randall Schweller's idea of "bandwagoning for profit," in which a country sees an "opportunity for [economic] gain" by "being on the winning side."[8] In this variant, bandwagoning means seeking a favorable relationship with a state (through, for example, granting a political concession such as diplomatic support) in order to gain the benefits of economic cooperation with that state. In the first case, the bandwagoning country perceives a dire threat and is motivated by its desire to survive. In the second case, the threat of attack may be low or non-existent and the motive for bandwagoning is greed. Some scholars have accepted the second variant, equating bandwagoning with a desire to trade with China.[9] In my view, however, bandwagoning should not be defined by heavy economic interaction. Such an approach strips the term of much of its relevance to a strategic analysis—relevance retained by the alternative definition of bandwagoning-for-security. Amitav Acharya points out correctly that economic cooperation with China does not imply, nor is it predicated upon, political alignment.[10] An economic relationship, even a robust one, does not constitute trust, submission, or assent to another state's security policies. Rather, it indicates that a government has concluded it is better off pursuing rather than avoiding opportunities for trade and investment with another state, or that the government cannot stand up to societal demands (which may be strategically short-sighted) for unrestrained international commerce. Strong trading relationships can coexist with substantial political tensions and do not necessarily prevent military conflict. Interest in increased bilateral trade and investment is in some cases an expression of strategic hostility, as a state uses economic penetration as a means of influencing a rival government. The familiar argument that liberal capitalist states can most efficiently subvert communist states through trade is illustrative.

Up to now I have discussed balancing and bandwagoning as general security policy options. Each of these security policy choices implies a particular supporting political and economic strategy. Assuming national policies are coherent and coordinated, a smaller state opting for a security policy of balancing would likely augment this strategy by attempting to discourage the international community from granting the rising state further prestige or influence. In its trade and investment with the rising power, the smaller state would seek to avoid economic cooperation that created vulnerabilities that could be exploited by its potential adversary or that abetted the rising state's relative strength in important capabilities. In stark contrast, a bandwagoning state would act as a cheerleader for the rising state in international discussions, supporting its agenda and leadership role. The counterpart of a bandwagoning security policy is, of course, "bandwagoning for profit." The smaller state would enthusiastically seek economic cooperation with the rising power, believing that the benefits outweigh concerns about vulnerability or relative gains.

Admittedly, these are simple conceptual archetypes. Foreign policymaking in the real world invariably involves mixtures and even contradictions. Nevertheless, these terms provide some useful touchstones for the analysis that will follow.

What about the oft-used term "hedging"?[11] It is not unusual for governments to pursue elements of more than one strategy concurrently toward a particular state. A common example is low-intensity balancing against a state while maintaining a healthy trade relationship with that state. This is where the hedging strategy becomes pertinent. As it is frequently used in the international relations literature, hedging applies when policymakers believe that a target state might pose a threat in the future, but also that a good relationship with the target state offers security and/or economic benefits today (or reduces the costs that a poor relationship would entail). Therefore the hedging state strives to prepare or maintain a channel for external defense assistance in case it proves necessary later, while in the meantime trying not to alienate the target state. The hedging state will likely make its efforts to maintain an insurance policy as discreet as possible and will attempt to offset these moves through cooperative signals toward the target state. Despite its popularity among analysts, especially in discussions of Asia's reaction to China, hedging is an imprecise and sometimes obfuscating term. In some sense, virtually every state that trades with and accords some respect to China but also has potential political or security concerns about China could be said to be hedging. This covers most countries in the Asia-Pacific region. I argue that Taiwan's cross-Strait policy may be best understood not as hedging in the sense of a government decision to prepare for two diverse but unpredictable contingencies, but rather as a result of a struggle between competing approaches in which each of two sides of a divided government has forced part of its package of preferences upon the other.

Simply put, Taiwan's cross-Strait policy is contested between the pan-Blue and the pan-Green factions, which have dramatically different views of China and of the Taiwan–China relationship. The pan-Blue believes Taiwan is part of China and should ultimately politically unite with the mainland. China's control by the Chinese Communist Party, the historical nemesis of the Kuomintang (KMT) (or Chinese Nationalist Party), complicates the situation. Viewing themselves as part of the Chinese nation, the Blues can cheer the rise of China. They can also sympathize with China's insistence on the eventual return of Taiwan to its former status as a Chinese province, and they see the Chinese "threat" largely as a response to Taiwan independence activities, which they join Beijing in opposing. Pan-Blue politicians and officials therefore tend to favor cross-Strait policies that will assure China (such as professing the one-China principle) and to avoid those that will antagonize China (such as "de-Sinification," acts hinting at formal independence, and building an offensive missile capability). They are also comparatively welcoming of a deeper cross-Strait economic relationship. These policy preferences could be considered bandwagoning. By contrast, the pan-Green camp is willing to risk offending China by identifying it as an enemy and by challenging what the Chinese have identified as one of their vital interests (ownership of Taiwan). Rather than accommodating China, the governments of both Lee Teng-hui (who ruled as a Kuomintang member, but in retirement has been identified with the pan-Green) and Chen Shui-bian tried to force Beijing to retreat from its claim over Taiwan. They also tried to marshal international support for resisting the PRC's military pressure. Taipei has worked assiduously to maintain a friendly relationship with the United States, upon which Taiwan relies to deter overt Chinese moves to gain dominance over the island. These actions are consistent with balancing behavior.

With a strong pan-Blue position in the legislature and a pan-Green executive, Taiwan's response to the rise of China during this decade has been primarily balancing mixed with elements of bandwagoning, an iron-and-clay policy reflecting the deep division in Taiwan's domestic politics.

Hard and soft balancing

Much of Taiwan's behavior vis-à-vis China is classic external balancing. In contrast to some other governments in Asia, Taiwan does not publicly deny that it considers China a threat or that its relationship with the United States is intended to counter China. On the contrary, high-ranking government officials routinely describe the PRC in adversarial terms, calling it, for example, an "aggressor" and a "trouble-making bully" that employs "terrorism" against Taiwan.[12] Although Taiwan's military stresses the need for self-reliance, analysts widely acknowledge that the island's objective in the event of a PLA attack will be to hold out until assistance arrives from the United States.[13]

To compensate for the PRC's huge numerical advantages in manpower and weapons systems, Taiwan relies heavily on arms sales from the USA.

Attempting to cultivate support from the international community could be viewed as a form of "soft" balancing.[14] Despite its disadvantages vis-à-vis China in the contest for diplomatic recognition, Taiwan tries to maintain its small stable of normal diplomatic partners and to enlarge it where possible. Since the early 1990s Taipei has sought unsuccessfully to rejoin the United Nations General Assembly (the ROC withdrew from the UN in 1971 when it was clear the organization was about to expel the ROC and give the "China" seat to Beijing). Says ROC Minister of Foreign Affairs James Huang:

> Suppose Taiwan had no diplomatic ties at all. That would justify what China has been saying: Taiwan isn't a sovereign, independent state, it's just a local government. . . . Eventually they [China] can say . . . "[n]obody recognizes you [Taiwan], how can you [Taiwan] call yourself a country?"[15]

These efforts to keep and win diplomatic allies often prompt charges of "dollar diplomacy"—a charge that also applies to China. In April 2007, Taiwan scored a minor success in the decision of the Caribbean island country of St. Lucia to switch diplomatic recognition from Beijing to Taipei, reversing the move St. Lucia's government made in 1997. St. Lucia's Foreign Minister Rufus Bousquet candidly said his country's policy is to "Support those who give you the most."[16] China was building the island a sports stadium and a mental hospital, but Taiwan countered with a sustainable development strategy, sharing its agricultural expertise and promising to help develop St. Lucia's agricultural, tourism, and information technology industries.

Chen has repeated countless times that "democracy is Taiwan's best defense." By this he appears to mean, at least in part, that a favorable image of Taiwan as a democratic country will increase the likelihood that the international community will stand up in defense of Taiwan in the event of a cross-Strait crisis. The Taiwan Foundation for Democracy, founded in 2003 and connected with Taiwan's Ministry of Foreign Affairs, styles itself as a supporter of democratization and human rights in Asia. Vice President Annette Lu's Democratic Pacific Union, founded in 2005, aims to deepen the informal ideological links between Taiwan and democratic states in the Asia-Pacific region. Chen has often expressed interest in strengthening Taiwan's relationship with Japan, a particularly sensitive and alarming issue for Beijing. Chen said in 2006, for example, "In the absence of formal diplomatic relations between Taiwan and Japan . . . Japan and Taiwan can surely form an excellent quasi-security-alliance relationship."[17]

Going on the offensive

The interest in an offensive missile capability appears to be the latest manifestation of a long search by strategists on Taiwan for an affordable way to deter the threat of a PRC military attack. This search led Taiwan to dabble in the development of nuclear weapons in the 1970s and 1980s, invoking strong US opposition. Once the developmental costs were paid, nuclear weapons would have been a relatively cheap (although not necessarily successful) answer to the problem of deterring China. Beginning in the 1990s, China's growing short-range conventional missile arsenal added another dimension to this problem. Referring to China's missiles, a Taiwan government official said bluntly, "Relying on purely defensive systems to protect ourselves from China means we will have to outspend them 10 to 1. . . . That is impossible in the long run."[18] For several years Chen's government hinted at its interest in deploying a conventionally armed missile force of its own to deter China's. Premier Yu Shyi-kun said in 2004 that Taiwan would be more secure if it achieved a "balance of terror" with China such as existed between the United States and the Soviet Union during the Cold War. Touting the deterrence value of an offensive capability, Yu said, "If you [China] fire[s] 100 missiles at me [Taiwan], I [Taiwan] should also be able to fire 100 missiles at you [China], or at least 50. If you [China] attack[s] Taipei and Kaohsiung, I [Taiwan] should at least be able to strike Shanghai."[19] In April 2007, Taiwan's Defense Minister Lee Jye publicly confirmed that Taiwan is developing missiles with a range of up to 1,000 km that could strike PLA missile bases inside mainland China.[20] American Institute in Taiwan Director Stephen Young quickly expressed US disapproval, saying, "The US view is that the focus should be on defensive weapons, not on offensive weapons."[21]

More external than internal balancing?

On one hand, Chen's government has appeared highly acceptant of the risks of provoking China. On the other hand, Taiwan has maintained relatively low levels of defense spending. In 2006, the ROC defense budget was only 2.2 percent of GDP, a strikingly small amount for a country facing such a concrete military threat.[22] Between 2000 and 2008, the Taiwan military cut the period of compulsory military service for its young men from 24 months to 12 months. Such statistics fed into a perception among some observers that Taiwan is not willing to pay the price of maintaining its autonomy from China. This perception became a problem in Taiwan–US relations with the debate surrounding the proposed US arms sale. In 2001 Washington offered Taipei an extraordinarily large arms package that included Patriot PAC-3 anti-missile batteries, P-3 Orion anti-submarine aircraft, and diesel submarines. Many US officials saw this as a generous offer that would help rectify years of unmet requests from Taiwan. The Americans were surprised, however, to see that the proposed arms deal became highly controversial in Taiwan. The Legislative Yuan's refusal to allocate funding to buy the weapons fueled a perception in the United States that Taiwan was free-riding on defense. In a February 2003 speech attended by ROC officials, Deputy Assistant Defense Secretary Richard Lawless said Taiwan "should not view America's resolute commitment to peace and stability in the Taiwan Strait as a substitute for investing the necessary resources in its own defense."[23] As the delay dragged into mid 2007, American Institute in Taiwan Director Stephen Young said, "We believe that Taiwan is not responding appropriately to the steady build-up of military across the Taiwan Strait," which "unfortunately also causes Taiwan's friend the United States to question whether our security partner here is serious about maintaining capable defense."[24]

Opponents of the arms sale in Taiwan have raised several arguments to explain their position. They assert that the Patriot PAC-3 anti-missile system on offer is an inadequate defense against the PLA ballistic missiles threatening Taiwan. The Patriots thus have more psychological than military value, acting as an assurance to Taiwan's people that their island is not defenseless against China's missiles. Critics say this limited utility does not justify purchasing the Patriot batteries. Opponents have complained that the weapons package is overpriced and amounts to a demand by the United States for "protection money." They have also argued that the systems offered by the US government are not necessarily the highest-priority items desired by Taiwan's defense officials, and that paying for the arms package would take too much funding away from more urgent domestic economic and social needs. These points serve as justifications for one of what may be the two most important reasons for the deadlock: the opposition pan-Blue sees in the proposed arms deal another opportunity to stymie Chen's government, which favors buying the weapons. The second of these most important factors is that Taiwan is not interested in challenging China to an arms race. This sentiment is bipartisan. Ma Ying-jeou, the Kuomintang candidate for the 2008 presidential election, has said, "We cannot depend on an arms race to maintain the peace. We have to establish a mechanism of mutual trust."[25] From the Green camp, Chen has promised "We will certainly not engage in an arms race with China."[26] Chen's support for moving ahead with the proposed arms deal may be based on a belief that the weapons package carries the political value of cementing US–Taiwan ties. Thus, the inaction on the arms sale proposed in 2001 appears to reflect not only the division in Taiwan between balancers and bandwagoners, but also shows the limits on the resources Taiwan is presently willing to devote to strengthening itself against China.

Distancing Taiwan from China

The political side of Chen's cross-Strait policy has involved distancing Taiwan from China, refusing to accept the Beijing government's notions of sovereignty over Taiwan or a superior status to the Taipei government, and attempting to reduce the military threat from China. Much of this policy could be considered akin to internal balancing, in the sense of mobilizing Taiwan's public for resistance to China's goal of unification. At minimum, Chen's policy could be called anti-bandwagoning. Chen has said publicly that "Taiwan is an independent country" and "Taiwan is an independent, sovereign country."[27]

His government has made a series of gestures with the common theme of distancing Taiwan from China. These include adding the word "Taiwan" to ROC passports; changing the logo of the Government Information Office to remove the map of China; revising secondary school textbooks to distinguish Chinese history from that of Taiwan; highlighting the culture of Taiwan's (non-Chinese) aboriginal peoples; renaming state-owned enterprises to replace the word "China" with "Taiwan"; announcing in 2006 that the National Unification Council had "ceased to function" and the Guidelines for National Unification "ceased to apply" (despite Chen promising in his 2000 inaugural address that he would not abolish the Council or the Guidelines); and attempting in 2007 to join the United Nations and the World Health Organization under the name "Taiwan." Each of these acts irritated China, but none was large or dramatic enough to trigger PRC military action. Instead there was a political reaction. The Chinese leadership appears to have written off working with Chen, absent a dramatic concession on his part, by 2001. The reaction in the United States was also negative. Chen pushed his agenda to the extent of annoying Taiwan's powerful friend.

Chen has continually expressed a desire for talks with China, but only under terms that implied a degree of status and flexibility for Taiwan that China was not willing to accept. Certainly for domestic political reasons and presumably for strategic reasons as well, Chen's government has sought to lower tensions across the Strait. Chen proposed, for example, that the two sides explore possibilities for arms control, confidence-building measures and a "code of conduct." He made several minor overtures that PRC officials ignored or rebuffed. An example was the statement in his December 31, 2000, New Year's address that "The integration of our economies, trade, and culture can be a starting point for . . . political integration," for which Chen drew criticism from some in his party.[28] Some of Chen's policies and statements that Beijing considered provocative were evidently expressions of frustration by Chen that the Chinese had not reacted positively to his proposals for improving cross-Strait relations. In May 2002, for example, Chen suggested private groups could carry out the negotiations over furthering the "three links," in accordance with a suggestion earlier floated by PRC Vice-Premier Qian Qichen. This was a concession on Chen's part, as previously he had insisted that the semi-official Straits Exchange Foundation should handle such negotiations on behalf of Taiwan. Beijing did not immediately respond to this offer by Chen, but a few weeks afterward announced the humiliating news that the government of Nauru was switching diplomatic recognition from Taipei to Beijing.

Early in his presidency, Chen said he could accept the "92 consensus" (i.e. the one-China principle with "China" not necessarily equated with the PRC), but under pressure from Green hardliners he soon moved toward a position that "one China" could not be a precondition of cross-Strait negotiations. Since Beijing was also willing to resume semi-official talks under the "92 consensus," it appears that the two sides were momentarily close to agreement, but the moment quickly passed. Thereafter Chen held to a position of ruling out neither independence nor unification as Taiwan's ultimate destiny (displeasing both Beijing and some independence advocates within his own party), and there was never a serious possibility of cross-Strait talks during his presidency. Later in his presidency, Chen, along with others in the pan-Green camp, took the position that there had in fact been no "consensus" on the one-China principle between the two sides in 1992, and that the only understanding was that the basis for cross-Strait talks would be equality and mutual respect.

Taipei's determination to avoid making compromises in certain areas as well as the tendency of all cross-Strait interaction to fall into the context of the sovereignty dispute between Taiwan and China are exemplified by Beijing's 2005 offer of two free pandas for Taiwan's zoos. This seemingly harmless gesture drew fire from critics in Taiwan who complained that it was a propaganda ploy by China, using the cute animals as goodwill ambassadors to divert attention from the Chinese missiles aimed at Taiwan. Furthermore, China argued that the panda gift was allowable under the Convention on International Trade in Endangered Species because it was a domestic rather than an international transfer. This meant that by accepting the gift Taiwan might implicitly acknowledge that it was part of China. In March 2006, Taipei rejected the pandas.

The dynamic between Chen's government and the Taiwanese public is an important factor in the shaping of Taiwan's cross-Strait policy. PRC analysts have frequently charged that Chen's "separatism" is unrepresentative of mainstream public opinion on the island or that Taiwanese nationalism results from Chen using his powerful political position to promote independence. Other analysts, however, see Chen as a moderate who is sometimes pushed by "dark Green" (pro-independence) elements to take hard-line anti-China positions.[29] In any case, one must take Taiwan society seriously as a player in the making of Taipei's policy toward China. In September 2003, for example, tens of thousands led by former President Lee marched in Taipei to demand that the ROC change its official name to Taiwan. The following day another 10,000 people participated in a rally against Taiwan independence. With China as an important (though often not the dominant) issue in Taiwan's electoral politics, Taipei's cross-Strait policies must be evaluated with the presumption that the intended audience may be inside Taiwan as much as across the Strait.

Although Taiwan's 2003 referendum law is largely an outgrowth of domestic politics, the context of a military threat from China shaped it and assisted in its passage. The law generally allows only the public or the legislature to initiate a referendum, but allows for the president to submit a "defensive referendum" if "the nation is threatened by an external force that could cause a change in the nation's sovereignty." The PRC certainly viewed Taiwan's referendum law as anti-China. "Clearly, the so-called 'referendum legislation' is just a step of the 'gradual independence' conspiracy," said a PRC government commentary.[30] Chen seemed at least as interested in the act of offering a referendum itself as he was in the content of the referendum. Originally he announced that the first referendum would ask if Taiwan's people believed the ROC should be allowed to join the World Health Organization. Since it was already clear how Taiwan's people felt about this issue, Taipei was already seeking WHO membership, and in any case the decision on Taiwan's membership was not in Taiwan's hands, there was little point to asking this question other than motivating Green-leaning voters and setting a precedent for employing the referendum mechanism. Arguing that the PRC missiles aimed at Taiwan fulfilled the criteria for a "defensive referendum," Chen invoked this loophole to present the voters with two re-worked referenda as part of the 2004 presidential election. The first question asked if Taiwan should acquire anti-missile defenses if PRC missiles continued to threaten the island. The second question asked if Taipei should negotiate a "peace and stability framework" with China. That the referenda were as much acts of Taiwan domestic politics as cross-Strait politics is evident from the fact that the opposition pan-Blue called on voters to boycott the referenda. Critics said the referenda were both illegal and unnecessary. The questions themselves were not controversial, each getting more than 90 percent affirmative votes, but both referenda failed because only about 45 percent of Taiwan's eligible voters cast ballots. The law stipulated that the passage of a referendum required the support of a majority of Taiwan's eligible voters.

Despite being weakened by a largely hostile legislature and later a corruption scandal during his second term, Chen refused to let Beijing relax. In April 2006 he asserted that the "four no's and one not" from his inaugural speech "were conditional upon China's having no intention to use military force against Taiwan. The situation has now changed" because of the growing number of PRC missiles aimed at Taiwan, he said.[31] In March 2007 he declared that "Taiwan wants independence, wants name rectification, [and] wants a new constitution."[32] "Name rectification" refers to using "Taiwan" rather than "Republic of China," and a "new" (as opposed to "revised") constitution implies an overhaul that might include changes to the passages that now formally acknowledge China as the mother country. These acts served both Chen's domestic and cross-Strait agenda. Domestically, they pleased and energized his dark Green supporters. These gestures also reiterated the distinction between Taiwan and China, part of Chen's campaign to force China to accept that Taiwan might choose a destiny other than unification.

Bandwagoning and the united front

The term "united front" dates back to attempts last century by the Kuomintang and Chinese Communist Party to temporarily lay aside their differences and cooperate against a common enemy (warlords in the 1920s and the Japanese in the 1930s and 1940s). Targets for recruitment into the united front today have been Taiwan politicians and business people. Originally Beijing reached out to pan-Blue politicians sympathetic to the one-China principle. More recently Beijing has also welcomed Democratic Progress Party (DPP) politicians who are willing to distance themselves from the independence platform in the DPP charter. Not surprisingly, pan-Green activists are quick to condemn Taiwan citizens who appear to be coordinating political activities with PRC officials as collaborators with the enemy.

In 2005 two of Taiwan's leading pan-Blue political figures, KMT Chairman Lien Chan and People's First Party Chairman James Soong, made separate high-profile visits to mainland China that included meetings with Chinese President Hu Jintao. Both Lien and Soong used these events to reaffirm the one-China principle and call attention to Taiwan's Chinese heritage. Chen initially criticized the visits, but reversed his position in light of public opinion polls showing most of the Taiwan public supported Lien and Soong going to China.

Lien's joint communiqué with Hu agreed that the two sides should "trust and help each other . . . so as to bring about brilliant and splendid prospects for the Chinese nation" as well as "[p]romote the unfolding of all-round cross-strait economic cooperation and establish close economic and trade cooperation ties."[33] In addition to affirming the one-China principle and condemning Taiwan independence, Soong said during his visit to the PRC that he saw China as the "workshop of the world and market for the prosperity of our world." He added, "I hope the people on both sides of the Strait will join hands, link each other heart to heart and work together to bring more glory to the Chinese nation in the twenty-first century."[34]

During several speeches in 2006 Ma Ying-jeou of KMT explained that his proposed cross-Strait policy, which he called the "five wants," included a resumption of talks, expanded economic ties including a common market, a peace agreement including provision for confidence-building measures, and more cultural exchanges.

The sentiments expressed by these pan-Blue leaders—a sense of a shared destiny with China and the willingness to bind themselves more closely with the rising regional power—are consistent with bandwagoning.

Cross-Strait economic integration

Taiwan's business community has long practiced the kind of economic band-wagoning with China (in the sense of a willingness to trade and to tolerate the consequent vulnerabilities) now seen throughout the Asia-Pacific region. If the "rise of China" became apparent by the early 1990s, this realization produced no reversal in the trend of rapidly growing Taiwan–PRC trade ties. Between 1991 and 2002, bilateral trade grew from $8.1 billion to $39.6 billion.[35] It has continued to expand since then, reaching $100 billion in 2006. The total value of Taiwan investment in China is estimated at between $100 and $150 billion.[36] China is Taiwan's largest trade partner.

Some analysts in Taiwan, and particularly the governments of both Lee and Chen, have continually warned of the risks of deepening economic interdependence with China and argued that the benefits to individual Taiwan firms often do not meet expectations. Lee's cross-Strait economic policy was known as "no haste, be patient" (*jieji yongren*). The purported dangers of trade with and investment in China are both economic and strategic. The economic danger is that the flight of Taiwan firms to China, where they can find lower labor and overhead costs, is resulting in the "hollowing out" and eventual loss of competitiveness of Taiwan's industrial base. Relocation of Taiwan business to China also speeds China's acquisition of advanced technology and managerial expertise, hastening the day when the Chinese will take over Taiwan's few remaining niches in the international economy. Strategically, Taiwan fears its increasing economic dependence on the PRC could eventually position Beijing to use economic leverage as a means of forcing Taipei to make political concessions such as agreeing to unification on China's terms.

An episode involving Hsu Wen-long, founder of Taiwan's giant petrochemical Chi Mei Corporation and long-term supporter of Taiwan independence and of Chen Shui-bian, clearly illustrated the kind of scenario feared by those in Taiwan who advocate caution in economic engagement with the mainland. Planning a large expansion into the Chinese market, Hsu found himself singled out for criticism by the Chinese media in mid-2004 as a Taiwan separatist. In March 2005, a Taiwan newspaper published a letter by Hsu in which he voiced support for the one-China principle, warned that Taiwan independence would lead to disaster, and put a positive spin on China's Anti-Secession Law. Hsu's recantation shocked Taiwan. Hsu later said he felt compelled to surrender to Chinese pressure out of concern for the welfare of his company's 20,000 employees.[37] Hsu's accommodation with China represents one possible Taiwanese response to the rise of China and epitomizes the concept of economic bandwagoning.

Chen's core supporters are divided on the question of cross-Strait trade and investment. Many DPP politicians and political activists see economic integration as a trap that can eventually cost Taiwan its autonomy. Much of the pan-Green Taiwanese business community, however, is focused on the potential profits to be made through strengthened economic ties with China, and hopes political disputes will not stand in the way. Chen himself showed an inclination to expand cross-Strait economic interaction as a means of maintaining Taiwan's prosperity within an increasingly competitive global marketplace. Chen also likely believed that progress on the bilateral economic front would strengthen his domestic credentials as a manager of cross-Strait relations. In late 2000, Taipei agreed to the "three mini-links," allowing trade and travel between the Taiwan-administered offshore islands of Jinmen and Matsu and ports on the nearby coast of mainland China. When an Economic Development Advisory Conference (EDAC) attended by a broadly representative group of experts recommended in 2001 that Taiwan's government reduce restrictions on investment in China, move toward opening Taiwan to Chinese investment and tourism, and establish direct trade and transportation with the mainland, Chen strongly supported the Conference's conclusions. This led to the replacement of Lee's "no haste, be patient" policy with a new approach called "active opening, effective management," premised on a more positive view of cross-Strait economic integration and involving a relaxation of restrictions along the lines advocated by the EDAC. In practice, however, Chen's government proceeded cautiously with the "active opening," and in 2006 Chen rephrased the name of the policy as "effective management, active opening," with the emphasis shifted from the first part of the original phrase to the second.

For Taiwan, the rise of China has meant increased pressure to accept the one-China principle and eventual unification. Taipei has generally matched that pressure with increased resistance. Chen Shui-bian has continued the general strategy of his predecessor Lee Teng-hui: attempting to stake out a position that would roll back Chinese constraints and give Taiwan more political freedom of maneuver. Chen has emphasized Taiwan's separation from China and demanded that China allow Taiwan's people to choose their own destiny. He has attempted strategic *jujitsu* toward the PRC military threat, arguing that the Chinese missiles arrayed against Taiwan justify the mechanism of a defensive referendum, and that in the event of a PRC attack he would declare Taiwan independent. The Lee and Chen governments sought to strengthen international support for Taiwan to balance the threat posed by China. Yet Taiwan's response to a rising China also includes elements of bandwagoning. The opposition pan-Blue views China as the mother country rather than the enemy to Taiwan. Blue politicians and officials have fought to position Taiwan for a closer emotional and economic association with China.

As we have seen throughout this discussion, domestic politics has been an inescapably important part of the cross-Strait relationship. Taiwan's politics has been a major driver of Chinese policies. Beijing has condemned Lee Teng-hui as "scum of the nation" and Chen Shui-bian as a "separatist."[38] The positions with regard to China taken by ROC politicians and officials are, in turn, often driven more by tactical electoral political considerations than by a strategic vision for promoting Taiwan's security and prosperity, as the relationship with China casts an ever-present shadow over the island's politics. Because the PRC perceived a heightened threat of Taiwan independence during the last decade, cross-Strait relations rose to a higher priority as a strategic issue than would have been the case if Taipei's executive branch of government was under the control of politicians who were unambiguously committed to the one-China principle and eventual unification. Chinese cross-Strait policy has been shaped by domestic politics not only in Taiwan, but also in China. The Chinese Communist Party leadership had to satisfy their fellow elites and the Chinese public that they were responding with sufficient toughness to what nearly all mainlanders saw as dangerous probing by Lee and Chen. China's March 2005 Anti-Secession Law, for example, stemmed at least partly from a demand inside China for a response to what the Chinese saw as a series of provocations from Taiwan. It seemed to acknowledge Chen's approach, recognizing that "secessionist forces" might act by some "means to cause the fact of Taiwan's secession from China" or that there might occur "major incidents entailing Taiwan's secession from China."

Taiwan's reaction to the rise of China is best seen as part of a continuous cycle of interaction between the two societies, and as a manifestation of the deep political division that runs through Taiwan.

Notes

1 "Three purposes of military maneuver at Dongshan Island," *People's Daily Online*, July 19, 2004, http://English.people.com.cn/200407/19/eng20040719_150106.html, accessed May 3, 2007.

2 Weixing Hu, "The Political-Economic Paradox and Beijing's Strategic Options," in Friedman, ed., *China's Rise, Taiwan's Dilemma and International Peace*, New York: Routledge, 2006, pp. 25, 35.

3 On Apr. 1, 2001, a US Navy EP-3 reconnaissance aircraft collided with a Chinese J-8 fighter aircraft over the South China Sea near Hainan Island. The collision destroyed the Chinese jet and killed its pilot, while the damaged EP-3 made an unauthorized emergency landing at a Chinese military airfield on Hainan Island. The following mutual recriminations created a temporary crisis in US–China relations.

4 CNN, "Bush vows 'whatever it takes' to defend Taiwan," April 25, 2001, http://archives.cnn.com/2001/ALLPOLITICS/04/25/bush.taiwan.03, accessed 12 April 2007; White House press release, "President Bush and Premier Wen Jiabao Remarks to the Press," December 9, 2003, www.whitehouse.gov/news/releases/2003/12/20031209-2.html, accessed April 12, 2007.

5 Randall Schweller, "Managing the Rise of Great Powers: History and Theory," in Alastair Iain Johnston and Robert S. Ross, eds, *Engaging China: The Management of an Emerging Power*, London: Routledge, 1999, pp. 7–16.

6 Joseph Nye, Harvard scholar and former Assistant Secretary of Defense, is usually credited with this formulation. Wu Xinbo, "Bush Should Act Now to Get Ties With Beijing Back on Track," *International Herald Tribune*, July 7, 2001, www.iht.com/articles/2001/07/07/edwu_ed3_.php, accessed May 11, 2007.

7 Stephen M. Walt, *The Origins of Alliances*, Ithaca, NY: Cornell University Press, 1987, p. 17.

8 Randall L. Schweller, "Bandwagoning for Profit: Bringing the Revisionist State Back In," *International Security*, 19(1), Summer 1994, pp. 72–107.

9 For example, although David Kang does not clearly lay out the case for his argument that "Asian states . . . seem to be bandwagoning" with China, he specifically notes "deep economic and cultural ties with China" in the cases of Singapore, Malaysia and Indonesia; that Japan and Taiwan have heavy trade with and investment in China; that "trade and other forms of economic cooperation have developed steadily between China and Vietnam"; and that South Korea and China have seen "rapid development of cultural and economic ties. Kang, "Getting Asia Wrong: The Need for New Analytical Frameworks," *International Security*, 27(4), Spring 2003, pp. 58, 69, 80, 81.

10 Amitav Acharya, "Will Asia's Past Be its Future?" *International Security*, 28(3), Winter 2003–2004, p. 152.

11 On hedging against China, see Evan S. Medeiros, "Strategic Hedging and the Future of Asia-Pacific Stability," *Washington Quarterly* 29(1), Winter 2005–2006, pp. 145–167.

12 The quotations are from, respectively, President Chen Shui-bian, Mainland Affairs Council Chairman Joseph Wu Jauhsieh, and Vice President Annette Lu Hsiu-lien. Huang Tai-lin, "Chen lashes out over China's law," *Taipei Times*,

March 17, 2005, p. 3; Joseph Wu Jauhsieh, "Democracy and peace to answer China's war-authorization law," *Taiwan Perspective*, Institute for National Policy Research, No. 69, March 25, 2005, online at www.tp.org.tw/eletter/story.htm?id=20007276, accessed March 25, 2005; Monique Chu, "Chen warns Asia of Chinese threat," *Taipei Times*, January 18, 2003, p. 1.

13   "US intervention is a realistic expectation, says Swaine," *Taipei Times*, June 4, 2000, p. 3; Reuters News Service, "Taiwan Could Fend Off China Attack for 2 Weeks—Paper," August 12, 2004, online at http://taiwansecurity.org/Reu/2004/Reuters–120804.htm, accessed March 24, 2005.

14   For discussions of the difference between "hard" and "soft" balancing, see Stephen M. Walt, "Keeping the World 'Off Balance,' " in G. John Ikenberry, ed., *America Unrivaled: The Future of the Balance of Power*, Ithaca, NY: Cornell University Press, 2002, pp. 121–154 and T.V. Paul, "The Enduring Axioms of Balance of Power Theory," in Paul, James J. Wirtz, and Michel Fortmann, eds, *Balance of Power Revisited: Theory and Practice in the Twenty-First Century*, Stanford, CA: Stanford University Press, 2004.

15   "Allies vital to survival: minister," *Taipei Times*, May 11, 2007, p. 3.

16   Guy Ellis, "Spurned for Taiwan, China berates St. Lucia," Associated Press, May 2, 2007, www.boston.com/news/world/articles/2007/05/02/spurned_for_taiwan_china_berates_st_lucia, accessed May 23, 2007.

17   ROC Government Information Office, "Excerpts of a Transcript of a Videoconference Question and Answer Session with UN Journalists," September 14, 2006, www.gio.gov.tw/Taiwan-website/4-oa/20060914/2006091401.html, accessed May 23, 2007.

18   Kathrin Hille, "Taiwan Speeds up Race to Match Beijing Missiles," *Financial Times* (Asia Edition), September 25, 2004, p. 3.

19   "China says Taiwan war-mongering," BBC News, September 29, 2004, http://news.bbc.co.uk/2/hi/asia-pacific/3699460.stm, accessed May 3, 2007.

20   Jimmy Chuang, "Taiwan developing more advanced offensive missiles," *Taipei Times*, April 27, 2007, p. 1.

21   Reuters News Service, "US opposes Taiwan missiles aimed at China: diplomat," May 3, 2007, www.reuters.com/article/topNews/idUSTP20113320070503, accessed May 4, 2007.

22   Ted Galen Carpenter, "Taiwan's Free Ride on US Defense," *Asian Wall Street Journal*, April 23, 2007, posted at www.cato.org/pub_display.php?pub_id=8203, accessed May 29, 2007.

23   John Pomfret and Philip P. Pan, "US Hits Obstacles In Helping Taiwan Guard Against China," *Washington Post*, October 30, 2003, p. A1.

24   "US Calls for Taiwan to Pass Arms Budget in Face of China Threat," Agence France Presse, May 4, 2007, posted at Taiwan Security Research, http://taiwansecurity.org/AFP/2007/AFP-040507.htm, accessed May 4, 2007.

25   Jewel Huang, "Ma Ying-jeou tells group it is too soon for a merger," *Taipei Times*, August 16, 2004, www.taipeitimes.com/News/Taiwan/archives/2004/08/16/2003198964, accessed May 15, 2007.

26   "Taiwan's President Chen Shui-bian," Washingtonpost.com, March 29, 2004, www.washingtonpost.com/ac2/wp-dyn?pagename=article&contented=A33322-2004Mar29&notFound=true, accessed May 21, 2007.

27   Agence France Presse, "President Chen Says Taiwan Is 'Fit' to be Independent," May 13, 2002, http://taiwansecurity.org/AFP/2002/AFP-051302.htm, accessed May 23, 2007; Shih Hsiu-chuan, "Chen urges unity to deal with China," *Taipei Times*, August 14, 2005, p. 1; "Strait Talking," *Time*, February 16, 2004, www.time.com/time/magazine/article/0,9171,501040223-591348,00.html, accessed May 23, 2007.

28 Chen Shui-bian, "Bridging the New Century," December 31, 2000, posted at ROC Government Information Office web site, www.taipei.org/chen/chen891 231.htm, accessed April 26, 2007.

29 See, for example, Richard C. Bush, *Untying the Knot: Making Peace in the Taiwan Strait* (Washington, D.C.: Brookings Institution Press, 2005), pp. 65–71.

30 "Taiwan separatists are doomed to fail: commentary (10/27/2003)," website of the PRC consulate in Houston, http://Houston.china-consulate.org/eng/nv/ t52818.htm, accessed April 23, 2007.

31 Jim Hwang, "No Bridging the Divide," *Taiwan Review*, vol. 56, no. 8 (August 2006), http://taiwanreview.nat.gov.tw/ct.asp?xItem=22910&CtNode=128, accessed May 11, 2007.

32 "Chen declares 'Four Wants and One Without,' " *China Post*, March 5, 2007, www.chinapost.com.tw/news/archives/front/200735/103826.htm,   accessed May 18, 2007.

33 "Text of KMT–Beijing agreement," BBC News, April 29, 2005, http://news. bbc.co.uk/1/hi/world/asia-pacific/4498791.stm, accessed May 14, 2007.

34 " 'Taiwan independence' a dead alley, Soong says," Chinanews, May 11, 2005, www.chinanews.cn/news/2004/2005-05-11/4263.shtml,   accessed   May   18, 2007; Xinhua, "Soong: Descendants of Cathay should never forget roots," *China Daily* Online, May 8, 2005, www.chinadaily.com/cn/English/doc/2005-05/08/content_440133.htm, accessed May 18, 2007.

35 Wayne M. Morrison, "Taiwan's Accession to the WTO and its Economic Relations with the United States and China," Congressional Research Service, May 16, 2003, http://fpc.state.gov/documents/organization/23370.pdf, accessed April 24, 2007.

36 Chen Ming-tong, *The China Threat Crosses the Strait: Challenges and Strategies for Taiwan's National Security* (Taipei: Taiwan Security Research Group, 2006), pp. 6–7.

37 Philip Liu, "Taiwan Business: Taiwan's China Investments Approach a Roadblock," *Taiwan Business TOPICS*, 35(9), September 2005, www.amcham. com.tw/publication_topics_view.php?volume=35&vol_num=9&topics_id=669, accessed April 24, 2007.

38 "China's PLA Daily Criticizes Lee Tung-hui's Divisiveness," *People's Daily* Online, August 20, 1999, http://English.people.com.cn/English/199908/20/enc_199 90820001036_TopNews.htm, accessed April 27, 2007; "一边一国' 论将两岸关系推向危机 ['A Country on Either Side of the Strait' Discussion Pushes Relations Toward Crisis]", *Renmin Ribao* Online, August 9, 2002, www.people.com.cn/GB/ paper39/6928/673160.html, accessed April 27, 2007.

7 Out of America, into the dragon's arms

South Korea, a Northeast Asian balancer?

Seong-Ho Sheen

In March 2005, in a speech at the Korean Air Force Academy, South Korean President Roh Moo-Hyun declared that the South Korean military should contribute to the peace of Northeast Asia as well as the Korean peninsula, and South Korea would play the role of balancer in the power politics of Northeast Asia.[1] The remarks, along with his administration's emphasis on "self-reliant defense capability," caused controversy and debates about South Korea's national security strategy. This chapter will discuss whether the new role proposed by the Roh administration represents a new thinking in South Korea's national security strategy. Especially, the statement raised questions regarding South Korea's future alliance strategy in the region. Does this mean South Korea will develop a more independent relationship with the United States? As some would predict, will South Korea fall into the expanding China's sphere of influence? Or, does it mean the third way of balancing itself between the United States and China?

South Korea's new strategic thinking represents a bold initiative taken by the Roh administration. Yet, the new thinking creates a confusion both domestically and outside about its real intention. The confusion comes from a desire to achieve a mixture of three different objectives. First, South Korea's obsession with its colonial past drives its quest for a self-reliant defense posture, thus autonomy from the United States. Second, South Korea's economic and political success drives a desire to take a more active role in emerging power politics in Northeast Asia as a new balancer. Third, however, the fundamental power gap with China and Japan drives South Korea's effort to strengthen the alliance with the United States despite its anti-American rhetoric, a compromise for the first two objectives. Despite its deepening ties with China in trade as well as in its political relationship, South Korea remains suspicious of Chinese hegemonic intentions as neighboring countries watch carefully the growing Chinese power in the region.

South Korea's new strategic thinking: out of America?

Amidst continuing debate about the uncertain future of bilateral relations between Seoul and Washington, many informed experts tend to see that the alliance is in trouble.[2] It is no secret that Washington and Seoul have serious disagreements over how to deal with North Korea and its nuclear development. Along with its reconciliation effort, South Korea tends to see North Korea as more in need of sympathy and aid while the United States gets deeply skeptical of the Kim Jong-il regime and its nuclear development. Recent restructuring of the US military on the Korean peninsula created further tension between the two governments. South Koreans are concerned that the US military restructuring aims to encircle rising China, which has become the number one trading partner of South Korea. South Korea's cooperation with the US effort would put Seoul's relations with Beijing in danger as South Korea's economy has become increasingly dependent on the growing Chinese market. Henry Kissinger said in a conference in Seoul that South Korea has made a different strategic choice as opposed to the United States in Northeast Asia.[3]

Meanwhile, there seems to be a more fundamental change in the South Korean society that drives the two allies along different paths. While the American people were shocked by the September 11, 2001, simultaneous terror attacks—the first ever direct attack on its soil since World War II—South Koreans have enjoyed half a century of peace since the Korean War. With the burgeoning democracy following economic development, memory of the Korean War is rapidly being forgotten. While US President George W. Bush finds and calls a new evil, North Korea is viewed as a subject of sympathy by the South Koreans. During the Cold War, South Korean politics was mostly shaped by foreign policy concerns such as the constant threat posed by the North. In recent years, however, domestic agenda have gained a more prominent role in Korean politics. While the United States and the international community regard North Korea's nuclear ambition as the most urgent issue, South Koreans are more concerned with such issues as where to build a new capital out of Seoul, what to do with past collaborators during the Japanese colonialism, and how to reform the social welfare and the private school systems.

With their economic and political success followed by growing confidence and national pride within Korean society, an increasing number of Korean people began to question the previously undisputed importance of bilateral relations with the United States. It was peculiar that South Korea has become one of the most anti-American societies in recent years. According to a survey in 2002, 44 percent of South Koreans looked unfavorably upon the United States, a much higher share than in France (34 percent), Germany (35 percent) or anywhere else in Europe or East Asia (except North Korea). Among non-Muslim countries, only Argentina had a larger share of people who actively disliked America.[4] Some unfortunate incidents, such as accidents and crimes involving US soldiers, the new revelation of atrocities by the US military in the small village of Nokunri during the Korean War, and controversial mishaps between Korean and American athletes in both the 2002 Salt Lake City Winter Olympics and the 2004 Athens Olympics, contributed to the rising anti-American sentiment. In particular, young Koreans began to see America with strong antagonism as they perceived it as an unruly hegemonic power that took advantage of South Korea's dependence for its selfish national interests.

Along with general concern over rising anti-Americanism among the South Korean public, informed Korean observers appear to be more worried about the changing attitudes among the elites, especially the government position on the alliance with the United States. Speaking of an anti-American rally in 2002, some cautious commentators pointed out that such public reaction toward America was nothing new in Korean politics. In the 1980s, the US embassy in Seoul and other facilities around the country often became targets of angry protesters. For example, in 1982 criticizing US support of the undemocratic military government in the aftermath of the Gwangju Uprising, a group of student activists occupied and set fire to the US Cultural Center in downtown Busan, the second largest city in South Korea. However, the important difference in the anti-American rallies now and then is the reaction from the South Korean government. Against public anger, the South Korean leadership had displayed firm support for the alliance in the past. The government actively denounced the anti-American movement and preached the importance of the alliance with the United States in South Korea's economic and security interests. Yet, in 2002, the South Korean government appeared to be less interested in defending its ally, when public anger toward the United States swept through the country over the death of two highschool girls in a tragic accident involving American soldiers on a training exercise.[5] Largely peaceful but strong anti-American protests in downtown Seoul continued throughout the last months of the 2002 presidential campaign without any government intervention.

The surprising victory of Roh Moo-Hyun amidst rising anti-American sentiment in 2002 appeared to confirm South Korea's growing discontent with the United States. A self-educated lawyer who defended labor activists in the 1980s, Roh distinguished himself from his predecessors vowing not to kowtow to American pressure. Supporters of the alliance in Seoul worried that the Roh government would seek military autonomy from the United States and try to break away from the alliance. Roh won a tight presidential race appealing to the popular anti-American sentiment. In his campaign, he declared himself a candidate more independent from American influence than his conservative opponent from the Grand National Party. To angry voters, Roh promised to demand more equal relations with the United States once he was elected.

Against criticisms, Roh defended his handling of the alliance by saying that he did not mean breaking the alliance, but simply wanted to lay the groundwork for building a self-reliant defense capability for Korea's future. He stressed that the ROK–US alliance would continue to play an important role in the security interests of Korea, and South Korea's increasing military capability would not go against the alliance. He argued South Korea needed continuing US support for its national security and would remain a key alliance partner for the United States in the coming years.[6] During his first visit to Washington in May 2003, Roh did his best to forge a strong relationship with his counterpart.[7]

Even though Roh has tried to emphasize a more pragmatic and balanced approach toward the United States, his tendency to follow largely nationalistic public sentiment appears to be sending mixed signals to the Americans. There have been continuing allegations about the unknown, if not antagonistic, nature of Roh's policy toward the United States. Critics argued the Roh administration's nationalistic policy seeking more autonomy would damage the 50-year alliance with the United States.

The controversy surrounding "strategic flexibility" of US Forces in Korea (USFK) was a good example of South Korean ambivalence toward future of the ROK–US alliance. In March 2005, Roh said that there would be no case in which South Korea will be involved in conflicts in Northeast Asia against its will.[11] The statement soon raised question about South Korea's commitment to the ROK–US alliance. Especially many questioned the conspicuous timing of the statement.[12] The US and South Korean officials were in the middle of negotiations over whether South Korea would acknowledge US rights to use American forces stationed in Korea for contingencies beyond the peninsula. Critics in Seoul argued that allowing "strategic flexibility" would put South Korea on a square with China in case Washington should confront Beijing over the Taiwan issue. The US effort to restructure and transform its forces on the Korean peninsula into a rapid deployment force was seen as a long-term strategy to contain China's rise in the region. Korea's active cooperation in this process would antagonize China. Amidst Beijing's growing influence over Seoul, allowing strategic flexibility of USFK became a litmus test for South Korea's commitment to the future of the ROK–US alliance from the US perspective. Roh's statement opposing South Korean involvement in regional great power struggles was understood as implicit, if not direct, rejection of the US military transformation effort in the region and represented a weakening of the South Korean commitment to the alliance with the United States.

Self-reliant defense: the past is still alive

Roh's efforts for less dependency on and more autonomy from the US security umbrella are driven by Korean nationalism rather than by its desire to build a new strategic relationship with China. Indeed, South Korea's quest for self-reliant defense represents the Korean desire to overcome its several thousand years' history of foreign interventions and invasions in which various Chinese empires played key aggressors until modern times. Critics question the future of the ROK–US alliance as Roh expresses a strong desire to build a self-reliant defense capability for South Korea. When newly-elected President Roh first met top generals from the ROK military in early 2003, he surprised them by asking whether South Korea could develop a self-reliant defense force.[13] The discussion of the subject with top military generals as a president-elect indicated that building an independent defense capability would become one of the primary objectives for the Roh government. The statement soon raised controversy about his position on the future military alliance with the United

States. Young and progressive supporters interpreted the president's statement as South Korea's legitimate quest for building an autonomous defense capability. Yet, conservatives accused Roh of endangering South Korea's national security based on reckless nationalism. Meanwhile, military experts doubted whether South Korea could have a truly independent defense capability without military assistance from the United States.

As for its broad foreign policy objectives, the Roh government established three principles: self-reliant defense, balanced diplomacy, and South–North reconciliation.[14] In the fall of 2005, the Ministry of National Defense announced its plan to achieve a self-reliant defense posture by 2020. The plan calls for a substantial increase of the defense budget by 11 percent every year for the next ten years. South Korea would build key strategic weapons systems, including Aegis-class destroyers, submarines, and airborne early warning systems.[15] Along with building a defense capability, the Roh administration agreed to take over the military missions that had been assigned to the USFK. The two governments agreed to complete transferring ten military missions from the USFK to the ROK army by 2008.[16]

The issue of returning wartime operational control (WOC) from the USFK to South Korea raised many questions about its timing and feasibility as well as political implications. Since the Korean War, wartime operational control was exercised by the USFK commander, who also plays the role of UN commander. The decision was the outcome of practical considerations based on the mutual security interests of the two allies. As a superior ally who will play a major role in military operations on the peninsula, the United States wanted to have the final authority regarding its troop operations. South Korea, as a country whose national security was solely dependent upon its alliance with the United States, understood the US position. As such American WOC on the peninsula was regarded as even more useful for South Korea's national security interests, as it was understood to assure US military intervention in the case of a North Korean invasion.

In the past, there was a talk of returning the WOC to South Korea as it was deemed natural for a sovereign country. However, it was regarded as premature given the unchanging military tension on the peninsula where South Korea faced the formidable North Korean army. Many assumed the WOC return would be possible only after many more years, if not decades, of preparation by the South Korean military followed by a major change in the military–political situation on the Korean peninsula. Some predicted that such a transition could be possible only after unification. Under the Kim Young-Sam administration, peacetime operational control (POC) was returned to South Korea in 1994. However, the returning of WOC was postponed indefinitely as the first nuclear crisis engulfed the Korean Peninsula in early 1994.

It was the Roh administration in 2003 that raised the WOC issue seriously. Indeed, the United States initiated negotiations for a fundamental change in the US military structure on the Korean Peninsula as part of worldwide US military transformation efforts. The main agenda included relocation of the

US main base in the Yongsan garrison into the Osan-Pyongtaik area, along with restructuring more than forty US bases into twenty, partial withdrawal of 36,000 US service personnel, and transfer of various military missions to the ROK army. However, the United States did not want to change the current command structure, in which WOC belonged to the Combined Forces Command (CFC) headed by a US general. It was the South Korean government which raised the question of transferring WOC.

Roh seems to be determined to speed up the process. In a press conference in 2006, he affirmed that he wanted to see a concrete resolution of the WOC issue by 2008. He stressed that there should be a certain closure to the issue within the remaining two years of his presidency.[17] It was unusual for the president to talk about the issue in such a specific manner. It showed Roh's resolve to irreversibly move the discussion during his presidency. One commentator said the return of WOC would mean dissolution of the current CFC structure, in which a US commander presided as the top military decision-maker with WOC. No US commander would take an order from the South Korean general who has WOC.[18] This change, if implemented, means the current system of combined command should be separated into two independent commands, in which each country exercises an operational control over its own military. The command structure would likely look more like the current parallel command system of the US–Japan alliance.

Splitting the CFC structure would bring about serious political implications to the ROK–US alliance. At a minimum, the current alliance structure—supposed to be most closely integrated—would be much loosened with the two militaries operating separately. As critics worry, the United States may feel less obliged to defend South Korea. South Korea will have more voice on its military operations. But, the military will shoulder a heavier responsibility to build its own capability and strategy to fight a possible invasion. The change will force the South Korean military to develop more independent war-fighting capability and defense strategies. This is exactly what the president has in mind in his push for WOC return—to create an irreversible momentum to build South Korea's self-reliant defense capability.

Indeed, the quest for a self-reliant defense capability has been an axiom of every Korean administration since the end of the Korean War. Two factors have shaped South Korea's peculiar emphasis on military autonomy in this regard. First, the tyranny of the geo-strategic situation surrounding the Korean peninsula has made Korea vulnerable to outside invasions for centuries. Surrounded by big neighbors, Korea has been the subject of great power struggles. Historically Korea has been a surrogate of various Chinese empires which often demanded contributions and took royal family members from Korea as hostages. Korea's history textbooks contain numerous cases of Chinese invasion during the Shilla, Korea, and Chosun dynasties.[19] The rise of Japan in modern times only worsened Korea's destiny as "a shrimp between whales." In the early twentieth century, the arrival of the Russians and the Americans to the geopolitical scene only deepened Korea's self-consciousness as a victim of power politics in the region. Today, Koreans often declare themselves a peace-loving nation, an effort to cast a positive spin on its self-perception as an innocent victim of the invasions by outside powers. Remembering the imperial power politics surrounding the Korean peninsula in the late nineteenth century, President Roh emphasized that Korean pacifism without a self-defense capability only led to Korea falling victim to the great power rivalry between Japan, China, and Russia.[20]

Second, the colonial experience under Japanese rule in the first half of the twentieth century had more direct impact on Korea's strong desire for military autonomy. The harsh rule by the Japanese colonial government created a strong attachment toward independence, which became a core value for the Koreans. Today, even after more than half a century since Korea's liberation in 1945, Korea still tends to approach its foreign relations in terms of foreign influence and its struggle to achieve independence. The Koreans see that the fate of their country is being heavily influenced by the power politics of the big countries including the United States.

Student activists in the 1980s defined South Korea as a colony of the United States and waged an "anti-American independence movement" during the period of the authoritarian governments. In their fight against the military dictatorships in the 1970s and 1980s, many student activists subscribed to the North Korean propaganda that South Korea was a colony of American imperialism. With its dependency on the US security umbrella during the Cold War, the undemocratic South Korean governments were supported by the puppet master in Washington. The remnants of such thinking can be observed today. Many of Roh's key advisors and staff in the Blue House came from the student activist groups of the 1980s. They are core members of the independent faction and yield strong influence on the policy of the Roh government. With blooming democracy and the twelveth largest economy in the world, time has come to finish the legacy of the colonial past once and for all. Building a self-reliant defense capability will be a testimony for Korea's long-awaited quest for true independence.

South Korean resentment of its colonial past is exacerbated by its recurring disputes with Japan over history issues. Despite growing exchanges in trade as well as social and cultural activities since the diplomatic normalization in 1965, the disputes over Japan's reluctance to come clean with its colonial past in Korea have been a recurring theme in the bilateral relations. The year 2005 was especially bad in this regard. In March, a Japanese municipal legislature passed a resolution to claim an island named Dokdo (Takeshima) in the East Sea (Japan Sea), which South Korea has long occupied as its legitimate territory. A month later, a passage in a new school textbook that grossly omitted Japanese wrong-doing in World War II, added another insult to the already angry South Korean public. The South Korean government reacted with strong protests. President Roh vowed to make every effort to correct the wrong approach by the Japanese government even at the risk of "diplomatic war" in his public message to the Korean people.[21] Japan's reluctance to admit its past has provided a useful staple for Korean nationalism, which has become more assertive with the success of the South Korean economy and the resulting growth of public pride and confidence.

South Korea's strong attachment to the value of independence appears to be an important factor to explain its quest for the development of a "self-reliant defense posture"—and the corollary concept of possessing a strong domestic arms industry—since the late 1970s.[22] This explains why South Korea continues to upgrade its military with an increasing defense budget despite the fact that its threat perception toward North Korea has rapidly decreased in recent years. In his annual meeting with newly appointed ambassadors in 2006, President Roh once again talked about Korea's bitter experience of making alliances with neighboring countries in the late nineteenth century. "A century ago, Korea tried China, Japan, and Russia as well as the United States as an ally to defend itself from imperial power politics in the region. But nothing worked, and Korea became a colony in the end."[23]

The Roh government's quest for a self-reliant defense capability has a more practical dimension as well. Along with a self-defense capability and balanced diplomacy, the North–South reconciliation has been a major policy objective of Seoul. There has been remarkable progress in this field since the 2000 summit between Kim Dae-Jung and Kim Jong-Il in economic and social exchanges. As far as military issues are concerned, however, Pyongyang tends to ignore Seoul, arguing that South Korea, a junior partner of the US forces on the peninsula, does not have much to say. The North Korean arrogance extends to the nuclear talks as well as other issues about which Pyongyang wants to talk to Washington only to marginalize Seoul's role. The Roh government believes that enhancing South Korea's autonomy in military affairs would give Seoul a stronger leverage in dealing with Pyongyang. The rationale appears ever more appealing as Seoul aims to take a leading role in the nuclear talks as a mediator between Pyongyang and Washington. Despite its support for Chinese efforts in the Six Party Talks, Seoul is weary of China's strong influence on North Korean economy and politics. In particular, South Korea is concerned about the possibility of Chinese intervention in the process of reunification of the Korean peninsula in the event of a regime collapse in North Korea and subsequent instability.[24]

Northeast Asian balancer: into the dragon's arms?

In March 2005, Roh surprised many observers by saying: "Depending on South Korea's choice, the Northeast Asian balance of power will be determined. Korea would play a balancer role to promote peace and prosperity of [N]ortheast Asia as well as the Korean peninsula."[25] The idea of becoming a Northeast Asian balancer represented a strategy to survive and play a more active role in uncertain power politics in the region. Some worried that the concept of balancer would imply neutrality of South Korea in the region, which practically would mean a departure from the US-ROK alliance. Others saw it as a sign of South Korea's growing affection toward China.

Since normalizing bilateral relations with China in 1992, South Korea's trade with that country has exploded at an annual rate of more than 20 percent, reaching $100 billion in 2005.[26] By 2004 China had become the number one trading partner of South Korea, replacing the United States. In 2002 China also replaced the United States as the top investment destination for South Korean companies. Bilateral social contacts are also substantial, with nearly two million Chinese people visiting South Korea annually and more than 22,000 South Korean students studying in Chinese universities.[27] With growing economic ties, China enjoys a more friendly relationship with South Korea. During his visit to Beijing in July 2003, President Roh emphatically called for unity with China in efforts to usher in a new era of peace and prosperity in Northeast Asia, saying: "The age of Northeast Asia is arriving. On the center stage are China and Korea."[28] More recently, China's growing influence on Korea has been most visible in its effort to mediate the North Korean nuclear crisis. Beijing plays an important role as host to the Six-Party Talks. Moreover, Seoul and Beijing appear to share the same approach in dealing with North Korea. While Washington has argued for more pressure against Pyongyang, the two tend to prefer more positive inducements to the North.

However, South Korea's drive for autonomy from the United States is not driven by its growing ties with China. It is true that China will enjoy a more friendly relationship, thus more influence on Seoul with deepening integration of the Korean economy with China. Given warming relations and great potential for economic cooperation, some analysts, including those in China, expect that in the long term Seoul will develop a closer and stronger relationship with Beijing than with Washington.[29] Yet, it is premature to predict that South Korea would simply trust China's benign intention of security matters on the Korean peninsula. The question still remains whether the two former enemies during the Korean War would achieve a full political partnership in Northeast Asia. In 2006, following a news report of Chinese researchers' claim that the ancient Koguryo kingdom belonged to China, the South Korean government issued a statement that the ancient kingdom of Northeastern China clearly belonged to the Korean nation. It was a good reminder that the bilateral relation was not without a trouble spot.[30]

Indeed, South Korea's vision of a Northeast Asian balancer does not mean that the Koreans want to switch their alliance partner from the United States to China. For one thing, China does not appear to be comfortable with the balancer role of Korea. For South Korea, the balancer represents independence from foreign influence, not the replacement of the old big brother with a new big brother. Indeed, before modern times, it was the Chinese who played the role of imperial power in the region for thousands of years. Despite the cultural affinity and rapidly increasing economic integration with China, the Koreans are suspicious of Chinese ambition in the region as the latter's power grows again. The dispute over the history of Korea's ancient kingdom in present northeastern China is just one example of potential conflicts between the two peoples.

Speaking of the balancer role, Roh said Korea should not be involved in rivalry between China and Japan. In other words, Korea's balancer role was supposed to be between China and Japan, not between China and the United States. However, critics pointed out that Japan was the most important ally of the United States. South Korea's neutral position vis-à-vis Japan would conflict with the US desire of building a strong US–Japan–Korea alliance axis in East Asia. South Korea's new thinking could pose a direct challenge to the US security interests in the region.[31] However, these critics do not appreciate South Korea's unique approach toward Japan. Compared to the casual approach taken by Washington on Japan's history issues with its neighbors, South Korea sees its history as a matter of national identity. As long as the Japanese government continues to provoke South Korea with the prime minister's visits to Yasukuni Shrine, whitewashing of history textbooks, and territorial disputes, South Korea will remain highly suspicious of Japanese intentions. The closure to the colonial past will remain unsolved. And full postwar reconciliation, such as that between Germany and France, will never become a reality. Accordingly, it will be difficult for South Korea to forget the past and forge a trilateral alliance that includes Japan. Instead, Japan will remain as a potential threat to Korea, as Japan tries to become a "normal" nation in the region. Most Koreans see Japan's effort to take a more active role in its defense and international arena with a dubious eye.[32]

Rather than bandwagoning with the growing Chinese power, South Korea as a Northeast Asian balancer represents a hedging strategy as well as ambition to play a more active role in the growing rivalry between China and Japan. Unsure of the intentions of both China and Japan, assuming a position of neutrality between the two neighbors would be in Korea's best interests. At the same time, the balancer role tries to take advantage of the two countries' rivalry. Fully aware of its geo-strategic importance in the region, South Korea expects it could maximize its national interests by playing one of the two big neighbors against the other. South Korea figures that the power rivalry could create competition between the two countries to court favors from South Korea. It could provide South Korea a useful leverage in dealing with them. For example, South Korea announced its position against the Japanese bid for permanent membership of the UN Security Council after protesting the Japanese mishandling of the history issue, a position shared by China.[33] The Korean government obviously wanted to create more pressure on the Japanese government in its dealing with the history issue using the Chinese veto against Japan's growing prominence in international politics.

However, skeptics criticized South Korea's ambition to play a bigger role as a facilitator of peace in the region and mediate future conflicts between the two rivals using its strategic position. Speaking of the balancer role, Roh made it clear that South Korea's military should contribute to the peace and prosperity of Northeast Asia as well as the Korean peninsula.[34] However, citing Great Britain during the eighteenth and nineteenth centuries in Europe, many experts doubt that South Korea's military capability is strong enough to become a balancer between the two Asian giants.[35] Certainly there is a gap between South Korea and its two big neighbors in terms of national wealth and power.

Japan has an economy six times larger than that of Korea (see Table 7.2) and spends three times more on defense than Korea (see Table 7.1). China has a population twenty times larger than that of South Korea (see Table 7.2). China already spends two to eight times more on military than South Korea (see Table 7.1), and its military spending and capability will continue to grow with its economy. Japan enjoys superior technological capability in a wide range of military equipment, while China has an arsenal of strategic nuclear weapons.

It is not very clear whether South Korea will be able to claim a bigger voice in the power politics of Northeast Asia in the near future. Yet, the concept of a Northeast Asian balancer represents South Korea's growing confidence and bold initiative to play a significant and more active role for the peace and security of the region.[36] Especially unification of Korea with continuing economic development would present Korea more as a power to be reckoned with in Northeast Asia.[37] One predicts that a unified Korea will have a population of 70 million compared to Japan's 110 million.[38]

Table 7.1 2005 Military spending in Northeast Asia

Country	In market exchange rate		In PPP dollar terms		
	World rank	Spending ($bn)	Spending (per capita)	World rank	Spending ($bn)
China	5	41	31	2	188.4
Japan	4	42.1	329	8	34.9
Russia	9	21	147	4	64.4
S. Korea	11	16.4	344	13	23.4
USA	1	478.2	1604	1	478.2

Source: SIPRI Yearbook 2006.

Table 7.2 People and wealth in Northeast Asia 2005

Country	In market exchange rate			In PPP dollar terms		
	World rank	GDP ($ t.)	Population (mn)	World rank	GDP ($ t.)	GDP per capita
China	6	1.8	1,306	2	8.15	6,200
Japan	2	4.95	127	3	3.86	30,400
S. Korea	12	0.72	48	14	0.98	20,300
USA	1	12.77	296	1	12.37	41,800

Source: CIA World Fact Book.

"Cooperative" self-defense: back to reality

South Korea's new and ambitious strategic thinking faces difficult challenges to overcome. Despite growing confidence and a desire to build an independent defense capability, South Korea largely lacks the capital and technology to achieve that goal. Even if South Korea fully develops its economic potential, the fundamental power gap between Seoul and its two neighbors will largely remain unchanged. The harsh reality drives South Korea's strategic calculation to seek refuge in its alliance with the United States.

Notwithstanding its desire and ambition for a self-defense posture and Northeast Asian balancer, South Korea is back where it started: promotion of the ROK–US alliance and taking full advantage of this alliance. Against the skeptics of his balancer concept, Roh later explained that South Korea's balancer role would be based on its strong alliance with the United States. Indeed, despite its rhetoric of autonomy, if not anti-Americanism, the record of the Roh administration's handling of sensitive issues with Washington shows more optimistic pictures. One commentator said that there was strong mistrust within Washington toward Seoul. Yet, he added that it was remarkable to see what the two governments had achieved over the past years in their bilateral relationship.[39] Some say as far as the bilateral relation with the United States is concerned, the Roh administration's deeds are much better than words. The track records of critical bilateral issues under the Roh administration show an interesting case as Seoul ended up in close cooperation with the United States in every important bilateral issue including base relocations, troop dispatches to Iraq, the alliance restructuring, strategic flexibility of US forces, non-proliferation efforts, and the bilateral free trade agreement.

The South Korean government was fully responsive to the US military transformation on the Korean peninsula. In 2003, as an effort to transform its military presence, the United States requested South Korea to cooperate in relocating and consolidating its forty bases scattered around the country into twenty, which would include moving the Yong-San base in Seoul into the Osan-Pyongtak. The move would provide greater flexibility and agility, and make US soldiers less vulnerable to possible attacks from the North. However, the bilateral negotiation became a subject of political debate within South Korea, with both the conservatives and the progressive liberals criticizing the Roh government's handling of the issue. For the conservatives, the relocation meant the United States was giving up the so-called "tripwire" function—a concept never assumed and loathed by the US military—that guarantees automatic involvement of US forces in case of a war on the Peninsula. They blamed the Roh government for not doing enough to convince Americans about South Korea's commitment to the alliance.[40] Meanwhile, the progressive liberals expressed concerns about a possible US military attack on North Korea. They suspected that the United States might launch a pre-emptive attack on North Korea should the nuclear situation escalate, and the relocation was part of a US contingency plan to minimize US casualties in case of war. Others questioned why South Korea should bear the bulk of the cost of moving US forces, estimated to be between $5 billion and $10 billion. They argued that it is unfair for South Korea to provide all the cost for the move, which in essence serves US military interest in the region.[41] Yet, the Roh administration argued that the move would not alter the fundamental deterrence capability of the alliance. South Korea would provide most of the money for base relocations as suggested. Against the criticism of unfair burden sharing, the government defended the agreement by saying that the move of the Yongsan base was originally made by the South Korean government back in the early 1990s.[42]

The dispatch of Korean troops to Iraq was another showcase of South Korea's commitment to the alliance. Amidst strong anti-war sentiment among the public, the government dispatched 3,600 troops to Iraq making it the third largest coalition force after the United States and Great Britain. Being a weak government challenged by a majority opposition party in the legislature, the Roh government tends to follow popular sentiment rather than lead it. Yet, amidst the widespread anti-war sentiment among the Koreans and severe criticism from his own supporters, Roh's decision to send 3,600 additional troops to Iraq along with 200 troops in Afghanistan was a clear indication that his government fully understands the importance of the US-ROK alliance for South Korea's national interest. Furthermore, the troop dispatch was extended twice by the Korean National Assembly after the government's request to extend the troop dispatch for a year.[43]

Third, in January 2006 the two governments announced a joint statement allowing strategic flexibility of USFK.[44] Previously, the US plan of transforming relocated bases as launch pads for regional operations beyond the Korean peninsula caused suspicion among the Koreans. Many worried that the new regional mission beyond the Korean peninsula would put South Korea's position in direct disputes with China, increasingly an important partner for South Korea's economy and security. The progressive liberals suspected that the United States was taking a pre-emptive move in preparing for a permanent post-unification presence on the peninsula, a subject yet to be discussed and decided by the Koreans. Against these critics, the South Korean government launched a new strategic consultation meeting with the United States. In the first meeting in Washington between the two foreign ministers, the two governments emphasized nurturing and protection of common values, such as respect for democracy, human rights, and the rule of law as the basis of the alliance. The two governments also made it clear that they would have regular high-level meetings to resolve pressing regional and global challenges.[45] This represented a major development for South Korea's approach to the objective of the alliance, which so far exclusively focused on the Korean peninsula. The broadening scope of the alliance missions beyond the Korean peninsula could mean South Korea's willingness to play a more active role in the global agenda of US national security interests.

South Korea's close cooperation with the US security demand was followed by a deepening of economic cooperation as well. In April 2007, the two governments announced the signing of the Korea–US Free Trade Agreement (KORUS FTA). Previously, South Korea had FTAs with only Chile and ASEAN. And the FTA discussion with Japan was suddenly stopped after disputes over the historical interpretations erupted in 2005. The agreement represented a major breakthrough in South Korea's quest for globalizing its economy. More importantly, it also symbolized the deepening integration of the South Korean economy with the much bigger US market. Many political supporters of Roh, especially the progressives and labor activists, strongly criticized the Roh administration for his pro-US policy. On the other hand, supporters of the KORUS FTA (the conservative opponents of Roh) welcomed Roh's leadership and argued that the FTA with the United States would reinforce the strong and mutually beneficial economic and strategic relationship between the two countries.

South Korea's close cooperation with the United States in key security fields is compelled by the two factors that bind the two allies: Northeast Asian geopolitics and its cost. While Americans are mostly concerned with security, South Koreans are determined to pursue economic prosperity that is unprecedented in their national history. Despite all the rhetoric about independence, national pride and confidence, self-reliant defense, and balancing diplomacy, the ultimate question of keeping the alliance with the United States may come down to the economic cost for South Korea: which is cheaper for South Korea— to keep Americans on the peninsula or not? In other words, how far is South Korea willing or able to pay for its autonomy? The answer will be decided by South Korea's perception of threat in Northeast Asia and its economic condition. Should South Korea feel no threat, there would be little reason to bother with paying billions of dollars in order to keep the US military on its soil, which causes political and diplomatic headaches.

The South Koreans are not so sure about their northern brethren and its two big neighbors. Notwithstanding the increasing exchange with North Korea, many South Koreans are still not convinced of the North Korean intension. According to a poll, even though an increasing number of South Koreans registered a positive view of North Korea, still a majority of the public (88.1 percent in 1998 and 81.8 percent in 2003) believed that North Korea's overall policy has remained unchanged. More than half of South Koreans think that North Korea's nuclear issue is likely to lead to another war on the Korean peninsula. The poll shows a persisting South Korean ambivalence toward North Korea with regard to their security. As such, almost two thirds of South Koreans still believe in the possibility of North Korea's armed aggression.[46] Interestingly enough, even many progressives in the Korean society acknowledge the importance of the US military presence on the peninsula until, if not after, unification.

Despite the increasing confidence in South Korea's military capability visà-vis North Korea, most South Koreans still appreciate the huge psychological as well as economic contributions made by the US military presence on the peninsula. Sudden withdrawal of US forces would cost South Korea at least tens of billions of dollars on top of the $15 billion defense budget. Replacing the 37,000-men strong heavily-armed US forces as well as the combat-related functions including intelligence gathering, air and naval support, and advanced military planning would be a huge undertaking for South Korea. Washington announced $11 billion extra spending just to help its military restructuring in South Korea.[47] The growing gap in military technologies and operational capability between the ROK and the US military, indeed a universal phenomenon in other countries as well, further increases the cost of replacing the US military role for South Korea.[48]

Indeed, many doubt the feasibility of such an ambitious military project by the Roh administration. First, critics question whether South Korea can afford such an expensive project. In 2004 South Korea's sluggish economic recovery prohibited even a moderate increase in defense spending from 2.7 percent of South Korea's gross national product (GNP) to 3.0 percent. In 2005 South Korea's defense spending was only 2.8 percent of its gross domestic product, while the average among developed countries was 3.5 percent. The newly-published military modernization plan required the government to spend more than $620 billion additional defense budget by 2020. The increase was mainly to occur for the first ten years by 2015 with an average 11 percent annual rise. However, the substantial increase in defense budget was based on the projection that the South Korean economy would grow by an average 7.1 percent until 2020. This economic projection was too optimistic. In fact, the Korean economy recorded less than a 4 percent GDP growth in 2005 and 5 percent in 2006.[49] The Korean Bank estimated South Korea's economic growth for the next ten years at an average rate of 4.6 percent. If the Korean Bank's more modest prediction is correct, the defense ministry will end up with $510 billion by 2020, $110 billion short of its current plan.[50]

Defense spending also competes against growing demands for government spending in other sectors. As its economy grows, the South Korean government feels a strong pressure to increase its spending on social welfare. Especially, the need is growing due to the country's rapidly aging population coupled with the lowest birth rate in the world. In August 2006 the government announced a new plan to increase its welfare budget by four times up to 50 percent of the national budget.[51] Meanwhile the government faces increasing fiscal pressure due to decreasing tax revenue as South Korea's working population declines and grows older. This will largely constrain the government's ability to address multiple social welfare demands as well as the military spending requests. Indeed, the defense budget for 2006, the first year of the ambitious 2020 defense reform project, showed a smaller increase in spending than in 2005.

Even if South Korea manages to afford the expensive project and accomplish its plan to modernize its military, it will still be far short of achieving an independent defense capability against China and Japan. Even after unification, US forces in Korea may remain an essential part of South Korea's defense against rising China and the rebuilt Japanese army. As for the continuing US military presence after unification, South Korea has not developed any specific vision in the absence of a serious debate on the subject matter. Many South Koreans, including Roh himself, appear to tacitly acknowledge a continuing presence for regional security. Lately, Roh asserted that even after dissolution of the North Korean threat, US forces' presence on the peninsula will be necessary as a "comprehensive deterrence capability" in the crucial role of "maintaining the balance of power in the region," reiterating his predecessors' position on South Korea's long-term commitment to the alliance.[52] The recent disputes with China over Korea's ancient history and with Japan over Dok-do (Takeshima) island may have strengthened the importance of the alliance with the United States in the post-unification era, in which the unified Korea may face unclear intentions of the two major powers in the region.

Conclusion

Under the Roh administration, South Korea developed a new strategic thinking. The new thinking could be summarized into two concepts; "cooperative self-reliant defense" and "Northeast Asian balancer." The new strategic concepts reflected the complicated nature of the security environment South Korea faced. Indeed, the new thinking was a partial reflection of South Korea's desire to be out of the American influence, a desire that is deeply rooted in its historical experience. It also represented South Korea's ambition to play a more active role in the emerging power politics of Northeast Asia between China and Japan. It represented South Korea's effort to have more voice in shaping its own destiny and desire to be recognized as a more meaningful actor in world politics. It was driven by growing confidence among the leadership after Korea's success in economic and political development. The changing power structure in Northeast Asia with rising China was another driver for South Korea's new thinking. However, this did not imply that Seoul wanted to create a new strategic partnership with Beijing at the expense of its alliance with Washington. Rather than falling into the sphere of China's growing influence, South Korea tried to be a balancer of conflicts and a facilitator of peace in Northeast Asia between China and Japan. Indeed this was a serious undertaking for South Korea (even for a unified Korea) given its unchanging power gap with the two big neighbors. The new approach deserves credit for its boldness in trying to think outside the box of South Korea's traditional dependence on the alliance with the United States. It represented South Korea's ambition to be more self-reliant and autonomous from the US security umbrella.

However, many doubted the feasibility of the new thinking. Cooperative self-reliant defense was a compromise between this bold new thinking and the challenges South Korea faced in reality. The more South Korea claims autonomy from the United States, the more it perceives the important contribution made by the United States in terms of money and the quality of defense. The more it tries to balance China and Japan, the more suspicion and mistrust it invites from both of them. South Korea is finally able to appreciate the value of the US alliance just as it tries to do without it. This explains the irony of the

Roh administration's policy toward Washington, which his anti-American supporters criticize for being too pro-American. The Roh government's bold approach to recover wartime operational control, the tendency to mediate between Washington and Pyongyang, its diplomatic war against Japan, its quest for a self-defense capability, and its demand for an equal partnership represent South Korean sentiment and confidence toward achieving more autonomy from the United States. But Seoul has still ended up closely cooperating with the United States on the alliance restructuring, North Korean nuclear issues, strategic flexibility of US forces in Korea, troop dispatch to Iraq, and free trade agreement.

South Korea's new strategic thinking under Roh was not complete. The country wanted more autonomy from America. However, complete autonomy might never be meant for Korea. Making one's own strategy means more responsibility and courage to make the tough choices that have to be made. It is a difficult process involving thorough assessment of one's own capability and creativity to achieve specific goals with limited resources. South Korea did not dare to take on this difficult task, finding refuge in the alliance with the United States. South Korea under Roh made the decision to explore the possibility of making its own grand strategy. So far it has caused confusion making mistakes and adjustments. At the end of the day, Korea may come back to the same old position of relying on the US alliance. Still, it was a worthwhile exercise for a country that has achieved a lot in the past, and it will have a better idea about itself and the world surrounding it.

Notes

1   Roh Moo-Hyun, "Speech to the Graduation Ceremony of Korean Air Force Academy," Seoul: Office of the President, March 8, 2005.
2   Oh Jong-Soo, "ROK–US in unprecedented difficult situation: A former US ambassador Bosworth speaks out," *Choongang Ilbo*, October 30, 2005.
3   A keynote speech at an international conference held by *Chosun Ilbo* in Seoul, March 3, 2005.
4   A survey conducted between July and October 2002 by Pew Global Attitudes Project, quoted in "A Survey of South Korea: Keeping the lights on," *The Economist*, April 19, 2003.
5   In fact, it was several months after the death of two schoolgirls that public anger erupted over the "not guilty" verdict by the US military court to the two US soldiers involved in the accident. The verdict, based on US law with due process, was largely viewed as a disgrace to Korean law and people who expected a criminal charge. Organized by young internet users, the anti-American movement rapidly spread into a peaceful but mass protest against the United States.
6   Roh, "Speech to the National Defense Force Day Ceremony," Office of the President, October 1, 2005.
7   During his visit, President Roh said that he would have been in North Korea's political prison camp had the United States not come to the rescue of South Korea during the Korean War, which angered many of his domestic supporters.
11 Roh, "Speech to the Graduation Ceremony of Korean Air Force Academy."

12 Editorial, "Speaking of 'Roh Moo-Hyun Doctrine," *Chosun Ilbo*, May 19, 2005.
13 *Wolgan Chosun*, February 2003, pp. 198–207.
14 National Security Council, *Pyonghwa bonyong kwa kukga anbo*, Seoul: NSC, March 1, 2004.
15 Ministry of National Defense, "Press Release on National Defense Reform 2020," September 13, 2005.
16 Kathleen T. Rhem, "US to Transfer 10 Missions to South Korean Military," *American Forces Press Service*, November 19, 2003. The missions include patrol of the Joint Security Area, anti-fire missions, and weather forecast.
17 Roh, "Speech to the 2006 Press Conference," Office of the President, January 26, 2006; www.president.go.kr/cwd/kr/archive/archive_view.php?meta_id=speech&id=53d7adb2c914007049f20ab7, accessed on Jan 29, 2006.
18 You, Yong-Won, "Dissolution of CFC could bring serious troubles for Korea's military capability," *Chosun Ilbo*, October 2, 2005.
19 In 2007, one of the most popular Korean writers, Kim-Hoon published a novel based on the historic event of the disgraceful sufferings of Chosun Dynasty under attack by the early Qing Dynasty in the seventeenth century. The book instantly became a best seller of the year.
20 Roh, "Speech to the Graduation Ceremony of Korean Air Force Academy."
21 Roh, "A letter to Korean People with regard to Korea-Japan Relations," Office of the President, March 23, 2005.
22 Richard A. Bitzinger and Mikyoung Kim, "Why Do Small States Produce Arms?: The Case of South Korea," *Korean Journal of Defense Analysis* XVII (2) Fall 2005, pp. 197–201.
23 Roh, "A meeting with ambassadors," Office of the President, February 16, 2006.
24 *Chosun Ilbo*, January 2, 2007.
25 Roh, "Speech to the Graduation Ceremony of Korea Third Military Academy," Seoul: Office of the President, March 22, 2005.
26 South Korean trade with China was especially sweet with $20 billion surplus while it recorded $22 billion trade deficit against Japan.
27 Denny Roy, "China and the Korean Peninsula: Beijing's Pyongyang Problem and Seoul Hope," *Asia-Pacific Security Studies* 3(1), January 2004 (Asia-Pacific Center for Security Studies).
28 Roh, "Speech to the Students of Chinghuia University," Office of the President, July 9, 2003.
29 Scott Snyder, "South Korea's Squeeze Play," *Washington Quarterly*, Autumn 2005, pp. 93–106; Doug Bandow, "Seoul Searching: Ending the US-Korean Alliance," *The National Interest*, Fall 2005, p. 115; Avery Goldstein, "The Future of US–China Relations and the Korean Peninsula," *Asian Perspective*, 26(3), 2002, pp. 124–127.
30 As for potential territorial disputes between the two countries, see Daniel Goma, "The Chinese-Korean Border Issue: An Analysis of a Contested Frontier," *Asian Survey*, XLVI(6), November/December 2006, pp. 867–880.
31 Bandow, pp. 112–116.
32 *Kyunghyang Shinmun*, August 25, 2006; *Munhwa Ilbo*, July 28, 2006; *Weekly Chosun*, July 4, 2006.
33 *Yonhap News*, May 10, 2005.
34 Roh, "Speech to the Graduation Ceremony of Korean Third Military Academy."
35 *Seoul Shinmun*, April 15, 2005.
36 According to a Goldman Sachs report, South Korea will be the third richest economy after Japan and the United States and richer than Great Britain and France by 2025 in terms of per capita income. By 2050, its economy would become the second richest in the world surpassing Japan. Lee, Ho Jin. "Korean

Economy in 2050 by Goldman Sachs Report," Korea Institute for International Economic Policy (KIEP), January 2, 2006, in Korean.

37 Unification could play both negative and positive roles for Korea's power projection. In the short term, it could put a severe strain on Korea's economic growth as it would require substantial capital to feed and rebuild the North Korean economy. In the longer term, it could reduce South Korea's heavy burden on defense spending. Despite the problem of political and social integration between the North and the South, a unified Korea would have much healthier and younger demographic trends than Japan or China as North Koreans would provide much needed labor.

38 Nicholas Eberstadt, "Power and Populations in Asia," *Strategic Asia, 2003–2004*, National Bureau of Asian Research, 2004.

39 Robert Einhorn in a public lecture, Seoul Press Center, Feburary 3, 2006.

40 They argued that the move could send a wrong message and invite adventurism from the North Koreans. Some even suspected that the US proposal was a retaliatory action from Washington against the latest anti-American movement in South Korea.

41 Kim, Tae-Kyoung, "US Commander says US will have to share 6 percent of base relocation cost in Korea," *Ohmynews*, January 25, 2006.

42 *Chosun Ilbo*, January 17, 2004.

43 *Yonhap News*, April 12, 2007.

44 *Chosun Ilbo*, January 20, 2006.

45 US Department of State, "United States and the Republic of Korea Launch Strategic Consultation for Allied Partnership," Press Release, January 19, 2006.

46 Chun Youngki, "Survey of Korean View of Other Countries," *Choongang Ilbo*, September 30, 2004. In a survey by the Korea Institute for National Unification, 57.7% in 1998 and 58.6% in 2003 said there is such a possibility.

47 Barbara Demick, "US Puts Its Latest Arms In S. Korea," *Los Angeles Times*, December 21, 2003.

48 For a detailed discussion of the US contributions to South Korea's defense, see Norman D. Levin, *Do the Ties Still Bind?: The US-ROK Security Relationship After 9/11*, Santa Monica, CA: RAND Corporation, 2004, pp. 11–19.

49 Bank of Korea, "2006 National Production," March 21, 2007.

50 Bruce Bennett, "Analysis of ROK's 'Defense Reform 2020,'" Office of National Assemblyman Hwang Jin-Ha, November 30, 2005. According to the report, the defense budget does not take 2.3% annual inflation into account. With the inflation, the budget would have to decrease by $100 billion.

51 Office of the President, *Vision 2030*, August 30, 2006. http://vision2030.korea. kr.

52 "An Interview with President Roh," *JoongAng Daily*, February 15, 2004. http:// joongangdaily.joins.com/200402/15/200402152259466439900090309301.html.

8 Southeast Asian responses to China's rise

Managing the "elephants"?

Evelyn Goh

Introduction

Historically, China's shadow has loomed large over Southeast Asia. In more recent times, during the Cold War, the People's Republic of China exported communist ideology to, and supported insurgencies in the post-colonial Southeast Asian states, and undertook military interventions in Indochina. It was the end of the Cold War though that catapulted China into the position of primary strategic worry for Southeast Asian states, which now had to cope with the twin uncertainties of American military withdrawal and Chinese strategic intentions, with its increasing material capabilities. China's claims to the South China Sea and a series of disputes with rival regional claimant states over islands there, exacerbated concerns about China's potentially aggressive ascendance. Since then, Southeast Asian states have been at the forefront of coping with the rise of China. With a fifteen-year track record of managing and adjusting to the China challenge, Southeast Asia provides an important and timely case study for a broader understanding of the rise of China and its implications for international order.

This chapter examines Southeast Asian states' responses to China's rise, and is organized in three parts. First, it reviews key Southeast Asian states' perceptions of rising China, and the main implications of China's rise for the military, economic, and political security of the subregion. The second section analyzes strategies of the Association of Southeast Asian Nations (ASEAN) to cope with the challenges posed by China. It identifies two key strategies of "omnienmeshment" and "complex balancing," and argues that these together seek peacefully to incorporate China into the region by facilitating the creation of a hierarchical regional order that maintains the US superpower overlay, but accords China a regional great-power position, while also incorporating other major regional players. The final section concludes that while there has been significant positive progress made in moderating regional threat perceptions of China, four problems remain: (a) the Sino–Southeast Asian relationship has been characterized thus far by low expectations and is untested by crises since 1995; (b) there is increasing divergence of views among ASEAN members regarding China; (c) Southeast Asia's strategic unimportance compared to Northeast Asia; and (d) the growing regional problems with non-traditional security issues.

Strategic implications of China's rise for Southeast Asia

Since the early 1990s, Southeast Asia's main preoccupation about regional security has centered on four key potential threats or challenges posed by a rising China.

First, they are wary about the territorial disputes over islands in the South China Sea, which involve China and four Southeast Asian countries. China and Vietnam had clashed over the Spratlys reefs in the late 1980s, but Beijing really worried its Southeast Asian neighbors when it laid claim to the whole South China Sea in 1992. Thereafter the Chinese occupied and built structures on reefs claimed by Vietnam and the Philippines in 1992, 1995, and 1999, the latter of which led to diplomatic confrontations and military tensions.[1] Despite the negotiation of a Declaration on the Code of Conduct in 2002, there remain internal divisions within ASEAN on the issue, and Vietnam and the Philippines continue to be wary of Chinese encroachment.

Second, Southeast Asian states are concerned about the fallout of a potential conflict between the United States and China if Beijing becomes more assertive or Washington decides to adopt a more aggressive containment policy toward Beijing. They particularly worry about a war over Taiwan, which would destabilize the whole region and force countries to choose sides. Third, these small and medium-sized countries perceive a medium- to long-term threat from regional dominance by the Chinese. This is most obvious if Beijing pursues aggressive policies in terms of territorial or resource domination. But short of such actions, Southeast Asian countries still remain wary of the potential domination of the regional security and economic landscape by China to the exclusion of other powers, particularly the United States. In this sense, Chinese regional unipolarity per se is regarded with suspicion because of uncertainties about Chinese intentions over the long term.

But the main challenge posed by a rising China is economic. China is the world's seventh-largest exporting nation and the top producer of grain, coal, iron, steel, and cement. In terms of GNP taking into account purchasing power parity, it has the second-largest economy after the United States, and its economy has averaged at least 7 percent annual growth over the last decade.[2] Although there is no agreement about the net outcome of China's economic growth on Southeast Asia, it is clear that this will bring both benefits and costs, and that a wide range of industries in the region will face stiff competition from their lower-cost Chinese counterparts.

China's altered approach toward Southeast Asia since the mid-1990s has significantly shaped the region's views of the China challenge. Beijing has succeeded in muting the worst of its Southeast Asian neighbors' threat perceptions and has managed to convey its current intentions for benign regional leadership. This positive state of affairs is due in part to the relatively high anxiety and low expectations with which Southeast Asia approached China in the early 1990s. But the explanation lies also in Beijing's strategic adaptation through a steep learning curve, resulting in policies since the mid-1990s characterized by multilateralism, mutual respect, and subscription to regional norms; conflict management; as well as an attitude of seeking mutual benefit, demonstrated through restraint and the bearing of cost burdens vis-à-vis less-developed neighbors.[3]

As a result, in Southeast Asia there is some evidence of a notable shift in perceptions of China as a potentially destabilizing force. On the one hand, policymakers still hold to their realist view that economic capacity will necessarily translate into military might and that sheer capability (intentions aside) has the potential to disrupt the region's strategic landscape by virtue of objective relative power deepening the security dilemma.[4] On the other hand, the same policy elites appear to have become more sanguine about the day-to-day policy implications of China's growth. They evince more comfort in walking in China's shadow—partly because of Beijing's successful regional diplomacy but also because they appear to have reconciled themselves to the reality of a resurgent giant neighbor. And the task of making the best of it has tended to normalize this state of affairs, rendering it less of an unknown quality and thus offering more possibilities of management.

Political challenges

The political front is where Southeast Asian evaluations of the impacts of China's rise have altered most over the last decade and a half. ASEAN's collective position on coping with the changing strategic landscape in the early 1990s encompassed a strong conviction that it was necessary to engage with rising China politically and economically. Apart from a reluctance to increase the region's dependence on the United States if it were to opt for containing China, there was a belief that it would not be wise to alienate China, given its geographical proximity and apparently inexorable rise.[5]

Southeast Asian political engagement of China has been advanced mainly through multilateral institutional membership and participation. Ostensibly, it is an attempt at "hegemonic entrapment," or, less antagonistically, a strategy to "socialize" China into adopting regional norms and by giving it a stake in regional goals and stability. This strategy accords well with ASEAN's "comprehensive security" concept, which emphasizes a multilevel and multi-issue approach to security concerns at the intra-states, intra-ASEAN and ASEAN-and-the-rest-of-the-region levels.[6] Thus, China was invited to become ASEAN's "consultative partner" in 1991, and was promoted to "full dialogue partner" in 1996. During this time, Sino–ASEAN cooperation was institutionalized with the creation of five dialogue mechanisms in the areas of political, scientific, technological, economic, and trade consultations. In the second half of the 1990s,

China began cooperating with ASEAN in its Mekong Basin Development Cooperation, on a range of issues including the control of illegal migration, drug trafficking, the spread of AIDS, and developing transport links in the basin which brings together China and mainland Southeast Asia. Crucially, in 1994, China joined in setting up the ASEAN Regional Forum (ARF), an Asia-Pacific gathering devoted to the discussion of security issues and under whose aegis China issued its first defense white paper in 2002.[7] In 1997, China, together with Japan and South Korea, inaugurated a new framework for regional cooperation in the ASEAN+3 summit track.

Within these multilateral institutional fora, Beijing has taken some important and consistent steps toward conforming to the status quo in terms of participating in regional institutions and adopting norms of conduct.[8] In general, the Chinese have upheld the prevailing diplomatic style of the region, called the "ASEAN way," which emphasizes informality, consensus, non-intervention in internal affairs, and moving at a pace that is comfortable for all members.[9] Beijing has also signaled its acceptance of the subregion's norms of peaceful settlement of conflicts and nuclear non-proliferation, first by signing the protocol to make Southeast Asia a nuclear-free Zone of Peace, Freedom, and Neutrality (ZOPFAN) in 2001, and then by being the first external power formally to accede to ASEAN's Treaty of Amity and Cooperation (TAC) in 2003.[10] The Joint Declaration on Strategic Partnership for Peace and Prosperity signed in October 2003 usefully indicated the range of political, economic, and cultural mechanisms that had been developed for close Sino–ASEAN cooperation, but it was also a significant indication of high-level Chinese commitment to positive engagement with Southeast Asia.[11] In terms of concrete policy outcomes, two substantive results that flowed out of these multilateral institutional processes most important to Southeast Asian states—the conflict management procedures for the South China Sea disputes and the commitment to an ASEAN–China Free Trade Area (ACFTA)—are discussed in the following sections.

Southeast Asians currently share a positive outlook regarding the political implications of China's rise thus far. By signaling its willingness to engage the subregion collectively and according to received norms, and through demonstrating its sensitivity to the comfort of smaller players by letting ASEAN retain the driver's seat in regional institutions, Beijing has managed to reassure its Southeast Asian neighbors about the benignity of its growing regional political clout.[12]

Now, the political challenge for Southeast Asia in coping with China's growing role in the region resides in whether and how Asian countries can build on existing institutions to achieve greater regional cooperation and integration. The desire certainly exists—though in different measures across the smaller countries—and China is lending its support, drive, and resources to developing particular institutions. Within Southeast Asia, one problem is that the concerns and perspectives of key ASEAN countries differ regarding which institutions to build up and how. There exists a quiet tussle over the shape regionalism should take, as amply illustrated in the bickering over membership for the East Asia Summit in December 2005. While China, Malaysia, and Thailand were happy to have an exclusively East Asian dialogue, Singapore, Japan, and Indonesia lobbied successfully to include India, Australia, and New Zealand in the summit, thereby undermining its potential as the premier China-led regional institution.[13] While this served to dilute the impact of the new institution, it also reflected the dilemma of ASEAN stalwarts, particularly the Indonesians, who are at the same time trying to resuscitate the organization (and Indonesia's leadership role in it) by forging the new ASEAN Economic and Security Communities, and who may view larger regional institutions as detracting from their enterprise. Since then, East Asian regionalism appears to have returned to the polarization between those who, like Beijing, prefer to have ASEAN+3 (ASEAN + Japan, China, and Korea) as the key regional institution, and those who prefer to retain the ASEAN Regional Forum (ARF) as the most important pan-regional, "open" institution.[14]

Military challenges

For American scholars particularly, debates about the strategic impacts of China's growing capabilities have tended to focus upon its potential military prowess.[15] For a time, Southeast Asian concerns, too, centered on the possibility of expansionist Chinese ambitions revolving around various outstanding territorial disputes, especially those in the South China Sea during the first half of the 1990s. Currently, Southeast Asian perspectives vary, with the Philippines and Vietnam most worried, but there is an almost determined effort to stress progress in ASEAN dialogue to resolve the issue and the conviction that China will not go to war over these islands.

This re-evaluation comes from demonstrations of Chinese willingness to settle general territorial disputes and Beijing's restraint on the South China Sea issue since the late 1990s. In the last fifteen years, the Chinese government has moved to resolve territorial disputes with its neighbors, such as Russia and India. In Southeast Asia, China signed an agreement with Laos in 1991 to delineate their land boundary, and negotiated with Vietnam throughout the 1990s to agree on their land and maritime boundaries.[16] The progress made in improving these relationships was followed by Beijing's gradual unbending toward multilateral discussions of the South China Sea disputes and its more restrained behavior in claiming the disputed islets from 1999 onwards. After much wrangling over the scope of a potential code of conduct, China and ASEAN signed a "Declaration on the Conduct of Parties in the South China Sea" on November 4, 2002, at the ASEAN summit in Phnom Penh.[17] This was an important achievement, though it fell far short of a binding Code of Conduct, and it was built upon in 2005, when the state-controlled oil companies of China, the Philippines, and Vietnam agreed to conduct joint surveys on oil and gas reserves in the area. The claimant states continue to discuss the implementation of the 2002 declaration, with the declared intention of eventually reaching agreement on a Code of Conduct.[18] It is pertinent to note, though, that Beijing has not withdrawn its territorial claims in principle to the whole of the South China Sea, and other disputed islands such as the Paracels are not included in the declaration. While Southeast Asian claimant states have been notably more sanguine in their attitude toward these disputes in the last two years, the effectiveness with which the conflict has been managed has yet to be tested.

Since the late 1990s, Southeast Asia and China have generally increased military contacts and exchanges. For instance, China has attended the annual "Cobra Gold" joint exercises involving the United States, Thailand, and Singapore since 2002, and invited ASEAN countries to observe one of its own major infantry exercises in 2004 and to participate in a joint military exercise in July 2007 dealing with peacekeeping and disaster management and reconstruction. Given that Southeast Asia is not a part of the world that enjoys particularly high levels of military transparency, it is often the politics of military relations that are most interesting. In the multilateral realm, for instance, Beijing has repeatedly suggested an annual Defense Ministers' meeting with ASEAN, implicitly offering an alternative to the lower-level Shangri-La Dialogue organized by the London-based International Institute for Strategic Studies. On the bilateral front, China has deftly played the politics of military contact and aid, particularly with ASEAN countries that have been least comfortable with its growing strategic weight. Thus, in 2005, Chinese leaders opened annual consultative defense talks with Vietnam and the Philippines and mooted a similar process with Indonesia. In addition, President Hu Jintao agreed to provide $1.6 billion in loans and investments to Manila in 2005, and in the following year China pledged its first military assistance to the Philippines of over $1 million.[19] Hu also signed a "Strategic Partnership" agreement with Indonesian President Susilo Bambang Yudhoyono in April 2005, which did not include an explicit military dimension, but nevertheless allowed the Indonesian military to add pressure on Washington to reinstate US–Indonesian military ties.[20]

While regional evaluations of the military implications of China's rise remain mixed, this combination of reassurance through the negotiation and settlement of territorial conflicts and strategic opportunity provided for some Southeast Asian countries seeking diversification of their military aid and supplies amount to a significant reduction of threat perceptions. For instance, President Hu's remarks emphasising Beijing's intention to build a strong blue water navy in December 2006, China's test of an anti-satellite weapon in January 2007, and the announced increase in military spending at the March 2007 National People's Congress met with very muted official response in Southeast Asia. On the one hand, these relatively sanguine evaluations may arise from the fact of low military capabilities in most Southeast Asian countries. Those with potential flash-points that may result in conflict with China have relatively ill-equipped and domestically preoccupied militaries (the Philippines and Indonesia) or are strategically conflict-averse for historical reasons (Vietnam),[21] while the countries with the most military advantage have no obvious reasons for military conflict with China (Singapore).[22] On the other hand, some Southeast Asian countries' growing confidence regarding China's challenges also stem from their relative success in maintaining and increasing US military and strategic support over the last fifteen years. The recent "war on terror" has notably benefited Singapore, which has expanded its strategic partnership with the United States; the Philippines and Thailand, which have been made major non-NATO allies enjoying better access to American training and equipment; and Indonesia, which has had military-to-military relations reinstated. These strategic ties with the United States are perceived to boost their ability to meet potential Chinese military threats, but more importantly, to facilitate a longer-term US military presence in the region that would deter Chinese ambitions.

Economic challenges

China's successful diplomacy vis-à-vis Southeast Asia has been expressed significantly on the economic front. For instance, Chinese restraint in its currency policy and aid to some Southeast Asian countries during the 1997 Asian financial crisis marked a significant turning-point in ASEAN perceptions of China. Its initiatives to promote economic regionalism in the ASEAN+3 grouping, which brings together Southeast Asian countries along with China, Japan, and South Korea, has also been one of the highlights of Beijing's multilateralist turn.

Yet, for Southeast Asia, a rising China will bring both economic benefits and costs. On the positive side of the ledger, as the Chinese economy continues to grow, its demand for exports from ASEAN will increase, particularly in terms of primary commodities and natural resources.[23] For instance, China's trade with Southeast Asia has already grown massively from $8 billion in 1981 to over $130 billion in 2005.[24] Furthermore, in a concrete indication of its desire to seek mutual benefits with the region through economic development, Beijing proposed in 2000 the idea of establishing a free trade area with Southeast Asia by 2010. If the ongoing negotiations are successful, the world's largest free trade zone will be created—comprising 1.7 billion people, a total GDP of $2 trillion, and total trade exceeding $1.2 trillion. It is estimated to have the potential of raising Southeast Asia exports to China by $13 billion (48 percent) and Chinese exports to ASEAN by $11 billion (55 percent).[25]

On the negative side, though, China and many Southeast Asian countries, at their present stages of economic development, tend to be more competitive than complementary in foreign direct investment (FDI) and manufactured exports in the developed-country markets. Southeast Asia worries primarily about China siphoning off foreign investments in the region: for instance, figures from 2001–2002 suggest that China attracted 50 to 70 percent of the FDI in Asia (excluding Japan), as opposed to the 20 percent that ASEAN received.[26] Even though the drop in the level of FDI flowing to ASEAN might have had more to do with the fallout of the 1997 financial crisis than direct competition from

China, the figures still pose questions about Southeast Asia's long-term ability to attract FDI.[27]

In addition, Southeast Asia faces stiff Chinese competition as rapid growth and foreign investment make China the world's pre-eminent low-cost manufacturer, not only of traditional labor-intensive goods like textiles, but increasingly of information technology, hardware, and electronics. The least developed ASEAN countries—Myanmar, Laos and Cambodia—are not in a position to compete with China, but rather have been at the receiving end of targeted Chinese investment and aid.[28] Countries such as Vietnam, Indonesia, and Thailand have been especially worried about intensifying Chinese competition in clothing and footwear manufacturing,[29] while the rapid expansion of China's non-traditional exports such as machinery and electronics is having the most disruptive impact on Indonesia, Thailand, Malaysia, Singapore, and Vietnam. Compared to these countries, China possesses a much larger pool of skilled as well as non-skilled labor. Furthermore, its massive domestic market provides considerable economies-of-scale opportunities. With lower marginal and average costs, China is thus able to enjoy a tremendous cost advantage over ASEAN. As a result, Southeast Asian countries face significant challenges of enhancing the price and quality of their products in order to remain competitive.

While the concern about Chinese competition is acute in the largest ASEAN economies, it is difficult to assess the relative gains and losses of each Southeast Asian country vis-à-vis China in terms of trade. For instance, there has been a significant change in the composition of ASEAN exports and imports to and from China since the mid-1990s. The top import–export items in ASEAN–China trade are now electrical and electronic products, parts, and components, constituting up to 50 percent of ASEAN-6 (Indonesia, Philippines, Singapore, Malaysia, Thailand, Brunei) exports to China, and 75 percent of ASEAN-6 imports from China. This reflects the growing integration of these economies as part of the same regional production networks of multinational firms. This not only complicates attempts to calculate relative gains and losses in trade from China's growth, but it also means that prospects for collective ASEAN action to cope with China trade competition are slim.[30] At the same time, ASEAN states' capacity to deal with Chinese FDI competition will critically depend first upon their ability to undertake domestic reforms necessary to enhance their economies' capacity to generate new capital.[31] Subsequently, ASEAN's competitiveness will depend also on its ability to enhance regional monetary and financial integration in the wake of the 1997 financial crisis. Here, the key challenges are exchange rate harmonization, the development of regional bond markets, and evolving regional financial arrangements.[32] In other words, whether the Southeast Asian economies can cope with China's rise depends in part on whether they can achieve national economic reform and resolve intra-ASEAN coordination problems. In addition, the overall effects of Chinese economic growth for Southeast Asia will also depend upon changing patterns of market access and investment. While the eventual ACFTA will liberalize the regional trade regime, Southeast Asian businesses currently have more limited access to important sectors of the Chinese economy than vice versa. In recognition of this, an accord was signed at the most recent China–ASEAN summit meeting to open up key Chinese service sectors including banking, transportation, real estate, and health, from July 2007. China will also need to demonstrate that it can invest much more significantly in its neighboring economies as its economy continues to grow, balancing out the balance of investments deficit with Southeast Asia.[33]

Southeast Asian strategies

The mixed record discussed so far suggests that Southeast Asian responses to China's rise have been marked by cautious optimism. There has been some speculation about whether Chinese ascendance has been so well managed over the last decade that Southeast Asia is moving into a Chinese sphere of influence. Yet, one ought not to ignore the common refrain in the region that the grass gets trampled, regardless of whether the elephants fight or make love. Southeast Asia is ultimately a collection of small and medium-sized states with significant internal and external insecurity, sharing two overwhelming strategic imperatives: anti-hegemony and diversification. Because of an intense post-independence struggle for bilateral and regional leadership between Indonesia and Malaysia, the core regional security principle of ASEAN has always been the prevention of intramural hegemony.[34] This renunciation of dominance by any single actor has extended to preventing the exercise of regional hegemony by any one external power. Thus, while the major Southeast Asian states—Indonesia, Malaysia, the Philippines, Singapore, Thailand, and Vietnam—acknowledge that they cannot avoid being part of the ambit of the big powers, they share a desire to not fall within the exclusive sphere of influence of one great power and assiduously explore options for diversifying dependence.[35]

In examining Southeast Asian approaches toward China, we can identify a broad maritime–continental divide. Continental Southeast Asian states, particularly the Indochinese states, have regional strategic outlooks that are dominated by the role of China. With the exception of Thailand, their relative deference to their huge neighbor is further necessitated by the lack of strategic ties with other major powers like the United States. Maritime Southeast Asia, by contrast, enjoys more room for maneuver because of geographical distance and strategic attraction for the United States. Singapore and the Philippines especially place more faith in leaning on their American partner, while Indonesia and Malaysia feel more confident in steering a middle path between China and the United States.

In spite of their differences, Southeast Asian states share some fundamental similarities in their perceptions of and strategic approaches to China. None of these Southeast Asian countries identifies China as a threat, preferring to discuss the "challenges" a rising China poses. They all ascribe to a strategy of vigorous engagement and attempted socialization of China, and uniformly see

China as an engine for economic growth in the region, even though they identify different degrees of individual economic opportunities in Chinese development. It is also true that policymakers commonly emphasize that Southeast Asia has no choice but to engage with China, as it is, by dint of geography and history, an intrinsic part of the region and a "true" regional great power. As a result too, all these countries unhesitatingly acknowledge rising Chinese influence in the region, mainly in terms of trade and investment, but also in the realm of regional political institutions. In particular, they agree that Beijing's record in the ASEAN Regional Forum, ASEAN+3, and other Sino–ASEAN institutions has been encouraging and improving over the last decade.

However, the Southeast Asian countries still appear to reserve judgment on whether China is ultimately a benign or threatening rising power. Almost every country's leaders express worries about the territorial disputes in the South China Sea and about potential conflict between China and the United States over Taiwan. Thus, while China's impressive diplomatic and economic engagement with the region in recent years is readily acknowledged, it is less clear whether the Southeast Asian countries in fact "buy" the idea of China's "peaceful rise" in the longer term. To some extent this is a conceptual problem, since the success or failure of their engagement strategy may ultimately depend on falsification based on future potential negative action by Beijing.[36]

Given this, it is premature to judge if Southeast Asia has been "won over," or, as Shambaugh puts it, "it remains far too early . . . to conclude that the regional order is becoming the modern version of the imperial 'tribute system' or that China is becoming the dominant regional hegemon."[37] More importantly, being absorbed into a Chinese sphere of influence, however apparently benign, is clearly not the Southeast Asian strategic preference, because of the region's twin imperatives of counter-hegemony and diversification. Indeed, the way the region has sought to adapt to and manage strategic changes since the early 1990s reflects a sophisticated strategy of "managing the elephant": creating and optimizing room for maneuver vis-à-vis China and other major powers. Southeast Asian strategic responses to China must be placed within the context of greater regional security strategies.

Regarding the China challenge, most analysts of Southeast Asia concur that the region has adopted a twin "hedging" strategy of deep engagement on the one hand and, on the other, "soft balancing" against potential Chinese aggression or disruption of the status quo. The latter strategy includes not only military acquisitions and modernization but also attempts to keep the United States involved in the region as a counterweight to Chinese power.[38] In the abstract, hedging refers to taking action to ensure against undesirable outcomes, usually by betting on multiple alternative positions. For Southeast Asia, hedging is a set of strategies aimed at avoiding (or planning for contingencies in) a situation in which states cannot decide upon more straightforward alternatives such as balancing, bandwagoning, or neutrality. Instead they cultivate a middle position that forestalls or avoids having to choose one side at the obvious expense of another.[39]

From a broader regional strategic perspective, hedging behavior in Southeast Asia comprises three elements. First is the complex engagement of China at the political, economic, and strategic levels with the hope that Chinese leaders may be persuaded or socialized into conduct that abides by international rules and norms. In this sense, engagement policies may be understood as a constructive hedge against potentially aggressive Chinese domination. Second, hedging entails indirect or soft balancing, which mainly involves persuading other major powers, particularly the United States, to act as counterweights to Chinese regional influence. The third element is a general policy of enmeshing a number of regional major powers to give them a stake in a stable regional order. All told, Southeast Asian states are in fact hedging against three key undesirable outcomes: Chinese domination or hegemony; American withdrawal from the region; and an unstable regional order.[40]

Engagement with China has already been discussed in the previous section. At the same time, since the end of the Cold War, key ASEAN states have tried to harness the superior US forces in the region to deter potential aggression from China. Two Southeast Asian states—the Philippines and Thailand—are formal allies of the United States, but neither plays host to American bases. Instead, they and a number of non-allied countries, including Singapore, Malaysia and Indonesia—provide military facilities and access to US naval and air forces. They also participate in bilateral and multilateral joint exercises and some countries have preferential military supply relations with the United States.[41] These policies are aimed at facilitating the continued military presence of the United States, and to consolidate and advance its power projection capabilities in the region. Rather than encouraging the United States to target its forces directly against China, though, the goal is to further buttress American military superiority in the region, and to demonstrate the ability to harness it, in order to persuade Beijing that any aggressive action would be too costly and/or unlikely to succeed.[42] Such balancing behavior is "soft" because it is indirect on the part of Southeast Asian states, which rely on the United States as the balancer of first resort against China.

Furthermore, ASEAN's engagement with China extends beyond this one great power alone. The former's efforts at developing closer economic relations; creating political/security dialogue, exchanges, and cooperation; and establishing military exchanges and relationships, are aimed not only at China, but also at the United States, as well as other major regional players such as Japan, South Korea, and India. This is an "omni-enmeshment" strategy that stems from the Southeast Asian imperative for diversification of dependence. By enmeshing these multiple large powers into regional institutions and norms, Southeast Asian states want to involve them actively in the region by means of good political relationships, deep and preferential economic exchanges, and some degree of defense dialogue and exchange. It is believed that this would translate into greater stability in the region. Certainly the major powers would be able to "keep an eye on each other" and act as mutual deterrents against adventurism. In this sense, enmeshment is about hedging against the possibility of violent rivalry between major powers in the region and major power aggression against smaller states. More constructively, however, these Southeast Asian countries want to buy time in the hope that these powers will discover they have common interests that are not mutually exclusive, such as the economic benefits of free trade and secure trading routes in the region. Thus they would be unwilling to disrupt the status quo at each other's expense—which would be more costly than if it were at the expense of the small or medium-sized states of the region alone. The major powers may then settle into a sustainable pattern of engagement and accommodation with the region and each other.[43]

The aim of the hedging strategy of great power enmeshment is not to produce a multipolar balance of power in the conventional sense, because the major powers involved here are not all in the same league. Rather, many Southeast Asian countries prefer to retain the United States as the preponderant great power, with China as the regional major power, and India, Japan, and South Korea as second-tier regional powers.[44] For instance, officials in Bangkok and Singapore hope that the gap between Chinese and American power and influence in the region will be maintained even as China grows stronger and, moreover, that Washington will continue to wield dominant influence.[45] As one Thai academic put it, the key task now is "to convince the US that its interests in the region are greater than anyone else's; to make China feel like its regional influence is on the rise; and to raise India's involvement in this part of the world."[46] Even in Hanoi, where the shadow of Chinese power is most keenly felt, the understanding is that the United States holds the primary strategic position in the region—and this pre-eminence is expected to continue as American economic ties with Vietnam and the region continue to grow.[47]

The implications of this broader regional security strategy is that, if one pays serious attention to Southeast Asian strategies and strategic preferences, then fears of Southeast Asia voluntarily moving exclusively into the Chinese sphere of influence or bandwagoning with China are misplaced.

Conclusion

The foregoing analysis suggests that in Southeast Asia, the China challenge has been transformed over the last fifteen years from being an unpredictable and thus threatening disruption to the regional status quo, to being an important source of continued economic development and diversified regional influence. Particularly over the last decade, the Southeast Asian regional security strategy of hedging by enmeshing China into regional norms while retaining American counterveiling power and engaging other major regional powers appears to have been successful in mediating the negative impacts of China's rise. This success must also be attributed to Beijing's altered approach to the region and its astute diplomacy, as well as the relative restraint exercised by China, the United States, and other major regional powers in regional security matters. Together, these trends have produced a reasonably stable regional order underpinned by continued American preponderance, growing Chinese engagement, and medium-power political activism.

However, this remains a period of strategic transition for East and Southeast Asia. While there has been significant positive progress made and regional threat perceptions have been mediated by Chinese diplomacy and successful mutual engagement, four problems remain, the trajectories of which will determine the future shape of regional order.

First, Southeast Asia started from a very low base in terms of expectations vis-à-vis China. Since the early 1990s, the key aim has been to "engage" with China, to develop economic and diplomatic relations with it, to cultivate political and strategic dialogue, and to include it in regional and international institutions. Engagement is not fundamentally a very demanding goal: Beijing has not only fulfilled ASEAN's expectations of participation in dialogue and uptake of ASEAN norms, but has at times surprised ASEAN, such as with its proposal for ACFTA, and at others surpassed them, as with its push for defense dialogues and exclusive Asian institutions. Because the Southeast Asians have not coherently adjusted their low initial expectations, ASEAN has been left in a position either of playing catch-up with China or of holding out against its more innovative initiatives. The difficulty of evaluating the benignity of China's rise is compounded by the fact that China–Southeast Asian relations have not been tested by crisis since 1995. There has not been an instance of outright dispute over an issue on which two or more parties have had clear divergent national interests that they were willing to act to protect. In the absence of such crises, it is difficult to test the substance and durability of current good relations.

Second, and central to ASEAN, is the concern that Southeast Asia is becoming increasingly divided by different priorities and preferences in coping with the further rise of China. There are several ways to draw the divide, but a crude one is the fault line between maritime Southeast Asia (the Philippines, Malaysia, Indonesia, and Singapore) and continental Southeast Asia (Cambodia, Laos, Myanmar, and Vietnam, with Thailand occupying an ambiguous position in between). The so-called CLMV countries of continental Southeast Asia have strategic landscapes that are dominated by China, due to a combination of geography, history, and the lack of alternatives. The maritime states, on the other hand, being more developed and the focus particularly of US regional strategy, have considerably more options vis-à-vis China, even though they also have differences in priorities among themselves.[48] Such fault lines will expand as Chinese influence in the region increases, with significant implications for ASEAN solidarity and thus its collective strategies and for the future of regional institutions such as the ARF and ASEAN+3. These divisions will also bring into question ASEAN's ability to maintain a coherent strategy toward the great powers, exacerbating the existing problem of lack of strategic thought regarding the "end-game" in the Southeast Asian strategy of great power engagement. While most regional policymakers profess to prefer good Sino–American relations and cooperation, they do not suggest how the two large powers will coexist—will it be the result of a balance of power brought about by mutual deterrence, or will it be a concert of powers with negotiated spheres of influence? This is partly due to the fact that relations between the great powers lie very much outside the influence of ASEAN states.

The third problem relates also to the limits of ASEAN influence: the main strategic issues in East Asia are located in Northeast Asia, whether it is the Taiwan Straits, the Korean Peninsula, or Sino–Japanese tensions. As a result, many policymakers and analysts either concentrate on these "East Asian" issues and regard the Northeast–Southeast Asia divide as artificial, or overlook Southeast Asia. In regional strategic terms, the most pertinent problem is the constant fear that ASEAN will become less and less relevant, as it cannot contribute to the management or resolution of any of these core security issues.

Finally, Southeast Asian states are also significantly limited in their ability to manage relations with China across the diverse spectrum of strategic issues in the region. Apart from the political, economic, and military issues discussed here, "non-traditional" security issues permeate the regional security agenda and constitute a large proportion of the cooperative endeavors of internal and external ASEAN relations. These are trans-boundary non-military security issues that include, most prominently, infectious diseases, trafficking, and environmental degradation, that require collective action, and that have significant potential to impact negatively upon the socio-political-economic stability of affected states. Yet, these are some of the issues on which ASEAN states themselves find most difficult to cooperate meaningfully.[49] These are also divisive issues because the costs and benefits of collective action are not usually evenly distributed, either within or across states. For instance, the Southeast Asian states that share the Mekong River with China have not been able to persuade it to participate in regional agreements on water utilization and basin planning, partly because of the power asymmetry, but also because of the shared concerns about sovereignty and non-intervention and the shared focus on economic growth.[50]

Ultimately, Southeast Asian countries remain deeply pragmatic, and we may expect them to continue to do their best to readjust to the changing strategic context in ways that enable them to balance or diversify their dependencies. However, Southeast Asia does face very significant limitations in terms of size and geography, which are exacerbated by severe limitations in strategic thinking and collective action. Whether the relative success of Southeast Asian responses to China's rise thus far can be built upon and deepened into a stable regional order will depend on whether these states can continue to find sufficient common interests and mechanisms to manage both the "elephants" and themselves.

Notes

1   Shee Poon Kim, "The South China Sea in China's Strategic Thinking," *Contemporary Southeast Asia* 19(4), 1998, pp. 369–387.

2   "Turning a Rising China into Positive Force for Asia," *Straits Times*, September 26, 2001.

3   A summary and reflection of this evolving approach can be found in Wang Jisi, "China's Changing Role in Asia," paper delivered at Salzburg Seminar, Session 415, 2003; and Alice Ba, "China and ASEAN: Renavigating Relations for a twenty-first Century Asia." *Asian Survey* 43(4), 2003, pp. 630–638. Wang suggests that Chinese assessments of the regional security environment are now more sanguine. He says that China's regional strategy is circumscribed by the issues of economic cooperation, developments on the Korean peninsula, efforts at forging regional security institutions, the Taiwan question, the Sino–Japanese relationship, and the US factor.

4   This realist predisposition is waived for only one state in the Asia-Pacific—the United States—which most Southeast Asian states have come to regard as a benign power that could act as arbiter. This somewhat complacent view may be changing, though, with concerns about US unilateralism and the fallout of US foreign policy since 9/11.

5   Alastair Iain Johnston and Robert S. Ross, eds, *Engaging China: The Management of a Rising Power*, New York: Routledge, 1999; Evelyn Goh and Amitav Acharya, "The ASEAN Regional Forum and Security Regionalism: Comparing Chinese and American Positions," in Melissa Curley and Nick Thomas, eds, *Advancing East Asian Regionalism*, London: Routledge, 2007, pp. 96–115.

6   James Shinn, ed., *Weaving the Net: The Conditional Engagement of China*, New York: Council on Foreign Relations, 1996; Alastair Iain Johnston, "Socialization in International Institutions: The ASEAN Way and International Relations Theory," in G. John Ikenberry and Michael Mastanduno, eds, *International Relations Theory and the Asia-Pacific*, New York: Columbia University Press, 2003, pp. 107–162; Pauline Kerr, Andrew Mack and Paul Evans, "The Evolving Security Discourse in the Asia-Pacific," in Andrew Mack and John Ravenhill, eds, *Pacific Cooperation: Building Economic and Security Regimes in the Asia-Pacific Region*, Boulder, CO: Westview, 1995, pp. 250–254.

7   Rosemary Foot, "China in the ASEAN Regional Forum: Organizational Processes and Domestic Modes of Thought," *Asian Survey* 38(5), 1998, pp. 425–440; Goh and Acharya, "The ASEAN Regional Forum." The first defense white paper, titled *China's National Defense in 2002*, is available at www. china.org/cn/e-white/, together with a list of other white papers, including subsequent defense white papers published in 2004 and 2006.

8   See Amitav Acharya, *Constructing a Security Community in Southeast Asia: ASEAN and the Problem of Regional Order*, New York: Routledge, 2000, chapter 6; Johnston, "Socialization in International Relations."

9   For a discussion of the "ASEAN way" see Hiro Katsumata, "Reconstruction of Diplomatic Norms in Southeast Asia: The Case for Strict Adherence to the 'ASEAN Way'," *Contemporary Southeast Asia* 25(1), April 2003, pp. 104–121.

10 "China Snuggles Up to Southeast Asia," *Asia Times*, October 7, 2003. ASEAN has invited all its dialogue partners to sign the treaty. China was the first to accede to the treaty, along with India, and they were followed in 2004 by Japan, South Korea, and Russia, leaving the United States as a conspicuous exception.

11 Avery Goldstein, *Rising to the Challenge: China's Grand Strategy and International Security*, Stanford, CA: Stanford University Press, 2005, pp. 173–174. The text of the Joint Declaration is available at: www.aseansec.org/15265.htm.

12 For a very positive review, see David Shambaugh, "China Engages Asia: Reshaping the Regional Order," *International Security* 29(3), Winter 2004/5, pp. 64–99.

13 See "New group for 'Asian century' shuns US," *International Herald Tribune*, December 12, 2005; Mohan Malik, "The East Asia Summit: More Discord than

Accord," *YaleGlobal*, December 20, 2005; Yang Razali Kassim, "The rise of East Asia? ASEAN's driver role key to ties between Japan and China," *IDSS Commentaries*, December 22, 2005.

14   See Zhai Kun, "Commonwealth offers bright future for East Asia," *China Daily*, January 15, 2007; Remarks by Christopher Hill, Assistant Secretary of State for East Asian and Pacific Affairs, to the Lee Kuan Yew School, Singapore, May 22, 2006.

15   See, for instance, Gerald Segal, "The Coming Confrontation between China and Japan," *World Policy Journal* 10(2), Summer 1993, pp. 27–32; Aaron Friedberg, "Ripe for Rivalry: Prospects for Peace in a Multipolar Asia," *International Security* 18(3), Winter 1993/4, pp. 5–33; Richard Bernstein and Ross Munro, "The Coming Conflict with America," *Foreign Affairs* 76(2), March/April 1997, pp. 18–32.

16   M. Taylor Fravel, "Regime Insecurity and International Cooperation: Explaining China's Compromises in Territorial Disputes," *International Security* 30(2), Fall 2005, pp. 46–83; Ang Cheng Guan, "Vietnam-China Relations Since the End of the Cold War," *Asian Survey* 38(12), 1998, pp. 1122–1141.

17   The implications of this non-binding declaration have been debated—see Ralf Emmers, "ASEAN, China, and the South China Sea: An Opportunity Missed," *IDSS Commentaries*, 2001; Leszek Buszynski, "ASEAN, the Declaration on Conduct, and the South China Sea." *Contemporary Southeast Asia* 25(3), 2003, pp. 434–463; Wu Shicun and Ren Huaifeng, "More Than a Declaration: A Commentary on the Background and Significance of the Declaration on the Conduct of Parties in the South China Sea," *Chinese Journal of International Law* 2(1), 2003, pp. 311–320.

18   See Michael Glosny, "Heading Toward a Win-Win Future? Recent Developments in China's Policy toward Southeast Asia," *Asian Security* 2(1), 2006, pp. 24–57 (pp. 37–38).

19   "Beijing offers Manila $2.6bn in funds," *Straits Times*, April 28, 2005; "Philippines warms to China with care," *Straits Times*, June 7, 2006.

20   "RI-China seal multibillion deal to strengthen trade," *Jakarta Post*, April 26, 2005; "Interview with Indonesia's Defence Minister: Running low on ammunition," *Straits Times*, May 13, 2005; "China offers arms to Indonesia," *South China Morning Post*, April 26, 2005.

21   See Evelyn Goh, *Meeting the China Challenge: The US in Southeast Asian Regional Security Strategies*, Washington, D.C.: East-West Center Washington Policy Studies Monograph no. 16, 2005, pp. 19–23.

22   For a contrasting, optimistic assessment of potential joint Southeast Asian capabilities to counterbalance Chinese power, see Bernard Loo, "Military Modernization, Power Projection, and the Rise of the PLA: Strategic Implications for Southeast Asia," in Evelyn Goh and Sheldon Simon, eds, *China, the United States, and Southeast Asia: Contending Perspectives on Politics, Security, and Economics*, London: Routledge, 2007, pp. 185–199.

23   "China's Rise: Export Boon for SE Asia," *Straits Times*, April 29, 2002; "China's Economic Prowess Is Not a Threat," *International Herald Tribune*, March 4, 2003.

24   "ASEAN Trade Prospects Bright," *China Daily*, September 7, 2006.

25   "China's Rise: Export Boon for SE Asia," *Straits Times*, April 29, 2002; ASEAN–China Expert Group on Economic Cooperation, *Forging Closer ASEAN–China Economic Relations in the 21st Century*, October 2001, available at www.aseansec.org. For a succinct analysis of the economic and political significance of the China–ASEAN negotiations see Ba, "China and ASEAN," pp. 622–647.

26 "China Boom Will Boost Region's Prosperity," *Straits Times*, April 25, 2002; "Turning a Rising China into Positive Force for Asia," *Straits Times*, September 26, 2001.
27 See Friedrich Wu *et al.*, "Foreign Direct Investments to China and ASEAN: Has ASEAN Been Losing Out?" *Economic Survey of Singapore*, 2003, available at www.mti.gov.sg/public/PDF/CMT/NWS_2002Q3_FD11.pdf?sid+92&cid=1418.
28 See Glosny, "Heading Toward a Win-Win Future?" pp. 30–31.
29 Note here that it has been difficult to gauge the impacts of recent changes in textile trading because currently available data do not yet reflect the impacts of the abolition of the Multi-Fiber Arrangement quota system from January 1, 2005, and the phasing out of the transitional arrangements accompanying China's accession to the WTO.
30 John Ravenhill, "Is China an Economic Threat to Southeast Asia?" *Asian Survey* 46(5), September/October 2006, pp. 671–672; Suthiphand Chirathivat, "China's Rise and Its Effects on ASEAN-China Trade Relations," in Goh and Simon, *China, the United States and Southeast Asia*.
31 Ravenhill, "Is China an Economic Threat to Southeast Asia?" pp. 655–664.
32 Tan Khee Giap, "ASEAN and China: Relative Competitiveness, Emerging Investment-Trade Patterns, Monetary and Financial Integration," in Goh and Simon, *China, the United States and Southeast Asia*.
33 Chinese firms only recorded overseas investments of US$16 billion in 2006, a "nearly negligible" amount, as Prime Minister Wen Jiabao noted. Robert Sutter and Chin-Hao Huang, "China-Southeast Asia Relations," *Comparative Connections*, April 2007, pp. 73, 78.
34 Michael Leifer, *ASEAN and the Security of South-East Asia* (London: Routledge 1989); Ralf Emmers, *Cooperative Security and the Balance of Power in ASEAN and the ARF* (London: RoutledgeCurzon 2003).
35 Alice Ba, "Southeast Asia and China," in Evelyn Goh, ed., *Betwixt and Between: Southeast Asian Strategic Relations with the US and China* (Singapore: IDSS 2005).
36 A systematic comparison of seven key ASEAN states' strategic perceptions of China and the US is found in Goh, *Betwixt and Between*.
37 David Shambaugh, "China Engages Asia: Reshaping the Regional Order," *International Security* 29(3), Winter 2004/5, p. 66.
38 Yuen Foong Khong, "Coping with Strategic Uncertainty: The Role of Institutions and Soft Balancing in Southeast Asia's Post-Cold War Strategy," in J.J. Suh, Peter J. Katzenstein, and Allen Carlson, eds, *Rethinking Security in Southeast Asia: Identity, Power, and Efficiency*, Stanford, CA: Stanford University Press, 2004.
39 The existing literature on hedging in the Asia-Pacific is unsatisfactory; the term is applied to multiple states acting in a variety of ways against a range of outcomes. See, for instance, Robert Manning and James Przystup, "Asia's Transition Diplomacy: Hedging Against Future Shock," *Survival* 41(3), 1999, pp. 43–67; C.P. Chung, "Southeast Asia–China Relations: Dialectics of 'Hedging' and 'Counter-Hedging,'" *Southeast Asian Affairs*, 2004, pp. 35–43; Evan Medeiros, "Strategic Hedging and the Future of Asia-Pacific Stability," *The Washington Quarterly*, 29(1), Winter 2005/6, pp. 145–167; Evelyn Goh, "Understanding 'Hedging' in Asia-Pacific Security," PacNet 43, August 31, 2006.
40 Goh, *Meeting the China Challenge*, pp. 1–4.
41 For details, see Evelyn Goh, "Great Powers and Southeast Asian Regional Security Strategies: Omni-enmeshment, Complex Balancing and Hierarchical Order," mimeo, 2006.
42 The United States is viewed as the key strategic force in the region for two reasons: its alliance with Japan forestalls Japanese remilitarization, and its military presence deters Chinese aggression in the Taiwan Straits and South China Sea.

43   See Amitav Acharya, "Regional Institutions and Security Order: Norms, Identity, and Prospects for Peaceful Change," in Muthiah Alagappa, ed., *Asian Security Order: Instrumental and Normative Features*, Stanford: Stanford University Press, 2002.

44   This is an initial finding based on interviews with officials. While the preference for US preponderance and China's secondary role is clear, it is at the moment more difficult to substantiate the suggested preference for the other nations as second-tier powers; how this would impact on relations and expectations; or how the hedging strategy is calibrated to incorporate these second-tier powers.

45   One Thai analyst has suggested that the current distribution of influence in the region is 80 percent US, 15 percent Japan, and 5 percent China. He ventures that so long as American influence exceeds 50 percent, stability will be maintained. Author interview, Bangkok, April 2004.

46   Author interview, Bangkok, April 2004.

47   For more details, see Goh, *Betwixt and Between*; Goh, *Meeting the China Challenge*; Goh, "Great Powers and Southeast Asian Regional Security Strategies."

48   See Goh, *Betwixt and Between*, Introduction.

49   One particular example is the annual problem of severe atmospheric haze in Malaysia and Singapore caused by massive forest fires in Indonesia.

50   See Evelyn Goh, *Developing the Mekong: Regionalism and Regional Security in China-Southeast Asian Relations*, Adelphi Paper 387, London: IISS, 2007.

9 India's response to China's rise

J. Mohan Malik*

At the beginning of the early twenty-first century, we are witnessing power transitions of the kind that usually take place once in 50 to 100 years in the international system. Power in the international system is always relative and ever-shifting.[1] It does not stay the same. Historically, long cycles of economic growth, wars, and imperial overstretch inevitably bring about changes in the geopolitical balance of power. No nation remains pre-eminent forever. The US National Intelligence Council and the investment banking and securities firm Goldman Sachs Inc. predict that, by 2040, the world's largest economies will be China, the United States, India, and Japan—in that order. Economic expansion inevitably leads to overseas military expansion and fuels grandiose geopolitical ambitions. More than a quarter century of exponential economic growth in China has been accompanied by nearly two decades of double-digit growth in its military expenditure, thereby creating geopolitical realignments and frictions around the world. However, China is not rising in a vacuum. India is also rising, so is Russia, and Japan is increasingly becoming a "normal nation." The Asia-Pacific of the early twenty-first century—home to several rising and contending powers as well as some weak and failing states—thus bears more resemblance to Europe of the late nineteenth and early twentieth centuries than to Europe of the early twenty-first century. This region is home to several rising and contending powers as well as some weak and failing states. Generally speaking, power transitions are usually dangerous periods when an established great power is challenged by the rise of a rival or peer competitors because rising powers are by nature revisionist, not status quo, powers. They seek to expand their power and influence in and beyond their regions mostly at the expense of established great powers.

The era of post-Cold War unipolarity—with the United States as the sole superpower—is fast fading into history. When historians look back in a few decades' time, the year 2001 will be seen as marking the beginning of the end of the "unipolar moment" in history. This was the year when the sole super-power, the United States, was challenged by both state and non-state actors—first by China in April 2001 over the EP-3 spy plane incident, and then by al-Qaeda via the 9/11 terrorist attacks. Though the United States still stands as a global colossus—economically, militarily, and culturally—the challenge to US global primacy today stems as much from China's rise as from sharpening conflicts over natural resources (particularly oil and natural gas), as from the emergence of new economic centers of gravity, as from ideological differences over democracy or human rights, and challenges posed by a trinity of non-state actors, Islamist terrorism and nuclear proliferation. In short, changes in comparative economic advantages have always preceded political competition in the international system. Rising powers thrive on picking up loose geopolitical change on their periphery. This is what the United States did in the nineteenth century in Latin America by proclaiming the Monroe Doctrine, and that is exactly what China is now doing in Central Asia (via the Shanghai Cooperation Organization), in Burma, Iran, and Pakistan, and in Africa where Beijing faces little or no competition. The key elements of China's grand strategy can be identified as follows:

*   Acquire "comprehensive national power" essential to achieving the status of a "global great power that is second to none" by 2049 (marking 100 years of the founding of the PRC);
*   Gain access to global natural resources, raw materials and overseas markets to sustain China's economic expansion. As an old Chinese proverb puts it, "*yang wei zhong yong*": make foreign resources, goods and technology help China become strong and powerful;
*   Pursue "three Ms": military build-up (including naval presence along the vital sea lanes of communication and maritime chokepoints), multilateralism, and multipolarity; and
*   Build a worldwide network of China's friends and allies through "soft power" diplomacy, trade and economic dependencies via free trade agreements, mutual security pacts, intelligence cooperation, and arms sales.

Asian responses to China's rise: three-tiers

The moment a country arrives on the international stage as "a great power of its age," it automatically generates envy, cooperation, opposition, and rivalry. How to adapt to China's growing power and influence is a question that dominates foreign policy establishment of nearly every country in the world. Among regional countries, China arouses unease because of its size, history, proximity, potential power, and more importantly, because the memories of "the Middle Kingdom syndrome" and tributary state system have not dimmed. Interestingly, a survey conducted in China in 2005 revealed that many interviewees thought that "a stronger China will try to restore its traditional vassal system." Once China emerges as an "unrivalled regional power and a major global actor, it will use its enhanced power to grant assistance and protection to 'the faithful countries,' in return for their alliance, obedience and inevitable submission and compliance."[2] Historically, there has never been a time when China has coexisted on equal terms with another power of similar or lesser stature. However, with the exception of a few, most Asian countries show no desire to live in a China-led or China-dominated Asia. Instead, they seek to preserve existing security alliances and pursue sophisticated diplomatic and hedging strategies designed to give them more freedom of action while avoiding overt alignment with major powers. Being a distant hegemon, the US still remains the balancer of choice for countries on China's periphery.

If one looks at the history of international relations over the last 500 years, the rise of a major continental power—especially one with an authoritarian regime nursing historical grievances with active territorial disputes—has always resulted in major geopolitical alignments, and led to the formation of a coalition of maritime powers to counter it. China is no exception to this rule. The US hedging strategy, the US–India nuclear deal, the growing warmth in India-Japan ties, the US–Japan–Australia–India quadrilateral (a.k.a. "concert of democracies") are all part of this—an inevitable response to the rise of China. By and large, countries on a rising power's periphery tend to either balance against or bandwagon with the rising power. Some, of course, choose to do both. Given China's centrality in Asian geopolitics, "hedging" against the rise of China is becoming the most preferred option, without giving up on the many benefits of engaging Beijing. In the early part of the twenty-first century, I would divide the Asian-Pacific states' responses to China's rise into three tiers:

- *First-Tier—Balancing*: India, Japan, Australia, Vietnam, Taiwan, Mongolia, and Indonesia are pursuing a clear balance-of-power or hedging strategy vis-à-vis China by strengthening their security ties with the United States as well as with each other (e.g. India's proactive courting of Japan, Taiwan, Vietnam, and Mongolia) to counterbalance China. The first-tier countries are obviously concerned about the strategic implications of China's ambitious military modernization program, which emphasizes preparations to fight and win short-duration, high-intensity conflicts along its periphery (esp. with those countries that have disputed borders with China).
- *Second-Tier—Balancing and Bandwagoning*: South Korea, Thailand, the Philippines, Malaysia, Laos, East Timor, and Singapore are both bandwagoning with and balancing against China. In other words, putting their eggs in both American and Chinese baskets. Most of these second-tier countries welcome the return of bipolarity and are already playing the reigning superpower off against the rising superpower to extract economic/diplomatic/military concessions.
- *Third-Tier—Bandwagoning*: North Korea, Pakistan, Iran, Burma, Russia, Cambodia, Bangladesh, Nepal, and most Central Asian countries are clearly bandwagoning with China—albeit for entirely different motives.

Against this backdrop of the broader geopolitical scene, this paper will examine the state of India–China relations by outlining the Chinese and Indian perspectives of each other and the historical, economic and strategic determinants of India's China policy. The last section focuses on the strategies and tools available to Indian policymakers to cope with China's rise. It is argued that an increasingly confident India is unveiling a comprehensive strategy that moves the country away from "non-alignment" to a multi-dimensional "multi-alignment" with the world so as to meet the growing China challenge as well as to facilitate its own rise as a great power.

Perceptions, misperceptions, expectations and illusions

At the beginning of the twenty-first century, India and China—the world's two oldest civilization-states, once great powers, and home to two-fifths of the world's population with the fastest growing economies are back as claimants to pre-eminence in Asia and the world. For the first time in more than half a millennium, both are on the march upward simultaneously on their relative power trajectories. Both see Asia's rise on the world stage as bringing about the end of Western dominance. Both have similar robust attributes of a strong power, i.e. a massive manpower resources, scientific, technological and industrial base, and formidable armed forces. Both are nuclear and space powers with growing ambitions. Historically too, both giants have demonstrated their will and capacity as hegemons who have dominated the security environment in this region. Both are engaging ever more deeply in the world economy. They also have a long history of bitter rivalry, and an unresolved border dispute that erupted in war in 1962 and armed skirmishes in 1967 and 1987. Each has its weak point—regional conflicts, poverty and religious divisions for India; the contradiction within the "Market-Leninist" system (between capitalist economy and communist politics) for China. Both are plagued with domestic linguistic, ethno-religious and politico-economic fault lines that could be their undoing if not managed properly.

Despite growing interaction at the political, cultural and economic levels, the gulf between China and India—in terms of their perceptions, attitudes and expectations from each other—has widened over the last half a century. There exists in the Chinese mind a deep distrust of India—with the converse also holding true. There has been a lot of talk from both countries about partnership and mutual progress but in reality each has sought to thwart the other. Publicly, diplomats from each capital point to declarations made on many occasions by both Prime Minister Wen Jiabao and Prime Minister Manmohan Singh that "China's development and India's development are each other's opportunity rather than a threat," their actual policies and actions, however, demonstrate that in fact the opposite is true. Apparently, Chinese and Indians continue to talk at, rather than talking to, each other.

Chinese perspectives on India: "big power dreams"

Chinese leaders and diplomats often call upon India to "change its attitude toward China". While Indians constantly benchmark themselves against China, the Chinese, masters of self-projection, do not project their country as an Asian power but a global one that compares itself *only* with the United States while making disparaging comments about India's "unrealistic and unachievable 'big power dreams' (*daguomeng*)."[3] China, in fact, hates being spoken of in the same breath as India. Many Chinese find the growing global tendency to compare their country with India as "offensive" and "demeaning." As one letter to *Asia Times online* noted derisively: "China is not competing with India . . . it is competing with the USA. Who wants to compete with India?" Traditionally, China has never looked at India as an equal, but merely as an upstart wannabe that likes to punch above its weight. Nor can Beijing comprehend the idea of India being China's equal in the future. China's leaders and strategic thinkers "do not hold warm or positive views of India for China's future." In particular, they remain dismissive of India's claims as "the world's largest democracy,"[4] and are convinced that India's fractious polity will continue to limit its economic and military potential. Nearly 43 percent of respondents in a Chinese opinion poll saw India as overly ambitious while 31 percent saw their southern neighbor as unstable, hostile, and aggressive.[5] The Chinese believe that their culture and governance system are superior to India.[6]

At best, India is seen, in Chinese eyes, as an emerging South Asian "regional power" (but one that can be easily contained) rather than a potential global player in a new Asian century. The opinion poll mentioned earlier found more than 47 percent seeing Beijing as following a containment policy toward India while 13 percent thought it was a mix of containment and cooperation.[7] Beijing has been making significant inroads into India's backyard through cross-border economic and strategic penetration of Bangladesh, Burma, Nepal, Pakistan, Sri Lanka, and the Maldives. A high degree of suspicion, mistrust and conflictual relations between India and its smaller South Asian neighbors provides Beijing with enormous strategic leverage vis-à-vis its southern rival, and thus prevents India from achieving optimal economic growth and spreading its wings on the global stage.[8]

Politically, Chinese strategic thinkers perceive the emerging multipolar world as strikingly similar to that of the Warring States era (475–221 BC) when wars were common, as were conferences, shifting alliances, betrayals, and the rise and extinction of some of the contending states. This period was characterized by power rivalries, with some competing to become a hegemon and others forming alliances to prevent any state from attaining that dominant status.[9] This outlook necessitates distrust of strong, powerful neighbors and preference for small, weak and subordinate or client buffer states.[10] Believing that Indian power contradicts Chinese power, the Chinese do not like the prospect of India raising its power, stature and profile regionally or internationally. In the power competition game, China has clearly surged far ahead of India by acquiring potent economic and military capabilities and the existing asymmetry in power and status serves Beijing's interests very well. Beijing's attitude to the expansion of the UN Security Council and India's nuclear program is an indication that China will not countenance the emergence of an Asian peer competitor.

However, over the last few years, China's India-watchers have started focusing on the strategic implications of India's high economic growth rates and New Delhi's efforts to forge strategic ties with the US, Japan, and other "China-wary" countries in Asia. Apparently, India's nuclear tests of 1998 did not cause as much concern in Beijing as India's success in sustaining a high economic growth rate of 8–9 percent since 2004. Though India's 1 trillion dollar economy is still less than half the size of China's, if it keeps growing at 8–9 percent per year, and if Beijing cannot indefinitely sustain its current economic growth rate, the gap between India and China would narrow. A recent *Renmin Ribao* [*People's Daily*] commentary articulated this concern: "Since India declared independence in 1947, it has always been determined to become a big power . . . *Although there are still people questioning the possibility*, India did make 'good achievement' in the following 60 years." The commentator accused New Delhi of seeking "big power status with Washington's backing" and "even stretch[ing] its tentacles outside Asia," and "actively chas[ing] after strategic cooperation with some African countries."[11]

The strategic consequences of India's economic resurgence coupled with the US secretary of state Condeleeza Rice's offer in March 2005 to "help make India a major world power in the twenty-first century" have greatly bothered the Chinese. This offer, and the long-term India–US defense cooperation framework and the July 2005 US–Indian nuclear energy deal that followed soon thereafter, have been compared by Chinese strategic analysts to "the strategic tilt" toward China executed by former US President Richard Nixon in 1971 to contain the common Soviet threat.[12] Claiming that these developments have "destabilising" and "negative implications" for their country's future, China's India-watchers have started warning their government that Beijing "should not take India lightly any longer."[13] Apparently, Chinese leaders were led to believe that China's growing economic and military might would eventually enable Beijing to re-establish the Sino-centric hierarchy of Asia's past as the US saps its energies in fighting small wars in the Islamic world, Japan shrinks economically and demographically while India remains subdued by virtue of Beijing's "special relationships" with its South Asian neighbors. However, a number of "negative developments," from Beijing's perspective, since early 2005—the Indian and Japanese bids for permanent seats on the UN Security Council, the formation of the East Asia Summit that includes India, Australia, and New Zealand, the US–India nuclear deal, India's ability to sustain its high economic growth rate of 8–9 percent, and the strategic implications of India's "Look East" policy—have upset the Chinese calculations.

Therefore, after a hiatus of a few years, Chinese media commentaries have resumed their criticism of Washington's "hegemonic ideas" of drawing "India in as a tool for its global strategic pattern," while accusing India of becoming a US monitoring station to collect intelligence on China. Some Chinese analysts express serious reservations about US efforts to draw "India in as a tool for its global strategic pattern," arguing that "India's DNA doesn't allow itself to become an ally subordinate to the US, like Japan or Britain."[14] Nonetheless, most see India as a "future strategic competitor," that would be an active member of an anti-China grouping due to the structural power shifts in the international system and advocate putting together a comprehensive "contain India" strategy based on both economic tools (aid, trade, infrastructural development) and enhanced military cooperation with "pro-China" countries. In response to a question on India's policy preferences, 49 percent of Chinese interviewees thought New Delhi would form an anti-China alliance with the United States, while only 37 per cent believed India and China would join hands to form an anti-US alliance (the remaining 16 percent were unsure).[15]

More importantly, an internal study on India undertaken in mid-2005 (with inputs from China's South Asia watchers such as Cheng Ruisheng, Zhou Gang, Ma Jiali, Sun Shihai, Rong Ying, Shen Dingli, amongst others) at the behest of the Chinese leadership's "Foreign Affairs Cell" recommended that Beijing take all measures to maintain its current *strategic leverage* (in terms of territory, membership of the exclusive Permanent Five and Nuclear Five clubs); *diplomatic advantages* (special relationships, membership of regional and international organizations); and *economic lead* over India.[16] Although the evidence is inconclusive, the most plausible deduction is that this internal re-assessment of India lies behind the recent hardening of China's stance on the territorial dispute and a whole range of other issues in China–India relations.[17]

The Chinese are concerned that the US–India nuclear deal and related agreements—if implemented—would bring about a major shift in the power balance in South Asia that is currently tilted in China's favor. The recent strengthening of China's strategic presence in Pakistan, Sri Lanka, Bangladesh, Burma, and overtures to the Maldives should, therefore, be seen against this backdrop. Despite protestations to the contrary from India and the United States that New Delhi is unwilling and unlikely to play the role of a closely aligned US surrogate as Japan or Britain, China's Asia strategy has come to be based upon the premise that maritime powers such as the US, Japan, Australia, and India would eventually form an informal quadrilateral alliance to countervail continental China.[18] This assessment is substantiated by a survey of Chinese public opinion undertaken by Silvia Sartori on the future of the US–China–India relationship and is shown in Table 9.1. This survey also identified issues that would negatively impinge upon the Sino–Indian relationship: the struggle for influence in East and Southeast Asia; energy and maritime security; and a nuclear confrontation.

Table 9.1 Chinese public views on India–China relations (%)

	Yes	No	Other
1 Does China intend to contain India?	**47**	40	13
2 Is an anti-Chinese US–Indian alliance likely?	**49**	33	18
3 Is an anti-American Sino–Indian alliance possible?	**23**	65	12

Source: Silvia Sartori, "How China sees India and the World," in *Heartland: Eurasian Review of Geopolitics*, No. 3, (Hong Kong: Cassan Press, 2005), pp. 48–58, www.heartland.it/_lib/_docs/2005_03_chindia_the_21st_century_challenge.pdf.

As a commentary in *Huanqiu Shibao* [*Global Times*] recently noted:

> The fact is that Japan, Australia, and India are respectively located at China's northeast, southeast, and southwest, and all are Asian powers, while US power in the Pacific is still unchallengeable. Hence, should the "alliance of values" concentrating military and ideological flavors in one body take shape, it will have a very great impact on China's security environment."[19]

From Beijing's perspective, the responsibility for this "negative development" lies solely at New Delhi's door. In their writings, Chinese analysts seem upset over their southern neighbor's all-consuming passion to become "a big power," and see the nuclear deal as its key to unlocking the door leading to the big league in world politics.[20] A *Renmin Ribao* commentary noted:

> The US–Indian nuclear agreement has strong symbolic significance for India in achieving its dream of a powerful nation . . . In recent years, it introduced and implemented a "Look-East" policy and joined most regional organizations in the East Asian region . . . In fact, the purpose of the United States to sign civilian nuclear energy cooperation agreement with India is to enclose India into its global partners' camp, so as to balance the forces of Asia [read, China]. This fits in exactly with India's wishes.[21]

Once the nuclear deal crosses all the "big four hurdles" (opposition from pro-Chinese Communist parties in India; negotiations on International Atomic Energy Agency (IAEA) safeguards; approval by the Nuclear Suppliers Group (NSG); and its passage by the US Congress), Beijing believes that it would end the nuclear symmetry between New Delhi and Islamabad (or, de-hyphenate the sub-continental rivals) and put India on par with nuclear China (re-hyphenate China with India). This, from Beijing's perspective, is quite disconcerting because a major objective of China's South Asia policy has been to perpetu-ate parity between India and Pakistan. Add to this India's military exercises with the US, Japan, and Australia, support for the concept of "concert of democracies," and attempts to establish strategic ties with countries that supposedly fall within China's sphere of influence (Mongolia, South Korea, Vietnam, the Philippines, Taiwan, and Myanmar)—all of these "new irritants" reinforce Beijing's fears about India's role in the US-led containment of China.[22] The Chinese have also made their strong displeasure over some Southeast Asian countries' attempts to draw India into the region (e.g. the East Asia Summit) known to regional capitals.[23] Beijing wants New Delhi to continue to abide by informal understandings (also known as "Five Nos") that laid the basis for the Sino–Indian rapprochement in the 1990s:

- Don't peddle "the China threat theory";
- Don't support Tibet or Taiwan's independence;

- Don't counter the Sino-Pakistani "all-weather relationship" or Sino-Burmese "special relationship";
- Don't align with the US and/or Japan to contain China; and
- Don't see or project yourself as an equal of China or as a nuclear and economic counterweight to China in Asia.

As long as New Delhi subscribes to these "five Nos" (or, "five principles"), both in words and deeds, Beijing is willing to develop its relations with India as part of its strategy to have good relations with all its neighbors.

Indian perspectives on China: "Rampant dragon on the prowl"

On the Indian side, a combination of emotions, illusions, and attitudes shape its China policy. While emotions range from the euphoria of misperceived Sino–Indian brotherhood in the 1950s, to the bitterness of India's 1962 military defeat by China, and back again to the illusion of imagined togetherness in the twenty-first century, policy attitudes are mostly underpinned by the visions of an expansionist, rampant Chinese dragon on the prowl blocking the Indian elephant's path to glory. At one end of the spectrum are those who envision "an India–China partnership that will produce an Asian Century" (very similar to former Prime Minister Jawaharlal Nehru's dream of joint Sino–Indian leadership of Asia, even though the Chinese show no enthusiasm for sharing leadership of Asia with anyone, least of all India). At the other end of the policy spectrum are those who retain anxieties about a resurgent and possibly revanchist, irredentist China.[24] Interestingly, they also quote none other than Nehru who reportedly said that: "A strong China is normally an expansionist China. Throughout history this has been the case."[25]

  If the Chinese are increasingly disillusioned with their southern neighbor, India's complaints are many. First, there is an unresolved border dispute of Himalayan proportions linked intrinsically to Tibet whose future evolution after the Dalai Lama remains uncertain, and has the potential to take China–India relations back to the 1950s. India is still sensitive to the fact that it was China which in 1962 suddenly abandoned the search for a negotiated settlement of the border dispute and invaded Indian-held territory. Apart from their territorial dispute over Tibetan lands, China's post-1962 "indirect strategy" of containing India through proxies—by arming Pakistan with conventional and nuclear weapons as part of the Sino–Pakistani "all-weather" relationship—is the second most important driver in India–China competition. For India, Pakistan cannot be a threat without China's military support just as Taiwan cannot constitute a threat to China without US support. Beijing's indirect support for separatist movements is another major source of friction. All separatist insurgencies inside India are fought mostly with Chinese small arms. Nor do China's concerns about growing instability and terrorism from Pakistan dovetail with India's concerns. For example, Beijing does not see acts of violence in India as cross-border terrorism emanating from Pakistan. At Islamabad's behest,

China recently blocked UN Security Council's move to declare *Jamat-ul Dawa* (formerly *Lashkar-e-Tayyeba*)—involved in numerous terrorist attacks in India—as an international terrorist organization under UN Security Council Resolution 1373. As Prime Minister Manmohan Singh in his address to the Combined Commanders' Conference on October 20, 2005 observed:

> We cannot also ignore the strategic cooperation that Pakistan secured from China in many ways. We cannot rule out the desire of some countries [read, China] to keep us engaged in low-intensity conflict with some of our neighbours as a means of getting India bogged down in a low equilibrium.[26]

Indian military officials routinely express anxiety regarding China's efforts to modernize its military and supply arms to India's neighboring countries. Delivering the B. C. Joshi Memorial Lecture in November 2005, Air Chief Marshal S. P. Tyagi, Chief of Indian Air Force, remarked that "China's strategic encirclement of India is already well under way . . . China is likely to view India as a regional economic threat and perhaps would be forced to attempt to stem its growth and influence in the region."[27] His successor Air Chief Marshal F. H. Major concurred: "There is considerable increase in Chinese power and influence in the countries surrounding us [at a time when] India faces the problem of terrorism and internal security."[28] Indian leaders routinely appeal to Beijing "to show greater sensitivity to [India's] security concerns," and to ensure that "each has sufficient strategic space in keeping with the principle of multipolarity".[29] However, according to one China-watcher, such appeals "are often ignored in Beijing as the cry of despair by the weak."[30]

Furthermore, Indian policymakers bristle at China's description of their country as a "regional player rather than a global player" entertaining "big power dreams" and insist that "India is not going to be defined by China but by itself."[31] India has long seen itself as the only Asian country with the size, resources, and all-round capabilities that is an equal of China. India certainly rivals China in terms of population, and, increasingly, in terms of its international stature and its actual and potential economic growth; India has a significant military and nuclear capability, with the former being expanded as India develops its blue water navy, with which China's navy may in future compete in the Pacific and the Indian oceans.

Claiming that derision and "exclusion of India has long been a running thread in Chinese policy," Indians hold China responsible for blocking their country's membership of regional and international institutions.[32] Beijing's "India allergy" led it to create hurdles in India's membership of the ASEAN Regional Forum (ARF), Asia-Pacific Economic Cooperation (APEC), Asia-Europe Summit Meeting (ASEM), and the Shanghai Cooperation Organisation (SCO). After offering support for India's UN aspirations in 2005, Beijing both overtly and covertly sabotaged India's bid for a UN Security Council permanent seat.

Then later that year, China sent special envoys to several East Asian countries to lobby against India's membership of the East Asia Summit (albeit, unsuccessfully) that held its inaugural summit in Kuala Lumpur in December 2005. The thrust of Chinese diplomacy is to confine India to the periphery of a future East Asia Community (EAC) by insisting on the ASEAN+3 (ASEAN + China, Korea, and Japan) framework as the core of regional community-building process. Beijing's stance on India's membership of the NSG is no different even as it supports Pakistan's nuclear ambitions.[33] To counter China's efforts to keep India out of regional arrangements in East and Southeast Asia by portraying India as an "outsider" and "interloper," India is "underlining the multi-millennia-old bond of Buddhism that it shares with these regions."[34]

Moreover, Indian observers point out that while forging all kinds of China-centered forums, dialogues and partnerships, Beijing loses no opportunity to criticize India for doing the same. A case in point is Beijing's unease over India-led regional cooperation forums such as the Mekong-Ganges Cooperation (MGC) and Bay of Bengal Initiative for MultiSectoral Technical and Economic Cooperation (BIMSTEC—Bangladesh, India, Myanmar, Sri Lanka, and Thailand). In May 2007, Beijing was furious over the first quadrilateral talks involving the US, Australia, Japan, and India on the sidelines of the ARF meeting in Manila, which were followed by the joint naval exercise in the Bay of Bengal in September 2007—seeing these moves as part of "contain China" strategy. However, Indian policymakers maintain that if the SCO member-states and the Russia–China–India triangle can hold high-level meetings to discuss issues of common concern and hold joint exercises, "then why should India, the United States, and Japan shy away from holding discussions on issues of common interest?"[35] Arguing that China has a habit of protesting too much, one Indian China-watcher asks:

> If India can openly join hands with China and Russia in a Eurasian strategic triangle intended to help promote global power equilibrium, why should it be diffident about partnering other states to seek democratic peace and stability in Asia? When China pursues actions overtly designed to contain India, does it bother to "explain" its actions to New Delhi? Rather, it determinedly presses ahead with steps antithetical to Indian interests, including a "string of pearls" strategy that aims to pin down India. Take the latest Chinese moves. Has Beijing cared to explain its new hardline stance on territorial disputes or its disinclination to set up what President Hu Jintao had agreed to during his visit to New Delhi last November—an interstate river-waters mechanism?[36]

For its part, New Delhi sees nothing sinister in having a common stake with Japan in developing a multipolar Asia to balance China's growing dominance, and interprets Beijing's opposition to India's strategic partnership with Japan and the US as an attempt to establish China-led unipolarity in the region. The US–Japan–India triangular partnership is seen as complementing the

Russia–China–India triangular cooperation. Asks C. Raja Mohan, a noted strategic affairs analyst:

> Will they [Japan and India] accept a subordinate status in a Sino-centric order that has begun to emerge in Asia? Or, will Tokyo and New Delhi persist with the construction of a multipolar Asia in the face of Chinese resistance at home and abroad? *If Japan and India want a place in Asia equivalent to that of China*, they have no alternative but to impart a strategic dimension to their bilateral economic engagement, deepen their political cooperation on issues ranging from maritime security, high technology transfers, regional stability and global warming.[37]

As regards Chinese concerns about India's pro-US tilt, Indian officials draw attention to their long-standing preference for independence and strategic autonomy in policymaking. The Indian Navy's decision to hold joint exercise with the Chinese Navy in 2006 soon after conducting trilateral US–Japan–India naval exercise in the Pacific Ocean and joint army exercises with China in December 2007 following the September 2007 quadrilateral naval exercises in the Bay of Bengal are cited as examples of India's engagement with all major powers. New Delhi claims to be cautious not to appear anti-China in its policies as China is likely to soon be its biggest trade partner. The Indians say they want to stay cautiously friendly as the dragon grows stronger. At the same time, they contend that

> just as China does not want India to object to Beijing's close strategic ties with India's neighbors, seeing them as part of "normal state-to-state relations", India hopes China would respect New Delhi's sovereign rights to build strategic partnerships and initiatives based on shared interests with like-minded countries in Asia and elsewhere.[38]

Some observers contend that the "Chinese fear not so much the military strengths of India and Japan despite their strong military capabilities, as their ideological strengths arising from their democratic roots."[39] Apparently, Beijing felt uncomfortable at India's participation in and co-sponsorship of a US-led initiative, the Community of Democracies, consisting of 100-plus nations, started at Warsaw in 2000. China and its Asian allies, such as North Korea, and Burma, saw themselves as the major targets of this *Pax Democratica* initiative.

The dramatic economic progress achieved by China in a quarter of a century evokes envy, admiration, and a desire for emulation among Indians who lament that whether China practices communism (under Mao) or capitalism (post-Mao), it always does it better than India. However, many Indians see China as predatory in trade, and look with worry at China's robust growth rates, fearing getting left behind. The Chinese economy is about 2.5 times greater than India and China receives four times more foreign direct investment than India ($63.81 billion for China and $16 billion for India in 2007). India's poor transport network and frequent power shortages remain the Achilles' heel of India's fast-growing economy that hinders its ability to compete with China. There is talk about partnering China's awesome manufacturing power with India's enviable IT and services sector which would make "Chindia" the factory and back-office of the world. But the reality is that China wants to beat India in the services sector, too. As one *Beijing Review* commentary "Hardnosed Software Battle" put it: in the IT software sector, "[a] fierce face-off with an old competitor—India—has [just] begun."[40] Bilateral trade flows are rising rapidly (from a paltry $350 million in 1993 to nearly $30 billion in 2007) and could cross $50 billion in 2010 and double again by 2015. But the bulk of Indian exports to China consist of iron ore and other raw materials while India imports mostly manufactured goods from China—a classic example of dependency. Nonetheless, unlike in the past, growing economic ties provide a cushion in times of crisis over territorial, nuclear, and military security issues in the future.

A recent survey conducted by the Pew Global Attitudes Project found that while China's image is generally positive in Asia, it has grown somewhat more negative in India with 43 percent expressing negative opinion about China compared to 20 percent in 2002. China's recent hardening of its stance on the territorial dispute with India and Indian losses in its fierce global competition with China for energy resources worldwide may have contributed to this shift in public opinion. In contrast, every major survey has shown that Indians overwhelmingly support closer ties with the US. Most Indians believe that while New Delhi has shown willingness to broaden relations with China, and demonstrated "extraordinary flexibility by discarding much of its past unrealistic posture and offering to negotiate on a practical and political basis, the final disposition of the Sino–Indian border, Beijing has not reciprocated in the same way."[41] An increasing number of Indians also view China's growing military might negatively. Similarly, more Indians see a growing Chinese economy as a bad thing than a good thing for their country (48 per cent versus 42 per cent).[42]

The fact of the matter is that China and India are locked in a classic security dilemma: one country sees its own actions as self-defensive, but the same actions appear aggressive to the other. Both the Indian and Chinese militaries see each other as future rivals and each points to threatening trends and behavior in the other. Both keep a close watch on changes in military doctrines and increases in defense spending, capabilities and related activities and remain committed to neutralizing perceived security gains of the other side. Unwilling to play second fiddle to China, rising India feels the need to take counter-balancing measures and launch certain initiatives, such as the "Look East" policy which are perceived as challenging and threatening China. Like China, India is actively seeking to reintegrate its periphery with the framework of regional economic cooperation. Like China, India seeks greater international status and influence commensurate with its growing economic power. However, like any other established status quo great power, China wants to ensure that its position remains strong vis-à-vis challenger India for strategic, economic, and geopolitical reasons. Through closer strategic ties with India's neighboring countries, China is warning India not to take any countermeasures to balance Beijing's growing might. Despite ever-increasing trade volumes, there is as yet no strategic congruence between the two. On almost all counts, the two Asian giants clash or compete, and they are vulnerable to any deterioration in relations. Differences in the philosophical approach to governance, political culture, values, and worldviews explain the lack of strategic congruence. Their burden of history, long memories, negative characterizations of each other in the media, deep-rooted prejudice, tensions over the unresolved territorial dispute, global competition for natural resources and markets, and new Chinese suspicions about India's evolving relations with the US and Japan add to mutual distrust and tensions. Indians see no sign of China giving up its "concircle India" (contain and encircle) strategy which takes several forms: an unresolved territorial dispute, arms sales to and military alliances with "India-wary countries" (Pakistan, Bangladesh, Burma, and now Nepal); nuclear and missile proliferation in India's neighborhood (Pakistan, Iran and Saudi Arabia); and opposition to India's membership of global and regional organizations.

Key issues in India–China relations in the twenty-first century

The India–China territorial dispute

Forty-six years after the 1962 war that erupted over their disputed border and after more than a quarter of a century of negotiations, the 4,056 kilometer (2,520 miles) frontier between India and China, one of the longest interstate borders in the world, remains the only one of China's land borders not defined, let alone demarcated, on maps or delineated on the ground. While Indians doubt China's sincerity in border negotiations, Chinese question Indian leaders' will and capacity to settle the dispute in a "give-and-take" spirit. Talks for a settlement have gone on since 1981—with a "big push" given to them by Prime Minister Rajiv Gandhi's visit to China in 1988, the second one by Atal Behari Vajpayee's sojourn in Beijing in 2003 and a third one by Manmohan Singh's talks with Premier Wen Jiabao in 2005 and President Hu Jintao in 2006—without producing any worthwhile result.

Up until 2005, there was a great deal of optimism about a possible break-through. Evidence of this came during Prime Minister Vajpayee's China visit in June 2003 when New Delhi's readiness to address Chinese concerns on Tibet was matched by Beijing's willingness to resolve the Sikkim issue by recognizing the trade route through the Nathu La pass on the China–Sikkim frontier with India and later showing Sikkim as part of India in its maps. For its part, New Delhi reiterated its stance on the Tibetan Autonomous Region as part of China. This visit also paved the way for border talks to be held through

Special Representatives of the leaders to find an early "political solution" to the boundary question, rather than going only by the legal and historical claims of the two sides. India indicated its willingness to settle for the territorial status quo by giving up claims to the Aksai Chin in Ladakh and hoped China would give up its claims to Arunachal Pradesh in the eastern sector and recognize the McMahon Line just as Beijing had accepted Xinjiang/Tibet's British-drawn colonial era boundaries with Afghanistan and Burma. In order to give a new thrust to the ongoing border negotiations, an "Agreement on the Political Parameters and Guiding Principles for the Settlement of the Boundary Question" was signed during Chinese Prime Minister Wen Jiabao's visit to India in April 2005. The Joint Statement issued at the end of the visit talked of a "Strategic and Cooperative Partnership" between India and China.

Since then, however, Beijing has upped the ante by demanding major territorial concessions in populated areas of Arunachal Pradesh on terms that many in New Delhi see as "humiliating and non-negotiable".[43] Tawang, in particular, has emerged as a sticking point since the Chinese claim it to be central to Tibetan Buddhism given that the sixth Dalai Lama was born there. Ties between China and India were strained even further in May 2007 when the Chinese government refused a visa to an Indian official from disputed Arunachal Pradesh to visit China, and the Indian government's invitation soon thereafter to Taiwan's opposition Kuomintang (KMT) Party presidential candidate, Ma Ying-jou to visit India in June 2007 to hold talks with senior Indian officials. China voiced its opposition to Ma's visit and called on India to abide by the "one China policy." Thereafter came media reports of the People's Liberation Army (PLA) encroachments across the Line of Actual Control (LAC), and Chinese small arms supplies to insurgents in India's volatile northeast via Bangladesh and Burma. Then in August 2007, Beijing demanded the removal of two old Indian Army bunkers near the tri-junction of Sikkim, Bhutan, and Tibet claiming that these were located on their territory.[44] This move raised questions about China's declared policy of treating Sikkim as part of Indian territory.[45] Not surprisingly, China's increasing assertiveness over the disputed Arunachal Pradesh has led to a remarkable meltdown in the Sino–Indian border talks and a "mini-cold war" has quietly taken hold at the diplomatic level in the past two years, despite public protestations of amity.

Some observers argue that Hu Jintao's desire to control the choice of the next Dalai Lama has led to pressuring India to concede access to the Tawang Monastery which is crucial to this choice.[46] The deterioration in Sino–Indian relations under Hu, however, should not have come as a surprise given his reputation as a hardliner over Tibet. (After all, Deng Xiaoping had groomed him for the Chinese Communist Party (CCP) leadership because of his claim to fame for the successful suppression of the Tibetan revolt in 1988.) In this context, the rapid pace development of road, rail and military infrastructure in Tibet close to its borders with India and Nepal is seen as pre-empting any possible destabilization of Tibet post-Dalai Lama, and to enable Beijing to exercise the military option to seize the Tawang Tract should that become necessary.[47]

Others, however, do not see any sinister designs in Western China's development. Instead, they attribute the recent downturn in Sino–Indian relations more to domestic power struggle within the CCP than to the Dalai Lama succession issue or to Chinese concerns about India's growing tilt toward the US.[48]

Tibet is the key

Tibet remains the key to China's policymaking on the India–China boundary dispute. The Chinese still suspect that India prefers an independent Tibet and covertly supports Tibetan separatists.[49] Unless and until Tibet is totally pacified and completely Sinicized as Inner Mongolia has been, Beijing would not want to give up the "bargaining chip" that an unsettled boundary vis-à-vis India provides it with. An unsettled border provides China the strategic leverage to keep India uncertain about its intentions, and nervous about its capabilities, while exposing India's vulnerabilities and weaknesses, and ensuring New Delhi's "good behavior" on issues of vital concern to China.[50]

Several recent commentaries in Chinese language sources confirm a shift toward a tougher Chinese stance on the territorial dispute with India. Articles on "Future Directions of the Sino–Indian Border Dispute" published in *Guogji Zhanlue* in November 2006, Liu Silu's "Beijing Should Not Lose Patience in Chinese–Indian Border Talks" in *Wen Wei Po* on June 1, 2007, and Professor Wang Yiwei's interview "Helping US May Derail Border Talks" with the *Asian Age* on July 25, 2007 are broadly representative of the official thinking in China's national security establishment on this subject. The key arguments and major themes presented in these and other similar writings are summarized below.

> First, since India controls 90,000 square kilometers of the richest part of Tibet and the Himalayan region, equivalent to two and a half Taiwans and as large as Jiangsu Province, "the Chinese government will not easily give up its territory." *Wen Wei Po* commentator Liu Silu contends that as "it is equally difficult to get India to spit out the fatty meat it is chewing . . . Beijing had better be patient at the negotiation table [because] time is on China's side." Apparently, many Chinese strategic thinkers believe that China's comprehensive national power vis-à-vis India is likely to increase over time, and that would enable Beijing to drive a better bargain on the boundary question in the future.[51]
>
> Second, as Professor Wang Yiwei puts it, "China showed 'greatness' once, after the 1962 Indo–China war, when it gave up the land it controlled [in Arunachal Pradesh] and it could not be expected to show magnanimity again . . . India 'lost an opportunity' to settle the boundary question when Deng Xiaoping and Mao Zedong were alive. President Hu Jintao is not Deng or Mao. He is strong but cannot be compared with them."[52] In other words, the ball is in India's court. If New Delhi wants a settlement, it must hand over a large chunk of territory in Arunachal Pradesh to China.

Third, the Sino–Indian border issue is linked with sovereignty, territorial integrity, and the respective status of the two countries in the global hierarchy. Hence, a *Guogji Zhanlue* commentary advises that Beijing "should not adopt any hasty step or make big compromises on principles" because this issue, "if approached in a hurry, could impact the respective rise of the two nuclear powers." One Chinese concern is that a border settlement, without major Indian territorial concessions, could potentially augment India's power position and thus impact negatively China's rise.[53] An unsettled boundary suits Chinese interests for the present because China's claims in the Western sector are complicated by the Indo–Pakistan dispute over Kashmir, Pakistan's interests in the Sino–Indian territorial dispute, and Beijing's interest in keeping India under strategic pressure on two fronts.[54]

Fourth, a "fair and reasonable settlement" implies that "India will need to give up something to get something."[55] Ideally speaking, *Wen Wei Po* argues that China should "recover the entire area. But it is negotiable for the disputed territory to be split equally between China and India, as was the case of Heixiazi [Bolshoy Ussuriysky] Island in the northeast [on the Russian border]. A third option would be for Beijing to recover at least the 2,000 square kilometers covering Tawang and Takpa Shiri. It is believed that this is Beijing's last resort and it will not accept any deal worse than this."[56] Apparently, having wrested substantial territorial concessions from Russia, Tajikistan, and Vietnam in their land border disputes with China, Beijing is now expecting the same from India.

Fifth, China should economically harmonize/integrate Tibet, Nepal and the border regions with India into China's economic sphere through increased economic links and infrastructure projects, such as the Qinghai–Tibet railway, before proceeding for a boundary settlement with India. Underlying this is the belief that economic interdependence would soften India's position, leading to a settlement on China's terms.

Last, if negotiations, coercive diplomacy and economic harmonization (a carrot and stick policy) fail to produce the desired outcome, the use of force at an appropriate time in the future to recover "China's Southern Tibet" (a new Chinese term for Arunachal Pradesh) is not ruled out.[57] Many Chinese analysts believe that the military balance has shifted in their favor with the completion of the 1,118-kilometre (695 miles) Qinghai-Tibet railway and other military infrastructure projects in Tibet and that negates the need for any territorial concession to India in the eastern sector.

These views and arguments clearly (a) advocate a "constraining India" strategy; (b) foretell a long and torturous course of future border negotiations; and (c) indicate an uncertain and unpredictable future for India's relations with China.

Hu is Hitler?

Chinese Foreign Minister Yang Jiechi's statement to his Indian counterpart Pranab Mukherjee made in June 2007 that the "mere presence of populated areas in Arunachal Pradesh would not affect Chinese claims on the boundary" should then be seen against this background. However, in Indian policy circles, this statement is seen as repudiating Article VII of the "Agreement on Political Parameters and Guiding Principles" signed during Chinese Premier Wen Jiabao's India visit in April 2005, which states: "In reaching a border settlement, the two sides shall safeguard populations in border areas." The inclusion of the phrase "settled population in the border areas" was then interpreted as a diplomatic concession that India had extracted from China as it protected India's interests against Chinese claims to Tawang and other areas in Arunachal Pradesh.[58] India reportedly conveyed to China in June 2007 that it could not be pushed beyond a point on the boundary dispute. Describing the Chinese move as "a serious retrograde step," Mukherjee publicly rebuffed Beijing, saying that New Delhi would not part with populated portions of the state of Arunachal Pradesh: "Any elected government of India is not permitted by the constitution to part with any part of our land that sends representatives to the Indian Parliament."[59] Sending a clear signal against any Chinese designs over Arunachal Pradesh, India's foreign minister added:

> The days of Hitler are over. After the Second World War, no country captures land of another country in the present global context. That is why there is a civilised mechanism of discussions and dialogue to sort out border disputes. We sit around the table and discuss disputes to resolve them.[60]

The Indian government has also responded by unveiling plans for economic development and major infrastructure projects (the building of 72 roads, three airstrips and numerous bridges) in the border areas along the undefined LAC that would enable the Indian military to "swiftly move forces into the region and sustain them logistically in the event of any untoward trouble or emergency." Indian Defence Minister A. K. Antony told the Combined Commanders' Conference in July 2007 that "China has been building a lot of infrastructure— railways, airports and roads [along the Indian border]. We are also doing the same thing."[61] In response to the establishment of four new airbases in Tibet and three in southern China, the Indian Air Force is reportedly beefing up its presence by deploying two squadrons of Sukhoi-30MKIs near the Chinese border.[62]

Although the probability of an all-out conflict is extremely low, the prospect that some of India's road building projects in disputed areas could lead to tensions, clashes, and skirmishes with Chinese border patrols cannot be completely ruled out. Should a conflict break out, the PLA's contingency plans emphasize a "short and swift localized" conflict (confined to the Tawang region, along the lines of the 1999 Kargil conflict) with the following objectives in mind: (i) capture the Tawang tract; (ii) give India's military a bloody nose; and (iii) deliver a knockout punch that punctures India's ambitions to be China's equal or peer competitor once and for all. The ultra-modern civilian and military infrastructure in Tibet is expected to enable Beijing to exercise the military option to achieve the above-mentioned objectives should that become necessary at some stage in the future.

In short, there is little or no sign of an early resolution to the conflicting claims, despite continuing negotiations and the recent upswing in diplomatic, political, commercial, and even military ties between the world's two most populous countries. The border disputes have simmered in the background for more than 50 years, threatening to disrupt relations between Asia's two giants. With China insisting on the return of Tawang on religious, cultural, and historical grounds, Indians have a more powerful case for the return of the sacred Mount Kailash-Mansarovar in Tibet, since it is a sacred religious place associated with the Hindu religion. Additionally, there is the contentious issue of the Shaksgam Valley that Pakistan handed over to China in 1963, which China's Foreign Ministry spokespersons now claim is a non-issue. Negotiating these issues will not be easy and will test diplomatic skills on both sides.

It is worth noting that historically China has negotiated border disputes with neighbors in their moment of national weakness (Pakistan, Myanmar in the 1960s, and the Central Asian republics in the 1990s) or only after the overall balance of power had shifted decisively in China's favor and/or after they had ceased to be a major threat (land border settlements with Russia and Vietnam in the 1990s). It has not, however, negotiated with those who are perceived as present rivals and future threats (India, Japan, Vietnam, the Philippines, and Taiwan). In the meantime, both sides will have to learn to live without an early resolution to the dispute. Even if the territorial dispute were somehow resolved, India and China would still compete over energy resources, markets and for geo-strategic reasons. A new potentially divisive issue for the future appears to be the ecological impact on the Indian subcontinent of Chinese plans to divert the rivers of Tibet for irrigation purposes in China. With China controlling the Tibetan plateau—the source of Asia's major rivers—there looms a potential conflict over depleting water reserves.[63]

Nuclear competition

While major Western powers have, however grudgingly, acknowledged the reality of India's *de facto* nuclear status, Beijing shows no sign of softening its demand that New Delhi initiate a complete rollback of its nuclear weapons programme and unconditionally sign the Comprehensive Test Ban Treaty (CTBT) and the Nuclear Non-Proliferation Treaty (NPT) as a Non-Nuclear Weapons State as per UN Security Council Resolution 1172 of June 6, 1998. China's nuclear diplomacy seeks to deny India entry into the exclusive N-5 Club and to foil any move that would acknowledge/legalize/legitimize India's status as a Nuclear Weapons State. Put it simply, China does not want India to get out of the nuclear doghouse to which it has been confined for nearly four decades. Not surprisingly, Beijing has been critical of the July 2005 US–India civilian nuclear energy deal. In the daily briefing on March 2, 2006, Chinese Foreign Ministry's spokesperson Qin Gang said:

India should sign the NPT and also dismantle its nuclear weapons. As a signatory country, China hopes non-signatory countries will join it as soon as possible as non-nuclear weapon states, thereby contributing to strengthening the international non-proliferation regime. China hopes that concerned countries developing cooperation in peaceful nuclear uses will pay attention to these efforts. The cooperation should conform with the rules of international non-proliferation mechanisms.[64]

Beijing is miffed at the nuclear deal not just because it will put India on par with China by conferring rights on India that are commensurate with China's in the nuclear domain—the right to have a nuclear arsenal as well as access to civilian nuclear technology—but will also provide access to advanced conventional weaponry and dual-use technologies from the West that are still denied to Beijing because of an arms embargo dating back to the Tiananmen massacre of 1989. A *People's Daily* commentary alluded to this concern: "The United States has explicitly proposed in the agreement that it would not hamper or intervene in the development of India's military nuclear plan, which will also help the country achieve its goals to be a nuclear power."[65] Once the nuclear deal crosses all the "big four hurdles" (opposition from pro-Chinese Communist parties in India; negotiations on IAEA safeguards; approval by the NSG; and its passage by the US Congress), then the balance of power between Beijing and New Delhi could shift in India's favor, and that would be quite unsettling.[66] However, despite its strong disapproval of a pact that would narrow the power gap between India and China, Beijing would not want to take a stance that pushes India further into Washington's camp. Most likely, Beijing would use its NSG membership to further its own and its allies' interests by:

- Using the "double standards" argument to question Washington's commitment to non-proliferation goals in light of its decision to back India's nuclear industry while opposing the right to nuclear energy for Iran and Pakistan[67];
- Insisting that any changes to the NSG guidelines to accommodate the deal must not be "country [i.e. India]-specific" but "universal criteria-based" so that "all countries [read, Pakistan] can benefit from the peaceful use of atomic energy under the IAEA safeguards." This formulation, outlined by Foreign Minister Yang Jiechi, would pave the way for the Chinese construction of the Chashma III and IV nuclear reactors in Pakistan[68];
- Using the deal to extract major concessions from Washington, including an end to the arms embargo and the lifting of bans on high-tech dual-use technology exports to China; and
- Seeking new assurances that US–India ties are not related to any "contain China" strategy.

Energy security spawns maritime rivalry: oil and water don't mix

The conventional wisdom is that China's growing ties to the world economy and its dependence on imported oil and raw materials will ensure China's "peaceful rise," as Beijing's leaders have pledged. But these same economic interests—and the need to defend them—are also forcing Beijing to pursue resource- and commodities-driven mercantilist foreign policy just as Britain and the United States did in the nineteenth and twentieth centuries. Chinese military journals stress the need to protect the country's sea-borne trade and energy supply routes, to blunt the US military's overarching superiority in the Pacific, and to disabuse New Delhi of the notion that the "Indian Ocean is India's ocean." For, as one Chinese daily editorial put it, in the twenty-first century, "whichever country controls the Indian Ocean controls East Asia."[69] China certainly seeks to be the dominant naval power in the region east of the ASEAN group of countries, especially in the South China Sea, just as India aspires to achieve the same capacity in the Indian Ocean and South Seas.

While China's economic boom offers profit and opportunity, Beijing's strategic ambitions and efforts to lock up a significant share of Central Asian, African, Latin American, Iranian, Burmese, and Russian energy resources and minerals for China's exclusive use generate suspicion, envy and fear. As India grows outwardly, the two Asian giants are beginning to rub shoulders in different parts of Asia, Africa and Latin America. With each passing year, as their economies grow, China and India's search for energy and raw resources to satisfy their industrial needs becomes more intense, and their desires to establish strategic links with their overseas suppliers and consumers will invariably create some friction and tension.

In the competition stakes, however, China currently has an overwhelming lead over India economically and diplomatically. China has been aggressively scouting for energy sources worldwide, as well as beating Indian firms in their own backyard—Kazakhstan, Iran, Bangladesh, Burma, Sri Lanka, and Cambodia. (For example, India lost out to China on importation of natural gas from Myanmar's offshore fields, even though Indian state-run firms have a 30 percent stake in those fields and it would have made more economic sense for Myanmar to send it to New Delhi.[70]) China's state-owned oil companies have outfoxed their Indian oil counterparts in securing oil deals in a number of countries because the former can draw on generous lines of credit from the Chinese government, which also offers military and diplomatic support to sup-plier states. Furthermore, Chinese oil companies are not averse to entering into uneconomic deals, driven as they are less by market and profit considerations and more by the Chinese government's strategy to establish strategic footholds and lock up resources.[71] As noted earlier, China is also the only major power that is lukewarm to India regaining access to the international nuclear energy market. Although the two countries concluded an energy cooperation pact in 2006, China shows willingness to cooperate with India in the energy sector only if the following three conditions are met:

1   Indian oil companies are willing to play the role of junior partner to China's state-owned oil conglomerates.
2   Energy resources do not lie in India's immediate neighborhood (Burma, Bangladesh, Central Asia, and Iran).

3   Energy resources lie in countries or regions (Syria, Sudan, Iran, Venezuela, Columbia, Russia, Yemen) where China–India cooperation would potentially cause a wedge between India and the United States. Apparently, China sees cooperation with India in pariah states such as Iran or Sudan as legitimizing the Chinese presence there. For, such cooperation makes it harder for Western critics to label China's foreign policy neocolonial and mercantilist.

The traditional Sino–Indian geopolitical rivalry has thus acquired a maritime dimension. China and India are among the world's top five energy consumers (China is second after the United States; India is fifth), making energy security an essential component of each country's strategic doctrine. Since nearly 70 percent of China's trade is carried by sea through the Strait of Malacca, the Indian Ocean, and the Suez Canal, China views the predominance of the US and Indian navies along these sea lanes of communication (SLOCs) as a major threat. As a major trading nation and a world power, Beijing is laying the groundwork for a naval presence along maritime chokepoints in the South China Sea, the Malacca Straits, the Indian Ocean, and the Strait of Hormuz in the Persian Gulf through acquisition of or access to naval bases in Cambodia, Burma, Bangladesh, Sri Lanka, and Pakistan to protect its long-term economic security interests. The Gwadar port in Pakistan at the mouth of the strategic Persian Gulf, about 400 km from the Strait of Hormuz, is being developed as a major conduit for global oil supplies to China. It would allow China to project its growing economic and military might westward, toward the Middle East, western India and eastern Africa, and down into the Indian Ocean.

For its part, India has countered by promoting defence cooperation with Iran, Oman, and Israel in the west while upgrading military ties with the Maldives, Madagascar, and Burma in the Indian Ocean, and with Singapore, Indonesia, Thailand, Vietnam, Taiwan, the Philippines, Australia, Japan and the United States in the east. India's new naval doctrine aims to influence events around the Indian Ocean—and beyond. As part of its "Look East" strategy, India has concluded over a dozen defense cooperation agreements over the last decade, and the Indian Navy has been holding joint naval exercises with Japan, the US, Australia, and Southeast Asian countries at regular intervals to signal to the Chinese navy that its future presence will not go unchallenged.[72] As James Holmes has stated: "Any Chinese attempt to control events in India's geographic vicinity would doubtless meet with Indian countermeasures. The Chinese recognize that India's energy needs, which resemble China's own, could impel New Delhi into zero-sum competition at sea."[73] Perhaps sooner rather than later, China's military alliances and forward deployment of its naval assets in the Pakistani, Bangladeshi, Sri Lankan, and Burmese ports would prompt India to respond in kind by seeking access to the Russian (Vladivostok), Vietnamese (Cam Ranh Bay), Taiwanese (Kao-hsiung), and Japanese (Okinawa) ports for the forward deployment of Indian naval assets to protect India's East Asian shipping and Pacific Ocean trade routes and access to energy resources from the Russian Sakhalin province. In short, maritime competition is intensifying as Indian and Chinese navies show off the flag in the Pacific and Indian oceans with greater frequency.

India bound to balance China: from "non-alignment" to "multi-alignment"

Of all the countries on China's periphery, India is in a category of its own because it is the only Asian power that has long been committed to balancing China, especially since the late 1950s.[74] During the Cold War era, India relied mainly on the Soviet Union and its leadership role in the Non-Aligned Movement (NAM) to counterbalance China. While the rest of the world started taking note of China's rise only in the 1990s, India has been warily watching China's rise since 1950 when the Chinese PLA marched into Tibet, and converted the traditional Indo–Tibetan frontier into a disputed India–China border that eventually culminated in the 1962 war. In other words, for New Delhi, China has been rising since the 1950s whereas the West took notice of China's rise only during the last decade of the twentieth century. True, the US (and Japan) balanced China from 1949 to 1971, but then they allied with Beijing from 1971 to 1989 to contain the common Soviet threat. Much of China's spectacular progress is owed to the massive inflow of American and Japanese capital and technology which contributed to China's rise as an economic and military power. In contrast, the strategic imperative to counterbalance China first drove "non-aligned" India into the Soviet camp during the Cold War years, then made it gate-crash the exclusive nuclear weapons club in the post-Cold War world, and has now made it tilt toward the United States in the early part of the twenty-first century. Since India was never part of the Sinic world order or tributary state system but a civilization-empire in and of itself, it remains genetically ill-disposed to sliding into China's orbit without resistance.

Long preoccupied with balancing its northern neighbor, India has unveiled a comprehensive strategy to meet the growing China challenge as well as to facilitate its own rise as a great power. This strategy consists of *internal balancing* (increasing comprehensive national strength through economic development), *external balancing* (via alliances, tilts, strategic partnerships with like-minded states), *bilateral cooperation and engagement* (with major power centres), *regional economic integration* (with Southeast and East Asia), and *soft power diplomacy* (via regional multilateral organizations). Since the twenty-first-century world is much more interdependent and strategically complex, an increasingly globalized India is moving away from "non-alignment" to a "multi-dimensional multialignment" with the world that seeks to establish a web of diverse partnerships with major powers and multilateral forums to pursue a wide variety of interests so as to avail itself of multiple strategic options and enhance India's strategic autonomy—the major Indian foreign policy objective. The premise underlying this strategy of forming a range of partnerships is to shape the strategic environment in ways that would induce

China to evolve as a constructive, rather than revisionist or irredentist power in Asia. In other words, since India is incapable of establishing the Asian power equilibrium on its own (despite being a rising power itself) because of its relatively weak economic base, fractious polity, preoccupation with internal security issues, and seemingly unresolvable tensions in its immediate neigh-borhood, it is on the lookout for credible, like-minded partners to help build a stable Asian security architecture.[75] This regional security structure would combine "the 'balancing' and 'integrative' processes to moderate a seem-ingly hegemonic China" (whose economic muscle, global reach and military power is being felt not only in the north, east, West, south of India but also increasingly reverberates within the country) and to maintain regional peace and security.[76] Thus, for historical, geopolitical, geo-economic, cultural, and civilizational reasons, India and other like-minded Asian countries (Mongolia, Japan, Vietnam, and Indonesia) are strengthening their security ties with the United States as part of their hedging and balancing strategy even as they become increasingly dependent on the Chinese market for trade, prosperity and economic well-being.

Minding the gap: economic strength

Having embarked upon economic liberalization 13 years after China and lagging behind China on all economic indicators, India has a lot of catching up to do in the economic sphere. So India's topmost priority is to seek closer eco-nomic ties with the world's largest and second largest economies—the US and Japan. From the US, India seeks synergy in the high-tech sector while Tokyo, as part of its "China plus" strategy, has offered to invest strategically in Indian infrastructure and manufacturing industries. Once the US–India free trade agreement and Indo–Japanese comprehensive economic partnership agreement are concluded, India's economy is expected to narrow the gap between itself and China's.

Sustained economic development in India is a strategic imperative because economic stagnation or slower economic growth under a centrist-left coalition government would heighten anxieties about China's greater power capabilities and prompt New Delhi to appease and/or bandwagon with Beijing. Conversely, slower economic growth under a nationalist-rightist government that worsens India's insecurities vis-à-vis China would see India overtly containing China by aligning itself with the US and reaching out to other "China-wary countries" (such as Japan, Taiwan, Vietnam, Russia). Or, it could resume nuclear testing. Such a posture could create regional tensions and sharpen internal divisions. However, a sustained economic growth rate of 8–10 percent would impart a greater sense of confidence and strength to pursue an independent, multi-aligned foreign policy—whether under Congress or BJP or coalition government—without any fear of China's ability to undermine India's vital interests. In other words, an economically strong India is less likely to give in to Chinese induce-ments and pressures to concede ground than a weak India. Robust economic growth in Asia's third largest economy would also ensure that Asian security architecture is not tilted in favor of China.

Strategic dynamics: triangles, tilts and trilateral equations

As China and India march upwards simultaneously on their relative power trajectories, geopolitical equations and power relations in Asia are undergoing significant realignments. All major powers, including China, are maneuvering for geopolitical advantage and economic leverage through new equations, permutations, and formations. The SCO, Russia–China–Iran and Russia–China–India triangles are good examples. China's best-case scenario is that the United States would over time willingly give up its insistence on maintaining the dominant strategic position in Asian and world affairs and reach an understanding with China just as Great Britain did with the US after World War II. However, the prospects of Sino–American accommodation, with the United States pulling back strategically from Asia as China rises to regional leadership, or a shared China–US hegemony or condominium seem remote for a variety of reasons. All the indications are that instead of walking away from the Asia-Pacific region or reducing its footprint, Washington is going to practice power balancing as it has vital political, economic, and strategic interests at stake in the region. This means that the US–China relations will be characterized by "Cold Peace" (or, "Cooperative Competition") for a long period of time, and the Asian security environment will be shaped by the state of US–China relations.

Just as Beijing is seeking friends and allies in Asia and far from its shores, other powers are also working to build new equations and partnerships. Even as they increasingly cooperate in the economic sphere and on transnational security issues (environment, energy, global warming, proliferation, and terrorism), China–India, China–Japan and China–US politico-military competition is a foregone conclusion. In the decades to come, the US–China–India triangular relationship and the US–Japan–India triangular relationships would be as important as was the US–Soviet–Chinese triangular relationship of the Cold War era. The US, Japan, and India's interests lie in ensuring that Asia is not dominated by China, and that the overall balance-of-power remains in favor of liberal democracies, not autocracies. The future of the Asian security environment will depend a great deal on how and in what ways the US manages the rise of China and how and in what ways China, in turn, manages the rise of India and accommodates India's interests. In fact, China's behavior toward India is not much different from that of the US' behavior toward China for the simple reason that China is a *status-quoist* power with respect to India while the US is a *status-quoist* power with regards to China. Beijing's reluctance to adapt its policies to accommodate India's rise, and the fact that both China and India value their ties with the United States more than with each other provides Washington with enormous leverage vis-à-vis the two Asian giants. For its part, New Delhi sees some degree of US–China competition as in its interest because it makes India the object of courtship by both Washington and Beijing.

For the first time in decades, New Delhi is working to establish a multi-dimensional engagement with Washington. Concerned about a shift in the regional balance of power in view of Indo–US strategic engagement, Beijing is simultaneously coercing and wooing India so as to prevent Washington and New Delhi from coming too close for China's comfort. How India and China manage their differences on border dispute, Pakistan, regional integration, and the UN Security Council reforms, will have significant implications on America's place in Asia. Other issues that will determine the nature of the India–China–US triangular dynamics include economic developments in India, nuclear proliferation, the war on terrorism, and the state of Sino–US ties. Strained US–China relations would make India the pivotal power ("the swing state") in the US–China–India triangle but tense India–China relations would put the US in a pivotal position. At the same time, India's historic quest for strategic autonomy, its self-identity as a great civilization-empire that rivalled China and great power ambitions of its own mean that it will never be the kind of junior ally the United States cultivated during the Cold War. Unlike Britain and Japan in the 1950s, India is a rising, not retiring, great power.

Just as India did not rely entirely on the Soviet Union to balance China during the second half of the twentieth century, India is surely not going to rely on the US alone to balance China in the twenty-first century. Indian strategists never forget to mention that the US and China were allies before and during World War II and in the second phase of the Cold War from 1971 to 1989. Should the US in the future reach a strategic accommodation with China, then India will move to seek closer relations with like-minded countries such as Japan, Vietnam, and Russia, in order to ensure a healthy balance of power is maintained in Asia. That would usher in triangular dynamics of a different kind (India–Russia–Japan or Japan–Vietnam–India). Much like India, Japan cannot be certain that the US and China will not reach an accommodation in the future again and deliver yet another "Nixon shock" once the Taiwan issue is settled between the two. Thus, India's drive for "strategic autonomy" and Japan's fear of "strategic abandonment" by Washington would bring the two closer to devise common strategies vis-à-vis China. While India has been seeking out Japan as a partner in the region for a long period of time, Japan warmed up to the idea of seeking partners, other than the US and Australia, only recently under the Koizumi and Abe administrations.

Given their geographical proximity to China and the direct impact Chinese power and ambitions hold for them, India and Japan view power equilibrium as a strategic imperative. New Delhi and Tokyo have witnessed Beijing's attempts to marginalize and relegate them to the periphery of the Sino-centric international order in Asia. Both India and Japan face hostile neighbors that are armed and backed by China—Pakistan and North Korea.[77] Moreover, both find common cause in their bid to be permanent members of the UN Security Council. Both prefer a multipolar Asia and are working together to avert a China-led unipolar Asia. Both are energy-dependent economies dependent on

SLOCs and are looking for ways to cooperate in alternate energy resources.[78] As India "Looks East," Tokyo is offering a helping hand in its quest for greater economic integration with the Asia-Pacific region. With Tokyo's support, India got invited to the inaugural East Asian Summit in December 2005, despite Beijing's efforts to keep its southern rival out.[79] As an Indian daily editorial commented recently:

> History is replete with China's repeated efforts to undermine India . . . Beijing keeps India out of the decision-making structures of East Asia Summit process and the Shanghai Cooperation Organisation. For the first time in decades, India is in a position to return the compliment by deepening its cooperation with Japan and the United States.[80]

Much to the chagrin of Beijing, Tokyo also took the lead in forming a regional quadrilateral arrangement of Japan, India, the US, and Australia, also called a "constellation of democracies." The fact that China is the largest or second largest trading partner of Japan, Australia, the US, and India gives the four democracies enormous leverage over China should they use it optimally and coordinate their policies vis-à-vis China on Taiwan, North Korea, nuclear proliferation, trade, and currency issues so as to ensure peace and prosperity in the region.

In short, closer Indo–Japanese ties are seen as benefiting the economic and security interests of both countries and the wider region. As China's power grows, the India–Japan relationship is becoming a key driving force in the construction of a new security architecture in Asia based on the protection of democratic values and market principles. By building strategic partnerships with two of China's biggest security concerns, the US and Japan, India also acquires useful leverage in its dealings with China. As one commentator observed:

> But niceties apart, Japan and India are telegraphing a message to China— if you can throw a cordon around marking your presence in Pakistan's Gwadar port, erect listening posts in Bangladesh, Myanmar, Cambodia and the South China Sea and work to politically limit India as a "regional player" and use history to browbeat Japan, others too can play the game.[81]

New Delhi's "quad" membership is a clear signal that India is not going to let China have its way in Asia. Privately, Indian officials say they are pleased that "China is finally getting the message," and hope that the India–US strategic partnership will impel Beijing not to trample upon Indian interests[82]: "Once Japanese investment, Australian uranium and American weaponry start flowing into India, Beijing would rethink the futility of its 'contain India' policy."[83] Eventually, a strong Japan, a strong China and a strong India will have to find ways to reconcile their interests so that they can peacefully coexist and prosper in Asia.

Containment begets counter-containment

India and China have long been involved in a zero-sum game in South Asia. Given their size and power, India in South Asia and China in Southeast and East Asia generate fear and suspicion ("big state versus small state syndrome") among their smaller neighbors respectively and exploit it to each other's advantage. For example, India's entry into the EAS and ASEM was backed by China's East Asian neighbors despite Beijing's opposition for the same geo-strategic reasons that India's South Asian neighbors backed China's admission into SAARC, despite New Delhi's opposition. China has perfected the art of exploiting India's troubled relations with its South Asian neighhbours to bolster its presence in the region. Nearly all of India's South Asian neighbors draw sustenance from the support they receive from China bound as they are with Beijing in a string of defence and security agreements. From India's per-spective, the Chinese investments in the strategic Trans-Karakoram highway and the Gwadar port in the west of India, the construction of the Lhasa rail-way that will enhance Chinese transport links with Nepal, Bhutan, Bangladesh and northeastern India and the building of the Irrawaddy Corridor (involving a combination of road, river, rail, and oceanic harbor infrastructure) linking Yunnan province with Burma ports on the Bay of Bengal in the east of India are all part of a wider strategy to contain India and draw South Asia into China's orbit.

But containment begets counter-containment. Since the late 1990s, India has responded by fishing in the troubled waters in Central Asia, East, and Southeast Asia where countries have unresolved territorial and maritime disputes with China. As part of its "Look East" strategy, New Delhi is forging economic and strategic partnerships with "China-wary" countries (Tajikistan, Mongolia, Japan, Taiwan, Vietnam, Indonesia, and Australia) to advance its security interests in Asia and beyond. An influential retired diplomat, G. Parthasarathy, wants New Delhi to counter Beijing's "containment of India" by "strengthening India's ties with countries like Japan and Vietnam and a review of the present limitations on contacts with Taiwan . . . Strategic ties with Vietnam should be strengthened with military supplies, including *Brahmos* and *Prithvi* missiles and a Plutonium Research Reactor."[84] During Vietnamese Prime Minister Nguyen Tan Dung's July 2007 visit to India, the conclusion of a defence agreement with Vietnam was interpreted as "furthering its [India's] fledgling China 'containment' strategy," in addition to furthering economic ties and cooperation at regional and multilateral forums with an old Southeast Asian ally.[85] India is also expanding its security links with Mongolia in a bid to monitor China's space and military activities in the region. Indian officials see military ties with China's neighbors as New Delhi's "tit-for-tat response for Beijing's strategic encirclement of India." As Lt. Gen. (Retd) V. K. Kapoor observes: "Through these alliances India is mirroring China's game plan of befriending neighbours in order to develop strategic leverage."[86] Apparently, the fear of becoming China's economic dependencies and security concerns regarding

China have prompted some Asian-Pacific countries to cultivate India as an alternative power so as to prevent the region from becoming an exclusive Chinese sphere of influence—an objective shared by the US and Japan. The navies of India, the Philippines, Indonesia, Singapore, and Thailand have agreed to cooperate in the Indian Ocean region to counter piracy, narcotics trafficking and any potential threat to commercial sea lanes. In a sense, India's "Look East" policy sends a signal to China that India can become part of an anti-Chinese coalition should China take stances that threaten the security of its neighbors. According to the Stockholm International Peace Research Institute, India is now the world's second largest arms importer—next only to China. It is projected to spend a staggering $60 billion over the next five years on its force acquisition and modernization plans for the three services—fighter and cargo aircraft, aircraft carriers, nuclear submarines, tanks, guns, helicopters.[87]

In short, as China and India's power and ambitions grow, nearly all regions of the world bear the marks of their competitive economic and geo-strategic outreach. In recent years, the resurgence in economic growth and growing self-confidence has emboldened them to employ strategic maneuvers so as to checkmate each other from gaining advantage or expanding spheres of influence. However, India suffers from the disadvantage of a latecomer and is still no match for China's economic clout and diplomatic influence in these regions. New Delhi's efforts to establish closer ties with Southeast and East Asian countries and to emerge as an independent power suggest future tension and friction between India and a China that aspires for regional and global dominance.

Soft power diplomacy

Both India and China are active participants in regional multilateral forums such as the ARF, ASEM, EAS, SCO, SAARC, and the Group of Eight. In addition, China is also a key member of APEC and ASEAN+3. The China–India rivalry for oneupmanship is increasingly being played out in regional multilateral forums as well where each seeks advantage over the other. Both put forward proposals for multilateral cooperation that seek to marginalize or exclude the other. The Mekong-Ganges Cooperation (MGC) and the Bay of Bengal Initiative for MultiSectoral Technical and Economic Cooperation (BIMSTEC) frameworks promoted by India are cases in point. After obtaining observer status in SAARC, China vowed to "dilute India's hold in the region as a major economic power." For its part, India offers solace to those in Southeast and East Asia who remain wary of Beijing's ambitions to establish an "East Asia Co-prosperity Sphere" under China's leadership.[88] Asia's regional organizations and institutions are either too weak to be effective in conflict management or remain susceptible to manipulation by great powers.

India and China are also engaged in a competition for soft power supremacy in Asia.[89] China's soft power is state-driven and a function of its economic success. In contrast, even though India lags behind China in economic development, Indian soft power—its music and movie industry, other art forms, literature, print and electronic media—is mostly culture-driven. An important element of their competition for soft power supremacy is the attraction of their respective developmental models. It is said that India's identity as a democratic Asian power—in contrast with authoritarian China—is also fueling the new warmth in India's relations with Tokyo and Washington. Ever since the 1950s, India and China have been seen as crucibles in which different developmental models are being tried and tested. That still remains the case, albeit with one important difference. During the 1950–1970s, it was socialist democracy in India and Marxism–Maoism in China. However, both have long abandoned dogmatic, doctrinaire approaches and embraced pragmatism. Economically, both China and India have now moved closer to market-driven capitalist policies. But politically, they still remain on divergent paths—multi-party democracy (with capitalism) in India and one-party authoritarianism (with capitalism) in China.

The Chinese government is using the full panoply of foreign aid, trade concessions, investment, infrastructure development, educational and cultural exchanges, diplomatic charm offensive, and peacekeeping to foster a more benign public image abroad of China's "peaceful rise." More importantly, the "successful Chinese model" of "development-without-democracy" or "development-before-democracy" is being sold to the developing world as an alternative model for ending poverty. And it resonates well across the world. Beijing's pitch for "non-interference in domestic affairs" and "development first" is certainly winning an audience in Central Asia, parts of South and Southeast Asia (Bangladesh, Burma, Nepal, Pakistan, Cambodia, Laos, Vietnam, Thailand), Africa, and Latin America. In a sense, this amounts to the revival of the old ideological debate over which political system—authoritarianism or democracy—delivers more people from poverty, and whether wealth or elections are a greater measure of freedom. This "contest of ideas" may bode ill for the UN efforts to promote transparency, accountability, good governance, and democracy in weak, failing states, but it opens the door for China to position itself to play the role of a balancer and enlarge China's own sphere of influence.

In this newly revived "battle of ideas," India plays an important role because it happens to be the world's fastest growing free market democracy, and thus offers a powerful alternative to China's authoritarian developmental model. India's experiment with democratic capitalism has appeal across borders. For, contrary to the conventional wisdom, the success of the Indian development model shows that a giant, poor country of billion-plus population with its vibrant civil society can achieve economic development and poverty reduction while remaining a liberal secular, multi-religious democracy. To all those enamored of the Chinese "Market-Leninist" developmental model of authoritarian capitalism, India's success further proves that "development-with-democracy" is the firmest foundation for the achievement of humankind's most basic aspirations.[90]

Concluding observations

With the rise of Asian powers—China and India—reclaiming their historic place in the world economy, power transitions of historic magnitude are taking place at the beginning of the twenty-first century. Just as the Indian sub-continental plate constantly rubs and pushes against the Eurasian tectonic plate and causes friction and volatility in the entire Himalayan mountain range, India's relations with China also remain volatile and friction-ridden because of past experience, war, territorial disputes, unparallel interests, conflicting world views, and divergent geopolitical interests. Asia's two giants hold different positions in the international system, have contrasting strategic cultures, clashing political systems and naturally competitive geo-strategic interests in overlapping spheres of influence. China has long figured in India's strategic calculus. As India gradually proceeds on its trajectory toward global power status, it is beginning to figure prominently in China's strategic calculus because India, just by being there as India—democratic, powerful, prosperous, successful—complicates Beijing's grand strategy and frustrates China's attempts to re-establish a Sino-centric international order. Their disputes are many, but both share an interest in avoiding overt rivalry, confrontation, and conflict given their current focus on acquiring comprehensive national power. A degree of pragmatism is informing their view of each other. Despite no breakthrough yet on finding a solution to the thorny boundary issue, confidence-building measures on the disputed border have been put in place. Trust between the two militaries is being established, especially through holding joint military exercises.

Optimists hope that as the relative weight of economic factors vis-à-vis military security concerns increases, the reality of the rapidly expanding bilateral engagement would provide a different template for addressing their disputes. With direct flights, tourism is taking off. Intensifying trade and commerce would hopefully eventually raise the stakes for China in its relationship with India and vice versa. While they are competitors for power and influence in Asia, China and India also share common interests in maintaining regional stability (for example, combating the growing Islamist fundamentalist menace, global warming, resource scarcity, terrorism, maintaining access to capital and markets, and benefiting from globalization). The normalization of relations is thus based on a need to focus on social and political stability, strong economic growth and a sense of security so they can concentrate on realizing their potential and avoid the perils of stagnation or decline.

Pessimists point to the territorial, strategic, economic, and geopolitical roots of the India–China rivalry and paint a very different picture. They argue that India–China ties remain fragile, and as vulnerable as ever to sudden deterioration as a result of misperceptions, unrealistic expectations, accidents, and eruption of unresolved issues. The combination of internal issues of stability and external overlapping spheres of influence forestall the chances for a genuine Sino–Indian rapprochement. Indeed, the issues that bind the two countries are also the issues that divide them and fuel their rivalry. Neither power is comfortable with the rise of the other. Each perceives the other as pursuing hegemony and entertaining imperial ambitions. Both are watching each other warily as they build up their respective militaries and jostle for power, influence and allegiance of small and medium-sized nations in Central, South, and Southeast Asia, seek access to natural resources in remote parts of the world, and compete for leadership positions in global and regional organizations. Their tandem emergence as global powers has evoked countervailing actions by both which invariably influences the security environment of the Asia-Pacific region. Each puts forward proposals for multilateral cooperation that exclude the other. Significantly, the future of the India–China relationship is increasingly being influenced by "the US factor." Both have been courting the US, each one seeking to move closer to Washington against the other. India has unveiled a comprehensive "multi-alignment" strategy to meet the growing China challenge as well as to facilitate its own rise as a great power. New Delhi is weaving a web of mutually inseparable relationships with an eye to opportunities and balance with great powers and trading partners, while trying to avoid alignment and overt confrontation. Still, a pro-US, pro-Japan tilt in India's national security policy—a reaction to the power projection capabilities of neighboring China—will be a defining characteristic of an increasingly globalized India.

Simmering tensions over territory, Tibet, energy resources, and rival alliance relationships ensure that Indian Prime Minister Manmohan Singh's assertion that "there is enough [geopolitical] space for the two countries to develop together" will remain more a "hope" than a conviction. The relationship between the two rising Asian giants with overlapping spheres of influence, disputed frontiers and ever-widening geopolitical horizons will therefore be characterized more by competition and rivalry than cooperation (or, "competitive cooperation"). Indeed, the possibility of confrontation cannot be ruled out completely.

Improvement in China–India relations over the long term will depend upon Beijing's assessment of India's evolving political cohesion, economic growth, and military potential. The existence of two economically powerful nations would create new tensions, as they both strive to stamp their authority on the region. It is possible that economically prosperous and militarily confident China and India might come to terms with each other eventually as their mutual containment policies start yielding diminishing returns but this is unlikely to happen in the short and medium term (i.e. before 2030s).

Notes

*   The views expressed here are author's own and do not reflect the policy or position of the Asia-Pacific Center for Security Studies or the US Department of Defense.

1   In assessing the notion of "national power" in today's world, factors such as technology, education, external respect and reputation, and economic growth and trade are as important as traditional power attributes of military, geography, raw

materials and population. In other words, "soft power" is as important as "hard power." Soft power seeks to achieve policy goals through attraction, appeal and persuasion rather than force and coercion.

2   Silvia Sartori, "How China sees India and the World," *Heartland: Eurasian Review of Geopolitics*, No. 3, (Hong Kong: Cassan Press, 2005), p. 57, www. heartland.it/_lib/_docs/2005_03_chindia_the_21st_century_challenge.pdf.
3   Andrew Scobell, " 'Cult of Defense' and 'Great Power Dreams': The Influence of Strategic Culture on China's Relationship with India," Chapter 13, in Malcolm R. Chambers (ed.), *South Asia in 2020: Future Strategic Balances and Alliances* (PA: US Army War College, Strategic Studies Institute, November 2002), pp. 329–359.
4   Scobell, " 'Cult of Defense' and 'Great Power Dreams' ", p. 347.
5   Sartori, "How China sees India and the World," pp. 48–58.
6   For details, see Mohan Malik, "Chinese conundrum: Mythical History," *Force*, August 2005, pp. 45–47; "Past Imperfect," *Force*, July 2005, pp. 40–43; "Partial Amnesia," *Force*, June 2005, pp. 45–47.
7   Sartori, "How China sees India and the World," pp. 49–50.
8   Mohan Malik, "China's Strategy of Containing India," *Power and Interest News Report*, February 6, 2006, www.pinr.com/report.php?ac=view_report&report_id=434.
9   See Michael Pillsbury, *China Debates the Future Security Environment* (National Defense University Press, 2000).
10   Hamish McDonald, "Beijing content with the devil it knows," *Age* (Melbourne), January 14, 2003.
11   Commentary, "Nuclear agreement and big power's dream," *People's Daily online*, August 30, 2007, http://English.people.com.cn/90001/90780/91343/6251506/html Italics mine.
12   A month after Rice's offer, Premier Wen Jiabao visited India in April 2005 and asked India not to sign a long-term military cooperation agreement with the US. Praful Bidwai, "Ties With China Sour as Alliance With US Grows," *Inter Press Service*, July 6, 2007, www.ipsnews.net/news.asp?idnews=38444.
13   Discussions and conversations with China's South Asia specialists in Beijing, Shanghai, Honolulu, 2006–2007. Bidwai, "Ties With China Sour . . ."
14   *People's Daily online*, August 14, 2007; *China Daily*, June 7, 2007.
15   Sartori, "How China sees India and the World," pp. 54–55.
16   Discussions and conversations with China's South Asia specialists, 2005–2006.
17   Arun Sahgal, "Blow Hot, Blow Cold," *Force*, July 2007; Ramesh Ramachandran, "Helping US May Derail Border Talks," *Asian Age*, July 25, 2007.
18   Rajat Pandit, "China's growing military clout worries India, US," *Times of India*, April 10, 2007, p. 1.
19   "Japan Still Pushing the 'Four-state Alliance,' " *Huanqiu Shibao* [*Global Times*], August 6, 2007.
20   M. K. Bhadrakumar, " 'Headless chickens' and the China threat," *Asia Times online*, August 23, 2007, www.atimes.com/atimes/South_Asia/IH23Df04.html.
21   Commentary, "Nuclear agreement and big power's dream."
22   For a review of Chinese media articles on India, see D. S. Rajan, "China: Media fears over India becoming part of Western Alliance," *Saag.org*, Paper No. 2350, August 29, 2007, www.saag.org/papers24/paper2350.html.
23   Seema Sirohi, "ASEAN: Ah, Singhapuram . . . China blocks India's attempts to join the powerful ASEAN plus," *Outlook.com*, December 3, 2007, www.outlookindia.com/full.asp?fodname=20071203&fname=Asean+%28F%29&sid=1.

24   For different schools of thought, see Mohan Malik, "Eyeing the Dragon: India's China Debate," in Satu Limaye, ed., *Asia's China Debate* (Honolulu: Asia-Pacific Center for Security Studies Special Assessments, December 2003), pp. 18, www.apcss.org/Publications/APSSS/ChinaDebate/ChinaDebate_Malik.pdf.

25   Nehru quoted in Sun Keqin and Cui Hongjian, eds., *Ezhi Zhongguo-Shenhua yu xianshi* [*Containing China-myth and reality*] (Beijing: Zhongguo yanshi chubanshe, 1996); B. Raman, "China: Through Indian Eyes," C3S Paper No. 12, May 14, 2007, www.c3sindia.org/India/87/china-through-indian-eyes/.

26   Quoted in K. Subrahmanyam, "Don't Get Fooled By China," *Times of India*, August 28, 2007.

27   R. Swaminathan, "India's Foreign Policy: Emerging Trends in the New Century," *Saag.org*, Paper No. 2194, April 5, 2007, www.saag.org/%5Cpapers22%5Cpaper2194.html.

28   PTI, "India's strategic thinking needs radical recast: IAF chief," *Times of India*, July 29, 2007.

29   Indian Foreign Minister Yashwant Sinha's speech at the Institute of Defence Studies & Analyses, New Delhi, November 22, 2003.

30   Comment by an Indian China-watcher, New Delhi, July 2007.

31   Former ambassador to China, Salman Haider, quoted in D. Srivastava and P. Andley, *Great Power Dynamics: India, US and China* (Report of Panel Discussion, May 5, 2007, sponsored by Indian Army 15 Corps HQ, Srinagar, and Institute of Peace and Conflict Studies, New Delhi), www.ipcs.org/DiscussionReport_May07.pdf.

32   Ibid.

33   J. Mohan Malik, "Security Council Reform: China Signals Its Veto," *World Policy Journal*, Vol. XXII, No. 1, Spring 2005, pp. 19–29; Mohan Malik, "The East Asia Summit: More Discord than Accord" *YaleGlobal Online*, December 20, 2005, pp. 1–4. http://yaleglobal.yale.edu/display.article?id=6645; Mohan Malik, "China Responds to the US–India Nuclear Deal," *China Brief*, Vol. 6, Issue 7, March 29, 2006. www.jamestown.org/publications_details.php?volume_id=415&issue_id=3670&article_id=237096.

34   Quoted in Indrani Bagchi, "Buddhism new obstacle between India, China," *Times of India*, June 21, 2007, p. 1.

35   B. Raman, "Tawang: Some Indian plain-speaking at last!" *Saag.org*, Paper no. 2273, June 22, 2007, www.saag.org/papers23/paper2273.html.

36   Brahma Chellaney, "The Quad: Australia–India–Japan–US Strategic Cooperation: A Concert of Democracies," *Asian Age*, July 3, 2007.

37   C. Raja Mohan, "Two PMs, one problem: China," *Indian Express*, August 21, 2007. Italics mine. www.indianexpress.com/story/211558.html.

38   Interview with an Indian diplomat, New Delhi, March 2007.

39   B. Raman, "America's Jihadists For Democracy," *Outlook*, August 22, 2007. www.outlookindia.com/full.asp?fodname=20070822&fname=ramanchina&sid=2.

40   Ding Wenlei, "Hardnosed Software Battle: India and China square up in IT ring," *Beijing Review*, March 25, 2004, Vol. 47, pp. 36–39.

41   Editorial, "Enter the Dragon? Beijing 'Not Serious' About Settling Border Dispute With India," *Indian Express*, May 29, 2007.

42   Agencies, "Growing Chinese economy bad, say Indians," *Times of India*, July 5, 2007, p. 1.

43   India reportedly conveyed to China in June 2007 that "it could not be pushed beyond a point on the boundary dispute." See Rajeev Sharma, "China Jams DD, AIR Signals in Border Area," *Tribune*, June 26, 2007.

44 Rajeev Sharma, "China objects to Sikkim bunkers," *Tribune*, September 3, 2007, www.tribuneindia.com/2007/20070903/nation.htm#7.

45 It is noteworthy that China has to date made no formal public declaration that it recognizes Sikkim as Indian territory. Ravi Velloor: "China's Position on Issues with India 'Hardening,'" *Straits Times*, June 12, 2007.

46 Raman, "Tawang: Some Indian plain-speaking at last!"

47 B. Raman, "Why I am wary of China," *Rediff.com*, November 14, 2006, http://in.rediff.com/news/2006/nov/14raman.htm.

48 Rajeev Sharma, "India–China Border Row—No Headway Expected This Year," *Tribune*, June 8, 2007.

49 Ma Jiali cited in Scobell, " 'Cult of Defense' and 'Great Power Dreams' . . .," p. 346.

50 G. Parthasarathy, "Disturbing signs flow from across the Himalayas," *Pioneer*, July 1, 2007.

51 Liu Silu, "Beijing Should Not Lose Patience in Chinese–Indian Border Talks," ["Zhongyin bianjie tanpan, Beijing bu neng ji (中印邊界談判北京不能急)"], *Wen Wei Po* (Hong Kong), June 1, 2007.

52 See interview with Prof. Wang Yiwei of Fudan University's Center for American Studies, in Ramesh Ramachandran, "Helping US May Derail Border Talks," *Asian Age*, July 25, 2007.

53 "Future directions of the Sino–Indian border dispute," *International Strategic Studies* [*Guogji Zhanlue*], November 2006; also see Sahgal, "Blow Hot, Blow Cold."

54 A resolution of the Sino–Indian border dispute would lead to the deployment of India's military assets on the India–Pakistan border, thereby tilting the military balance decisively in India's favor, much to China's ally Pakistan's disadvantage.

55 Prof. Wang Yiwei's interview in Ramachandran, "Helping US May Derail Border Talks."

56 Liu, "Beijing Should Not Lose Patience . . ."

57 "Future directions of the Sino–Indian border dispute"; Sahgal, "Blow Hot, Blow Cold. . . ."

58 Indrani Bagchi & Saibal Dasgupta, "India red-faced as China gets tough," *Times of India*, May 27, 2007; Seema Mustafa, "New PRC Foreign Minister Hardens Border Dispute," *Asian Age*, August 4, 2007.

59 Reuters, "India rebuffs Beijing on disputed border," *International Herald Tribune*, June 17, 2007.

60 "Pranab says can't give any part of Arunachal," *Indian Express*, June 17, 2007; Raman, "Tawang: Some Indian plain-speaking at last!"

61 Rahul Bedi, "India develops infrastructure on Chinese border," *Jane's Defence Weekly*, July 18, 2007.

62 Bappa Majumdar, "China in mind, India to boost eastern air power," *Reuters*, August 8, 2007.

63 "Melting glaciers threaten Indus, Ganges," *Southasiamedia.net*, July 25, 2007, www.southasianmedia.net/index_story.cfm?id=409988&category=frontend&Country=main&pro=0.

64 Chinese Foreign Ministry's daily briefings, March 2, 2006, www.china-embassy.org/eng/fyrth/t238267.htm.

65 Commentary, "Nuclear agreement and big power's dream."

66 Bhaskar Roy, "123 Agreement and the People's Republic of China," *Saag.org*, Paper No. 2324, August 8, 2007, www.saag.org/papers24/paper2324.html.

67 Wang Peng, "The US–Indian Nuclear Agreement: Cooperation or Threat?" *People's Daily*, August 11, 2007, p. 8.

68 This formulation by foreign minister Yang Jiechi would pave the way for the Chinese construction of Chashma III and IV nuclear reactors in Pakistan. Chris Buckley, "China likely to swallow anger over Indo-US N-deal," *Reuters*, August 29, 2007.

69 Cited in James Holmes, "China's Energy Consumption and Opportunities for US–China Cooperation," Testimony before the US–China Economic and Security Review Commission, June 14, 2007, www.uscc.gov/hearings/2007 hearings/written_testimonies/07_06_14_15wrts/07_06_14_holmes_statement.pdf.

70 PTI, "India loses to China on Myanmar gas," *Rediff.com*, August 23, 2007, www.rediff.com/money/2007/aug/23gas.htm.

71 Sanjay Dutta, "Government to set up energy security panel to counter China," *Times of India*, March 7, 2007.

72 Sudha Ramachandran, "India promotes 'goodwill' naval exercises," *Asia Times online*, August 14, 2007, www.atimes.com/atimes/South_Asia/IH14Df01. html.

73 Holmes, "China's Energy Consumption and Opportunities for US–China Cooperation . . .," p. 2.

74 Many argue that India and China have been rival civilizations for millennia in the grand scheme of events. See Rajeev Srinivasan, "A millennia-old tussle," *Rediff.com*, November 22, 2002, www.rediff.com/news/2002/nov/23chin.htm.

75 Brahma Chellaney, "The Quad: Australia-India-Japan-US Strategic Cooperation," *Asian Age*, July 3, 2007.

76 Rahul Bedi, "India eyes major player status," *Jane's Defence Weekly*, July 18, 2007.

77 Brahma Chellaney, "A yen for closer ties," *Hindustan Times*, August 9, 2007; "Look East, At Japan, Not China," *Asian Age*, September 7, 2007.

78 Srikanth Kondapalli, "Why Japan and India are moving closer," *Rediff.com*, August 23, 2007, www.rediff.com/news/2007/aug/23guest.htm.

79 Anirudh Suri, "India and Japan: Congruence, at last," *Asia Times online*, June 9, 2007, http://a.tribalfusion.com/i.click?site=AsiaTimes&adSpace=ROS&size= 468x60&requested=587334943.

80 Editorial, "Love with Tokyo," *Indian Express*, August 24, 2007.

81 Seema Sirohi, "Japan: The Sake Is Warming," *Outlook*, 27 August 27, 2007.

82 Praful Bidwai, "Five-Nation Naval Drill Presages 'Asian NATO'?" *Inter-Press Service*, September 7, 2007, www.ipsnews.net/news.asp?idnews=39175.

83 Correspondence with senior diplomats and military officers, August 2007.

84 G. Parthasarathy, "China remains a challenge," *Pioneer*, December 14, 2006, p. 5.

85 Madhur Singh, "India, Vietnam deepen defence, nuclear ties," *Hindustan Times*, July 6, 2007, p. 1.

86 Indian government officials quoted in Rahul Bedi, "Defence ties with Mongolia expanded: Bid to monitor China's military activities," *Tribune*, August 9, 2007, www.tribuneindia.com/2007/20070810/main5.htm; "India: Early Warning Radar In Mongolia?" *Stratfor.org*, August 9, 2007, www.stratfor.com/products/ premium/read_article.php?id=293768.

87 "Global Military Spending Hits $1.2 Trillion-Study," *Reuters*, June 13, 2007.

88 Bruce Loudon, "India, China in clash at summit," *Australian*, April 4, 2007, p. 7.

89 "The rising 'Soft Power' of China and India," *Business World*, May 30, 2005, www.ibef.org/artdisplay.aspx?cat_id=54&art_id=6275.

90 Greg Sheridan, "China lobby keeps India on the outer," *Australian*, March 17, 2007.

10 Political construction of human rights

With a focus on North Korean refugees in China

Mikyoung Kim

Introduction: China's place in the human rights debates

The heinous atrocities committed during World War II alerted the international community to the importance of human rights. People were appalled to learn that "inconceivable acts" were actually carried out at Nazi camps, and after Hiroshima and Nagasaki even human extinction itself seemed a possibility. Science and technology suddenly seemed more likely to damn than save, and humanity had to confront its dark side. Existential questions such as "what is it to be human?" and "what is history?" dominated contemporary discourse. Amid such serious soul searching, the Declaration of Universal Human Rights was announced at the United Nations in 1948. The Declaration, not a binding treaty but rather a statement of principles, was a reaffirmation that humanity was capable of saving itself from its own destructive impulses.

The end of the Cold War signaled the advent of the globalization of universal human rights. The American "victory" over the former Soviet Union was regarded by many as undeniable empirical evidence in support of participatory democracy. The alternative regime types of totalitarian and authoritarian rule were becoming passé. The values embedded in Western thought such as individual rights, equality, and freedom were revered as the winning ideational combination for social progress. Despite this grand transformation, however, the world continued to witness "crimes against humanity." The African continent suffered from genocidal acts, massive famine, dire poverty, and ceaseless internal strife. A good part of Asia was also experiencing tumultuous times. A hypothetical causal linkage among economic growth, political development, and human rights improvement has put the rising economic power of Asia, China, at the center of global scrutiny regarding human rights.

China poses as an interesting case for analysis by revealing how multi-faceted human rights situations and debates are. Unlike the West, which took more than two hundred years to experience the Industrial Revolution and the ensuing democratization, Chinese society is under intense pressure as it has been undergoing simultaneous economic, social, and political transformative processes since the end of the 1970s. Its aspirations to achieve "a peaceful rise" and "world harmony" entail multitasking rather than sequential progress.

In this vein, Beijing's handling of "the others," the escapees from neighboring North Korea, sheds an illuminating light on Beijing's strategic ambivalence about human rights. This chapter aims to discuss issues pertinent to the Chinese human rights debate, and assess the situation of North Korean escapees within that context.

Theoretical issues

While no social science research can be purely scientific, scientific rigor is highly sought after in social science research praxis. Human rights may be even more difficult to research than other areas of social science,[1] as such a "para academic" field has sufficient "gray area" to be at risk of politicization. With that caveat, however, research into theoretical issues will be revisited in the following.

Particularism vs. universalism: does culture equal destiny?

It was not very long after its issuance that the 1948 UN Declaration began to face resistance. With memories of colonial subjugation still fresh, non-Western governments and peoples rebutted the Declaration's assertions of universality. They criticized it as a self-righteous attempt to impose Western values on non-Western societies. Ethos and worldviews are culture-bound, and human rights, therefore, should be understood within each particular cultural context, they argued. As Western imperialism was spearheaded by the evangelical Judeo-Christian tradition in the nineteenth century, the Declaration was regarded as a velvet fist to punish those deviating from Western mores. The 1993 Bangkok Declaration of Human Rights represented direct resistance against "human rights" as defined by the world's power centers. Two of the clauses, quoted below, explicitly argue against the politicization of human rights and the use of pressure or force to bring about compliance:

*   *Stressing* the universality, objectivity and non-selectivity of all human rights and the need to avoid the application of double standards in the implementation of human rights and its politicization.
*   *Recognizing* that the promotion of human rights should be encouraged by cooperation and consensus, and not through confrontation and the imposition of incompatible values.

In the East, the universality assertion of the UN Declaration was taken as an extension of pre-existing ideas in the West that the East was an object to be enlightened. In 1911, for example, American sociologist Edward Warren Capen drew up a long list of areas in which the West could exert a positive influence on "the Orient." These areas included "ignorance, the low standard of living, economic insufficiency, physical suffering due to ignorance of sanitation and medical science, the lack of individual opportunity and responsibility, the corruption and inefficiency of government, and low ethical standards."[2] Together, the legacies of Orientalism and the celebrated democratic values of the twentieth century represented a powerful force pressing for the implementation of universal human rights in Asia.

The Bangkok Declaration was not the only expression of Asian dissent from Western concepts of human rights. The phenomenal economic growth of the Four Little Dragons (Taiwan, Singapore, Hong Kong, and Korea) was cited as evidence against the notion that Asian cultural values were incompatible with competitive capitalism. In his seminal work, *The Protestant Ethic and the Spirit of Capitalism*, Max Weber argued that the capitalist mentality was on the same continuum as that of Protestant ethics, and that the two worldviews when combined provided a powerful impetus for societies and individuals to succeed materially.[3] With the Four Little Dragons ascending, the Asian Confucian heritage was seen as just as compatible with the current capitalist mentality as Protestantism, argued Singaporean leader Lee Kuan Yew. Despite profound differences in human beings' relations to their God/gods, both traditions instill similar virtues in their adherents, such as industriousness, frugality, and perseverance. In other words, the Asian values of Confucianism are as relevant as the Western ethos in framing the mindset to excel materially.

In the universality vs. particularity debate, the Chinese government takes a jaundiced view of American criticism of its human rights record. Such outside criticism is often construed as unjustifiable interference in internal affairs and as a breach of sovereignty.[4] Since Beijing sees itself as just having begun to move beyond a tumultuous century characterized by foreign subjugation, internal strife, and civil wars,[5] Washington's pressure is deemed to be inappropriate. Further complicating matters, Beijing tends to regard American criticism of its human rights situation as political rather than purely humanitarian. But the PRC is far from the only Asian country that objects to Western concepts of human rights and especially to the use of pressure to impose them. For example, Singapore's Lee added, "It is not my business to tell people what's wrong with their system. It is my business to tell people not to foist their system indiscriminately on societies in which it will not work."[6]

Indeed, Chinese circumstances differ significantly from those of the West. "A history of cruelty" is one way to describe the trajectory of Chinese history.[7] Leaving aside ancient civil strife, the trauma of recent internal convulsions, such as the Great Leap Forward and the Cultural Revolution, is still vivid in the Chinese collective memory.[8] Nathan offers a long list of the Chinese government's human rights offenses, including imprisonment, arbitrary detention, forced exile, religious repression, violations related to criminal procedure, torture and abuse of inmates of prisons and labor camps, forced resettlement, and forced abortion and sterilization.[9] Reflecting on the cruel realities that the Chinese people have had to survive, Xu states that "theoretical discussions of subjectivity, identity, individuality and universalism may seem remote and disconnected from harsh realities."[10]

The power dimensions: securitization of human rights

With pluralism rising in world politics, issues formerly not regarded as security concerns began emerging as legitimate security areas.[11] These include piracy, drug trafficking, illegal migration, and environmental degradation. Human rights were also added to the list, as it was argued that states that did not respect the human rights of their citizens would be more likely to engage in aggressive and dangerous behavior abroad as well. The 2004 North Korean Human Rights Act passed by the US Congress is a good case in point. The Bush administration and especially Republican members of Congress decided to focus on the abysmal human rights situation inside North Korea as part of their overall foreign policy agenda toward North Korea, and they manifested their will to do so by allocating significant resources to the project. Another example is the 1998 legislation passed by the US Congress authorizing the State Department to assist non-governmental organizations (NGOs) that could foster democracy in China.[12]

The increasing attention to non-traditional security concerns may be the result of increasing globalization as well as the decline of traditional security threats such as arms races. This paradigmatic shift in threat perception changes the focus regarding security architecture from "hardware," such as military weaponry, to "software," the treatment of peoples and even individuals by their governments and societies. This new focus is contributing to the rising importance of identity politics in international affairs.

Identity politics

The politicization of human rights entails the (re-)construction of identity in international society. The framing of charges against Beijing by the US reflects "the construction effects of interaction on identities and interests."[13] In other words, the United States, as the hegemonic power, seeks to exert its influence on the rising power, China, which can pose a threat to the status quo in a unipolar world. As China's visibility increases, countervailing forces to check its international advance tend to become equally strong. Critics argue that to be a responsible power Beijing should transform its political system to that of liberal democracy and loosen up the tight grip on its populace. The heightened prestige that Beijing desires can come only by fulfilling moral obligations such as respect for human rights, they assert. All the mounting pressure suggests China's changing identity from that of a developing Socialist country to that of a regional (or an emerging world) power.

The United Sates has been at the forefront in pushing Beijing toward democratic reform. Following up on the Carter administration's positioning of human rights at the top of the diplomatic agenda, it was the Clinton administration that actually tried to link the issue to trade sanctions.[14] In response to the US Department of State's publication of its annual *Human Rights Report*, the Beijing government began releasing its own *White Paper on Human Rights* since 1991. In addition, as part of the PRC's counter-attack, its Ministry of Foreign Affairs has frequently criticized the United States for domestic human rights violations.

Concerns about applying American standards to other countries also come from within the United States. The late Jeane Kirkpatrick, for example, wrote that "No idea holds greater sway in the mind of educated Americans than the belief that it is possible to democratize governments, anytime and anywhere, under any circumstances."[15] For the United States as a self-designated moral crusader, the politicization of human rights is an ideational device to boost its own standing, and Beijing's existence accentuates this self-proclaimed US identity within the world community. Riles observes that

> The field of human rights is predominantly US projects; hence, it raises questions about US global domination, in particular. One also cannot discuss human rights without analyzing the influence of large donors based primarily in the United States and Europe who, whether purposefully or not, promote certain local intellectuals and projects that fit more closely with their own agendas while ignoring others.[16]

The US government's "shaming tactics" can lead to a situation in which China comes to play the role of a reluctant advocate of Asian values. Given the country's recent history of violence and trauma, this scenario will lose its viability only when the United States stops setting the stage for such role playing.

Following up on Blumer, a nation's behavior "arises . . . from how he interprets and handles these things [environmental pressure, stimuli, motives, attitudes, and ideas] in an action which he is constructing."[17] In this socially constructed world, the interactions between the United States and China on human rights can help Beijing establish its own new identity as a torch-bearer of culture-bound human rights. Creating confrontations sets up a stage where "actors learn identities and interests as a result of how significant others treat them."[18] Actors play out their parts as they understand what others expect them to do. It is the perception that prescribes a certain behavior, which is not necessarily an outcome of a rational cost–benefit analysis.[19] Thus, the more the United States presses Beijing using its own moral values as a weapon, the likelier Beijing is to act like a moral opponent equipped with its own set of values. The environment of states, domestic and international, is the theater where actors contest and challenge each other's norms. The reciprocal interactions construct and reconstruct identities that are played out during negotiation processes.[20]

Conceptual qualifiers

Considerable differences exist between the United States and China in their definitions of human rights. Americans, for instance, attach supreme importance to the rights of the individual, while the Chinese place higher priority on group rights. In addition, the Chinese ascribe more authority to the state's moral leadership than their American counterparts. These perceptual differences are indicative of just how different the worldviews of the two peoples are.

Individual vs. group

Harmony is a central concept in Chinese thinking. Group harmony is more important in the creation and maintenance of social order than respecting individual rights regulating relational norms between the two.[21] Such a norm is a continuing legacy from ancient agrarian times when class-based group cooperation was essential for the functioning of a hierarchy-driven society. The only probable exception to this order of priority in the Chinese tradition was "the great man." His influence was almost limitless, and yet an imputed lack of selfish interests was the core element of his authority.[22] An individual could supersede a group only when his individuality was sacrificed for the collective cause. With the arrival of Marxism, the imagery of the great man was transformed into that of a selfless proletariat. A person who would sacrifice himself for the proletarian revolution, *the* cause of the working class, could exercise influence as the moral harmonizer of society.[23]

The supremacy of collective norms over individual rights help the Chinese understand democracy, a Western introduction, from their unique cultural standpoint. The Chinese view democracy "as a symbol of harmony of interests" rather than as a "means of reconciling differences."[24] Amid rapid global integration, the populace is becoming more aware of the democratic system, and they believe that Western democracy would lose its relevance if it failed to harmonize the individuality of the majority of citizens.[25] The concept of an individual born with innate rights does not exist in the Chinese mind, a striking demarcation from that of "an entitled individual" in Western thought.

The state and law

The Chinese believe that the state bears primary responsibility for protecting individuals; the concept of individual rights is missing in traditional thought. Qi writes that

> . . . in modern society, the only body of power sufficient to suppress human rights is state power. The Chinese have never understood human rights in this way. In China, the traditional view has been that it is the state's duty

to take care of the people's welfare. In this sense, China has never had an innate view of human rights as derived from their indigenous culture.[26]

In ancient times, the ruler, an entity of a higher moral order, often enjoyed unrestrained power to create law to strengthen his state. Law, in that regard, was inherently pro-status quo and conformed to the Confucian world order. Virtues such as filial piety, loyalty and compassion were accentuated, and yet harsh laws providing for severe punishment were often enacted in the belief that they would be more effective than lenient versions.[27]

Despite the lingering residue of ancient norms on the state and law, the Chinese government in recent years has promulgated a series of laws to limit the discretionary power of the state. They are the Administrative Law (1990), State Compensation Law (1992), Administrative Penalties Law (1996) and Lawyer's Law (1997). Under these, citizens are permitted to sue the state for a variety of excesses and infractions. They also provide a clearer outline of governmental transparency and accountability. Most importantly, those with limited finances now have recourse to free legal representation.[28] With the number of law schools and lawyers increasing dramatically since 1979, Moore reports that "the number of commercial disputes adjudicated by the courts rose from about 15,000 a year in the early 1980s to 1.5 million a year in the mid-1990s. The number of civil cases also increased from approximately 300,000 in 1978 to 3 million in 1996."[29] This phenomenal increase, however, does not necessarily mean that law enforcement is fair and even throughout the country. Rural and inland areas still lag in implementing a fair judicial process.

The ubiquitous acknowledgment of rights in the current Chinese constitution can be misleading. The state still exerts near absolute power in protecting as well as sanctioning its populace. The idea of engaging in subversive acts to challenge state authority in order to win individual rights over those of the collective continues to be outside the boundaries of the acceptable in terms of Chinese views.

Economic rights vs. political rights

China and the United States approach each other from different standpoints originating from different domestic priorities. During a speech to the 1993 Vienna World Conference on Human Rights, PRC Ambassador Liu Huaqiu stated:

> The concept of human rights is an integral one, including both individual and collective rights. Individual rights cover not only civil and political rights but also economic, social, and cultural rights. The various aspects of human rights are interrelated and interdependent and both necessary for safeguarding personalities.[30]

Liu's statement appeared to have been directed primarily at the United States. Unlike the United States, the Chinese government's concept of human rights parallels the definition of basic rights as "security from arbitrary violence and minimum subsistence rights."[31] While the US government has consistently and frequently downplayed economic rights as a legitimate human rights concern, the Chinese government has argued for "subsistence rights (*shencun quan*)." For the PRC, on the other hand, political rights exist to serve social utility, with the building of a strong state being the top priority.[32]

On explaining different stance between Washington and Beijing, Qi explains that

> There is no doubt that different political systems are the essential reason for the conflicts between the United States and China. However, more profound causes of the disagreement between the United States and China on human rights issues lie in the different levels of economic development and the divergent cultures and basic values of the two countries.[33]

Given the different levels of economic development, the United States seems oblivious to the pressing needs of the majority Chinese populace in meeting the basic human needs as human rights.

Domestic policy priorities

Despite continuing speculation that Beijing's ambition is to take a leadership role in the international arena, regime survival remains the pressing concern among the PRC's top leadership.[34] China's economic reform brought redistribution of wealth away from the state toward the society, and this empowerment has led to increasing incidents of challenging, if not subversive, acts by the people against state authority.[35] As workers continue to move from the public to the private sector, the government finds that traditional methods of control such as surveillance of work units (*danwei*) are inadequate and that new means are required. Beijing has become preoccupied with domestic issues as its ability to control the society declines.

China's increasing integration into the global economy is turning out to be a mixed blessing. While it fills the nation's coffers, it is also becoming a cause of rising social discontent. Beijing faces a wide range of problems including the widening gap between rich and poor, the developmental gap between coastal regions and interior provinces, discontent on the part of ethnic minorities, Falun Gong, and the "floating" population in search of work, environmental degradation, and energy shortage. The central government is particularly wary of increasing foreign influence as potentially subversive.[36] According to China's Ministry of Public Security, in 2004 there were 74,000 mass incidents— demonstrations, riots, and other acts of civil disobedience—an average of 200 incidents per day.[37]

North Korean escapees in China

Making an assessment of Beijing's policy toward North Korean escapees will help us understand China's balancing act between *realpolitik* and moral obligations. Both China and North Korea have been targets of harsh criticism by Washington of their treatment of their own people, criticism against which both have been vigilant in their self-defense.[38] An irony, though, is that China is also criticized for its treatment of North Korean refugees who are the victims of their own state, North Korea. Another irony stems from the tumultuous contemporary history of the region. China was the beneficiary of North Korean assistance when it suffered the trauma of a great famine between 1959 and 1961 that claimed 20–30 million lives. Now, China is finding itself having to deal with starving escapees from North Korea.

Push and pull factors

The world today has approximately 20.8 million displaced people.[39] The broad category of "displaced people" includes refugees, internally displaced, externally displaced, and illegal migrants. We can make the following general definitional distinctions based on the causes of displacement. Refugees are people who have fled persecution for primarily political reasons. They are entitled to protection under international law. When it is adjudged that they would be subject, upon repatriation, to oppression for political and ideological reasons, the host country is theoretically obligated to provide them with legal counsel and protection. Internally displaced people are those who fled from one area to another within the same sovereign territory. While the causes vary, such people are vulnerable to political persecution as well as economic hardship. Tutsis during the 1994 Rwanda genocide and Sunnis in post-Saddam Iraq are two current examples of internally displaced groups. External displacement occurs when a persecuted group flees its own country seeking protection and means of survival. In the case of illegal migration, the main factors behind the international relocation are economic, such as the search for food and employment.

As for the conditions of the various modes of (in-)voluntary relocation, there exists a synchronizing mechanism: push from the country of origin and pull from the country of reception. Push factors include internal strife and conflict, the danger of criminal punishment, political oppression, systemic discrimination and oppression, economic deprivation, and family dissolution. On the other hand, the prospect of physical safety, the availability of support networks, and the possibility of employment and educational opportunities are significant pull factors. North Korean escapees are not a major exception to this general mechanism, even though the potential repercussions for them of attempting to escape and also of being forcefully repatriated are relatively very serious. They risk their lives crossing the Sino–DPRK border in search of food and a better life as well as out of fear of severe punishment for petty crimes.[40]

The massive famine in the DPRK in 1995 was the catalyst for a large-scale migration within and outside of the country. The pull factors included the existence of support networks among ethnic Chinese-Koreans in the PRC as well as helpful NGOs, better employment opportunities, demand for marriageable women among the Chinese male population, family reunions, and the South Korean government's supportive policy.

Current status of North Korean escapees in China

Number estimates and locales for hiding

Ever since famine struck North Korea in 1995, China has been on the receiving end of a massive influx of Korean escapees. Pyongyang's failure to feed its own people has driven a starving population in search of food across the dangerous 850-mile-long border between the two countries. With the zone dividing South and North Koreas highly fortified, the Sino–DPRK border is the best route by which these hungry masses can flee the North. The exact number of North Korean escapees in China is open to debate. The Chinese government's conservative estimate is 10,000; Seoul's calculation is between 10,000 and 30,000; and humanitarian organizations put the figure as high as 300,000. According to Lee, the number of escapees reached a peak in 1998–1999.[41] There has been a gradual decline since the year 2000, when the estimated number of escapees was 75,000–125,000. By 2005 the number was down to 30,000–50,000. The number will likely grow again as North Koreans try to find a better life than the continuing shortage of food and tepid economic growth in the DPRK permits. The refugees' usual hideouts are the DPRK border regions inside China densely populated by ethnic-Koreans, such as Liaoning and Jilin provinces as well as the Dandong, Tumen, Yanbian, and Yanji areas.[42]

The experiences of escapees in China reveal salient gender dynamics. Escapees often fall victim to human trafficking in the form of (in-)voluntary marriages and prostitution. Table 10.1 shows that over half of the respondents are residing with spouses. In the aftermath of the Chinese government's one-child policy, the gender ratio in the PRC has been greatly distorted, resulting in the majority of Chinese men in rural areas having very limited marriage prospects. For instance, Charny reports a staggering 14-to-1 male–female ratio among the unmarried age group in rural Yanbian.[43] There is thus a high demand for women willing to live in rural areas, and women escapees from North Korea voluntarily and involuntarily fill in the demographic void.

Women comprise two-thirds of all North Korean escapees, and those who are in hiding are often forced into violent marriages or sold into sexual slavery. But their legal status strips them of any legal recourse. These women most often must endure rape, assault, torture, or other forms of abuse and violence for the sake of survival. Fear of being turned in to the authorities by their spouses or pimps further locks them into their situation.[44]

Table 10.1 Types of residential support for North Korean refugees (1998–1999)

Residential Type	Number	Percentage
Relatives, Acquaintances	3,051	10.7
Strangers	10,642	37.4
Marriage	**14,769**	**51.9**
No answer	10	0.0
Total	28,472	100.0

Source: Good Neighbors, *Dumangangeul Gunneuon Saramdul: Jungkuk Dongbukbujiyok 2,479gae Maeul Buhan 'Shikryangnanmin' Shiltaejosa [The Border Crossing People: A Study of North Korean Food Migrants in 2,479 Villages in Northeast China]* (Seoul: Jungto Publishing, 1999), p. 50.

Most escapees rely on random acts of kindness by strangers. Chinese who survived their own recent famine (1959–1961) and the social chaos and economic hardships of the Cultural Revolution (1966–1976) remember the assistance they and their relatives received from North Koreans, and they try to reciprocate.[45] Table 10.2 shows that most escapees rely on local Chinese to find shelter and procure the necessities for survival. They also find work nearby their hiding places.

Most Chinese, however, are hesitant to assist the escapees as the ramifications for being a good Samaritan are too substantial to ignore. One escapee stated that[5]:

> We had high hopes for China, but it was a foreign country. We had no place to go, and no place to hide. We decided to ask the village head for help, so I went to his house and asked him, "Don't you know what's happening in the North? I came here for help because you are a Chinese-Korean. Please help us." "I cannot help you," he said, "because if I get caught helping North Koreans, I will have to pay a five-thousand yuan fine."[46]

The push–pull mechanisms explain the North Korean out-migration to China. The existence of various support networks in the hiding locale plays a crucial role as a pull factor. The women escapees' experiences are gendered due to the high demand for females in rural China. Their dependence on assistance from the local Chinese, while crucial, is limited due to the government's policy. The following is an assessment of Beijing's policy toward the escapees.

The Chinese government's policy and North Koreans' exit tactics

Beijing has been trying to minimize the negative impact from the existence of the North Korean escapees. As the number of escapees increased, so did the number of forced returnees. For example, the number of confirmed repatriations rose from 580 in 1996 to 5,400 in 1997, and from 2,300 in 1998 to 8,000 in 2003.[47]

Table 10.2 Types of living environment in China (2004)

Type	Relatives (Korean-Chinese)	Local (Chinese)	Hideouts	NGO & Church Facilities	SK Gov't Facility	Floating	Others	Combination	Total
Number (%)	20 (18.7)	**43 (40.2)**	4 (3.7)	4 (3.7)	10 (9.3)	15 (14.0)	9 (8.0)	2 (1.9)	107 (100.0)

Source of Living Expenses	Relatives in China	Relatives in SK	Chinese-Koreans	NGOs & S. Koreans	Earned from Labor	SK Gov't	Begging	Others	Total
Number (%)	14 (13.6)	10 (9.7)	18 (17.5)	7 (6.8)	**42 (40.8)**	5 (4.4)	1 (1.0)	6 (5.8)	103 (99.7)

Source: Yoon Yeo Sang. 1998. "Talbukja Shiltaewa Jiwonchaegae: Jungkukjiyokeul Jungshimuro [The Reality of North Korean Refugees and Support System: With a Focus on China]," Tongil Yongu Nonchong 7(2), p. 106.

Currently, Beijing designates North Korean escapees as "illegal economic migrants." The United Nations, along with a majority of legal experts, regard them as refugees who should be granted refugee status on the grounds of *refoulement*, as returnees to North Korea are known to suffer severe repercussions, including capital punishment. Defining North Korean escapees as "illegal economic migrants" goes beyond a simple difference in preferred terminology. It is the conscious byproduct of Beijing's carefully calculated effort to evade any legal or political responsibility for these people. By designating the escapees as "illegal economic migrants," Beijing exempts itself from any legal, moral, and ethical obligations in assisting them. Police crackdowns, cash rewards for turning in escapees, and the levying of hefty fines on citizens who aid them are therefore regarded as legitimate and justifiable.

The bilateral agreements between Beijing and Pyongyang as well as Chinese domestic laws on border patrol lay the legal ground for Beijing's repatriation policy. The bilateral agreements are the Agreement on Repatriation of Illegal Entrants of the early 1960s,[48] the Border Area Task Agreement of 1986,[49] and the Jilin Province Border Area Management Clause of 1998. Intergovernmental talks were also held to address the escapee problems. During a 1996 meeting between Li Jizou, deputy director of Chinese Public Security, and Lee Myung Un, deputy director of the DPRK Border Patrol, China reportedly requested that Pyongyang take stern measures against illegal border crossings from the North Korean side. In March 1997, the PRC National People's Congress passed a resolution adding the crime of "border management hindrance" to the Chinese Criminal Law. The Chinese government began levying fines against people who provide shelter to North Korean escapees. The fine is calculated based on the distance between the place of arrest and the border. The farther away from the border that an arrest is made, the larger the fine is.[50]

Even though China bears the primary responsibility to protect the escapees, it has not been enthusiastic about fulfilling its normative duty to protect them. The North Korean escapees are not free from needs and fear in China.[51] Beijing cares about its traditional alliance relationship with Pyongyang in addition to the security need to control and eradicate elements causing potential domestic instability. It does not welcome the crimes committed by the floating North Korean escapees or the increase in black market activity due to cross-border smuggling. It is also concerned that rising ethnic consciousness among Chinese-Koreans could pose a threat to its minority policy. While the PRC repatriates escapees when they are caught, it has been lenient about South Korean NGOs' provision of assistance across the border for the civilian, not official, nature of the humanitarian work. The Border Screening and Detention Center of Chinese Public Security are in charge of detaining the escapees for a certain period of time and repatriating them back on average once a week. During special campaign periods, the frequency is determined by the number of refugees in detention: the more detainees, the more frequent the number of repatriations.

The escapees' constant fear of being apprehended by local police makes China a less than desirable place for them to settle down. Most hope to move to South Korea because of existing family ties, linguistic homogeneity and cultural affinity. An escapee stated the following during an interview:

> I felt that I was not strong enough to make it all the way to the South, so I wanted to go to deep into the countryside in China to live off farming. But the police kept on hunting for us. We kept getting caught, bribing them, and then being set free, only to be caught again. Since it was impossible to find a hideaway in China, we followed our relatives to the South.[52]

The Seoul government's engagement policy also helps make the settlement process less strenuous. The refugees often take diverse routes to South Korea. Some undertake the arduous journey to China's neighboring countries, such as Mongolia, Vietnam, and Thailand, before reaching their final destination. Once arriving in these countries, the refugees declare themselves to be political asylum seekers, and the South Korean diplomatic mission begins processing their requests accordingly.

Others take more drastic measures. They attempt to gain illegal entry into foreign establishments in China, such as embassies, consulates and foreign schools, and then request political asylum. NGOs such as Life Funds for North Korean Refugees often work very closely with these refugees, sometimes informing the foreign news media of such plans prior to the actual attempt, in order to publicize and dramatize their plight and thereby pressure Beijing into permitting their release to South Korean authorities.

Beijing's strategy of ambivalence

In responding to the rising influx of escapees, China has shown both a friendly face and come down with an iron fist, depending on the situation. When it comes to the breaching of foreign diplomatic compounds, for example, Beijing has been generally lenient. Unless they are caught by the Chinese security police prior to entry, those who manage to aenter foreign embassies have a good chance of being granted asylum in South Korea. At the same time, the Chinese government has employed punitive measures against other refugees. The police actively hunt down North Korean escapees, primarily in the most susceptible border areas, such as Jilin and Dandong. Beijing also offers cash rewards to those who turn in escapees, while those suspected of helping escapees can be fined up to $3,500. Beijing has avoided coming up with concrete policy measures in its handling of escapees. When the South Korean media report on the escapee situation, the PRC engages in crackdowns. But when Seoul becomes relatively quiet about the issue, the PRC tends to turn a blind eye to the escapees. Beijing's ambivalent policy stance is a reflection of the Chinese concern of losing its face under the watchful eyes of external observers.

The continuing influx of North Korean refugees is pushing Beijing to address the current situation in a more straightforward manner—but this will not be an easy matter. Beijing naturally wants to maintain its increasing economic ties with Seoul, now its third-largest trading partner. And while Beijing wants to prove its respect for human rights to the international community, it does not wish to damage its alliance with Pyongyang, with which it shares a mutual security pact.

China has enough social woes of its own, and it does not need any additional, externally imposed burdens. Under the circumstances, Beijing cannot welcome another source of strain by having to deal with a massive influx of famished people from its neighboring country. Beijing is therefore faced with several dilemmas at once. China obviously wishes the North Korean refugee problem would simply go away, but the issue has grown too big to ignore. In trying to deal with it, however, Beijing is trapped between encouraging Pyongyang to reform its economic practices, in order to ease the influx, and at the same time working to prevent the collapse of the DPRK regime. Beijing tries to appease and prod North Korea toward reform by aligning with it. Assigning "refugee" status to the North Korean escapees would be an admission that Kim Jong-il's leadership is politically repressive and is therefore a non-starter for the PRC.

At the same time, to prevent another massive exodus from North Korea into its territory, Beijing needs to ensure that the current regime does not collapse abruptly, causing chaos in the region. That would be a major disaster for the PRC's booming economy. During the latter half of 2004, the Chinese military deployed its elite troops along the Sino–DPRK frontier to tighten border control. Beijing's provision of oil and food to the DPRK is another way it seeks to sustain the failing regime. China is also the second-largest provider of humanitarian aid to Pyongyang, behind only Seoul.

Conclusion: the middle ground

This case study reveals many hidden dynamics to Beijing's handling of the North Korean escapees. Since Pyongyang's nuclear test in October 2006, China is under even greater pressure to work with North Korea. As the host of the Six-Party talks involving Pyongyang, Seoul, Washington, Tokyo, and Moscow, Beijing bears the primary responsibility for persuading North Korea to engage more actively with the international community. Beijing also knows that it can play an important international role as a mediator between Pyongyang and other regional powers, elevating its own status in the process. At the same time, China cannot afford to lose its alliance with North Korea. As much as Pyongyang needs Beijing as its sole ally, Beijing, as the leader and mediator of the Six-Party framework, needs to stay in close touch with Pyongyang.

The PRC's rising economic and military power entails higher expectations of its moral leadership in the region, and yet, its history is riddled with bloody sanctions against anti-regime challenges. The memories of the 1989 Tiananmen

Square massacre have not faded, nor has Beijing's decades-old brutal crackdown in Tibet. Complicating the issue, Beijing has been voicing concerns over the unilateral imposition of universal human rights in non-Western contexts. The advocacy of individual rights, for instance, has been deemed a Western invention with limited validity in more group-oriented Confucian cultural contexts such as that of China. Beijing has never supported the Bush administration's elevation of human rights as a core item on the international agenda. Note, for example, how it kept its silence on Secretary of State Condoleeza Rice's naming of the six "outposts of tyranny"—North Korea, Cuba, Myanmar, Iran, Belarus, and Zimbabwe.

At the same time, winning the bid to host the 2008 Olympics was a great boost to China's national pride. It was a vindication of China's economic accomplishments and recognition of its emergence as a respected power in the world. Beijing cannot afford to tarnish this image by being viewed as a violator of human rights because of the North Korean escapees. Such negative images would damper the nation's newly celebrated wealth, status, and leadership.

China is undergoing a grand transformation. Its economic reform led to its integration into global society, which in turn brought about a heightened awareness of democracy among the Chinese people.[53] The area of human rights, one indicator of democratization, has been a thorny issue for China both at home and abroad. Despite mounting pressure, primarily from the United States, to improve its human rights situation, the PRC has been slow to respond.

The Chinese worldview regarding the individual, the state, and law does not constitute a good fit for Western-style democracy. China is a society with a resilient historical tradition. The directionality of reforms will also defy the usual top-down vs. bottom-up dichotomy. Changes will have to be made in both directions, and the result will be distinctly Chinese, not Western.

Angle writes:

> Is skepticism, subjectivism, or even nihilism a sensible response to pluralism? I believe not. They are overreactions to pluralism, reactions based on the unrealistic expectation that there should be a single set of concepts to which all people should adhere to. I will argue that we can retain commitment to our own values through reliance on local justifications.[54]

China's efforts to improve its human rights will find a middle way, harmonizing the particular and the universal elements. Sadly, in this complicated equation of security and human rights, the plight of North Korean refugees and the debate as to their human rights continues to fall between the cracks.

Notes

1   Joan Acker, Kate Barry, and Johanna Esseveld, "Objectivity and Truth: Problems in Doing Feminist Research," *Women's Studies International Forum* 6(4), 1983, pp. 423–435.

2   Edward Warren Capen, "Sociological Appraisal of Western Influence in the Orient," *The American Journal of Sociology* 16(6), May 1911, pp. 735–736.

3   Max Weber, *The Protestant Ethic and the Spirit of Capitalism*, translated by Talcott Parsons and introduction by Anthony Giddens (London and New York: Routledge, [1930] 1992).

4   Xu Xiaoqun, "Human Rights and the Discourse on Universality: A Chinese Historical Perspective," in the Quest for Human Rights," in Lynda S. Bell, Andrew J. Nathan, and Ilan Peleg, eds., *Negotiating Culture and Human Rights* (New York: Columbia University Press, 2001), pp. 153–196.

5   Kishore Mahbubani, "Understanding China," *Foreign Affairs* 84(5), 2005, p. 51.

6   Fareed Zakaria, "Culture is Destiny, A Conversation with Lee Kuan Yew," *Foreign Affairs* 73(2), March/April 1994, p. 39.

7   Alastair Iain Johnston, *Strategic Culture and Grand Strategy in Chinese History* (Princeton, NJ: Princeton University Press, 1995); Johnston, "Cultural Realism and Strategy in Maoist China," in Peter J. Katzenstein, ed., *The Culture of National Security: Norms and Identity in World Politics* (New York: Columbia University Press, 1996), pp. 216–270; Andrew J. Nathan (with contributions by Tianjian Shi and Helen V.S. Ho), *China's Transition* (New York: Columbia University Press, 1997), p. 16.

8   Anne F. Thurston, "Community and Isolation: Memory and Forgetting—China in Search of Itself," in Gerrit W. Gong, ed., *Memory and History in East and Southeast Asia: Issues of Identity in International Relations* (Washington, D.C.: The Center for Strategic & International Studies, 2001), pp. 149–172.

9   Nathan, *China's Transition*, pp. 249–250.

10   Xu, "Human Rights and the Discourse on Universality," p. 217.

11   O. Weaver, "Securitization and Desecuritization," in R. D. Lipschutz, ed., *On Security* (New York: Columbia University Press, 1995), pp. 46–86.

12   Rebecca R. Moore, "Outside Actors and the Pursuit of Civil Society in China," in Mahmood Monshipouri, Neil Englehart, Andrew J. Nathan, and Kavita Philip, eds., *Constructing Human Rights in the Age of Globalization* (Armonk and London: M.E. Sharpe, 2003), p. 159.

13   Alexander Wendt, *Social Theory of International Politics* (London: Cambridge University Press, 1999), pp. 170–171.

14   Bill Clinton, *My Life, Vol. II: Presidential Years* (New York: Vintage Press, 2005), pp. 433–435; Qi Zhou, "Conflicts over Human Rights between China and the U.S.," *Human Rights Quarterly* 27, 2005, pp. 106–111.

15   Jeanne Kirkpatrick, "Politics and the New Class," *Society* 16(2), 1979, p. 33.

16   Annelise Riles, "Anthropology, Human Rights, and Legal Knowledge: Culture in the Iron Cage," *American Anthropologist* 19(1), 2006, p. 56.

17   Herbert Blumer, "Society as Symbolic Interaction Theory," in Arnold M. Rose, ed., *Human Behavior and Social Processes: An Interactionist Approach* (Boston: Houghton Mifflin, 1962), p. 183.

18   Wendt, *Social Theory of International Politics*, p. 171.

19   The Bush administration's labeling practice is a powerful example of identity politics. It has a long record of name-calling in regard to unfriendly regimes, starting with President Bush's labeling of North Korea, Iran and Iraq as an "axis of evil" in his 2002 State of the Union address, and including Secretary of State Condoleeza Rice's more recent labeling of North Korea as an "outpost of tyranny." This is a reflection of the Bush administration's worldview, which divides the states of the international community into "good" and "evil" and those who are "with" and "against" the United States. Kim Mikyoung, "North Korea: Beyond the Name Game," *The Oregonian*, July 25, 2005.

20   Peter Katzenstein, "Introduction: Alternative Perspective on National Security," in Katzenstein, ed., *Culture of National Security: Norms and Identity in World Politics* (Ithaca and London: Cornell University Press, 1996), p. 25.

21   Tsuchiya Hideo (土屋英雄), 中国の人権論の歴史的位相: 「群」優先の論理お中心 として [Historical Status of the Chinese Human Rights: With a Focus on Group Priority]," *Human Rights International* 7, 1996, pp. 44–47.

22   Andrew J. Nathan, "Sources of Chinese Rights Thinking," in R. Randle Edwards, Louis Henkin, and Andrew J. Nathan, eds., *Human Rights in Contemporary China* (New York: Columbia University Press, 1986), p. 138.

23   Ibid, pp. 141–142.

24   Stephen C. Angle, *Human Rights and Chinese Thought: A Cross-Cultural Inquiry* (Cambridge: Cambridge University Press, 2002), p. 229.

25   Ibid, p. 229.

26   Qi, "Conflicts over Human Rights between China and the U.S.," p. 113.

27   Nathan, "Sources of Chinese Rights Thinking," p. 127.

28   Moore, "Outside Actors and the Pursuit of Civil Society in China," p. 149.

29   Ibid, p. 150.

30   Angle, p. 243.

31   Nicholas S. Wheeler, *Saving Strangers: Humanitarian Intervention in International Society* (Oxford: Oxford University Press, 2002), p. 27.

32   From a holistic point of view, the three aspects of human rights—cultural, economic and political—are difficult to separate from one another. For example, given the empirical validity of a positive causal link between economic growth and political development, many argue for the supremacy of economic subsistence rights over those of a political nature in Third World countries (see Shashi Tharoor, "Are Human Rights Universal?" *World Policy Journal* XVI(4), winter 1999/2000. See www.worldpolicy.org/journal/tharoor.html). In addition to cultural particularity, the level of economic growth is also an important variable in explaining the status of human rights. These examples suggest how problematic it can be to make ethno-centric judgments about another society while being oblivious to its pressing needs.

33   Qi, "Conflicts over Human Rights between China and the U.S.," p. 105.

34   Robert G. Sutter, *China's Rise in Asia: Promises and Perils.* New York: Rowman & Littlefield, 2005), pp. 58–59.

35   Moore, "Outside Actors and the Pursuit of Civil Society in China," p. 152.

36   *International Herald Tribune*, January 30, 2006; December 10 and 11, 2005.

37   *Time*, October 24, 2005.

38   Unlike China, the North Korean constitution does not acknowledge individual rights. Clause 49 states that "The citizen's rights and duties in Democratic People's Republic of Korea are based on the group principles. Asia Watch— Minnesota Lawyers International Human Rights Committee, *Bukhaneui Inkwon* [North Korean Human Rights] (Seoul: Koryowon, 1990), p. 208. In other words, the distinction between the individual and the collective is vague; both share the goals of nation-building and protection of sovereignty.

39   United Nations High Commissioner for Refugees. www.unhcr.org accessed on March 7, 2007.

40   Lee Geum Soon, *Bukhanjumineui Kukgyongidong Shiltae: Byonwhawa Jungmang* [The North Korean Border Crossing: Changes and Prospects] (Seoul: Korean Institute for National Unification, 2005).

41   Ibid, p. 41.

42   Kim Mikyoung, "Nukes and Human Rights: North Korean Escapees in China," *Jamestown Organization* 5(5), March 2005. See www.jamestown.

org/publications_details.php?volume_id=408&issue_id=3246&article_id=
2369336.
43 Joel R. Charny, *Acts of Betrayal: The Challenge of Protecting North Koreans in China*, report (Washington, D.C.: Refugee International, 2005), pp. 10–11. www.refugeesinternational.org accessed April 2, 2008.
44 Norma Kang Muico, *An absence of choice* (London: Anti-Slavery International, 2005).
45 Charny, *Acts of Betrayal*, p. 7.
46 Interview on July 29, 2000. The qualitative data come from 15 interviews the author conducted with North Korean refugees in South Korea between June and August, 2000.
47 Ministry of Unification (South Korea), *Bukhan Inkwon Baekseo* [White Paper on Human Rights in North Korea] (Seoul: Ministry of Unification, 1998); Choi Gyu Yeop, "Bukhan Ingwoneui Shilatae [North Korean Human Rights]," a paper presented at International Symposium on North Korean Human Rights, December 1, 2004, Seoul, South Korea.
48 This agreement was signed in secrecy between the two governments.
49 The Border Area Task Agreement ceased being effective in 2006, twenty years after its enactment. It provided a legal basis for mutual cooperation on illegal entries and the provision of personal information on the illegal entrants.
50 Lee, *Bukhanjumineui Kukgyongidong Shiltae*, p. 70.
51 Anwar Dewi Fortuna, "Human Security: An Intractable Problem in Asia," in Muthiah Alagappa, ed., *Asian Security Order: Instrumental and Normative Features* (Stanford: Stanford University Press, 2003), p. 540.
52 Interview by author, July 11, 2000.
53 Rhonda E. Howard-Hassmann, "The Second Great Transformation: Human Rights Leapfrogging in the Era of Globalization," *Human Rights Quarterly* 27, 2005, pp. 14–16; Kokubun Ryosei (国分良成), 序論: 中国の政治外交---天安門事件とその後 [Introduction: Chinese Politics and Foreign Relations—The Tiananmen Incident and After]," *International Relations: China after the Tiananmen Incident* 145, August 2006, pp. 1–16.
54 Angle, *Human Rights and Chinese Thought*, p. 53.

11 Conclusion

China in the eyes of Asia and America

*Yoichiro Sato**

Spectacular economic growth of China during the past fifteen years resulted in a rush of books centered on the theme of rising China. Among literature on international relations and foreign policy, there have been two groups of books. Books in the first group have examined China's bilateral relations with its neighbors and the United States. The key debate within this group has been whether the rising China will be a peaceful and cooperative international actor or an aggressive challenger to the existing international order.[1] The traditional geopolitical thinking has been dominant within this group. Robert G. Sutter, a China expert, looks at drivers of China's foreign policy mainly from domestic perspectives and then moves on to examine China's bilateral relations with major powers (United States, Japan, Russia) and others (Taiwan, Korean Peninsula, Central Asia, Southeast Asia, and South Asia).[2] Analysis of the bilateral relations in this book is largely state-centric. David Shambaugh's edited book has collected essays by many China experts and is a little more open to discussions of non-state actors than Sutter's, but such discussions are mostly limited to business relations in the region.[3]

Books in the second group have examined China's growth from internal perspectives and looked into various domestic consequences. The key debate within this group has revolved around China's social and political stability, including prospects for its democratization.[4] Gilley, for example, sees compatibility between the Chinese culture and democracy and argues that the contradiction between openness of the market economy and the restricted political system would solve itself through transformation of elite political values.[5] The division between the two groups overlaps the division between theoretically oriented international relations scholars and more traditional area (China) studies scholars, but some books can be considered hybrids of these two streams.[6]

Aside from these two main groups, there has been a growing volume of works which examine China's governance from the perspective of its implications for transnational security.[7] The economic growth of China, initially started in the late 1970s with domestic and rural reforms, has been increasingly driven by China's integration into the regional and global markets, industrialization, and urbanization. The increased openness of China, however, has exposed

China's closest neighbors and even more remote countries to its various (previously "internal") problems, and the lagging "political" openness of China has impacted on cooperation with other countries in dealing with these problems (i.e. trans-border pollution, epidemics, illegal migration, organized crime, financial management, etc.), often negatively, but not always so. Paying attention to these transnational issues not only significantly broadens the "domestic" literature's scope, but also provides a bridge between the international relations literature and domestic literature.

This book has incorporated all three streams of research, thereby offering a comprehensive view of China's "rise" and its implications to the East Asian region (and beyond). For the purposes of this book, China was seen as the independent variable with various chapters focusing on the nations of the region reacting from a security perspective to China's rise (except Jian Yang in Chapter 2, who looked at China's internal debate on its strategy, and Mikyoung Kim in Chapter 10, who looked at China's balancing act between its *realpolitik* and international normative considerations). Each chapter, with differing proportions of mix, examined both traditional and alternative views of security. While many of the recent China-related books have been written by China experts, this book looked at the bilateral relations with China from the perspectives of China's diplomatic partners. In this collective book, experts of these countries' (rather than China's) foreign policy wrote chapters on bilateral relations with China, thereby giving more emphasis on responses of these countries to the growing China.

Realism vs. liberalism on transnational issues

Additional attention to transnational issues in this book has expanded the scope of theoretical discussions beyond the traditional liberal–realist dichotomy. For behaviors of China's counterparts in international relations, the state-centric approach and the emphasis on military security by realists would yield a fairly simple set of predictions: pre-emption, counterbalancing, and bandwagoning. Liberals' emphasis on multilateral diplomacy and economic interests leads to predicting engagement of the rising China by its counterparts.

Unlike military procurement and deployments, or legitimate overseas trade and financial transactions, some transnational activities are hard to attribute to state authorities. Transnational criminal activities may defy the laws of both the source and the host countries. Such illegal activities may take place because of the lack of enforcement power in either country, or perhaps the lack of willingness. The complexity of transnational issues has been troublesome for realist analysis, because it does not neatly sit with the state-centric assumption of realism. When realists do pay attention to transnational entities—such as terrorists and criminal organizations, or business corporations, they tend to be treated as agents of the state, rather than more autonomous actors.

Openness of liberalism to more pluralistic views of policymaking is more comfortable with the transnational issues, but its ideological commitment to multilateral cooperation among states tends to overly focus on common economic interests at the neglect of other divergences. Liberalism's lack of attention to the possibility that states may deliberately decide not to cooperate with other states in dealing with transnational issues is attacked by realists.

Utilitarianism vs. constructivism: the role of perceptions

While the debate between realists and liberals centered on material interests— whether military security or economic—constructivists have challenged this utilitarian bias of the two paradigms and focused instead on intangible values and ideas.[8] Constructivists' new focus on intangibles added a new dimension to the dichotomous realist–liberal debate in the international relations discipline.

True to its activist origin, earlier constructivism was overwhelmingly liberal. Countering the pessimistic predictions of realism about international cooperation in general and cooperative management of security in particular with optimism and faith in grassroots movements meant that the ideas these constructivists focused on were heavily drawn from what Farrell calls "good norms"[9]—or others might call ethics. As the basic tenet of constructivism that intangibles matter in international relations received a broader acceptance, realists could no longer simply ignore constructivist scholarship. Instead, realists viewed the role of intangibles in a top-down manner (as opposed to bottom-up), in order to strengthen their arguments that intangibles (such as ideas) are utilized by the state elite to justify or mask their material interests.[10]

China's ongoing industrialization has led the country to face various social issues derived from economic, social, and cultural transformations similar to those the more advanced industrial countries have experienced several decades ago. Political scholars in particular paid great attentions to prospects of China's democratic transformation and human rights consciousness at the time of the country's industrialization, but in a new context of global information age.[11] Externally, China's entry into the world economic system raised not only "quantitative" issues—impacts due to the growing size of the Chinese economy— but also qualitative issues about its participation. The industrial policy debate of the 1970s and 1980s focused on the then rising economic power—Japan. In the twenty-first century, China passed Japan as the country most accountable for America's trade deficit and Treasury bond sales, and both China's foreign economic policy and the underpinning economic ideology received scholarly attentions. In particular, the question of whether China will be a status quo state conforming to the existing rules of international economic relations (neoclassical liberalism)—or a challenger state seeking alteration of the existing rules—has been hotly debated. China's neighbors' perceptions of China's economic ideology and policy are of particular importance, for they affect the course of their cooperation or competition with China. The book collectively displayed diverse views and perceptions of China's neighbors on these questions.

In Chapter 2, Jian Yang presented China's domestic debate over its strategy. With the country's economic growth, the Chinese are gradually regaining confidence in their country as a truly great power. The benign self-image of such a great power conflicts with the emerging "China threat" theories abroad, and has resulted in resentment particularly against Western countries. Chinese strategic thinkers see today's world as neither multipolar nor unipolar, but in a transitional stage in-between moving toward the former. This stage is likely to last for several decades, and this will give China time to enjoy peace and focus on development. However, China sees the present international order as unfair and is determined to challenge it in the long term. Based on this observation, Yang warns of the gap in perceptions between China and the international society about China's growth, which may prevent both healthy maturation of China into a responsible great power and the acceptance of China's rise by the international society. While China shows some signs of a benign great power by getting acquainted with liberal norms, taking up international responsibilities, and paying attentions to other countries' concerns, its foreign policy will continue to exhibit realist characteristics, such as strong insistence on national sovereignty and national interests.

In Chapter 3, Kevin Cooney examined the strategic role of US policy in East Asia in light of international relations theory, American national security interests, and strategic theory. China's growth does offer the world increased opportunities, but this does not make the world dependent on China. Quite conversely, it is China whose continued growth is dependent on the world. Despite the high rate of annual economic growth, China's catch-up with the United States would be of a medium- to long-term prospect. Technologically, China's dependence on the world is an effective deterrence against the former's hegemonic ambition. Therefore, for a foreseeable future, China will seek "peaceful coexistence" with the current superpower—the United States. However, the search for an agreeable boundary between the two countries may be tenuous. Meanwhile, American policy toward China will be a simultaneous pursuit of military containment and economic and political engagement. The current asymmetrical nature of any potential conflict with China gives the United States greater ability to experiment with multilateralism without sacrificing its dominant power status. Cooney has illustrated that much of the discussions about China's rise is a hype that needs to be dealt with caution. He showed that despite the presence of some exaggerated views about China's challenge against the United States, US policy remains rationally realist.

Evelyn Goh in Chapter 4 examined three alternative scenarios in negotiating Sino–American coexistence: maintenance of the *status quo* of US strategic dominance over the region, while China concentrates on internal consolidation and development; *negotiated change* through forming a concert (duet) of power and eventually a regional security community; and *power transition*, in which a rising China challenges US dominance with a range of possible outcomes. Goh challenges the dominant (realist) view in the United States that

China will soon challenge US hegemony, leading to power transition scenarios. While leaving open such a possibility in the medium to long terms, Goh has argued that China is playing according to the international rules and will concentrate on domestic consolidation for the short to medium term. In addition, Goh has illustrated a range of possible trajectories that the US–China relationship could traverse before reaching a power transition. Accommodating the changing power balance between the United States and China entails consideration of not only the military balance of power, but also the more complex competition of influence in the arenas of economy and diplomacy. Availability of positive-sum cooperation in the latter arenas, according to Goh, could pave the way toward a negotiated change.

Yoichiro Sato in Chapter 5 illustrated Japan's careful balancing of its enhanced alliance with the United States (in anticipation of conflicts with China) and its increasing economic interdependence with China. The deep-rooted sense of war guilt among the Japanese, which supported Japan's conciliatory diplomacy toward China, has barely survived the revisionist drives by the domestic conservatives. However, the sense of war guilt also serves as a source of increasing fear, as the growing China continues to hold a grudge against Japan's past misbehavior. Japan sees China's commitment to the existing multilateral economic institutions as tactical, half-hearted, and insufficient to guard Japan's economic interests. Therefore, Japan tries to discipline China's economic behaviors through bilateral and multilateral venues. While Japan continues to search for diplomatic maneuvering space in its China policy, Japan's utility for the United States in the changing contexts of US–China relations has also affected Sino–Japanese relations. The "lost years" of Sino–Japanese relations during the latter part of the Koizumi administration represented an exceptional period, during which Japan did not follow the conventional pattern of placing itself between the United States and China. Maturing of the Japanese democracy since the end of the Liberal Democratic Party dominance in 1993 opened a venue for a new generation of politicians with no personal memory of war to assert more influence over foreign policy—a field which was traditionally dominated by bureaucrats and a small number of senior politicians. This new generation of politicians was heavily in the conservative camp and championed the importance of democratic values in Japan's relations with the authoritarian China. The negative stereotype of China as an irresponsible international actor strongly persists among the Japanese populace and provides a fertile background for realist policies.

In Chapter 6, Denny Roy argued that China's improving military capabilities and global economic and political importance have raised the likelihood of involuntary unification of Taiwan. Taiwan has tried through various avenues to distance itself from China and strengthen international linkages. Taiwan's increasing economic linkages with China coexist with political and military tensions, and by no means indicate Taiwan's security "bandwagoning" with China. Roy attributes Taiwan's cross-Strait policy to a political struggle within the divided Taiwanese government. A sense of a shared destiny with China and the willingness to more closely integrate with the rising regional power is present in Taiwan and is consistent with the notion of "bandwagoning." On the other hand, portraying a favorable image of Taiwan as a democratic country has been Taiwan's strategy to increase the likelihood that the international community will stand up in defense of Taiwan in the event of a cross-Strait crisis. Like in Japan, maturing of the Taiwanese democracy and the changes in public perceptions of China in the domains not directly related to economic or security interests seem to have played a critical role in Taiwan's policy.

Seong-Ho Sheen in Chapter 7 described South Korea's view of China's role in the context of the former's new security thinking. The Roh administration's new strategic thinking represented South Korea's bold initiative, but it was poorly understood. The confusion resulted from the country's desire to achieve a mixture of three somewhat conflicting objectives: a self-defense posture and autonomy from the United States, a more active role as a new balancer in emerging power politics of Northeast Asia, and a strengthened alliance with the United States to enhance its own balancer role between China and Japan. Despite its deepening economic and political relations with China, South Korea remains suspicious of Chinese hegemonic intentions. South Korea's new strategic thinking represented the country's effort to have more voice in shaping its own destiny and its desire to be recognized as a more meaningful actor in world politics. It was driven by growing confidence among the leadership after Korea's success in economic and political development. The changing power structure in Northeast Asia with rising China was another driver for South Korea's new thinking, but this did not imply that Seoul wanted to create a new strategic partnership with Beijing at the expense of its alliance with Washington. Rather than falling into the sphere of China's growing influence, South Korea tried to be a balancer of conflicts and a facilitator of peace in Northeast Asia between China and Japan. Cooperative self-reliant defense was a compromise between the bold new thinking and the challenges South Korea faced in reality. Sheen's analysis shed light on the continuity and change in the Korean perceptions. The longstanding mistrust of the Chinese is keeping Korea's foreign policy from tilting toward China despite the changes in geopolitical and economic interests. On the other hand, the ever present anti-Americanism since the Korean War seems to take less priority than the tangible security benefits of the alliance with the United States in Korea's neighborhood of competing and superior powers.

In Chapter 8, Evelyn Goh reviewed key Southeast Asian states' perceptions of rising China, and the main implications of China's rise for the military, economic, and political security of the subregion. On one hand, the end of the Cold War placed China into the position of primary strategic worry for Southeast Asian states, due to the twin uncertainties of American military withdrawal and Chinese strategic intentions with its increasing material capabilities. On the other hand, the China challenge has been transformed over the last fifteen years from being an unpredictable and thus threatening disruption to the regional status quo, to being an important source of continued economic development and diversified regional influence. She identifies two key strategies of "omni-enmeshment" and "complex balancing" in her analysis of ASEAN's strategies and argues that these together seek to peacefully incorporate China into the region by facilitating the creation of a hierarchical regional order, which simultaneously maintains the United States superpower overlay, accords China a regional great power position, and incorporates other major regional players. The Southeast Asian hedging strategy has mediated the negative impacts of China's rise. Beijing's "smile diplomacy" and relative restraints exercised by all major powers contributed to a stable regional order. The increasing diversity among the ASEAN countries (such as maritime vs. continental) in terms of priorities and preferences in coping with China will bring into question ASEAN's ability to maintain a coherent strategy and affect the future of regional institutions such as the ARF and ASEAN+3. This limitation may most prominently manifest in ASEAN countries dealing with China on non-traditional and transnational security issues, such as the water rights concerning the Mekong River.

Mohan Malik in Chapter 9 examined the key issues of commonalities and differences between China and India—Asia's two rising powers. India's response to China's rise is likely to lead to significant new geopolitical realignments in the region, including changes in the China–India–US triangular relationship in the twenty-first century. Malik views the simultaneous rise of China and India in the context of major power competitions that also include Russia and Japan, rather than post-Cold War unipolarity of the United States as the sole superpower. Malik points out India's uniqueness as the only Asian power that has long been committed to balancing China. The strategic imperative to counter China first drove India into allying with the Soviet Union during the Cold War years, developing nuclear weapons in the post-Soviet years, and cooperating with the United States during the first decade of the twenty-first century. The increasingly globalizing India is moving away from "non-alignment" to a "multi-alignment" with the world to both meet the growing China and to promote its own rise as a great power. India's relations with China are full of disputes—be it historical, geopolitical, or cultural, but it prefers to avoid overt conflicts and focus on achieving comprehensive national power. India's normalization of relations with China is based on a need to focus on social and political stability, and strong economic growth under a sense of security. For this pragmatic reason, India prefers to avoid entangling alliances in order to leave more options available to itself. Instead, incremental pro-US, pro-Japan tilts in reaction to the rising China will characterize India's national security policy.

In Chapter 10, Mikyoung Kim examined China's handling of trans-border North Korean refugees. The Chinese government designates North Korean escapees as "illegal economic migrants," thereby exempting itself from any legal, moral, and ethical obligations to provide protection to these persons. China's history of bloody crackdowns against anti-regime challenges betrays the higher expectations of its moral leadership in the region accompanying its rising economic and military power. Beijing's interests in maintaining a primary diplomatic role over North Korea and avoiding its collapse lead to preferences for appeasement. An ironical consequence of this formulation is that when the South Korean media report on the escapee situation, China is pressured to crack down on the refugees, but silence in Seoul allows China to turn a blind eye to them. China's aspirations to achieve "a peaceful rise" and "world harmony" are under watchful eyes of outside observers, and its handling of the escapees from North Korea illuminates Beijing's strategic ambivalence about human rights. Despite the heightened awareness of democracy among the Chinese people as a result of China's economic reforms and integration with the global economy, its social and political transformations will likely take a distinctive form.

China's rise in military, economic, or diplomatic terms has attracted the attentions of scholars and practitioners alike. However, major disagreements exist about the pace of China's ascent and the timing of, if at all, catching up with the United States as a superpower. Overly inflated images of the ascent, in economic terms, may have contributed to economic bubbles in China through infusion of hot money and unrealistic expectations of future economic opportunities in China in the minds of its foreign counterparts. The more pessimistic assessments of China's military ascent may have led the regional countries to respond to the emerging security threat by coming out of their ambiguities and adopting a more explicit stance one way or the other between China and the United States. Chapters in this volume illustrated the diverse views on these very basic points.

The book also collectively addressed diverse views about integration of the emerging China into the structure of global politics. Two contrasting yet overlapping images of a China seeking hegemonic dominance and a China seeking a beneficial accommodation were presented in this volume. Furthermore, some contributors (i.e. Yang in Chapter 2, Sato in Chapter 5, and Kim in Chapter 10) extended their analysis into China's positions vis-à-vis international norms. By shedding light on the underlying gap in perceptions of certain norms between China and the Western democratic countries (including Japan), these chapters provided comprehensive accounts of China's behavior and other countries' responses to the rising China.

Having examined various reactions of the regional countries to China's growth, the book laid a solid foundation on which to build sound forecasts about the regional alignment. The latter task is beyond the scope of this book, but some chapter authors (i.e. Goh in Chapter 4 and Malik in Chapter 9) have successfully brought in such broader future considerations into their analysis. Equally useful in forecasting are analyses of Chinese strategic thoughts and foreign policy norms. Yang's analysis of the victim mentality of the Chinese (Chapter 2) and Kim's analysis of China's image problem associated with the human rights issues (Chapter 10) add subtle nuances to more strictly utilitarian analysis.

All of the relations with China considered in this volume encompass both security and economic dimensions. While a country's foreign policy is expected to integrate both aspects, diverse patterns among the countries examined in this volume reveal differing conceptualizations of security. Southeast Asian countries, Taiwan, Korea, and India seem to have set aside their doubts about the growing China to concentrate on taking full advantage of economic interactions with the growing Chinese market. These countries have smaller domestic economies than China and many of them see continuing economic growth as a key factor that enhances their fragile domestic governance. Taiwan and Korea's maturing democracies lack the stability of one-party dominance as seen in Japan during the Cold War or the stability of the American democratic regime under intense two-party competition. On one hand, reliance on economic growth for domestic political legitimacy may continue to lead these countries' China policies. On the other hand, a reversal of their current policies may take place to emphasize external security threats of the Chinese military growth and negatively affect economic relations with China (or urge these countries to at least diversify their economic relations by cultivating other partners). In contrast to these countries, Japan and the United States (which possess potent leverages to control China's economic growth) have clearly been utilizing both bilateral and multilateral venues to discipline China's integration with the world economy. China's entry into the WTO was just the beginning of this control through engagement, and their continuing efforts (often in cooperation with the European Union) to enhance the rules of global economic interactions in areas such as investment rules and IPR protections are consistent with the realist view of institutionalism—where international rules are manifestations of power relations. Japan and the United States in the military-security domain demonstrate even clearer realist inclinations.

The book collectively contributed to the discussions of China's growth in four major ways. First, it challenged the fundamental assumption behind the discussions by showing a range of forecasts about China's growth. Second, the book brought in historical and cultural roots of Chinese foreign policy, which both explain its generally realist orientations and modify deductive predictions about Chinese foreign policy based on realist theories. Third, the authors in this volume presented a great diversity in regional perceptions about China's growth. It is hoped that perhaps discussions in this concluding chapter have at least raised enough theoretical questions about this diversity and provided some orientations for future researches on Asia-Pacific security. Although each chapter has addressed relations with China mainly through bilateral lenses, analysis of each bilateral relations with China was placed in the contexts of trilateral relations that included the United States or a broader multilateral context involving other major powers—such as Japan, India, Australia, and Russia. What emerged collectively—a synthesis of multiple regional perspectives and a comprehensive analysis of China's significance in the region—can be claimed as the fourth contribution.

Notes

* The views expressed here are the author's own and do not reflect the policy or position of the Asia-Pacific Center for Security Studies or the US Department of Defense.

1 Robert G. Sutter, *China's Rise in Asia: Promises and Perils*, Lanham, MD: Rowman and Littlefield, 2005; David Shambaugh, ed., *Power Shift: China and Asia's New Dynamics*, Berkeley: University of California Press, 2006.

2 Sutter, *China's Rise in Asia*, 2005.

3 Shambaugh, ed., *Power Shift*.

4 Bruce Gilley, *China's Democratic Future: How It Will Happen and Where It Will Lead*, New York: Columbia University Press, 2004.

5 Ibid.

6 Deng Yong, *China Rising: Power and Motivation in China's Foreign Policy*, Lanham, MD: Rowman and Littlefield, 2004; Peter Gries, *China's New Nationalism: Pride, Politics, and Diplomacy*, Berkeley: University of California Press, 2004.

7 Elizabeth Economy, *The River Runs Black: Environmental Challenge to China's Future*, Ithaca: Cornell University Press, 2004; Richard Louis Edmonds, ed., *Managing the Chinese Environment*, Oxford: Oxford University Press, 2000.

8 Alexander Wendt, *Social Theory of International Politics*, Cambridge: Cambridge University Press, 1999; John Gerard Ruggie, *Constructing the World Polity: Essays on International Institutionalization*, London: Routledge, 1998.

9 Theo Farrell, "Constructivist Security Studies: Portrait of a Research Program," *International Studies Review* 4(1), Spring 2002, pp. 58–59.

10 J. Samuel Barkin, "Realist Constructivism," *International Studies Review* 5(3), September 2003, pp. 336–339.

11 Shi Yin-hong, China's prominent Japanologist, warns against simplistic application of Western modernization paths as a lens through which to look at China. "China's embryonic civil society simultaneously has both 'civilized' and 'uncivilized' natures, and this is the most prominent characteristic of Chinese society as it stands now." Shi, "The Issue of Civil Society in China and Its Complexity," in Yoichiro Sato, ed., *Growth and Governance in Asia*, Honolulu: Asia-Pacific Center for Security Studies, 2004, p.226.

Bibliography

Acker, Joan, Kate Barry and Johanna Esseveld. 1983. "Objectivity and Truth: Problems in Doing Feminist Research." *Women's Studies International Forum* 6(4), pp. 423–435.

Adler, Emmanuel. 2001. "The Change of Change: Peaceful Transitions of Power in the Multilateral Age." In Charles A. Kupchan, Emmanuel Adler, Jean-Marc Coicaud, and Yuen Foong Khong, *Power in Transition: The Peaceful Change of International Order.* Tokyo: United Nations University Press.

Alagappa, Muthiah, editor. 2003. *Asian Security Order: Instrumental and Normative Features.* Stanford, CA: Stanford University Press.

Acharya, Amitav. 1999. "A Concert of Asia?" *Survival* 41(3), autumn, pp. 84–101.

——. 2001. *Constructing a Security Community in Southeast Asia: ASEAN and the Problem of Regional Order.* London: Routledge.

——. 2003. "Regional Institutions and Security Order: Norms, Identity, and Prospects for Peaceful Change." In Muthiah Alagappa, editor, *Asian Security Order: Instrumental and Normative Features.* Stanford, CA: Stanford University Press.

——. 2003–2004. "Will Asia's Past Be Its Future?" *International Security* 28(3), winter, pp. 149–164.

Ang Cheng Guan. 1998. "Vietnam–China Relations since the End of the Cold War." *Asian Survey* 38(12), December, pp. 1122–1141.

Angle, Stephen C. 2002. *Human Rights and Chinese Thought: A Cross-Cultural Inquiry.* Cambridge: Cambridge University Press.

Anwar Dewi Fortuna. 2003. "Human Security: An Intractable Problem in Asia." In Muthiah Alagappa, editor, *Asian Security Order: Instrumental and Normative Features.* Stanford: Stanford University Press, pp. 536–567.

ASEAN–China Expert Group on Economic Cooperation. 2001. *Forging Closer ASEAN–China Economic Relations in the 21st Century,* October. Available at: http://www.aseansec.org.

Ba, Alice. 2003. "China and ASEAN: Renavigating Relations for a 21st Century Asia." *Asian Survey* 43(4), pp. 622–647.

——. 2005. "Southeast Asia and China." In Evelyn Goh, ed., *Betwixt and Between: Southeast Asian Strategic Relations with the U.S. and China.* Singapore: IDSS, pp. 93–108.

——. 2006. "Who's Socializing Whom? Complex Engagement and Sino–ASEAN Relations." *Pacific Review* 19(2), June, pp. 157–179.

Bandow, Doug. 2005. "Seoul Searching: Ending the U.S.–Korean Alliance." *National Interest,* fall, pp. 111–116.

Barkin, J. Samuel. 2003. "Realist Constructivism." *International Studies Review* 5(3), September, pp. 325–342.

Beason, Doug. 2005. *The E-Bomb.* Cambridge, MA: Da Capo Press.

Bernstein, Richard and Ross Munro. 1997. "The Coming Conflict with America." *Foreign Affairs* 76(2), March/April, pp. 18–32.

Betts, Richard K. 1993–1994. "Wealth, Power, and Instability: East Asia and the United States after the Cold War." *International Security* 18(3), winter, pp. 34–77.

Bitzinger, Richard. 2004. "Civil-Military Integration and Chinese Military Modernization." *Asia-Pacific Security Studies* 3(9), December. Honolulu: Asia-Pacific Center for Security Studies. http://www.apcss.org/Publications/APSSS/Civil-MilitaryIntegration.pdf

Bitzinger, Richard A. and Mikyoung Kim. 2005. "Why Do Small States Produce Arms? The Case of South Korea." *Korean Journal of Defense Analysis* XVII(2), fall, pp. 197–201.

Blum, Samantha. 2003. "Chinese Views of U.S. Hegemony." *Journal of Contemporary China* 12(35), May, pp. 239–264.

Blumer, Herbert. 1962. "Society as Symbolic Interaction Theory." In Arnold M. Rose, editor, *Human Behavior and Social Processes: An Interactionist Approach.* Boston: Houghton Mifflin, pp. 179–192.

Broomfield, Emma V. 2003. "Perceptions of Danger: the China Threat Theory." *Journal of Contemporary China* 12(35), pp. 265–284.

Brown, Michael E. et al, editors. 2000. *The Rise of China.* Cambridge, MA: MIT Press.

Bush, Richard C. 2005. *Untying the Knot: Making Peace in the Taiwan Strait.* Washington, D. C.: Brookings Institution Press.

Buszynski, Leszek. 2003. "ASEAN, the Declaration on Conduct, and the South China Sea." *Contemporary Southeast Asia* 25(3), December, pp. 434–463.

Buzan, Barry, Ole Wæver, and Jaap de Wilde. 1997. *Security: A New Framework for Analysis.* Boulder, CO: Lynne Rienner.

Buzan, Barry and Rosemary Foot, editors. 2004. *Does China Matter? Essays in Memory of Gerald Segal.* London: Routledge.

Calder, Kent. 2006. "Coping with Energy Insecurity: China's Response in Global Perspective." *East Asia* 23(3), fall, pp. 49–66.

Callahan, William A. 2005. "How to Understand China: The Danger and Opportunities of Being a Rising Power." *Review of International Studies* 31(4), pp. 701–714.

Capen, Edward Warren. 1911. "Sociological Appraisal of Western Influence in the Orient." *The American Journal of Sociology* 16(6), May, pp. 734–760.

Carpenter, Ted Galen and Justin Logan. 2005. "The Pentagon's Surprisingly Sober Look at China." *National Interest* 16, August.

Chang, Gordon G. 2001. *The Coming Collapse of China.* London: Random House.

———. 2006. "Halfway to China's Collapse." *Far Eastern Economic Review* 169(5), June.

Checkel, Jeffrey T. 2001. "International Institutions and Socialization in the New Europe." ARENA Working Paper 01/11, May.

Chen, Rosalie. 2003. "China Perceives American: Perceptions of International Relations Experts." *Journal of Contemporary China* 12(35), pp. 285–297.

Cheng, Joseph Y. and Zhang Wankun. 2002. "Patterns and Dynamics of China's International Strategic Behaviour." *Journal of Contemporary China* 11(31), pp. 235–260.

Chen Ming-tong. 2006. *The China Threat Crosses the Strait: Challenges and Strategies for Taiwan's National Security.* Taipei: Taiwan Security Research Group.

"China's Position Paper on the New Security Concept." 2002. July 31. Available at http://www.fmprc.gov.cn/eng/wjb/zzjg/gjs/gjzzyhy/2612/2614/t15319.htm

"Chinese Military Power: Council on Foreign Relations Independent Task Force Report." 2003. June. Available at http://www.cfr.org/pdf/China_TF.pdf

Christensen, Thomas J. 1996. "Chinese Realpolitik." *Foreign Affairs* 75(5), September–October, pp. 37–52.

——. 2000a. "Posing Problems without Catching Up: China's Rise and Challenges for U.S. Security Policy." *International Security* 25(4), spring, pp. 5–40.

——. 2000b. "Theatre Missile Defense and Taiwan's Security." *Orbis* 44(1), winter, pp. 18–32.

Chung, C. P. 2004. "Southeast Asia–China Relations: Dialectics of 'Hedging' and 'Counter-Hedging.'" *Southeast Asian Affairs*, pp. 35–43.

Clinton, Bill. 2005. *My Life (Vol. II: Presidential Years).* New York: Vintage Press.

Cooney, Kevin. 2007. *Japan's Foreign Policy Since 1945.* New York: M. E. Sharpe.

Curley, Melissa, editor. 2007. *Advancing East Asian Regionalism.* London: Routledge.

De Castro, Renato Cruz. 2006. "Exploring the Prospect of China's Peaceful Emergence in East Asia." *Asian Affairs: An American Review* 33(2), summer, pp. 85–102.

De Soysa, Indra, John O'Neal, and Yong-Hee Park. 1997. "Testing Power Transition Theory Using Alternative Measures of National Capabilities." *Journal of Conflict Resolution* 41(4), August, pp. 509–528.

Deng Xiaoping. 1994. *Selected Works of Deng Xiaoping 1982–1992.* Beijing: Foreign Language Press.

Deng Yong. 1998. "The Chinese Conception of National Interests in International Relations." *China Quarterly* 154, June, pp. 308–329.

——. 2004. *China Rising: Power and Motivation in China's Foreign Policy.* Lanham, MD: Rowman and Littlefield.

Deng Yong and Fei Ling, editors. 2005. *Rising China: Power and Motivation in Chinese Foreign Policy.* Lanham, MD: Rowman and Littlefield.

Deutsch, Karl W. and J. David Singer. 1964. "Multipolar Power Systems and International Stability." *World Politics* 16(3), April, pp. 390–406.

Doran, Charles F. and Wes Parsons. 1980. "War and the Cycle of Relative Power." *American Political Science Review* 74(4), December, pp. 947–965.

Drifte, Reinhard. 1991. *Japan's Foreign Policy for the Twenty-first Century: From Economic Superpower to What Power?* New York: St. Martin's.

——. 2006. "The Ending of Japan's ODA Loan Programme to China—All's Well that Ends Well?" *Asia-Pacific Review* 13(1), pp. 94–117.

Dumbaugh, Kerry and Larry Niksch. 2003. *U.S. Congressional Attitudes toward China: Recent Trends and Their Implications.* Washington, D. C.: Congressional Research Service.

Eberstadt, Nicholas. 2004. "Strategic Implications of Asian Demographic Trends." In *Strategic Asia, 2003–2004.* Seattle, WA: National Bureau of Asian Research, pp. 453–485.

Economy, Elizabeth. 2004. *The River Runs Black: Environmental Challenge to China's Future.* Ithaca, NY: Cornell University Press.

Edmonds, Richard Louis, editor. 2000. *Managing the Chinese Environment.* Oxford: Oxford University Press.

Elrod, Richard B. 1976. "The Concert of Europe: A Fresh Look at an International System." *World Politics* 28, January, pp. 159–174.

Emmers, Ralf. 2001. "ASEAN, China, and the South China Sea: An Opportunity Missed." *IDSS Commentaries*.

———. 2003. *Cooperative Security and the Balance of Power in ASEAN and the ARF.* London: RoutledgeCurzon.

Farrell, Theo. 2002. "Constructivist Security Studies: Portrait of a Research Program." *International Studies Review* 4(1), spring, pp. 49–71.

Foot, Rosemary. 1998. "China in the ASEAN Regional Forum: Organizational Processes and Domestic Modes of Thought." *Asian Survey* 38(5), pp. 425–440.

———. 2003. "Bush, China and Human Rights." *Survival* 45(2), summer, pp. 167–186.

———. 2006. "Chinese Strategies in a US-hegemonic Global Order: Accommodating and Hedging." *International Affairs* 82(1), pp. 77–94.

Fravel, M. Taylor. 2005. "Regime Insecurity and International Cooperation: Explaining China's Compromises in Territorial Disputes." *International Security* 30(2), fall, pp. 46–83.

Friedberg, Aaron. 1993. "Ripe for Rivalry: Prospects for Peace in a Multipolar Asia." *International Security* 18(3), winter, pp. 5–33.

———. 2002. "11 September and the Future of Sino–American Relations." *Survival* 44(1), spring, pp. 33–50.

———. 2005. "The Future of U.S.–China Relations: Is Conflict Inevitable?" *International Security* 30(2), fall, pp. 7–45.

Gill, Bates. 2001. "Discussion of 'China: A responsible great power.'" *Journal of Contemporary China* 10(26), pp. 27–32.

Gilley, Bruce. 2004. *China's Democratic Future: How It Will Happen and Where It Will Lead.* New York: Columbia University Press, 2004.

Gilpin, Robert A. 1981. *War and Change in World Politics.* Cambridge: Cambridge University Press.

Glaser, Bonnie S. 2007. "Ensuring the 'Go Abroad' Policy Serves China's Domestic Priorities." *China Brief* 7(5), March 8. The Jamestown Foundation. Available at: http://www.jamestown.org/publications_details.php?volume_id=422&issue_id=4030 &article_id=2371986

Glaser, Bonnie S. and Philip C. Saunders. 2002. "Chinese Civilian Foreign Policy Research Institutes: Evolving Roles and Increasing Influence." *China Quarterly* 171, September, pp. 597–616.

Glosny, Michael. 2006. "Heading Toward a Win–Win Future? Recent Developments in China's Policy toward Southeast Asia." *Asian Security* 2(1), pp. 24–57.

Goh, Evelyn. 2004. "The ASEAN Regional Forum in United States East Asian Strategy." *Pacific Review* 17(1), pp. 47–69.

———. 2005a. *Constructing the U.S. Rapprochement with China, 1961–1974: From Red Menace to Tacit Ally.* New York: Cambridge University Press.

———. 2005b. "The Role of Great Powers in Southeast Asian Regional Security Strategies: Omni-enmeshment, Balancing and Hierarchical Order." IDSS working paper 84, July. Singapore: Institute of Defence and Strategic Studies.

———. 2005c. "The US–China Relationship and Asia-Pacific Security: Negotiating Change." *Asian Security* 1(3), pp. 216–244.

———. 2005d. *Meeting the China Challenge: The U.S. in Southeast Asian Security Strategies.* Policy Studies Monograph 16. Washington, D. C.: East–West Center Washington.

——. 2007. *Developing the Mekong: Regionalism and Regional Security in China–Southeast Asian Relations.* Adelphi Paper 387. London: IISS.

Goh, Evelyn, editor. 2005. *Betwixt and Between: Southeast Asian Strategic Relations with the U.S. and China.* IDSS Monograph 7. Singapore: Institute of Defence and Strategic Studies.

Goh, Evelyn and Amitav Acharya. 2007. "The ASEAN Regional Forum and Security Regionalism: Comparing Chinese and American Positions." In Melissa Curley and Nick Thomas, editors, *Advancing East Asian Regionalism.* London: Routledge, pp. 96–115.

Goh, Evelyn and Sheldon Simon, editors. 2007. *China, the United States, and Southeast Asia: Contending Perspectives on Politics, Security, and Economics.* London: Routledge.

Goldstein, Avery. 1997. "Great Expectations: Interpreting China's Arrival." *International Security* 22(3), winter, pp. 36–73.

——. 2002. "The Future of U.S.–China Relations and the Korean Peninsula." *Asian Perspective* 26(3), pp. 111–129.

——. 2005. *Rising to the Challenge: China's Grand Strategy and International Security.* Stanford, CA: Stanford University Press.

Goma, Daniel. 2006. "The Chinese–Korean Border Issue: An Analysis of a Contested Frontier." *Asian Survey* XLVI(6), November/December, pp. 867–880.

Grieco, Joseph M. 1988. "Anarchy and the Limits of Cooperation: A Realist Critique of the Newest Liberal Institutionalism." *International Organization* 42(3), summer, pp. 485–507.

Gries, Peter. 2004. *China's New Nationalism: Pride, Politics, and Diplomacy.* Berkeley, CA: University of California Press.

Hao Yufan. 1998. "Interpreting Chinese Foreign Policy: The Micro–Macro Linkage Approach" (book review)." *American Political Science Review* 92(2), June, pp. 510–511.

Harding, Harry. 1992. *A Fragile Relationship: The United States and China since 1972.* Washington D. C.: Brookings Institution.

Harris, Stuart. 2000. "The People's Republic of China's Quest for Great Power Status: A Long and Winding Road." In Hung-mao Tien and Yun-han Chu, editors, *China under Jiang Zemin.* Boulder, CO and London: Lynne Rienner Publisher, pp. 165–182.

Howard, Russell D. and Albert S. Willner. 2003. "The Rise of China and the U.S. Army: Strategic and Operational Change." A Paper Presented at the Annual Convention of the International Studies Association, Portland, Oregon, February 26–March 1.

Howard-Hassmann, Rhoda E. 2005. "The Second Great Transformation: Human Rights Leapfrogging in the Era of Globalization." *Human Rights Quarterly* 27, pp. 1–40.

Hu Weixing. 2006. "The Political–Economic Paradox and Beijing's Strategic Options." In Edward Friedman, editor, *China's Rise, Taiwan's Dilemma and International Peace.* New York: Routledge, pp. 22–38.

Hund, Markus. 2003. "ASEAN Plus Three: Towards a New Age of Pan-Asian Regionalism? A Skeptic's Appraisal." *Pacific Review* 16(3), August, pp. 383–417.

Huntington, Samuel P. 1988–1989. "The United States: Decline or Renewal." *Foreign Affairs* 67(2), winter.

Hwang, Jim. 2006. "No Bridging the Divide." *Taiwan Review* 56(8), August. http://taiwanreview.nat.gov.tw/ct.asp?xItem=22910&CtNode=128, accessed May 11, 2007.

Inoguchi Takashi. 2002. "Japan Goes Regional." In Inoguchi, editor, *Japan's Asia Policy: Revival and Response*. New York: Palgrave, pp. 1–34.

Jervis, Robert. 1985. "From Balance to Concert: A Study of International Security Cooperation." *World Politics* 38, pp. 58–79.

——. 1988. "Realism, Game Theory, and Cooperation." *World Politics* 40, pp. 317–349.

——. 1992. "A Political Science Perspective on the Balance of Power and the Concert." *American Historical Review* 97(3), June, pp. 716–724.

Jia Qingguo. 2005a. "Learning to Live with the Hegemon: Evolution of China's Policy toward the U.S. since the End of the Cold War." *Journal of Contemporary China* 14(44), August, pp. 395–407.

——. 2005b. "Peaceful Development: China's Policy of Reassurance." *Australian Journal of International Affairs* 59(4), December, pp. 493–507.

Johnson, Chalmers A. 1992. "Japan in Search of a 'Normal' Role." *Daedalus* 121, fall, pp. 1–33.

Johnston, Alastair Iain. 1995. *Strategic Culture and Grand Strategy in Chinese History*. Princeton, NJ: Princeton University Press.

——. 1996. "Cultural Realism and Strategy in Maoist China," in Peter J. Katzenstein, editor, *The Culture of National Security: Norms and Identity in World Politics*. New York: Columbia University Press, pp. 216–270.

——. 2001. "Treating International Institutions as Social Environments." *International Studies Quarterly* 45, pp. 487–515.

——. 2003a. "Is China a Status Quo Power?" *International Security* 27(4), spring, pp. 5–56.

——. 2003b. "Socialization in International Institutions: The ASEAN Way and International Relations Theory." In G. John Ikenberry and Michael Mastanduno, editors, *International Relations Theory and the Asia-Pacific*. New York: Columbia University Press, pp. 107–162.

——. 2003c. "The Correlates of Nationalism in Beijing Public Opinion." IDSS working paper 50, September. Singapore: Institute of Defence and Strategic Studies.

Johnston, Alastair Iain and Robert S. Ross, editors. 1999. *Engaging China: The Management of an Emerging Power*. London: Routledge.

Kang, David C. 2003. "Getting Asia Wrong: The Need for New Analytical Frameworks." *International Security* 27(4), spring, pp. 57–85.

Katsumata Hiro. 2003. "Reconstruction of Diplomatic Norms in Southeast Asia: The Case for Strict Adherence to the 'ASEAN Way.'" *Contemporary Southeast Asia* 25(1), April, pp. 104–121.

Katzenstein, Peter. 1996. "Introduction: Alternative Perspective on National Security," in Katzenstein, editor, *Culture of National Security: Norms and Identity in World Politics*. Ithaca and London: Cornell University Press, pp. 1–32.

Kelly, James A. 2004. "An Overview of U.S. East Asia Policy." Testimony before the House International Relations Committee, Washington D. C., June 2. Available at http://www.state.gov/p/eap/rls/rm/2004/33064pf.htm

Kennedy, Paul. 1987. *The Rise and Fall of the Great Powers*. New York: Random House.

Kenny, Henry J. 2004. "China and the Competition for Oil and Gas in Asia." *Asia-Pacific Review* 11(2), pp. 36–47.

Kerr, Pauline, Andrew Mack, and Paul Evans. 1995. "The Evolving Security Discourse in the Asia-Pacific." In Mack and John Ravenhill, editors, *Pacific Cooperation: Building Economic and Security Regimes in the Asia-Pacific Region*. Boulder, CO: Westview, pp. 233–255.

Kim Mikyoung. 2005a. "Nukes and Human Rights: North Korean Escapees in China," *Jamestown Organization* 5(5), March. www.jamestown.org/publications_details. php?volume_id= 408&issue_id= 3246& article_id=2369336.
——. 2005b. "North Korea: Beyond the Name Game," *The Oregonian*, July 25.
Kim, Samuel S. 2004. "China in World Politics." In Barry Buzan and Rosemary Foot, editors, *Does China Matter? Essays in Memory of Gerald Segal.* London: Routledge, pp. 37–53.
Kim Shee Poon. 1998. "The South China Sea in China's Strategic Thinking." *Contemporary Southeast Asia* 19(4), March, pp. 369–387.
Kim Woosang and James Morrow. 1992. "When Do Power Shifts Lead to War?" *American Journal of Political Science* 36(4), November, pp. 896–922.
Kirkpatrick, Jeanne. 1979. "Politics and the New Class," *Society* 16(2), pp. 42–48.
Kupchan, Charles A., Emmanuel Adler, Jean-Marc Coicaud, and Yuen Foong Khong. 2001. *Power in Transition: The Peaceful Change of International Order.* Tokyo: United Nations University Press.
Lampton, David M., editor. 2001. *The Making of Chinese Foreign and Security Policy in the Era of Reform, 1978–2000.* Stanford, CA: Stanford University Press.
Lampton, David M. and Richard Daniel Ewing. 2003. *The U.S.–China Relationship Facing International Security Crises.* Washington, D. C.: Nixon Center.
Larson, Deborah Welch. 1985. *Origins of Containment: A Psychological Explanation.* Princeton, NJ: Princeton University Press.
Layne, Christopher. 1997. "From Preponderance to Offshore Balancing: America's Future Grand Strategy." *International Security* 22(1), summer, pp. 86–124.
Lee Jung Nam. 2006. "The Revival of Chinese Nationalism: Perspectives of Chinese Intellectuals." *Asian Perspective* 30(4), pp. 141–165.
Lee, Pak K. 2005. "China's Quest for Oil Security: Oil (Wars) in the Pipeline?" *Pacific Review* 18(2), June, pp. 267–269.
Leifer, Michael. 1989. *ASEAN and the Security of South-East Asia.* London: Routledge.
Lemke, Douglas and Suzanne Werner. 1996. "Power Parity, Commitment to Change and War." *International Studies Quarterly* 40(2), June, pp. 235–260.
Levin, Norman D. 2004. *Do the Ties Still Bind? The U.S.–ROK Security Relationship After 9/11.* Santa Monica, CA: RAND.
Levy, Jack S. 1987. "Declining Power and the Preventive Motivation for War." *World Politics* 40(1), October, pp. 82–107.
Li Bin. 2003. "Absolute Gains, Relative Gains, and U.S. Security Policy on China." *Defense and Security Analysis* 19(4), December, pp. 309–317.
Li Nan. 2004. "The Evolving Chinese Conception of Security and Security Approaches." In See Seng Tan and Amitav Acharya, editors, *Asia-Pacific Security: National Interests and Regional Order.* Armonk, NY: M.E. Sharpe, pp. 53–70.
Li Qinggong and Wei Wei. 1997. "Chinese Army Paper on New Security Concept." *Jiefangjun Bao*, December 24, 1997. Translation available at FBIS–CHI–98–015, January 15, 1998.
Liao Xuanli. 2006. *Chinese Foreign Policy Think Tanks and China's Policy towards Japan.* Hong Kong: Chinese University Press.
——. 2007. "The Petroleum Factor in Sino–Japanese Relations: Beyond Energy Cooperation." *International Relations of the Asia-Pacific* 7, pp. 23–46.
Lincoln, Edward J. 2004. *East Asian Economic Regionalism.* Washington, D.C.: Brookings Institution Press.

Liu Ming. 2003. "China and the North Korean Crisis: Facing Test and Transition." *Pacific Affairs* 76(3), fall, pp. 347–374.

Loo, Bernard. 2007. "Military Modernization, Power Projection, and the Rise of the PLA: Strategic Implications for Southeast Asia." In Evelyn Goh and Sheldon Simon, editors, *China, the United States, and Southeast Asia: Contending Perspectives on Politics, Security, and Economics.* London: Routledge, pp. 185–199.

Mahbubani, Kishore. 2005. "Understanding China." *Foreign Affairs* 84(5), pp. 49–60.

Malik, Mohan. 2003. "Eyeing the Dragon: India's China Debate." In Satu Limaye, editor, *Asia's China Debate.* Honolulu: Asia-Pacific Center for Security Studies, Special Assessments, December, pp. 6.1–6.8. <http://www.apcss.org/Publications/APSSS/ChinaDebate/ChinaDebate_Malik.pdf>.

——. 2005a. "Security Council Reform: China Signals Its Veto." *World Policy Journal* XXII(1), spring, pp. 19–29.

——. 2005b. "The East Asia Summit: More Discord than Accord." *YaleGlobal,* 20 December.

——. 2006. "China Responds to the U.S.–India Nuclear Deal." *China Brief* 6(7), March 29. <http://www.jamestown.org/publications_details.php?volume_id=415&issue_id=3670&article_id=237096>

Manning, Robert and James Przystup. 1999. "Asia's Transition Diplomacy: Hedging Against Future Shock." *Survival* 41(3), pp. 43–67.

Mearsheimer, John. 2001. *The Tragedy of Great Power Politics.* New York: Norton.

Medeiros, Evan S. 2005–2006. "Strategic Hedging and the Future of Asia-Pacific Stability." *Washington Quarterly* 29(1), winter, pp. 145–167.

Medeiros, Evan and M. Taylor Fravel. 2003. "China's New Diplomacy." *Foreign Affairs* 82(6), November/December, pp. 22–33.

Modelski, George. 1978. "The Long Cycle of Global Politics and the Nation State." *Comparative Studies in Society and History* 20, pp. 214–235.

Moore, Rebecca R. 2003. "Outside Actors and the Pursuit of Civil Society in China." In Mahmood Monshipouri, Neil Englehart, Andrew J. Nathan, and Kavita Philip, editors, *Constructing Human Rights in the Age of Globalization.* Armonk and London: M.E. Sharpe, pp. 145–177.

Morgenthau, Hans J. 1985. *Politics among Nations: The Struggle for Power and Peace.* New York: Alfred A. Knopf.

Morrison, Wayne M. 2003. "Taiwan's Accession to the WTO and its Economic Relations with the United States and China." Congressional Research Service, May 16. http://fpc.state.gov/documents/organization/23370.pdf. Accessed April 24, 2007.

Muico, Norma Kang. 2005. *An absence of choice.* London: Anti-Slavery International.

Mulvenon, James C. Murray Scot Tanner, Michael S. Chase, David Frelinger, David C. Gompert, Martin C. Libicki, and Kevin L. Pollpeter. 2006. *Chinese Responses to U.S. Military Transformation and Implications for the Department of Defense.* Santa Monica, CA: RAND.

Nathan, Andrew J. 1986. "Sources of Chinese Rights Thinking," in Edwards, R. Randle, Louis Henkin and Andrew J. Nathan, editors, *Human Rights in Contemporary China.* New York: Columbia University Press, pp. 125–164.

—— (with contributions by Tianjian Shi and Helen V. S. Ho). 1997. *China's Transition.* New York: Columbia University Press.

Noble, Gregory W. 2006. "New Breakthroughs and Enduring Limitations in Japan's Special Relationship with Taiwan." In Yoichiro Sato and Satu Limaye, editors, *Japan* in *A Dynamic Asia: Coping with the New Security Challenges.* Lanham, MD: Lexington Books, pp. 89–116.

Odgaard, Liselotte. 2002. *Maritime Security between China and Southeast Asia: Conflict and Cooperation in the Making of Regional Order.* Aldershot, Hampshire, UK: Ashgate.

Office of the President (South Korea). 2006. *Vision 2030.* August 30. http://vision2030.korea.kr

O'Neill, Tip and Gary Hymel. 1994. *All Politics is Local: And Other Rules of the Game.* Holbrook, MA: Bob Adams.

Organski, A.F.K. 1958. *World Politics.* New York: Knopf.

Organski, A.F.K. and Jacek Kugler. 1980. *The War Ledger.* Chicago: University of Chicago Press.

Osius, Ted. 2001. "Discussion of 'The Rise of China in Chinese Eyes.'" *Journal of Contemporary China* 10(26), pp. 41–44.

——. 2002. *The U.S.–Japan Security Alliance: Why It Matters and How to Strengthen It.* Washington Papers Number 181. West Port, CT: Praeger and Washington, D. C.: Center for Strategic and International Studies.

Pang, Zhongying. 2006. "China, My China.' *National Interest* 83, spring, pp. 9–10.

Pastreich, Emanuel. 2006. "Is China the Nemesis in a New Cold War?" *Policy Forum Online* 06-18A. San Francisco, CA: Nautilus Institute. March 2. http://www.nautilus.org/fora/security/0618Pastreich.html

Pei, Minxin. 2002. "Beijing Drama; China's Governance Crisis and Bush's New Challenge." *Policy Brief* 21, November. Washington, D. C.: Carnegie Endowment for International Peace. http://www.carnegieendowment.org/files/Policybrief21.pdf

Peters, Ralph. 2005. *New Glory: Expanding America's Global Supremacy.* New York: Penguin Group.

Pillsbury, Michael. 2000. *China Debates the Future Security Environment.* Washington, D. C.: National Defense University Press, January. http://www.fas.org/nuke/guide/china/doctrine/pills2/. Accessed June 7, 2007.

Powell, Robert. 1991. "Absolute and Relative Gains in International Relations Theory." *American Political Science Review* 85(4), December, pp. 1303–1320.

——. 1994. "Anarchy in International Relations Theory: The Neorealist–Neoliberal Debate." *International Organization* 48(2), spring, pp. 313–344.

Pramit Mitra. 2003. "A Thaw in India–China Relations." *South Asia Monitor* 62, September 1.

Qin Yaqing. 2001. "A Response to Yong Deng: Power, Perception, and the Culture Lens." *Asian Affairs: An American Review* 28(3), fall, pp. 155–158.

Rajan, D. S. 2007. "China: Media Fears over India Becoming Part of Western Alliance." *Saag.org*, paper no. 2350, August 29. http://www.saag.org/papers24/paper2350.htm1

Raman, B. 2007. "China: Through Indian Eyes." C3S Paper, no. 12, May 14. http://www.c3sindia.org/india/87/china-through-indian-eyes/

——. 2007b. "Tawang: Some Indian plain-speaking at last!" *Saag.org*, paper no. 2273, June 22. http://www.saag.org/papers23/paper2273.html

Ravenhill, John. 2006. "Is China an Economic Threat to Southeast Asia? *Asian Survey* 46(5), September/October, pp. 653–674.

Riles, Annelise. 2006. "Anthropology, Human Rights, and Legal Knowledge: Culture in the Iron Cage." *American Anthropologist* 19(1), pp. 52–65.

Roh Moo-Hyun. 2003. "Speech to the Students of Chinghuia University." Seoul: Office of the President, July 9.
——. 2005a. "Speech to the Graduation Ceremony of Korean Air Force Academy." Seoul: Office of the President, March 8.
——. 2005b. "Speech to the Graduation Ceremony of Korea Third Military Academy." Seoul: Office of the President, March 22.
——. 2005c. "A letter to Korean People with regard to Korea–Japan Relations." Seoul: Office of the President, March 23.
——. 2005d. "Speech to the National Defense Force Day Ceremony." Seoul: Office of the President, October 1.
——. 2006. "Speech to the 2006 Press Conference." Office of the President, January 26. http://www.president.go.kr/cwd/kr/archive/archive_view.php?meta_id=speech& id=53d7adb2c914007049f20ab7, accessed on 29 January 2006.
Ross, Robert. 1995. *Negotiating Cooperation: The United States and China, 1969–1989.* Stanford, CA: Stanford University Press.
——. 1997. "Beijing as a Conservative Power." *Foreign Affairs* 76(2), March/April, pp. 33–44.
——. 1999a. "Engagement in U.S. China Policy." In Alastair Iain Johnston and Ross, editors, *Engaging China: The Management of an Emerging Power.* London: Routledge.
——. 1999b. "The Geography of the Peace: East Asia in the Twenty-first Century." *International Security* 23(4), spring, pp. 81–118.
——. 2002. "Navigating the Taiwan Strait: Deterrence, Escalation Dominance, and U.S.–China Relations." *International Security* 27(2), fall, pp. 48–85.
——. 2005. "Assessing the China Threat." *The National Interest*, fall, pp. 81–87.
Roy, Denny. 1994. "Hegemon on the Horizon? China's Threat to East Asian Security." *International Security* 19(1), summer, pp. 149–168.
——. 2003a. "China's Reaction to American Predominance." *Survival* 45(3), autumn, pp. 57–78.
——. 2003b. "Rising China and U.S. Interests: Inevitable vs. Contingent Hazards." *Orbis*, winter, pp. 125–137.
——. 2004. "China and the Korean Peninsula: Beijing's Pyongyang Problem and Seoul Hope." *Asia-Pacific Security Studies* 3(1), January. Honolulu, HI: Asia-Pacific Center for Security Studies.
——. 2006. "Stirring Samurai, Disapproving Dragon: Japan's Growing Security Activity and Sino–Japan Relations." In Yoichiro Sato and Satu Limaye, editors, *Japan in A Dynamic Asia: Coping with the New Security Challenges.* Lanham, MD: Lexington Books, pp. 69–87.
Rozman, Gilbert. 2002. "China's Changing Images of Japan, 1989–2001: The Struggle to Balance Partnership and Rivalry." *International Relations of the Asia-Pacific* 2(1), pp. 95–129.
Ruggie, John Gerard. 1998. *Constructing the World Polity: Essays on International Institutionalization.* London: Routledge.
Rutherford, Geddes W. 1926. "Spheres of Influence: An Aspect of Semi-Suzerainty." *American Journal of International Law* 20(2), April, pp. 300–325.
Sartori, Silvia. 2005. "How China sees India and the World," *Heartland: Eurasian Review of Geopolitics*, No. 3. Hong Kong: Cassan Press. http://www.heartland.it/ _lib/_docs/2005_03_chindia_the_21st_century_challenge.pdf

Sato Yoichiro. 1999. "Will the US–Japan Alliance Continue?" *New Zealand International Review* XXIV(4), July/August, pp. 10–12.

———. 2006a. "Japan's Reactions to the DPRK Missile Tests of July 2006." In Yongjin Zhang, editor, *Whither the Six Party Talks? Issues, Stakes and Perspectives*. Auckland: New Zealand Asia Institute, pp. 35–44.

———. 2006b. "US North Korea Policy: the 'Japan Factor.'" In Linus Hagström and Marie Söderberg, editors, *North Korea Policy: Japan and the Great Powers*. European Institute of Japanese Studies, East Asian Economics and Business Series 9. London: Routledge, pp. 73–94.

———. 2006c. "Japan and the Emerging Free Trade Agreements in the Asia-Pacific: An Active Leadership?" In Sato and Satu Limaye, editors, *Japan in A Dynamic Asia: Coping with the New Security Challenges*. Lanham, MD: Lexington Books, pp. 37–68.

———. 2007. "Southeast Asian Receptiveness to Japanese Maritime Security Cooperation." Asia-Pacific Papers. Honolulu, HI: Asia-Pacific Center for Security Studies.

———. Forthcoming. "Role of Norms in Japan's Overseas Troop Dispatch Decisions." In Sato and Keiko Hirata, editors, *Norms, Interests, and Power in Japanese Foreign Policy*. New York: Palgrave.

Sato Yoichiro, editor. 2004. *Growth and Governance in Asia*. Honolulu, HI: Asia-Pacific Center for Security Studies.

Sato Yoichiro and Satu Limaye, editors. 2006. *Japan in A Dynamic Asia: Coping with the New Security Challenges*. Lanham, MD: Lexington Books.

Schroeder, Paul W. 1992. "Did the Vienna Settlement Rest on a Balance of Power?" *American Historical Review* 97(3), June, pp. 683–706.

Schweller, Randall L. 1994. "Bandwagoning for Profit: Bringing the Revisionist State Back In." *International Security* 19(1), summer, pp. 72–107.

———. 1999. "Managing the Rise of Great Powers: History and Theory." In Alastair Iain Johnston and Robert S. Ross, editors, *Engaging China: The Management of an Emerging Power*. London: Routledge, pp. 7–16.

Scobell, Andrew. 2002. "'Cult of Defense' and 'Great Power Dreams': The Influence of Strategic Culture on China's Relationship with India." In Malcolm R. Chambers, editor, *South Asia in 2020: Future Strategic Balances and Alliances*. PA: U.S. Army War College, Strategic Studies Institute, pp. 329–359.

Segal, Adam, Joseph Prueher, and Harold Brown. 2003. *Chinese Military Power*. Independent Task Force Report, May. New York: Council on Foreign Relations.

Segal, Gerald. 1993. "The Coming Confrontation between China and Japan." *World Policy Journal* 10(2), summer, pp. 27–32.

———. 1994. *China Changes Shape*. Adelphi Papers 287. London: IISS.

Shambaugh, David. 2000. "Sino–American Strategic Relations: From Partners to Competitors." *Survival* 42(1), spring, pp. 98–104.

———. 2001. "China or America: Which is the Revisionist Power?" *Survival* 43(3), autumn, pp. 25–30.

———. 2002. "China's International Relations Think Tanks: Evolving Structure and Process." *China Quarterly* 171, September, pp. 575–596.

———. 2003a. *Modernizing China's Military: Progress, Problems and Prospects*. Berkeley, CA: University of California Press.

———. 2003b. "China and the Korean Peninsula: Playing for the Long Term." *Washington Quarterly*, spring, pp. 43–56.

——. 2004–2005. "China Engages Asia: Reshaping the Regional Order." *International Security* 29(3), winter, pp. 64–99.

Shambaugh, David, editor. 2006. *Power Shift: China and Asia's New Dynamics.* Berkeley, CA: University of California Press.

Sheives, Kevin. 2006. "China Turns West: Beijing's Contemporary Strategy Towards Central Asia." *Pacific Affairs* 79(2), pp. 205–224.

Shi Yin-hong. 2004. "The Issue of Civil Society in China and Its Complexity." In Yoichiro Sato, editor, *Growth and Governance in Asia.* Honolulu, HI: Asia-Pacific Center for Security Studies, pp. 225–232.

Shin Eui-Soon. 2005. *Joint Stockpiling and Emergency Sharing of Oil: Update on the Situations in the ROK and on Arrangements for Regional Cooperation in Northeast Asia.* www.nautilus.org/archives/energy/AES2004Workshop/SHIN_ROK.ppt

Shinn, James, ed. 1996. *Weaving the Net: The Conditional Engagement of China.* New York: Council on Foreign Relations.

Simon, Sheldon W. 1995. "International Relations Theory and Southeast Asian Security." *Pacific Review* 8(1), pp. 5–24.

Snyder, Scott. 2005. "South Korea's Squeeze Play." *Washington Quarterly*, autumn, pp. 93–106.

Storey, Ian. 1999–2000. "Living with the Colossus: How Southeast Asian Countries Cope with China." *Parameters*, winter, pp. 111–125.

Stuart, Douglas T. 1997. "Toward Concert in Asia." *Asian Survey* 37(3), March, pp. 229–244.

Stuart-Fox, Martin. 2003. *A Short History of China and Southeast Asia: Tribute, Trade and Influence.* Crows Nest, New South Wales: Allen & Unwin.

Suh, J. J., Peter J. Katzenstein, and Allen Carlson, editors. 2004. *Rethinking Security in East Asia: Identity, Power, and Efficiency.* Stanford, CA: Stanford University Press.

Sutter, Robert G. 2005a. "China's Rise in Asia—Promises, Prospects and Implications for the United States." Occasional Paper. Honolulu: Asia-Pacific Center for Security Studies, February. http://www.apcss.org/Publications/Ocasional%20Papers/OP ChinasRise.pdf

——. 2005b. *China's Rise in Asia: Promises and Perils.* Lanham, MD: Rowman and Littlefield.

Suzuki Shogo. 2007. "The Importance of 'Othering' in China's National Identity: Sino–Japanese Relations as a Stage of Identity Conflicts." *Pacific Review* 20(1), March, pp. 23–47.

Swaine, Michael. 1996. "China." In Zalmay Khalilzad, editor, *Strategic Appraisal 1996.* Santa Monica, CA: RAND.

——. 2003. "Reverse Course? The Fragile Turnaround in U.S.–China Relations." *Policy Brief* 22, February. Washington, D. C.: Carnegie Endowment for International Peace. http://www.carnegieendowment.org/files/Policybrief22.pdf

Swaminathan, R. 2007. "India's Foreign Policy: Emerging Trends in the New Century." *Saag.org*, paper no. 2194, April 5. <http://www.saag.org/%5Cpapers22%5Cpaper 2194.html>

Takamine Tsukasa. 2006. "The Role of Yen Loans in China's Economic Growth and Openness." *Pacific Affairs* 79(1), spring, pp. 29–48.

Tan See Seng and Amitav Acharya, editors. 2004. *Asia-Pacific Security: National Interests and Regional Order.* Armonk, NY: M.E. Sharpe.

T'Ang Leang-Li. 1927. *China in Revolt: How a Civilization Became a Nation.* London: N. Douglas. <http://www.questia.com/library/book/china-in-revolt-how-a-civilization-became-a-nation-by-tang-leang-li.jsp>, accessed June 11, 2007.

Tang Shiping and Zhang Yunling. 2006. "China's Regional Strategy." In David Shambaugh, editor, *Power Shift: China and Asia's New Dynamics.* Berkeley, CA: University of California Press, pp. 48–68.

Tanner, Murray Scot. 2002. "Changing Windows on a Changing China: The Evolving 'Think Tank' System and the Case of the Public Security Sector." *China Quarterly* 171, September, pp. 559–574.

Taylor, Brendan. 2005. "US–China Relations after 11 September: A Long Engagement or Marriage of Convenience?" *Australian Journal of International Affairs* 59(2), June, pp. 179–199.

Tellis, Ashley J. and Michael Wills, editors. 2005. *Military Modernization in an Era of Uncertainty: Executive Summary.* Seattle, WA: National Bureau of Asian Research.

Terasawa Katsuko. 2003. "Labor Law, Civil Law, Immigration Law and the Reality of Migrants and Their Children." In Mike Douglass and Glenda S. Roberts, editors, *Japan and Global Migration: Foreign Workers and the Advent of a Multicultural Society.* Honolulu, HI: University of Hawaii Press, pp. 219–243.

Tharoor, Shashi. 1999/2000. "Are Human Rights Universal?" *World Policy Journal* XVI(4), winter. www.worldpolicy.org/journal/tharoor.html.

Thurston, Anne F. 2001. "Community and Isolation: Memory and Forgetting—China in Search of Itself." In Gerrit W. Gong, editor, *Memory and History in East and Southeast Asia: Issues of Identity in International Relations.* Washington, D.C.: Center for Strategic and International Studies, pp. 149–172.

Tow, Shannon. 2004. "Southeast Asia in the Sino–U.S. Strategic Balance." *Contemporary Southeast Asia* 26(3), pp. 434–459.

Tyler, Patrick. 1999. *A Great Wall: Six Presidents and China An Investigative History.* New York: Century Foundation, pp. 105–180.

United States Department of Defense. 2001. *Quadrennial Defense Review, 2001.* Available at: http://www.defenselink.mil/pubs/qdr2001.pdf.

——. 2004. "Department of Defense Background Briefing on Global Posture Review." 16 August. Available at: http://www.defense.gov/transcripts/2004/tr20040816-1153.html.

——. 2005. *The Military Power of the People's Republic of China 2005: Annual Report to Congress.* Washington, D. C.: Department of Defense.

——. 2006. *Annual Report to Congress: Military Power of the People's Republic of China 2006.* Washington, D. C.

United States National Security Council. 2002. *The National Security Strategy of the United States of America,* September. Available at: http://www.whitehouse.gov/nsc/nss.html.

United States National Security Council. 2006. *The 2006 National Security Strategy.* http://www.whitehouse.gov/nsc/nss/2006/

Urayama Kori. 2004. "China Debates Missile Defense." *Survival* 46(2), summer, pp. 123–142.

Vasquez, John. 1993. *The War Puzzle.* New York: Cambridge University Press.

Wallerstein, Immanuel. 1984. *The Politics of the World Economy.* Cambridge: Cambridge University Press.

Walt, Stephen M. 1987. *The Origins of Alliances.* Ithaca, NY: Cornell University Press.

——. 2002. "Keeping the World 'Off Balance,'" in G. John Ikenberry, editor, *America Unrivaled: The Future of the Balance of Power.* Ithaca, NY: Cornell University Press, pp. 121–154.

Waltz, Kenneth. 1979. *Theory of International Relations*. Reading, MA: Addison-Wesley.

Wang Jisi. 2003. "China's Changing Role in Asia." Paper delivered at Salzburg Seminar, Session 415.

Ward, Adam. 2003. "China and America: Trouble Ahead?" *Survival* 45(3), autumn, pp. 35–56.

Weaver, O. 1995. "Securitization and Desecuritization." In R.D. Lipschutz, editor, *On Security*. New York: Columbia University Press, pp. 46–86.

Weber, Max. [1930] 1992. *The Protestant Ethic and the Spirit of Capitalism* (translated by Talcott Parsons and introduction by Anthony Giddens). London and New York: Routledge.

Weitz, Richard. 2001. "Meeting the China Challenge: Some Insights from Scenario-Based Planning." *Journal of Strategic Studies* 24(3), September, pp. 19–48.

Wendt, Alexander. 1999. *Social Theory of International Politics*. Cambridge: Cambridge University Press.

Wheeler, Nicholas S. 2002. *Saving Strangers: Humanitarian Intervention in International Society*. Oxford: Oxford University Press.

Whiting, Allen S. 1989. *China Eyes Japan*. Berkeley: University of California Press.

Wohlforth, William. 1999. "The Stability of a Unipolar World." *International Security* 24(1), summer, pp. 5–41.

Wong, John and Sarah Chan. 2003. "China–ASEAN Free Trade Agreement." *Asian Survey* 43(3), May/June, pp. 507–526.

Wu, Friedrich, et al. 2003. "Foreign Direct Investments to China and ASEAN: Has ASEAN Been Losing Out?" *Economic Survey of Singapore, Third Quarter*. Available at: http://www.mti.gov.sg/public/PDF/CMT/NWS_2002Q3_FDI1.pdf?sid+92&cid=1418.

Wu, Joseph Jauhsieh. 2005. "Democracy and Peace to Answer China's War-Authorization Law." *Taiwan Perspective* 69, Institute for National Policy Research, March 25. http://www.tp.org.tw/eletter/story.htm?id=20007276, accessed March 25, 2005.

Wu Shicun and Ren Huaifeng. 2003. "More than a Declaration: A Commentary on the Background and Significance of the Declaration on the Conduct of Parties in the South China Sea." *Chinese Journal of International Law* 2(1), pp. 311–320.

Wu Xinbo. 2005–2006. "The End of the Silver Lining: A Chinese View of the U.S.–Japan Alliance." *Washington Quarterly* 29(1), winter, pp. 119–130.

Xia Liping. 2001. "China: A Responsible Great Power." *Journal of Contemporary China* 10(26), pp. 17–25.

Xiang Lanxin. 2001. "Washington's Misguided China Policy." *Survival* 43(3), autumn, pp. 7–23.

Xu Xiaoqun. 2001. "Human Rights and the Discourse on Universality: A Chinese Historical Perspective," in the Quest for Human Rights." In Lynda S. Bell, Andrew J. Nathan, and Ilan Peleg, editors, *Negotiating Culture and Human Rights*. New York: Columbia University Press, pp. 153–196.

Yan Xuetong. 2001. "The Rise of China in Chinese Eyes." *Journal of Contemporary China* 10(26), pp. 33–39.

———. 2006. "The Rise of China and Its Power Status." *Chinese Journal of International Politics* 1(1), pp. 5–33.

Yang Bojiang. 2006. "Redefining Sino–Japanese Relations after Koizumi." *Washington Quarterly* 29(4), autumn, pp. 129–137.

Yang Jian. 2006. "China's Security Strategy and Policies." In Stephen Hoadley and Jürgen Rüland, editors, *Asian Security Reassessed.* Singapore: Institute of Southeast Asian Studies.

Yang, Razali Kassim. 2005. "The Rise of East Asia? ASEAN's Driver Role Key to Ties between Japan and China." IDSS Commentaries, 22 December. Singapore: Institute of Defence and Strategic Studies.

Yee, Herbert and Ian Storey, editors. 2002. *The China Threat: Perceptions, Myths and Reality.* London and New York: RoutledgeCurzon.

Yu Bin. 1994. "The Study of Chinese Foreign Policy: Problems and Prospect." *World Politics* 46(2), January, pp. 235–261.

Yuan Jing-dong. 2001. "Regional Institutions and Cooperative Security: Chinese Approaches and Policies." *Korean Journal of Defense Analysis* XIII(1), autumn, pp. 263–294.

Yuen Foong Khong. 1997. "Making Bricks without Straw in the Asia Pacific?" *Pacific Review* 10(2), pp. 289–300.

——. 2004. "Coping with Strategic Uncertainty: The Role of Institutions and Soft Balancing in Southeast Asia's Post-Cold War Strategy." In J. J. Suh, Peter J. Katzenstein, and Allen Carlson, editors, *Rethinking Security in East Asia: Identity, Power, and Efficiency.* Stanford, CA: Stanford University Press, chapter 5.

Zakaria, Fareed. 1994. "Culture is Destiny, A Conversation with Lee Kuan Yew." *Foreign Affairs* 73(2), March/April, pp. 36–42.

Zhang Juyan and Glen T. Cameron. 2003. "China's Agenda Building and Image Polishing in the U.S.: Assessing an International Public Relations Campaign." *Public Relations Review* 29(1), March, pp. 13–28.

Zhao Quansheng. 2005. "Impact of Intellectuals and Think Tanks on Chinese Foreign Policy." In Yufan Hao and Lin Su, editors, *China's Foreign Policy Making: Societal Force and Chinese American Policy.* Aldershot, Hampshire, UK: Ashgate.

Zhao Suisheng. 1998. "A State-Led Nationalism: the Patriotic Education Campaign in Post-Tiananmen China." *Communist and Post-Communist Studies* 31(3), pp. 287–302.

Zheng Bijian. 2005. "China's 'Peaceful Rise' to Great-Power Status." *Foreign Affairs* 84(5), September/October, pp. 18–24.

Zhou Qi. 2005. "Conflicts over Human Rights between China and the U.S." *Human Rights Quarterly* 27, pp. 105–124.

[In Japanese]

Hara Kimie (原貴美恵). 2005. サンフランシスコ平和条約の盲点 *San Francisco Heiwa Jouyaku no Mouten* [The Blind Spots of the San Francisco Peace Treaty]. Hiroshima: Keisui-sha.

Iijima Isao (飯島勲). 2007. 実録・小泉外交 *Jitsuroku Koizumi Gaikou* [Documentary of Koizumi Diplomacy]. Tokyo: Nihon Keizai Shimbunsha.

Kokubun Ryosei (国分良成). 2006. 序論：中国の政治外交—天安門事件とその 後 [Introduction: Chinese Politics and Foreign Relations—The Tiananmen Incident and After]. *International Relations: China after the Tiananmen Incident* 145, August, pp. 1–16.

Sato Yoichiro (佐藤洋一郎). Forthcoming. 日本の海外派兵決定の分析 "Nihon no Kaigai Hahei Kettei no Bunseki" [Analysis of Japan's Overseas Troop Dispatch Decisions]. In Kimie Hara (原貴美恵), editor, 在外日本人研究者が見た日本外交 *Zaigai Nihonjin*

Kenkyusha ga Mita Nihon Gaikou [Japanese Diplomacy as Seen by Overseas Japanese Scholars] (tentative title). Manuscript under review.

Tsuchiya Hideo (土屋英雄). 1996. 中国の人権論の歴史的位相:「群」優先の論理お中心として [Historical Status of the Chinese Human Rights: With a Focus on Group Priority]. *Human Rights International* 7, pp. 44–47.

[In Korean]

Asia Watch—Minnesota Lawyers International Human Rights Committee. 1990. *Bukhaneui Inkwon* [North Korean Human Rights]. Seoul: Koryowon.

Choi Gyu Yeop. 2004. "Bukhan Ingwoneui Shilatae" [North Korean Human Rights]. A paper presented at International Symposium on North Korean Human Rights, December 1, Seoul, Korea.

Good Neighbors. 1999. *Dumangangeul Gunneuon Saramdul: Jungkuk Dongbukbujiyok 2,479gae Maeul Buhan 'Shikryangnanmin' Shiltaejosa* [The Border Crossing People: A Study of North Korean Food Migrants in 2,479 Villages in Northeast China]. Seoul: Jungto Publishing.

Lee Geum Soon. 2005. *Bukhanjumineui Kukgyongidong Shiltae: Byonwhawa Jungmang* [The North Korean Border Crossing: Changes and Prospects]. Seoul: Korean Institute for National Unification.

Ministry of Unification (South Korea). 1998. *Bukhan Inkwon Baekseo* [White Paper on Human Rights in North Korea]. Seoul.

Yoon Yeo Sang. 1998. "Talbukja Shiltaewa Jiwonchaegae: Jungkukjiyokeul Jungshimuro" [The Reality of North Korean Refugees and Support System: With a Focus on China]. *Tongil Yongu Nonchong* 7(2), pp. 33–48.

[In Chinese]

Chu Shulong and Wang Zaibang. 1999. "Guanyu guoji xingshi he wo duiwai zhanlue ruogan zhongda wenti de sikao" [Some Thoughts on Several Major Issues about International Situation and Our External Strategy]. *Xiandai Guoji Guanxi* [*Contemporary International Relations*] 8.

Guo Wanchao. 2004. *Zhongguo Jueqi* [*Rise of China*]. Nanchang, Jiangxi: Jiangxi renmin chubanshe [Jiangxi People's Publishing House].

Guo Xuetang. 2005. "Guoji zhuyi yu Zhongguo waijiao de jiazhi huigui" [Internationalism and the Return to Traditional Values in Chinese Foreign Policy]. *Guoji Guancha* [*International Observation*] 1, pp. 35–38.

Li Baojun and Xu Zhengyuan. 2006. "Lengzhanhou Zhongguo fuzeren daguo shenfen de goujian" [The Construction of China's Identity as a Responsible Great Power since the End of the Cold War]. *Jiaoxue yu Yanjiu* [*Teaching and Research*] 1, pp. 49–56.

Liu Yantang and Liu Xinyu. 2005. "Guoji biange: Shijie yu Zhongguo de zhanlue hudong" [International Changes: Strategic Interactions between the World and China]. *Liaowang Xinwen Zhoukan* [*Liaowang Weekly*] 9, February 28.

Liu Yi and Wang Xialing. 2005. "Dui Zhongguo jueqi de sikao" [Thoughts about the Rise of China]. *Dangdai Yatai* [*Contemporary Asia Pacific*] 2, pp. 19–23.

Meng Xiangqing. 2002. "Lun Zhonguo de guoji juese zhuanhuan yu duiwai aiquan zhanlue de jiben dingwei" [On the Changes to China's International Role and the Fundamentals of China's External Security Strategy]. *Shijie Jingji yu Zhengzhi* [*World Economics and Politics*] 7, pp. 10–15.

Pang, Zhongying. 2005. "Dui 'Zhongguo weixielun' caiqu xin zhitai" [New Attitude towards the "China Threat Theory"]. *Liaowang Xinwen Zhoukan* [*Liaowang Weekly*] 9, February 28.

Qian Wenrong. 2004. "Duojihua shi dangjin shijie geju fazhan de keguan qushi" [Multipolarization Is the Actual Trend of the Development of Today's World Order]. *Heping yu Fazhan* [*Peace and Development*] 3, pp. 16–18.

Sha Qiguang. 2000. "Dui xifang meiti sanbu 'Zhongguo weixielun' de pingxi" [An analysis of the "China threat theory" spread by Western media]. *Guoji Zhengzhi Yanjiu* [*International Political Studies*] 3, pp. 113–125.

Shi Aiguo. 2004. *Aoman yu Pianjian: Dongfang zhuyi yu Meiguo de "Zhongguo weixielun" yanjiu* [*Pride and Prejudice: A research on Orientalism and the "China threat theory" in the United States*]. Guangzhou: Zhongshan Daxue Chubanshe [Zhongshan University Press].

Sun Keqin and Cui Hongjian, editors. 1996. *Ezhi Zhongguo-Shenhua yu xianshi* [*Containing China-myth and reality*] Beijing: Zhongguo yanshi chubanshe.

Tao Jiyi. 2005. "Meiguo zhengzhi xuezhe dui 'Zhongguo weixielun' de pibo tanxi" [An analysis of American honest scholars' rebuttal of the "China threat theory"]. *Guoji Wenti Yanjiu* [*International Studies*] 3, pp. 20–24, 33.

Wang Yizhou. 1998. "Sikao 'duojihua'" [Thoughts about "Multipolarity"]. *Guoji Jingji Pinglun* [*International Economic Review*] 9/10, pp. 26–27.

——. 2003. *Quanqiu Zhengzhi yu Zhongguo Waijiao* [*Global Politics and China's Foreign Policy*]. Beijing: Shijie zhishi chubanshe [World Knowledge Publishing House].

Wang Yunxiang. 1996. "'Zhongguo weixielun' xi" [An Analysis of the "China Threat Theory"]. *Guoji Guancha* [*International Observation*] 3, pp. 35–40.

Xiao Feng. 2002. "Shijie 'duojihua' qushi hui nizhuan ma?" [Will the Trend of World Multipolarity Be Reversed?]. *Dangdai shijie* [*The Contemporary World*] 8, pp. 7–8.

Yan Bai. 2005. "'Zhongguo weixie lun' de sici chaoliu" [The Four Waves of the "China Threat Theory"]. *Shishi Baogao* [*Current Affairs Report*] 10, p. 70.

Yan Xuetong. 1996. *Zhongguo Guojia Liyi Fenxi* [*An Analysis of China's National Interests*]. Tianjin: Tianjin renmin chubanshe [Tianjin People's Publishing House].

Yu Sui. 2004. "Shijie duojihua wenti" [The Issue of Multipolarization of the World]. *Guoji Zhengzhi yu Guoji Guanxi* [*International Politics and International Relations*] 3, pp. 15–20.

Zhou Fangyin. 2000. "Dui dangqian guoji gejiu de julei fengxi" [A Categorized Study of Current International Order]. *Xiandai Guoji Guanxi* [*Contemporary International Relations*] 12, pp. 40–43.

Index

Abe, Shinzo 98, 107, 110, 112, 115, 202
ABM (see Anti-Ballistic Missile Treaty)
absolute gains 7–10, 12, 86, 248
alternative security 4–6
American power 1, 12, 45, 50, 56, 67, 71, 81, 170
anti-Americanism 3, 142, 151, 237
Anti-Ballistic Missile (ABM) Treaty 73
anti-hegemon 167
anti-satellite (ASAT) 82
APEC (Asia-Pacific Economic Cooperation) 105, 112, 186, 205
ARF (ASEAN Regional Forum) 9, 77, 91, 162–163, 171, 175, 186–187, 205, 238, 245
arms sales to Taiwan 22
ASAT (anti-satellite) 82
ASEAN (Association of Southeast Asian Nations) 1, 3, 6–7, 9–10, 12, 18–19, 33, 64, 72, 74, 76, 78, 85, 87–88, 90–91, 96, 105–106, 153, 159–169, 171–175, 186, 197, 209, 238, 242–243, 245–248, 255–256
ASEAN China Free Trade Area (ACFTA) 162, 166, 171
ASEAN Regional Forum (ARF) 9, 77, 91, 162–163, 171, 175, 186–187, 205, 238, 245
ASEAN+3 64, 77, 162–163, 165, 168, 171, 187, 205, 238
ASEAN-6 166
Asia's rise 180, 207
Asian geopolitics 153, 179
Asian values 76, 215, 217
Asia-Pacific Economic Cooperation (APEC) 105, 112, 186, 205
Association of Southeast Asian Nations (ASEAN) 1, 3, 6–7, 9–10, 12, 18–19, 33, 64, 72, 74, 76, 78, 85,

87–88, 90–91, 96, 105–106, 153, 159–169, 171–175, 186, 197, 209, 238, 242–243, 245–248, 255–256
asymmetrical conflict 60, 81
avian flu 113

balancer 3, 125, 130, 140, 147–151, 155, 169, 179, 206, 237
balancing 2–3, 62–63, 77, 81, 83, 88–89, 91, 124–130, 138, 140, 153, 159, 167–169, 175, 179, 189, 199–201, 221, 233, 236, 238, 245, 248, 256
ballistic missiles 120
bandwagoning 89, 124–127, 130, 133–137, 149, 168, 170, 179, 233, 236–237, 252
Bangkok Declaration of Human Rights 214
Bay of Bengal Initiative for MultiSectoral Technical and Economic Cooperation (BIMSTEC) 187, 205
Beijing Olympics 228
bipolarity 69, 71, 81, 179
Brooks, David 52, 58
Bush Administration 40
Bush, George W. 40, 53, 57, 62, 66–67, 70, 72, 75, 77, 87–88, 124, 137, 139, 141, 216, 228, 245, 250

Cambodia, Laos, Myanmar, and Vietnam (CLMV) 171
CCP (Chinese Communist Party) 191–192
CFC (Combined Forces Command) 145, 157
Chan, Lien 134
Chen Shui-bian 3, 106, 122, 127–139

China
  comprehensive national power
    (CNP) 17, 24, 66, 178, 192,
    207
  famine 223
  foreign policy 1, 4, 12–16, 31–32,
    36–37, 63–65, 72, 76, 198, 233,
    239–241, 244–246, 248
  foreign policy making 14, 256
  Question 39
  rise 1–7, 9, 11, 13, 18–27, 30–33,
    35–39, 46, 48, 55–56, 59–61, 63,
    68, 76, 81, 83, 85–86, 104, 117,
    120, 127, 135–137, 143, 159–162,
    164, 166–168, 170–172, 174–175,
    177–180, 193, 197, 199, 201,
    206–207, 230, 233, 235, 237–239,
    241, 243–244, 246, 250, 253, 255,
    257
  self-perception 13, 24
  strategy of ambivalence 226
  think tanks 1, 13–16, 29, 32, 248,
    252, 256
  threat theory 1, 13, 16, 18–23, 27,
    29–30, 32–36, 184, 243, 258
China National Offshore Oil
  Corporation (CNOOC) 20
China-India relations 183, 185, 208
Chinese Communist Party (CCP)
  191–192
Chinese power 49, 60–61, 67, 83–85,
  140, 149, 168, 170, 174, 181, 186,
  202
CIA 41, 150
Clinton, Bill 6, 34, 40, 216–217, 229,
  244
CLMV (Cambodia, Laos, Myanmar,
  and Vietnam) 171
CNOOC (China National Offshore Oil
  Corporation) 20
Cold War 3, 7–9, 13, 17, 19, 25, 27, 31,
  34, 37, 38, 41, 44, 45, 53, 58–59,
  71, 73–74, 76–77, 79–80, 83–84,
  89–90, 92, 94, 105–106, 108,
  115–116, 120, 129, 141, 146, 159,
  169, 174, 177, 191, 199, 201–202,
  213, 237–238, 240, 242–243, 247,
  250, 256–257
Combined Forces Command (CFC) 145,
  157
communist 7, 14, 17, 19, 28, 34, 46,
  76–77, 84, 95, 105, 108, 117–118,
  121, 124, 126–127, 133, 136, 159,
  180, 184, 196, 256

comprehensive national power (CNP),
  China 17, 24, 66, 178, 192, 207
Comprehensive Test Ban Treaty
  (CTBT) 195
cooperative security 76–77, 82, 175, 245
cross-Strait
  policy 120, 126–127
  trade 122, 135
CTBT (Comprehensive Test Ban
  Treaty) 195

David Brooks 52, 58
defense spending 129, 154, 158, 189
Democratic People's Republic of Korea
  (DPRK) 74, 106, 118, 221–222,
  225, 227, 252
Democratic Progress Party (DPP)
  133–135
Deng Xiaoping 17, 24, 26, 46, 63, 72,
  90, 191–192, 244
de-securitize 63
development assistance 100–102, 112,
  117, 244
Dokdo (or Takeshima) 146
DPP (see Democratic Progress Party)
DPRK (see Democratic People's
  Republic of Korea)
DPRK border regions 222

EAS (see East Asian Summit)
East Asia Community (EAC) 187
East Asia Summit 163, 173, 182, 184,
  187, 203, 210, 249
East Asian Summit (EAS) 77, 105, 115,
  163, 173, 182, 184, 187, 203–205,
  210, 249
East Sea (or Sea of Japan) 146
Economic Development Advisory
  Conference (EDAC) 135–136
economic partnership agreement (EPA)
  99–100
economic rights 219–220
EDAC (see Economic Development
  Advisory Conference)
EEZ (see exclusive economic zone)
energy 2, 4, 11, 19–20, 42, 47–49, 54,
  108, 111–112, 118–119, 182–184,
  189, 195–198, 201–203, 208, 212,
  220, 243, 248, 253
engagement policy 226
EPA (economic partnership agreement)
  99–100
exclusive economic zone (EEZ)
  110–111

famine 213, 221–222
  China 223
  North Korea 222
FDI (see foreign direct investment)
Federation of Economic Organizations
    (Keidanren) 97, 99, 116–117
food safety 113, 114
foreign direct investment (FDI) 18–19,
    165–166
foreign policy 7–9, 15, 17, 21, 26, 34,
    92, 117, 126, 141, 144, 178, 197,
    200, 216, 232, 235–236, 240
  China 1, 4, 12–16, 31–32, 36–37,
    63–65, 72, 76, 198, 233, 239–241,
    244–246, 248
  India 199, 210, 253
  Japan 102, 107, 118, 237, 244, 252
  the US 173
foreign policy making, China 14, 256
foreign policy-making 14
Free Trade Agreement (FTA) 19, 87,
    96, 99, 106, 118, 151, 153, 156,
    178, 200, 252, 255
Fukuda, Yasuo 107, 110

gross domestic product (GDP) 18, 44,
    50–53, 129, 150, 154, 165
gross national product (GNP) 154, 160
Guidline (The 1997, of US-Japan
    Defense Cooperation) 47

hedging 3, 36, 39, 53, 61, 70, 126, 137,
    149, 168–170, 175–176, 179, 200,
    238, 244–245, 249
hegemon 1, 6, 8–9, 17, 21, 24, 27–29,
    34, 36, 38–40, 42, 45–46, 50,
    54–56, 58, 61–62, 68, 70–73, 75,
    77, 79–86, 88–92, 104–105, 124,
    140, 142, 161, 168–169, 179–182,
    200–201, 208, 216, 235–237, 239,
    243, 245, 247, 251
hegemonic competition 38, 54
history card 95, 103, 115
Hsu Wen-long 135
Hu Jintao 27, 31, 35, 46, 76, 110, 134,
    164, 187, 190–192
Hussein, Saddam 12, 42, 221

IAEA (International Atomic Energy
    Agency) 184, 196
idealism 39
identity politics 216, 228
illegal economic migrants 225, 238
independence 70, 92, 146

India
  foregin policy 199
  foreign policy 210, 253
  rise 201, 207
individual vs. group 218
institutionalism 3, 7–9, 12, 240, 246
institutionalists 7, 10, 60, 68
intellectual 100
intellectual property rights (IPR) 96,
    100, 240
intellectual property(ies) 34, 95–96,
    115
International Atomic Energy Agency
    (IAEA) 184, 196
international order 2, 27–30, 36–37, 68,
    79–80, 88, 159, 202, 207, 232, 235,
    242, 248, 258
Iraq 11, 42, 45, 53–54, 62, 67, 72, 81,
    86, 92, 112, 151–152, 156, 221,
    229
Islamic extremism 59

Japan 1–3, 6–7, 11–12, 14, 17–21,
    23–24, 32, 34, 39, 41, 45–48,
    53–54, 57–58, 64, 69–70, 72–74,
    77, 79, 81–82, 85, 87, 90, 92–100,
    102–108, 110–119, 123, 128, 140,
    145–147, 149–150, 153, 155–158,
    162–163, 165, 169–170, 173–177,
    179, 182–185, 187–188, 195, 198,
    200–204, 208–209, 212, 234,
    236–238, 240, 244, 247–252,
    255–256
  colonial government 146
  foreign policy 102, 107, 118, 237,
    244, 252
Japan and Taiwan 128, 137
Japan External Trade Organization
    (JETRO) 99
Jia Qinqguo 22, 34–35, 247
Jiang Zemin 33, 46, 64, 76, 100, 246

KEDO (see Korean Energy
    Development Organization)
Keidanren 97, 99, 116–117
Kelly, James 66
Kim Jong-il 4, 141, 147, 227
Kissinger, Henry 55, 141
KMT (Kuomintang Party) 127, 134,
    139, 191
Koguryo kingdom 148
Koizumi, Junichiro 46, 58, 96–97,
    102–103, 107, 110, 115, 117–118,
    202, 236, 255–256

Korean Energy Development
    Organization (KEDO) 106
Korean nationalism 143, 147
Korean War 1, 19, 42, 141, 144–145,
    148, 156, 237
Korea-US Free Trade Agreement
    (KORUS FTA) 153
Kuomintang Party (KMT) 127, 134,
    139, 191

LAC (see Line of Actual Control)
Lee Teng-Hui 106, 122, 127, 136
Line of Actual Control (LAC) 191,
    194
Lu, Annette 122, 128, 137

Ma Ying-jeou 130, 134, 138
Malacca Strait 111, 198
Manchuria 48, 95
Mao Zedong 14, 35, 42, 74, 188, 192
maritime competition 199
Mekong-Ganges Cooperation (MGC)
    187, 205
METI (see Ministry of Economy, Trade,
    and Industry)
MGC (Mekong-Ganges Cooperation)
    187, 205
Middle East 25, 45, 48–49, 59, 62, 67,
    77, 111, 115, 198
migration 18, 114, 162, 216, 221–223,
    233, 254
military transformation 57, 143–144,
    151, 249
Ministry of Economy, Trade, and
    Industry (Japan) (METI) 99
Ministry of Foreign Affairs (Japan)
    (MOFA) 117
missile defense 54, 70, 73, 89, 104, 244,
    254
missiles 43–44, 104, 129–130, 132–133,
    136, 138, 204
    ballistic 120
multipolarity 1, 27–29, 36–37, 71, 178,
    186, 258
multipolarization 28, 37, 258
Mutually Assured Destruction (MAD)
    58

NAM (see Non-Aligned Movement)
Nathan, Andrew J. 230–231, 249
National Security Strategy 65–66, 88,
    140, 254
NATO (see North Atlantic Treaty
    Organization)

neoliberal 7–10, 12, 250
newly industrializing country (NIC) 100
Non-Aligned Movement (NAM) 199
non-governmental organization(s)
    (NGO) 216, 222, 224–226
North Atlantic Treaty Organization
    (NATO) 25,165, 212
North Korea 4, 8, 25, 41, 46, 59, 70, 85,
    103–104, 106, 115, 118, 141, 144,
    146–148, 151, 153, 155–156, 158,
    179, 188, 202–203, 213–214, 216,
    221–223, 225–231, 239, 248–249,
    252, 257
    famine 222
    refugees 221, 226–229, 231, 238, 257
North Korean refugees 221, 226–229,
    231, 238, 257
Northeast Asia 3, 74, 90, 94, 140–141,
    143, 147–151, 153, 155, 160, 172,
    237, 253
NSG (see Nuclear Suppliers Group)
Nuclear Non-Proliferation Treaty (NPT)
    195–196
Nuclear Suppliers Group (NSG) 184,
    187, 196

ODA (see Official Development
    Assistance)
Official (Overseas) Development
    Assistance (ODA) 100–102, 112,
    117, 244
oil 20, 27, 34, 47–49, 65, 108, 111–112,
    115, 118–119, 141, 153, 163, 178,
    195–198, 227, 247–248, 253
Okinotori-shima 110
one-China principle 122, 127,
    131–136
Osan-Pyongtaik 145

pacific fleet 54
Pakistan 75, 112, 178–179, 181,
    183–187, 190, 193, 195–196, 198,
    202–203, 206, 211–212
pan-Blue 127, 130, 133–134, 136
Pang Zhongying 22, 29, 35–37
pan-Green 127, 132, 134–135
particularism 214
peaceful coexistence 2, 55, 60, 76, 235
peacetime operational control (POC)
    144
People's Liberation Army (PLA)
    41–42, 44, 49, 55, 65, 87, 92,
    121, 123–124, 127, 129–130,
    139, 174, 191, 194, 199, 249

People's Republic of China (PRC)
15–16, 19, 23, 34, 42, 44, 48,
120–125, 127–129, 131–136, 139,
178, 211, 215, 217, 219–220, 222,
225–228
Persian Gulf War 42, 54
piracy 100, 112, 205, 216
PLA (see People's Liberation Army)
political rights 219–220
PRC (see People's Republic of China)
President
  Bill Clinton 6, 34, 40, 216–217, 229,
    244
  Chen Shui-bian 3, 106, 122,
    127–139
  George W. Bush 40, 53, 57, 62,
    66–67, 70, 72, 75, 77, 87–88,
    124, 137, 139, 141, 216, 228,
    245, 250
  Hu Jintao 27, 31, 35, 46, 76, 110,
    134, 164, 187, 190–192
  Jiang Zemin 33, 46, 64, 76, 100, 246
  Roh Moo-Hyun 3, 140, 142–145,
    147–149, 151–158, 237, 251
Prime Minister
  Junichiro Koizumi 46, 58, 96–97,
    102–103, 107, 110, 115, 117–118,
    202, 236, 255–256
  Shinzo Abe 98, 107, 110, 112, 115,
    202
  Yasuko Fukuda 107, 110
pull factors 221–222
push factors 221

realism 3–4, 7–10, 31, 39, 88, 230,
  233–234, 247
refugees, North Korea 221, 226–229,
  231, 238, 257
rejuvenation, China 21, 23, 30
relative gains 8–12, 66, 86, 126, 166,
  248, 250
Republic of China (ROC) 121–123,
  128–129, 131–132, 136, 138–139
Republic of Korea (ROK) 64, 69, 74,
  87, 142–145, 147, 151–152, 154,
  156, 158, 248, 253
Revolution in Military Affairs (RMA)
  42, 53
rise (of)
  Asia 180, 207
  China 1–7, 9, 11, 13, 18–27, 30–33,
    35–39, 46, 48, 55–56, 59–61, 63,
    68, 76, 81, 83, 85–86, 104, 117,
    120, 127, 135–137, 143, 159–162,

164, 166–168, 170–172, 174–175,
177–180, 193, 197, 199, 201,
206–207, 230, 233, 235, 237–239,
241, 243–244, 246, 250, 253, 255,
257
India 201, 207
rivalry 19, 42, 85, 94, 105, 107–108,
  112, 114–115, 117, 146, 149, 170,
  174, 178, 180, 196, 198, 205,
  207–208, 245, 251
RMA (see Revolution in Military
  Affairs)
ROC (see Republic of China)
Roh Moo-Hyun 3, 140, 142–145,
  147–149, 151–158, 237, 251
ROK (see Republic of Korea)
Russia 20, 24–25, 43, 48–49, 62, 68–69,
  74, 81, 86, 90, 146–147, 150, 163,
  173, 177, 179, 187–188, 193, 195,
  198, 200–202, 232, 238, 240
Russia–China–India triangle 187

SAARC (see South Asian Association
  for Regional Cooperation)
San Francisco system 69
SARS (see Severe Acute Respiratory
  Syndrome)
school textbook 131, 146
SCO (see Shanghai Cooperation
  Organization)
sea lanes of communication (SLOC) 11,
  109, 111, 198, 203
Sea of Japan (or East Sea) 146
securitization of human rights 216
securitize 5–6
self-perception, China 13, 24
self-reliant defense 3, 140, 142–147,
  153, 155, 237
Senkaku Islands 110
Seventh Fleet 48–49
Severe Acute Respiratory Syndrome
  (SARS) 49, 113, 122
Shanghai Cooperation Organization
  (SCO) 77, 86, 186–187, 201, 205
Siberia 48
Six Party Talks 62, 118, 147, 252
SLOC (see sea lanes of communication)
South Asian Association for Regional
  Cooperation (SAARC) 204–205
South Korea 1, 3–4, 62, 90, 102–103,
  105, 137, 140–158, 162, 165,
  169–170, 173, 179, 184, 226, 237,
  243, 250, 253, 257
  engagement policy 226

Soviet Union 5, 17, 19, 25, 27, 38, 44–45, 58, 73, 108, 129, 199, 202, 213, 238
Spratlys 160
state and law 218–219
status quo 21, 41, 47, 59–62, 64–71, 73, 81–87, 108, 121, 124, 162, 168, 170, 177, 190–191, 216, 219, 234–235, 238, 247
strategic flexibility 143, 151–152, 156
strategy of ambivalence, China 226
student activist 142, 146

Taiwan 1–3, 7, 18–19, 21–22, 26–27, 41–42, 44–46, 49, 57, 59–60, 62, 64–65, 72–73, 75–77, 79, 81–87, 89–90, 93, 100, 103, 106–108, 110–111, 116, 118, 120–138, 143, 160, 172–173, 175, 179, 184–185, 191–192, 195, 198, 200, 202–204, 215, 232, 236–237, 240, 243–244, 246, 249, 251, 255
   independence 22, 44, 74, 77, 106, 121, 124, 127, 132–136, 139, 184
Takeshima (or Dokdo) 146
territorial dispute 20, 27, 64, 72, 87, 149, 157, 160, 163, 168, 174, 179, 183, 185, 187, 189–190, 192–193, 195, 207, 245
   China and Japan 2
   India and China 4
   US and China 3
think tanks, China 1, 13–16, 29, 32, 248, 252, 256
threat theory, China 1, 13, 16, 18–23, 27, 29–30, 32–36, 184, 243, 258
Three Gorges Dam 48
Tiananmen Square 24, 43, 96, 107, 115
Tibet 26, 184–185, 190–195, 199, 208, 228
Treaty of Amity and Cooperation (TAC) 162
triangle 201

US Forces in Korea (USFK) 143–144, 152
US–China–India triangle 202

US–Japan alliance 103–104, 118, 145, 252, 255
US–Japan security treaty 45
Union Oil Corporation of California (UNOCAL) 20, 49, 57, 65
United Nations 9, 27, 72, 76, 88, 123, 128, 131, 213, 225, 229, 242, 248
United Nations Security Council (UNSC) 103–104, 117
United States and Taiwan 83
universalism 214, 216
UNOCAL (see Union Oil Corporation of California)
UNSC (see United Nations Security Council)
UNSC reform 103
USFK (see US Forces in Korea)

Vice-President Annette Lu 122, 128, 137

wartime operational control (WOC) 144–145, 156
WHO (see World Health Organization)
WOC (see wartime operational control)
World Health Organization (WHO) 133
World Trade Organization (WTO) 19, 31, 62–63, 73, 96, 98, 100, 115, 123, 139, 175, 240, 249
World War II 5, 46–47, 53, 94, 100, 102–103, 105, 114, 141, 146, 202, 213
WTO (see World Trade Organization)

Yan Xuetong 23–25, 30, 33, 36, 255, 258
Yasukuni Shrine 46, 58, 102–103, 149
Yongsan garrison 145, 152
Young, Stephen 129–130

Zone of Peace, Freedom, and Neutrality (ZOPFAN) 162
ZOPFAN (see Zone of Peace, Freedom, and Neutrality)